HOSTILE BROTHERS

GOVERNMENT–INDUSTRY RELATIONS

Editors: Maurice Wright and Stephen Wilks

Volumes within this series incorporate original research into contemporary policy issues and policy-making processes in the UK, Western Europe, the United States, and South-East Asia.

ALREADY PUBLISHED

Comparative Government–Industry Relations: Western Europe, the United States, and Japan
edited by Stephen Wilks and Maurice Wright

Government and the Chemical Industry: A Comparative Study of Britain and West Germany
Wyn Grant, William Paterson, and Colin Whitston

Capitalism, Culture, and Economic Regulation
edited by Leigh Hancher and Michael Moran

FORTHCOMING

Regulating for Competition: Government, Law, and the Pharmaceutical Industry in the United Kingdom and France
Leigh Hancher

HOSTILE BROTHERS

Competition and Closure in the
European Electronics Industry

ALAN CAWSON
KEVIN MORGAN
DOUGLAS WEBBER
PETER HOLMES
ANNE STEVENS

CLARENDON PRESS · OXFORD
1990

Oxford University Press, Walton Street, Oxford OX2 6DP

Oxford New York Toronto
Delhi Bombay Calcutta Madras Karachi
Petaling Jaya Singapore Hong Kong Tokyo
Nairobi Dar es Salaam Cape Town
Melbourne Auckland
and associated companies in
Berlin Ibadan

Oxford is a trade mark of Oxford University Press

Published in the United States
by Oxford University Press, New York

British Library Cataloguing in Publication Data

Hostile brothers: competition and closure in the European
electronics industry—(Government – industry relations; 4)
1. Western Europe. Electronics industries. Policies of governments
I. Cawson, Alan 1947– II. Series
338.4' 7621381' 094
ISBN 0–19–827568–4

Library of Congress Cataloging-in-Publication Data

Hostile brothers: competition and closure in the European electronics
industry/Alan Cawson . . . [et al.].
p. cm.—(Government–industry relations; 4)
Includes bibliographical references.
1. Electronic industries—European Economic Community countries—
Case studies. 2. Telecommunication—European Economic Community
countries—Case studies. 3. Competition—European Economic
Community countries—Case studies. I. Cawson, Alan. II. Series.
HD9696.A3E935 1990   338.6' 048—dc20   89–26483
ISBN 0–19–827568–4

Typeset by BP Integraphics, Bath
Printed and bound in
Great Britain by Bookcraft (Bath) Ltd,
Midsomer Norton, Avon

TP

Preface

This book reports the results of a two-year research project directed by Alan Cawson which was financed by the Economic and Social Research Council as part of its Government–Industry Relations research initiative. The Chairman of the ESRC sub-committee, Professor Maurice Wright, and the research co-ordinator, Dr Stephen Wilks, have been sympathetic academic critics as well as unfailingly supportive administrators.

The field research comprised over 300 interviews conducted in the three countries and at the European Commission. Amongst those interviewed were senior managers, civil servants, trade association and trade union officials, and industry and academic experts. Many respondents requested confidentiality, so we have decided not to attribute information to named individuals. We are grateful to all of those who gave so generously of their time—only a handful of interviews lasted less than one hour and many extended to several hours. The interviews were conducted in the period from March 1985 to December 1986, and as will be evident from the chapters which follow, this was a period of considerable change in the pattern of government–industry relations in all of the three countries, and we have tried to identify the underlying processes which continue to refashion the relationships between the major actors.

Successive drafts of the various chapters were discussed by all of the authors, so that the book is a genuine collective effort. Interviewing and the preparation of initial drafts was carried out as follows: Alan Cawson researched the British consumer electronics industry and the process of internationalization of the European industry, and developed the theoretical framework for the study; Kevin Morgan carried out the study of telecommunications in Britain and the European dimension, and collaborated on the French case-study; Douglas Webber studied the telecommunications and consumer electronics sectors in the Federal Republic of Germany; Peter Holmes conducted the case-study of French consumer electronics and collaborated on French telecommunications; and Anne Stevens researched the national frameworks of government–industry relations drawing on work contributed by Douglas Webber and Peter Holmes.

We would like to record our special thanks to a number of people who were particularly helpful in our research: Elie Cohen, Jean-Pierre Coustel, Kenneth Dyson, Josef Esser, Henry Ergas, Peter Forster, Edgar Grande, Wyn Grant, Gareth Locksley, Takao Negishi, Karl Heinz Neumann, Wolfgang Raabe, Wolfgang Streeck, and Harro Welzel. Finally we would like to thank Geoffrey Shepherd who helped to design the project and contributed to the early stages of the research, and Susan Cory-Wright who provided invaluable administrative support.

Brighton
September 1989

Contents

List of Abbreviations   viii

1. Studying Government–Industry Relations   1

2. Markets as Systems of Power   15

3. National Frameworks: Britain, France, and
   Germany   38

4. Telecommunications: Politics, Technologies, and
   Markets   77

5. Breaching the Monopoly: The Neo-liberal
   Offensive in Britain   87

6. France: The Rise and Fall of *Dirigisme*   121

7. Germany: Defending the Monopoly   150

8. Telecom Strategies in Europe: The End of
   Parochialism?   182

9. Consumer Electronics: Politics, Technologies, and
   Markets   218

10. Britain: Arrival and Departure   233

11. France: The Illusion of State Control   262

12. Germany: Holding the Ring?   289

13. European Consumer Electronics: The Rise of the
    Transnationals   318

14. Conclusions   348

    Bibliography   379

    Index   391

List of Abbreviations

ACARD	Advisory Council for Applied Research and Development
ACE	Action for Communications and Electronics
AEG	Allgemeine Elektrizitätsgesellschaft
AFUTT	Association Française des Utilisateurs du Téléphone et Télécommunications
AGSD	Advisory Group on System Definition
AIT	Association des Ingénieurs des Télécommunications
APEX	Association of Professional and Executive Staffs
ASEAN	Association of South-East Asian Nations
ASIC	application specific integrated circuit
ASTMS	Association of Scientific, Technical and Managerial Staffs
AT&T	American Telephone and Telegraph
AUEW	Amalgamated Union of Engineering Workers
BBC	British Broadcasting Corporation
BCG	Boston Consulting Group
BDI	Bundesverband der Deutschen Industrie (Federation of German Industry)
BKA	Bundeskartellamt (Federal Cartel Office)
BOC	Bell Operating Company
BREMA	British Radio and Electronic Equipment Manufacturers' Association
BRITE	Basic Research in Industrial Technologies in Europe
BT	British Telecom
BTS	British Telecommunications Systems
CBI	Confederation of British Industry
CCIR	Comité Consultatif International du Radio
CCITT	Comité Consultatif International pour Téléphone et Télégraphe
CD	compact disc
CD–A	Compact Disc—Audio
CD–I	Compact Disc—Interactive
CD–ROM	compact disc—Read Only Memory
CDU	Christlich Demokratische Union (Christian Democratic Union)
CE	consumer electronics

CEPT	Conference of European Post and Telecommunications Administrations
CGE	Compagnie Générale d'Électricité
CNCL	Commission Nationale des Communications et Libertés
CNET	Centre National d'Études des Télécommunications
CNPF	Confédération National du Patronat Français (National Federation of Employers' Organizations)
CNT	Caisse Nationale des Télécommunications
CPE	customer premises equipment
CSU	Christlich Soziale Union (Christian Social Union—Bavaria)
CTV	colour television
DAII	Direction des Affaires Industrielles Internationales
DAT	digital audio tape
DBP	Deutsche Bundespost
DBS	Direct Broadcast by Satellite
DEC	Digital Equipment Corporation
DG	Directorate General (of the Commission of the European Communities)
DGB	Deutsche Gewerkschafts Bund (German Trade Union Federation)
DGP	Direction Générale de la Poste
DGT	Direction Générale des Télécommunications
DIELI	Direction des Industries Électroniques et de l'Information (Directorate of the Information and Electronic Industries)
DIHT	Deutscher Industrie- und Handelstag (German Chamber of Industry and Commerce)
D.o.I.	Department of Industry
DPG	Deutsche Postgewerkschaft (German Post Office Workers' Union)
DRAM	Dynamic Random Access Memory
DTI	Department of Trade and Industry
EACEM	European Association of Consumer Electronics Manufacturers
EC	European Communities
ECU	European Currency Unit
EDC	Economic Development Committee (of the National Economic Development Council)

EDS	Electronic Data Systems
EEC	European Economic Community
EETPU	Electrical, Electronic, Telecommunications and Plumbing Union
EIAJ	Electronic Industries Association of Japan
EITB	Engineering Industry Training Board
ESPRIT	European Strategic Programme for Research on Information Technology
ESRC	Economic and Social Research Council
ETSI	European Telecommunications Standards Institute
FCC	Federal Communications Commission
FDP	Freie Demokratische Partei (Free Democratic Party)
FIEE	Fédérations des Industries Électriques et Électroniques
FRG	Federal Republic of Germany
FTZ	Fernmeldetechnisches Zentralamt (Central Telecommunications Office)
GATT	General Agreement on Tariffs and Trade
GDP	gross domestic product
GEC	General Electric Company (UK)
GPT	GEC-Plessey Telecommunications
HDTV	high definition television
IBC	integrated broadband communications
IBM	International Business Machines
ICL	International Computers Limited
IG Metall	Industrie Gerwerkschaft-Metall (German Metal Workers' Union)
IHS	Interactive Home Systems
INTUG	International Telecommunications User Group
ISDN	Integrated Services Digital Network
IT	Information Technology
ITA	Independent Television Authority
ITT	International Telephone and Telegraph
ITU	International Telecommunications Union
J2T	Japan Victor Company–Thorn-EMI–Telefunken Joint Venture (now JVC–Thomson)
JVC	Japan Victor Company
LCD	liquid crystal display
MAC	Multiplexed Analogue Components
MAFF	Market Access Fact Finding

MDA	Microelectronics Design Associates
MDNS	Managed Data Network Services
MET	Matra-Ericsson Communications
MITI	Ministry of International Trade and Industry (Japan)
MMC	Monopolies and Mergers Commission
M.o.D.	Ministry of Defence
MUSE	Multiple Sub-Nyquist Encoding
NEB	National Enterprise Board
NEC	Nippon Electric Company (Japan)
NEDC	National Economic Development Council
NEDO	National Economic Development Office
NET	Normes Européennes de Télécommunications
NHK	Japanese State Broadcasting Organization
NIC	newly industrialized country
NTSC	National Television System Committee
NTT	Nippon Telephone and Telegraph (Japan)
OECD	Organization for Economic Co-operation and Development
OEM	original equipment manufacturer
ONA	Open Network Architecture
ONP	Open Network Provision
OSI	Open Systems Interconnection
PABX	Private Automatic Branch Exchange
PAL	Phase Alternation by Line
PDG	Président-Directeur-Général
PKI	Philips Kommunikations Industrie
POEU	Post Office Engineering Union
POUNC	Post Office Users' National Council
PTT	Post, Telegraph, and Telephone (Organization)
R. & D.	research and development
RACE	Research on Advanced Communications for Europe
RAI	Italian State Broadcasting Organization
RCA	Radio Corporation of America
RETRA	Radio, Electrical and Television Retailers' Association
RIC	Radio Industry Council
SECAM	Séquence à Mémoire
SEL	Standard Elektrik Lorenz
SNA	Systems Network Architecture

SPD	Sozialdemokratische Partei Deutschlands (German Social Democratic Party)
STAR	Special Telecommunications Action for Regional Development
STC	Standard Telephone and Cable
SWP	Sector Working Party (of the National Economic Development Council)
TGWU	Transport and General Workers' Union
TMA	Telecommunications Managers' Association
TUA	Telephone Users' Association
UPW	Union of Post Office Workers
VADS	value added and data services
VANS	value added network services
VCR	video cassette recorder
VDMA	Verband Deutscher Maschinen- und Anlagenbau (German Mechanical Engineering Association)
VER	voluntary export restraint
VHS	video home system
VLSI	very large scale integration
VPB	Verband der Postbenutzer (Association of Post Office Users)
ZVEI	Zentralverband der Elektrotechnischen Industrie (Central Association of the Electrical Engineering and Electronics Industry)
ZZF	Zentrales Zulassungsamt für das Fernmeldewesen (Central Telecommunications Equipment Approval Office)

A portion of the old capital has to lie unused under all circumstances; it has to give up its characteristic quality as capital, so far as acting as such and producing value is concerned. The competitive struggle would decide what part of it would be particularly affected. So long as things go well, competition effects an operating fraternity of the capitalist class, as we have seen in the case of the equalisation of the general rate of profit, so that each shares in the common loot in proportion to the size of his respective investment. But as soon as it no longer is a question of sharing profits, but of sharing losses, everyone tries to reduce his own share to a minimum and to shove it off upon another. The class, as such, must inevitably lose. How much the individual capitalist must bear of the loss, i.e. to what extent he must share in it at all, is decided by strength and cunning, and competition then becomes a fight among hostile brothers. The antagonism between each individual capitalist's interests and those of the capitalist class as a whole, then comes to the surface, just as previously the identity of these interests operated in practice through competition. (Karl Marx, *Capital*, iii (Moscow: Progress Publishers, 1954), 253.)

Participation in a 'market' . . . encourages association between the exchanging parties and a social relationship, above all that of competition, between the individual participants who must mutually orient their action to each other. But no further modes of association develop except in cases where certain participants enter into agreements in order to better their competitive situations, or where they all agree on rules for the purpose of regulating transactions and of securing favourable general conditions for all. (Max Weber, *Economy and Society*, ed. G. Roth and C. Wittich (Berkeley and Los Angeles: University of California Press, 1978), i. 43.

1

Studying Government–Industry Relations

Introduction

The 1970s and 1980s have witnessed an extraordinary period of instability and uncertainty in the economies of the major industrialized countries. After nearly thirty years of relative stability and consistent growth, suddenly the practical and theoretical assumptions which were taken for granted by academics and policy-makers alike were subject to challenge. The shockwaves generated by the oil crisis of 1973 are still being felt in the political and economic institutions of the OECD countries, as they struggle to adapt themselves to a changed and continually changing economic world. Almost everywhere 'deregulation' and 'privatization' are on the political agenda, and traditional ideas of state intervention and industrial policy are being revised.

The danger we have tried to avoid in writing a book like this one in such a period of ferment is that of mistaking the trivial for the profound, while overlooking the important. If one simply takes as evidence the pronouncements of the leading exponents of the currently fashionable neo-liberal ideology, one is likely to overestimate the likely impact of these changes, and neglect the relative permanency of established institutions and traditions. On the other hand, things *are* changing, but the significance of the changes can only be analysed in terms of a secure understanding of the historical and institutional context in which they are taking place. It is precisely the emphasis on context and history which marks the contribution of academic analysis, and which differentiates it from the contributions of industry consultants and political and economic journalists.

We have chosen to study two important sectors in what has come to be seen as perhaps the most important industry of the future—information technology (IT). Some commentators have argued that information has become as significant a factor of production in the contemporary world economy as land, labour, and raw materials were to the nineteenth-century industrial revolution. The production, management, and utilization of 'information' are sometimes seen as the crucial element of contemporary political economy, and those firms, organizations and governments which develop effective techniques of information handling are likely to emerge as the most powerful international actors in the 1990s. This, some would argue, constitutes an industrial revolution just as important as that which transformed agrarian societies into industrial societies.

This book, however, does not address such broad questions directly. Rather, it is premissed on the belief that before we can reliably generalize about the significance of such changes, we need to know a good deal more than we know at present about what changes are taking place within firms, trade unions, branches of industry, and governments. What are the predominant patterns of interaction between the various actors who make up the field of 'government–industry relations'? What levels of government are involved, and how do these relate to economic organizations in a period where more and more markets for products and services are becoming international?

In the mid-1970s the characteristic patterns of government–industry relations were largely contained within established boundaries set by the role and scope of national governments and traditional definitions of 'consumer electronics' and 'telecommunications'.

The 'brown goods' (television and audio) industry in Europe at that time consisted principally of segmented national markets, in which domestic producers were subject to increasing levels of import penetration from Japan, especially in the audio sub-sector. There was very little intra-European trade in consumer electronics products, and each country had its own national industry and national trade association. Issues such as tariff levels and the responses to rising levels of imports tended to be handled by negotiations between firms, trade associations, and national governments on the one hand, and, just beginning, negotiations at an industry-wide level between European producers and the Japanese and later other Far Eastern countries such as Taiwan, Hong Kong, and Korea.

In the telecommunications sector, established patterns were more firmly entrenched because all of the national governments had set up public sector telephone network providers (the PTTs) who were given a legal monopoly to provide telecommunications services to individual and business users. The PTTs' relationships to their equipment suppliers were tightly controlled, with only a few favoured firms allowed to tender for the supply of exchanges and customer premises equipment. Each government privileged its own domestic industry, and within Europe there was very little inter-country trade in telecommunications products. The international telephone networks were in turn tightly controlled by international bodies dominated by the PTTs, who were largely the bearers of the various national governments' interests.

We chose to compare these sectors in Britain, France, and the Federal Republic of Germany (FRG) in order to discover the pro-cesses which underlie the different patterns we observed. We were interested in whether these differences could best be explained by either the special characteristics of each industry, or the particular national frameworks and traditions, or some combination of these two. In the case of telecommunications, we found that, until the impact of the push and pull towards deregulation (which we later argue to be *re*regulation), the special nature of telecommunications as a perceived natural monopoly tended to explain the similar tele-communications 'regimes' in the three countries. But once a combi-nation of 'imported' deregulation from the United States and a vigorous neo-liberal government in the UK had made itself felt throughout Europe, the regimes tended at least initially to follow divergent paths, which we explain in Chapters 5–8 to be traceable to the unique combination of industry characteristics and political pressures in each country.

In consumer electronics the effects of international competition were felt much earlier and much more sharply than in telecommuni-cations. The relentless pace of product and process innovation, spearheaded by the major Japanese electronics firms, forced a radical restructuring of the European industry, and a very significant shift in the pattern of government–industry relations. Previously seg-mented national markets were carved open, as in Britain and the FRG with the support of governments for inward investment around a market-led strategy, or more reluctantly as in France with a change in the pattern of state intervention. A wave of mergers, acquisitions, joint ventures and radical restructuring began in the late 1970s and was still unfolding while this book was being written. National governments began to play a reduced role as trade politics in consumer electronics took on a European focus, with the EEC and particularly the European Commission taking a lead in policy-making.

Governments were thus implicated deeply in these sectors at a number of different levels. At the most superficial level, industry actors were in almost constant communication with government officials, and we were interested in the scope and intensity of these relationships, and particularly in the interests and strategies of different kinds of actor. At a deeper level we were concerned to understand how these interests were shaped, and what structural factors constrained those strategies. It is at this level that the separation between politics and economics implied in the term 'government–industry relations' needs to be subjected to critical analysis. The most appropriate set of concepts for exploring political economy through empirical research seemed to us to be found in Weber, and the most significant issues those which have been explored in the debate over neo-corporatism.[1]

Our Approach to Analysing Government–Industry Relations

There is no need for us to begin this book with an extensive survey of the existing academic literature on government–industry relations, since others have already done this.[2] What we will do in this section is to situate our approach within the broad concerns identified in that body of writing. In particular, we will suggest that the perspective offered by corporatist theory has been unjustly neglected by students of government–industry relations, and, anticipating Chapter 2, that the theory of social closure offers a useful way of developing that perspective in a way which is appropriate for empirical study at the level of industry sectors, and which can be extended to examine links across sectoral and national boundaries.

One of the trends apparent in recent writing on government–industry relations has been towards more empirical studies, especially at the sectoral level, which may in turn lead to a more focused attempt to reconsider more general theories of the relationship between politics and economics, between state and industry, in the light of their findings.[3] This is, of course, the underlying aim of this book, and of the research initiative of which it is a part. But empirical research is never carried out without some principle of selectivity, whether or not this is derived from a theoretical model or set of abstractions. It is thus important at the outset to make clear how this study was guided.

Corporatism and social closure

Modern (or neo-) corporatist theory was developed in the 1970s out of a profound sense of dissatisfaction with available pluralist and neo-Marxist paradigms for understanding state–society relationships in industrialized countries.[4] Its early emphasis was on the comparison of national-level systems, and the major finding was that in some countries major economic policy and welfare decisions were reached by a process of bargaining between state agencies and peak-level monopolistic class organizations, and implemented through the capacity of those organizations to bind their memberships to accept agreed policies. Anti-inflationary and economic growth coalitions were forged between organizational leaders representing the interests of capital, labour, and the state.[5] Corporatist approaches were from the outset 'state-centric'; corporatism was part of a move to overcome the limitations of pluralist analysis by 'bringing the state back in'. It shared with neo-Marxist writing a concern to explore the linkages between politics and economics that had been neglected as those disciplines became more specialized.

As the study of political economy from this perspective developed, it became clear that corporatism, understood as a process of confining policy-making and implementation to a restricted group of socio-economic organizations, was not found only at the national level, and was not the province only of peak-level class organizations.[6] Many examples were found, even in supposedly neo-liberal settings of closed circuits of policy-making, where unwanted and potentially destabilizing actors were excluded. The concept 'incorporation' implies the exclusion of those who are not incorporated, and parallels very closely Claus Offe's arguments concerning the attribution of 'public status' to interest groups, which leads to a category of 'policy-makers' (the incorporated) and a category of 'policy-takers' (the excluded).[7]

Which actors are excluded, and which are included, depends on a number of factors. Corporatist theory recognizes that interests are not pre-given and then simply aggregated by organizations; the process of forming organizations is itself a process of shaping interests.[8] Corporatism thus involves a process of bargaining between actors representing monopolistic organizations and (because we are speaking here of 'public' policy) actors representing the state. Following Weber, the state can be defined as that organization which can successfully uphold a claim to a monopoly of the legitimate use of coercion. Many organizations in society employ legitimate coercion, but the state is the only body which does not derive its capacity to coerce from another body. It can be understood from this that the sociological boundary of the state does not necessarily coincide with the geographical boundary of the nation: supranational bodies such as the International Monetary Fund, the EEC, and the GATT can exercise legitimate coercion as well. During the period of our study we found a tendency for the determination of some aspects of public policy to migrate to Brussels, which in turn stimulates the development of interest organizations at the European level. The insight of the corporatist writers is that the process of interest formation is bound closely to the process whereby those interests are organized, and this in turn both shapes and is shaped by the organization of state structures. This perspective helps to avoid the error of seeing public policy as a simple resultant of the mobilization of pressures, since we can pose the problem of how public policy influences the identification of shared interests as well as their organization.

The next step is to try to capture the social processes which produce monopolistic organizations; or, more precisely, the social processes which permit some organizations to achieve monopolistic power by the exclusion of others. If we are looking at government–industry relations, we are examining the role of actors defined in terms of a process of production and exchange. The kinds of organizations which are initially included in our search are defined in terms of the characteristics of production: firms, associations of firms, trade unions, groups organizing the interests of users of particular products or services, and so on. The strength of particular organizations bears a relationship to the nature of the industry: if it is dominated by a very small number of very big firms, then the trade associations will tend to be weak, or at least dominated by the major firms. But some of the opportunities and constraints on organization arise from the wider society: legal frameworks, cultural order, etc. What we are interested in doing is analysing over time a sequence of changes in the mode of organization of different actors (including state actors), to explain why it is that state actors sometimes attempt to achieve their objectives through incorporating organizations into policy formation and implementation; and why it is that non-state actors often attempt to pursue their interests through, in effect, 'borrowing' the legitimacy and coercive power of the state. At one extreme, actors 'capture' the state, and public policy and the public interest become identical with the private interests of the non-state organization. At the other extreme, state actors legitimately coerce non-state organizations into pursuing state-defined objectives. In between these extreme positions there is an enormous variety of combinations of public and private interests in the making and implementing of 'public' policy.

Corporatism is pre-eminently a theory of the 'in between'. It has eschewed grand theory building in preference for 'middle range' generalizations of restricted scope, and it has challenged the conventional understandings of 'public' and 'private' which are part of pluralism's inheritance from liberalism. Corporatist theorists have, for the most part, tended to reject the economistic conceptions of the competitive market as the foundation for theory-building, although they have recognized the force of neo-liberal rhetoric, not least in prising open some of the established corporatist structures. But, in the same way that we argue in this book that 'deregulation' is really 'reregulation', the news of the death of corporatism under the recent onslaught of neo-liberalism is premature. 'Reincorporation' of the previously excluded in a new kind of combination is a more likely outcome than an organizational free-for-all. For example, trade unions may be excluded from participating in policy-making with the demise of tripartism and national incomes policies, as in Britain since 1979, but they may at the same time be incorporated into further policy networks for specific purposes, for example in the extension of industrial training and job creation schemes. Corporatist practices may well shift levels from the macro- to the meso- or micro-levels.[9]

The suggestion that corporatism, in this sense of the closed circuit between state and monopoly interest, may occur at the micro-level, has caused particular difficulties for sympathizers as well as sceptics and detractors.[10] But if we find evidence that a particular market (understood as a system of power as we explain in the next chapter) is dominated by a firm or small group of firms, and if those firms bargain 'public' policy objectives with state actors, and themselves implement those objectives, then it is difficult to see why this should not be seen as a particular kind of corporatist process. The particularity lies in the absence of intermediary organizations, such as trade or employer associations, so that in effect firms represent their own interests. What element of corporatist intermediation is present in such a case? Here we need to go much further towards analysing firms than we have done so far, or indeed are able to in this book, although we will return to the subject in the closing chapter. If firms are themselves systems of power, with consitutent groups (e.g. of engineers, managers, workers, R. & D. staff) challenging each other's power, then to an important extent firms are involved in intermediating between society and the state. If, moreover, as we will try to show in the empirical chapters of this book, transnational firms are becoming the most significant collective actors in the process of production, their relationship to state and supra-national state actors needs to be understood as a power relationship. To the extent that such firms have achieved monopoly power, or have had that power conferred upon them within an extended state system, we can speak of as corporatism the particular combination of exclusive bargained policy formation and implementation.

It is necessary systematically to explore this middle territory in order to differentiate bargained outcomes from those in which the state is captured by the firm, or in which the firm's strategy is subordinated to state directives. The first case refers to what Americans refer to as 'agency capture', and some Marxists as 'state monopoly capitalism'. The second is most characteristic of modernizing capitalist states such as France in the 1940s and 1950s (and in telecoms as late as the 1970s) and Korea at the present time. The successful capitalist developmental state breeds successful firms which sooner or later will flex their muscles and force a bargained rather than a directed form of relationship with the state. Reiterating what we said earlier, we must emphasize that there is no such thing as the stable state–economy–society relationship; constant pressures not least from technological change force any apparently stable pattern to be continually reproduced. This is costly in terms of resources, especially in the face of strong external challenges.

Thus corporatism contains an inherent process, that of concentration or closure. 'The process of social closure is a part of the concentrative dynamic argued here to be the essential independent variable in the development of corporatism.'[11] It would perhaps have been better to say that concentration or monopolization is part of the fundamental process of social closure, as suggested in Chapter 2. The antithesis of corporatism is liberalism, and the tensions between competition and closure which form the heart of this book can be seen as a tension between liberalizing and corporatizing tendencies within society. Neo-liberal strategies, such as those of 'Thatcherism', can thus be interpreted as attempts to dissolve existing patterns of closure, and are overtly anti-corporatist. Corporatist strategies are aimed at privileging specific groups within the state system, and are thus anti-liberal. The character of the neo-liberalism, and the prospects for its success, can then be seen to turn on the specific nature of the corporatist system under scrutiny, and the degree to which closed groups can mobilize to protect their interests. This in turn must be related to the rules of inclusion and exclusion of the organized groups themselves.

An interdisciplinary perspective

What is it that propels social action towards specific kinds of strategies which involve different kinds of relationship such as competition and collaboration? What are the objectives of the actors, and how do they act? It is surely necessary to develop a theoretical understanding of action, before one can understand the patterns of action. In this book we follow Wilks and Wright[12] in suggesting that analytical frameworks and typologies can be *built on* the categories of competition and closure, which are contradictory action impulses common to all kinds of human relationships. It is the way in which the tension between these impulses is resolved, temporarily or relatively permanently, which gives us the basis for a typology of relationships. Thus a long-term 'solution' may be found in the creation of institutions where closure is achieved by relatively low-cost solutions (in terms of the cost of securing compliance) involving a group accepting the legitimacy of an established order. But even here actors from outside the institution may be able to harness competitive pressures to dissolve the order and substitute a new, and different, one. The point that must be stressed here is that the basic concepts we are using assume a constant process of change which is implicit in the term 'action'; stability is the successful resistance of change, which in turn implies action. Once again, we must stress that actors do not simply have 'relationships'; they act.

Part of the problem of studying such processes arises from an increasingly common understanding (which we share) that the perspective of a single social science 'discipline' is inadequate to comprehend real-world phenomena. What do we do to overcome this problem? To simplify a quite complex problem, we can say that there are two broad strategies: the *multi*disciplinary and the *inter*disciplinary. What are the advantages and disadvantages of the two research strategies?

The multidisciplinary approach defines as 'given' the existing fiefdoms of academic knowledge and its arbitrary boundaries between 'politics', 'economics', 'sociology', 'psychology', and so on. Its adherents seek to mobilize the expertise of political scientists, economists, sociologists, and others to attack real-world problems from a number of different directions. In such a way, they believe, the truly multifaceted nature of government–industry relations will be understood. The essence of this approach is 'from each according to his perspective; to each according to others' perspectives'.

We would agree that this is a major advance on the view that government–industry relations can be understood from the vantage-point of *any* one discipline. The danger is that each discipline exports to the endeavour its entire theoretical baggage, and not just the slim suitcase that may be hoped for. In order to cope, the baggage handlers have to devise more and better storage systems (the conceptual typologies) which require ever larger warehouses. Somewhere there is likely to be a useful set of interpretative ideas, but all the onlooker can discern is warehouses and suitcases. The possible outcome is theory as a complex of chaotic conceptions, which, to use Wilks's graphic expression, piles 'obfuscation upon mystification'.[13] If there were space here to do so, it would be interesting to reinterpret the drawing of disciplinary boundaries as closure strategies (in the Weberian sense) around identifiable and defensible and preferably unique bodies of knowledge, which may have as much to do with interest group politics as they have with the pursuit of knowledge. Readers interested in exploring a much wider application of closure theory than is attempted in this book should consult Raymond Murphy's excellent development of Weber's ideas in *Social Closure: The Theory of Monopolization and Exclusion*.[14]

The alternative strategy to the multidisciplinary one, which like the latter is trying to grapple with the lack of fit between the real world and the boundaries of academic disciplines, is the interdisciplinary approach. The two approaches are confused so often that it is worth saying what we mean by 'interdisciplinary'. The central point is the selection of a methodology and an appropriate set of concepts which *transcends rather than reproduces* the boundaries set by academic disciplines. The most impressive theorist (apart from Weber) to have done this is undoubtedly Karl Marx, and at the risk of being anachronistic, the testimony to the ease with which Marx's ideas transcend disciplines is the activities of 'Marxists' in every branch of every grove of academe. There are, however, very serious difficulties with the methodology and concepts of Marxism, and part of Weber's work was concerned with addressing them. Recent Weberian scholarship has emphasized the extent to which Weber built on the insights of Marx, rather than refuted them. Weber's view was that Marx gave unwarranted privilege to the economic, and failed to grasp that economic action was one possible kind of social action, so that non-class non-economic factors have to be given equal weight. The precise configuration of factors which explain any given outcome has to be empirically determined. Thus, for Weber, there are no deterministic historical laws, but only tendencies and probabilities, and the future is always indeterminate.

In their introduction to the 'sprawling essays that were to congeal posthumously into *Economy and Society*[15] Weber's editors aptly encapsulate our notion of interdisciplinarity:

Economy and Society was the first strictly empirical comparison of social structure and normative order in world-historical depth. In this manner it transcended the plenitude of 'systems' that remained speculative even as they claimed to establish a science of society.[16]

Weber's contribution was to identify basic social relations and categories of social action in a *dynamic* fashion, and his intellectual method was constantly to reinterpret theoretical categories by a dialogue with empirical cases. The abstract 'ideal types' for which Weber became famous in the English-speaking world, such as his distinctions between three pure types of legitimate domination—rational, traditional, and charismatic—were the end-product, and not the starting-point, of his work.

Unless it can be convincingly shown that human beings have

changed fundamentally in the last century, it seems to us premature to claim that we lack appropriate theoretical tools to analyse contemporary society. Certainly Weber lived in a very different world from ours, but his ideas were developed on the basis of an extraordinary historical range and depth, so that if they can be shown to be equally applicable to cases as different as classical Greece and early twentieth-century Germany, there is no reason to expect that they have no purchase on the study of government–industry relations in the 1980s. Of course the process of iterative interrogation between abstractions of the world and the world itself cannot stop, and our task is to continue this process so as further to refine the categories. The aim must continue to be, as was Weber's, to *interpret*, and thereby to explain, the world.

It is for this reason that we see *synthesis* as well as analysis as a necessary component of social inquiry. Our objective in this book is to make sense of the two industries in the three countries we have chosen to study. We proceed by analysis, that is breaking down the subject-matter into its various parts, and this is part of a process of learning and reflective judgement, guided by sociological understandings. But in order to fit the pieces together again—to see what picture is formed from the jigsaw puzzle pieces of our data—we need to achieve a synthesis which identifies the major characteristics and explains them in an intelligible fashion. This synthesis is as empirical as it is theoretical: we arrive at the end of our research with a view that internationalized firms are the key players in the unfolding drama of government–industry relations; we started with a view but our starting-point gave no particular privilege to firms, governments, trade associations, or trade unions. In the final section of the book we suggest some theoretical issues which arise from the search for explanation of the power and role of these firms.

But first we need to explore in some detail the application of Weberian social closure theory to interpret the competitive struggle within markets. In doing so we are seeking to develop the argument that the relationship between firms in a market should be analysed as power relations mediated through the state. Firms can defend and advance their interests in a variety of ways, some of which involve enlisting the state's capacity to coerce other actors, which implies revision of the existing patterns of exclusion and privilege. We argue that firms are essentially political as well as economic actors, not only in the sense of seeking to influence public policy, but also in the sense of exercising their market power and resisting or accommodating to the market power of other firms. As we shall see, how 'the market' is defined is itself the subject of a political process.

Notes

1. In part this is because of our empirical concern with industrial sectors and the political role of firms. We do not wish to imply that the alternative approaches which we do not consider here are irrelevant where other kinds of questions are to be asked.
2. See especially D. R. Steel, 'Review Article: Government and Industry in Britain', *British Journal of Political Science*, 12 (1983), 449–503; and S. Wilks, 'Government–Industry Relations: A Review Article', *Policy and Politics*, 14 (1986), 491–506. A comprehensive, although now somewhat dated, bibliography was compiled by Stephen Young for the ESRC. Most of the material listed is pre-1980, which means that it is based on data gathered even earlier, often pre-oil crisis. See S. C. Young, *An Annotated Bibliography on Relations Between Government and Industry in Britain 1960–82*, 2 vols. (London: Economic and Social Research Council, 1984).
3. Wilks, 'Government–Industry Relations', p. 492. See also S. Wilks and M. Wright, 'Introduction' to Wilks and Wright (eds.), *Comparative Government–Industry Relations: Western Europe, the United States and Japan* (Oxford: Clarendon Press, 1987).
4. Lack of space precludes a lengthy excursus on corporatism at this point. The reader is referred to two recent books which provide an overview of the debate: Alan Cawson, *Corporatism and Political Theory* (Oxford: Basil Blackwell, 1986); and Peter J. Williamson, *Corporatism in Perspective* (London: Sage Publications, 1989).
5. For source material on these theoretical debates and their empirical applications, see in particular, P. C. Schmitter and G. Lehmbruch (eds.), *Trends Toward Corporatist Intermediation* (London: Sage Publications, 1979); G. Lehmbruch and P. C. Schmitter (eds.), *Patterns of Corporatist Policy-Making* (London: Sage Publications, 1982); S. Berger (ed.), *Organizing Interests in Western Europe: Pluralism, Corporatism and the Transformation of Politics* (Cambridge: Cambridge University Press, 1981); and W. Grant (ed.), *The Political Economy of Corporatism* (London: Macmillan, 1985).
6. See Cawson, *Corporatism and Political Theory*, and A. Cawson (ed.), *Organized Interests and the State: Studies in Meso-Corporatism*

(London: Sage Publications, 1985) for a discussion of corporatism at the 'meso' and 'micro' levels.

7. Claus Offe, 'The Attribution of Public Status to Interest Groups: Observations on the West German Case', in Suzanne Berger (ed.), *Organizing Interests in Western Europe: Pluralism, Corporatism and the Transformation of Politics* (Cambridge: Cambridge University Press, 1981), pp. 123–58.

8. Cawson, *Corporatism and Political Theory*, ch. 1.

9. K. Bonnett, 'Corporatism and Thatcherism: Is There Life After Death?', in Cawson (ed.), *Organized Interests and the State*.

10. This point has been the subject of recent exchanges between one of the present authors and critics of corporatism. See A. Cox, 'The Old and New Testaments of Corporatism' and A. Cawson, 'In Defence of the New Testament: A Reply to Cox', *Political Studies*, 36 (June 1988), 294–308, 309–15; and Leo Panitch, 'Review of Corporatism and Political Theory' and 'Reply' by A. Cawson, *Canadian Journal of Political Science*, 21 (1988), pp. 813–22.

11. *Corporatism and Political Theory*, p. 38.

12. *Comparative Government-Industry Relations*, p. 307.

13. Wilks, 'Government-Industry Relations', p. 497.

14. Oxford: Clarendon Press, 1988.

15. The phrase is Frank Parkin's, taken from his excellent introduction to Weber's sociology, *Max Weber* (Chichester: Ellis Horwood, and London: Tavistock, 1982). Weber's classic work *Economy and Society* was first published in English in 1968 by the Bedminister Press, New York, under the editorship of Guenther Roth and Claus Wittich. It was reissued by The University of California Press in 1978 in two volumes.

16. *Economy and Society*, xxxiii.

2

Markets as Systems of Power

Introduction

In the previous chapter we suggested that competition and collaboration can be seen as as two basic conflicting social forces whose interaction provides the dynamic of industrial change.[1] Our aim in the book is in part to study the different ways in which these forces are combined in different types of 'hostile brotherhoods'. The task in this chapter is to develop a theoretical understanding of modes of competition and modes of collaboration in different kinds of markets, so that we can set the chapters which follow into a more general context. In this way we hope to show what remains distinctive about the telecommunications and consumer electronics industries of the three countries, despite an increasing similarity as the scale of market competition expands to embrace European and global markets, and the apparent convergence of discrete sectors into 'information technology'.

What is the theoretical significance of the erosion of sectoral boundaries? How far can the difficulty of maintaining a definition of 'telecommunications equipment' or 'consumer electronics' during a period of rapid technological change be explained by available paradigms in economics and political science? We do not propose here to dwell on the manifest shortcomings of neoclassical economic theory—whether macro ('the economy'), micro ('the firm') or even meso ('the industry')—since these have been well discussed elsewhere.[2] In a sense the problem is more serious for political science, because with very few exceptions[3] political scientists have neglected to study the political role of the most important organization discussed in this book—the firm. Students of organized interests, whether operating in terms of pluralist or corporatist frameworks, have tended to study only those organizations to which firms belong, such as trade and employer associations. Rather like neoclassical economists or lawyers they have preferred to treat firms as 'fictitious individuals', as *members* of organizations, rather than organizations in their own right.

The same cannot be said of organization theorists, who have contributed a theoretical base for management consultants who earn their living by studying the internal organization of firms and their relationships to markets. These approaches, of which perhaps that of the 'Carnegie school' is the most famous,[4] focus on the different tasks performed by firms, and show that managers tend to 'satisfice' rather than 'maximize' in pursuing goals such as making profits. Furthermore managers face a 'bounded rationality problem' in that perfect information on which to base decisions is never available.

As useful as these insights are, they do not speak to the issues raised in our research. The relationships in which we are interested are not contained within the boundary of the firm or its position in the market. We are just as concerned with how governments influence firm behaviour (and vice versa) as we are with how firms perceive the market and adjust their behaviour to those perceptions.

This chapter will thus present a framework for understanding government–industry relations by setting out as systematically as possible some basic concepts of competition and closure. Neither of these concepts is either a purely economic or a purely political one; both concepts require an elaboration of both dimensions.

It is perhaps fitting then that we turn to one of the classic writers of sociology for our starting-point. Max Weber's celebrated work combines the economic and political within his concept of the 'social': human interaction at different levels is the basic building material with which the analytic structure is constructed. One form of human interaction is *competition*, which Weber defines as 'a formally peaceful attempt to attain control over opportunities and advantages which are also desired by others'.[5] There is no element of the impersonal mechanism or hidden hand in Weber's work: economic exchange is more like warfare pursued by other means where the 'visible fist' is the more appropriate metaphor. But peace can break out in competitive struggles, and they can become regulated, i.e. governed by rules or, as Weber puts it, where 'end and means are oriented to an order'.[6] Thus all markets contain elements of regulation.

Successful competitors in markets tend to want to preserve their advantages by excluding others from participation. It is perhaps unfortunate that Adam Smith is remembered for the idea of the hidden hand, when he also observed (as Weber did subsequently) that when sellers get together socially they tend to develop a common interest in insulating themselves from the market in a way which runs counter to the wider public interest.[7] How they accomplish this may vary considerably, in ways which are discussed later in this chapter. Just as important, therefore, as competition is what happens when competitors win: the process of *closure*. Closed social relationships guarantee monopolized advantages to groups by excluding others, but then the excluded groups may in turn struggle (more or less successfully) to undermine the basis of their exclusion.

The interaction of these social processes—that is, the constant tensions between them and the outcome of attempts to resolve the tensions—constitutes a dynamic account of the evolution of markets. For Weber, markets are social relationships, and any attempt to enforce a market on the basis of an impersonal mechanism confronts the human impulse to personalize them. In a neglected but vital passage of his *Economy and Society*, Weber writes:

The 'free' market, that is, the market which is not bound by ethical norms, with its exploitation of constellations of interests and monopoly positions and its dickering, is an abomination to every system of fraternal ethics. In sharp contrast to all other groups which always presuppose some measure of personal fraternization or even blood kinship, the market is fundamentally alien to any type of fraternal relationship.[8]

Given that Weber's account of human interaction necessarily involves the formation of *social* relationships based on ethical norms, the creation and sustaining of an impersonal market mechanism requires a set of rules which prevent closure. Thus regulation and the market are inseparable; what varies is the *type* of regulation and the *type* of market.

A crucial characteristic of market relationships is that, to the extent that they remain market relationships in any real (that is, impersonal) sense, they are relatively open to participation. In general, sellers and buyers are permitted to enter the market freely according to the formal rules of the market. Of course, in practice there may be many barriers to entry and market participation, but these are not generally enshrined in any formal rules of exclusion. But even within a market which is open in practice as well as in principle, there are inescapable social impulses towards closure and exclusion. This is the inherent dynamic of the market.[9] To quote from Weber again:

Market relationships are in most, or at least in many, cases essentially open. In the case of many relationships, both communal and associative, there is a tendency to shift from a phase of expansion to one of exclusiveness ... There is a ... close relationship between the extension of market relationships in the interest of increased turnover on the one hand, [and] their monopolistic restriction on the other.[10]

But at the same time Weber stresses that there is a wide variety of different degrees of closure and of conditions of participation in markets, so that openness and closure, regulation and order are *relative* concepts. In subsequent chapters we will show that a comparison of market dynamics and political struggles in telecommunications and consumer electronics permits us to state confidently that consumer electronics markets have been more open than telecommunications markets, and thus there have been fewer barriers to market expansion in search of increased turnover. In the latter sector public network providers (PTTs) have tended to choose alternative strategies reliant on exploiting advantages and creating privileges within closed markets based on exclusive procurement relationships (monopsony) and exclusive selling rights (monopoly).

The tensions between competition and closure, paradoxically encapsulated in the title of this book in a quotation from Marx rather than Weber, are central to our analysis of government–industry relations. It is worth signalling briefly at this stage the relationship between this dynamic and that of Schumpeter, who identified the essence of capitalist development as a process of 'creative destruction'. In *Capitalism, Socialism and Democracy*, Schumpeter identifies the creative dimension of capitalism with the entrepreneurial spirit characteristic of small firms owned and managed by a single proprietor.[11] Schumpeter's pessimism about the future of capitalism, and his argument concerning the inevitability of Socialism, is based on an analysis which directly parallels Weber's rationalization thesis, whereby bureaucracy and rational economic calculation come to dominate all forms of social organization. Socialism will triumph because capitalism will lose its creative aspect, and thereby its capacity to legitimate itself, since it is hardly possible to engender mass loyalty to a system of destruction alone.

But neither Weber nor Schumpeter, writing respectively in the 1920s and 1940s, could have predicted the emergence of business corporations which could combine entrepreneurial and bureaucratic elements within a single organization.[12] In one important sense the principle of hostile brotherhood, or competitive collaboration, can be applied *within* the firm, as well as between firms, which is the more commonly identified case of strategic alliances discussed in general terms in this chapter, and in empirical terms later in the book. In the conclusion to this book, based on observations of the 'secret' of Japanese competitive strength, especially in consumer electronics but increasingly in telecommunications and other branches of IT, we point to the importance of understanding the differences between the way in which European firms are organized and the organization of Japanese firms, including their relationships to sub-contractors and suppliers as well as customers. If there is one single conclusion to emerge from this book, it is that the most important factors we have identified are not technical, legal, economic, or political, but *social* (in the Weberian sense). What determines how successful economic organizations will be is the manner in which the contradictory impulses of competition and closure are socially organized, whether at the level of the state or the firm, or at different (meso) levels in between.

In the remainder of this chapter we will develop the implications of this central tension by examining the possible range of competitive strategies and closure strategies open to different kinds of actor, both governmental and non-governmental. We shall see that what distinguishes the role of government from other organized groups is the specific capacity of governments to regulate through the ultimate sanction of the employment of *legitimate* coercion.

Economics and Politics

Markets are social institutions in which sellers and buyers interact. The conceptual problem is to identify what factors shape these interactions, and to what extent, if any, they can be subsumed under general statements such as the claim that firms' interactions are governed by a search for profit. To say that markets are social institutions is to reject any a priori claim that they are the product of some 'hidden hand' or determined by the operation of the 'law of value'. It is, at the same time, however, a claim that transactions occur within the context of a set of rules, some of which are necessarily framed by public authorities, by which we mean the state.

Whether maintaining the value of currencies, or the ultimate enforcement of contracts, the state is ever-present in market relationships. Without a state system or, rarely, its functional equivalent, goods and services cannot be exchanged in the market-place. Thus it makes no sense to maintain a sharp distinction between 'the state' and 'the market', as if either institution could exist in isolation from the other. The ability of buyers and sellers to fix prices by haggling—the limiting case of the bazaar—itself depends on social institutions such as trust.[13]

Only in a case where buyers just bought once from any one seller, or conversely sellers never needed to sell to the same buyer twice, could we describe the aggregate of exchanges between buyers and sellers of a product (or set of substitutable products) as 'a market' and explain its rules by reference to impersonal mechanisms. In *all* contemporary sectors these limiting conditions will never fully obtain, but it is clearly possible to determine how closely specific empirical cases approximate to the pure type. Indeed, one of the main points of contrast examined in this book between telecommu-nications equipment and consumer electronics arises because the latter sector comprises a few sellers and many buyers, whereas the former comprises a few sellers and a single buyer.

Producers tend to orientate their actions, not towards some amor-phous conception of 'the market', but towards each other.[14] Con-sumer signals may play an important part in the strategies of producers, but each producer will be just as concerned with how his competitors read market signals—and act or fail to act—as he is with the content of the signals themselves. If all the manufacturers of, say, portable radios share a common position in relation to the customer—which generates a social relationship between them which may be formalized in a trade association—then, as long as each producer continues to play by the (written or unwritten) rules, there is no need to be overly concerned about whether customers are satisfied as long as no producer rocks the boat. As we shall see, this can only obtain where market relationships coincide with social and political groups: there is little international trade, and there are no industry mavericks.

Social networks, as often institutionalized in trade associations, are always a mild form of cartel, and often they may be more than this. As we show in Chapter 10 British television manufacturers in the 1960s did not directly fix prices in the manner of a cartel, but did reinforce each other's unwillingness to engage in sharply competitive practices by moderating their price competition and adopting a leisurely attitude towards such things as product reliability and technical change.

At the same time that producers form social relations from which cartel-like behaviour arises they may or may not adopt the same attitude towards their suppliers. As Oliver Williamson has continued to remind us,[15] firms may choose whether to procure components in 'spot' markets, or try to form longer-term 'obligational' relationships with suppliers, or may start to make the components themselves by replacing market with hierarchy and expanding the boundary of the firm.

Apart from the quite extraordinary case of producers not bound by social relationships who buy factors of production and sell finished goods repeatedly only on the basis of spot transactions, all markets involve a combination of competition and solidarity. Exchanges across the boundaries between firms and their environments will thus almost always involve some element of hierarchy, or, in other words the exercise of *power*. Weber recognized this clearly, when even in an apparently 'free' transaction, such as the purchase of a pair of shoes, some element of power is present.

... where a customer places with a shoemaker an order for a pair of shoes, can it be said that either one has control over the other? The answer will depend on the circumstances of each individual case, but almost always it will be found that in some limited respect the will of the one has influenced that of the other even against the other's reluctance and that, consequently, to that extent one has dominated over the other.[16]

Thus different types of market involve different degrees of the exercise of power, which in turn can be understood in terms of the idea of social closure. We need to recognize also, however, the different strategies by which market participants seek to exercise power through a variety of forms of closure. Not all of these strategies will be equally available to each participant, and it is the task of the next section to undertake some preliminary explorations of 'markets'.

Recognizing Varieties of 'Markets'

All market participants will seek to insulate themselves from the disadvantages of unrestrained competition, and it is an important part of the analysis of markets to differentiate between different closure strategies. It is especially important, in the context of international markets, to recognize that one strategy of closure involves co-opting state power to insulate territorially based economic interests from the threat from outsiders. Protectionism, in one form or another, either active or passive,[17] tariff or non-tariff, and so on, is essentially part of the process of closing ranks against the threat from outsiders. It is by no means the only response to competitive pressures, and we need to be able to explain why it is that some firms attempt to compete by avoiding competition, whereas others avoid the temptation of pushing for protectionism by strategies aimed at improving competitive performance. We shall return to this problem later in this chapter when we contrast closure strategies with usurpation strategies. At this stage such action will be considered as one possible kind of closure strategy.

We can distinguish the following types of strategic action aimed at securing a dominant position in the market, within which we include the system of government–industry relationships:

1. *Closure by securing a dominant competitive position* vis-à-vis *other competitors*. Such a strategy is market-orientated, or, more accurately, orientated aggressively (rather than co-operatively) towards other producers rather than towards public authorities. In such strategies the hostility is more evident than the brotherhood, but even here common interests may be recognized and pursued, for example over common technical standards. There are many different ways of achieving closure through competitive strategies, but with respect to our concerns the following two are particularly relevant:

   (a) The attempt to secure through successful competition the position of monopoly producer, which may involve first mover advantages arising out of the successful exploitation of new products or processes; and
   (b) The attempt to secure privileges by the successful upholding of property rights in a given innovation through patenting.

2. *Closure by associative action* where producers define their collective interest as lying in the avoidance of the kind of competition involved in strategy (1) above. Such an interest may be forged in response to pressure from outside, but it is equally likely to arise

from the process of concentration within an industry. Competition becomes personalized as numbers become smaller, and the effect of disruptive action becomes more serious. Such cartel-like strategies may or may not actually become cartels, whether legal or illegal. More often they arise from the formation of trade associations, which provide an organizational framework for common interests to be perceived. There is considerable variation among trade associations, within countries and between countries, in the extent to which they are able to discipline their members to accept and enforce a common policy. The most powerful trade associations can exercise sanctions against any member violating collective agreements (to restrain competition). At the extreme such organizations can expel members or exact severe penalties; in other cases loss of honour or face is sufficient to maintain the line. This is the phenomenon of 'private interest government',[18] and in many cases the regulations become absorbed within the state system by the devolution of state authority. Weber sees such processes as an inescapable feature of market competition:

In spite of their continued competition against one another, the jointly acting competitors now form an 'interest group' towards outsiders; there is a growing tendency to set up some kind of association with rational regulations; if the monopolistic interests persist, the time comes when the competitors ... establish a legal order that limits competition through formal monopolies ... In such a case, the interest group has developed into a *legally privileged group* and the participants have become *privileged members*. Such closure, as we want to call it, is an ever-recurring process ...[19]

3. *Closure through the state.* In this case an economic organization attempts to consolidate its monopoly position by invoking the authority of the state; instead of using economic power to induce compliance even against resistance, the dominant group may try to achieve the same result at lower cost by in effect 'borrowing' the authority of the state. A firm which can protect its position in the market by the enactment of laws which restrain competitors has succeeded in passing on to the public purse the costs of maintaining its privileged position. Such an outcome may be the result of successful pressure applied to national governments, but equally it may be a consequence of the firm being granted privileged status by the state because of its significance for the achievement of the policy

goals of government. The important point, which has been grasped by corporatist theorists but which still seems to elude those who view markets through the rose-tinted spectacles of pluralist theory, is that pressure will be successful because the firm is able to exercise monopoly power. Its collaboration is considered necessary by the government; such collaboration is obtained by the conferment of legitimacy. But just as governments privilege firms, so, in changed circumstances, can successor governments remove these privileges.

The breaking of the British Telecom monopoly, examined in Chapter 5, was possible in part because the older arguments that telecommunications was a 'natural monopoly' were increasingly challengeable as technical change eroded traditional conceptions of products, services, and markets. This process of challenge began in the United States, and was later 'imported' first into Britain and then into other European countries, including France and West Germany. That the outcomes were not the same in each country arises because importation faced a different set of barriers examined in Chapters 6 and 7. Likewise the attempt to persuade governments to pass anti-dumping laws, local content regulations, and so on reflect this type of strategy, as does the enactment of regulations which restrict public purchasing to national firms.

Thus, for Weber, it is the phenomenon of competition which requires just as much explanation as the phenomenon of monopoly. Far from being an aberration, the development of monopoly is seen as integral to the process of competition. Those who are excluded from the privileges conferred by monopoly have a direct interest in challenging the basis of such closure, and, following Frank Parkin's pioneering analysis,[20] we shall call such a process usurpation. This aspect of the theory of social closure is discussed below. But before doing so, we consider the specific position of the firm.

Bringing the Firm as well as the State into the Analysis

Both orthodox economic theory and conventional political science have neglected to examine the firm as a significant object of study. The assumptions underlying the neoclassical approach are those of consumer sovereignty and the subordination of the firm to the market. As Galbraith has observed, such assumptions exclude a priori the role of power within the system, whether it is the power of producers to shape consumer preferences, or of firms to influence, even control, the market. In his presidential address to the American Economic Association in 1972, Galbraith pointed to the importance of analysing the firm in order to understand differences between different types of market:

In fact the neoclassical model has no explanation of the most important microeconomic problem of our time. That problem is why we have a highly unequal development as between industries of great market power and industries of slight market power, with the development, in defiance of all doctrine, greatly favouring the firm.[21]

If we are to treat firms as systems of power—that is, as organizations with their own internal modes of closure—and as organizations which shape as well as are shaped by their interaction with other organizations, then we need to unpack the concept of the firm in much the same way as has recently been done for 'the state'. Recent writing on the state has refused to see it as torn by societal pressures or its role determined by class struggle. Instead state theorists are beginning to analyse its independent sources of power and its internal divisions.[22] The difficulty is, however, that neither of these processes of disaggregation can be done independently, because of the point made earlier that neither states nor markets can exist independently of each other. Again to quote Galbraith, the state must perform regulatory tasks in relation to markets, while at the same time it is influenced by constellations of power arising from market relations.

... when we make power and therewith politics a part of our system, we can no longer escape or disguise the contradictory character of the modern state. The state is a prime object of economic power. It is captured. Yet on all the matters I have mentioned—the restrictions on excessive resource use, organization to offset inadequate resource use, controls, action to correct systematic inequality, protection of the environment, protection of the consumer—remedial action lies with the state.[23]

Galbraith's prescriptive approach, which specifies what tasks states *ought* to be performing, depends on an adequate explanatory theory of what tasks states *actually* perform. The case material in later chapters provides considerable evidence, for our two sectors, of the variety of such tasks, and the extent to which different national frameworks embrace distinct conceptions of the role of the state is examined in Chapter 3.

In earlier attempts to develop state theory[24] a case was made for disaggregating the state into its constituent levels and parts, free of the a priori assumption that the state possesses an 'essential unity' which allows its role to be explained by a single general theory such as those developed by the neo-Marxists. An analysis of the range of tasks actually performed by modern states, including those which by implication ought not to be performed according to pre-scriptions such as Galbraith's, shows considerable variety in organi-zational structure (mode of closure) as well as in the substance of the tasks themselves. Some of these organizational structures will correspond to Weber's famous ideal type of bureaucracy, but others will differ considerably. Weber clearly did not anticipate the extent to which the evolution of patterns of formal organization has revealed an important variety of structure, particularly in the extent to which decentralized administration can be combined with centra-lized financial control. Such differences call for a set of distinct ideal types of bureaucracy, rather than the distinction between bur-eaucratic, traditional, and charismatic means of domination which was elaborated in *Economy and Society*. Such a task is unfortunately beyond the scope of this chapter, but we can give some indications of how it might be approached.

A starting-point would be to subject the firm to the same process of 'unpacking' that we have previously applied to the state. It is no longer sufficient (indeed it never was) to treat the firm as a 'black box' which somehow transforms the factors of production into mar-ketable products. We cannot simply describe product markets and factor markets on the assumption that their characteristics will somehow determine the nature of the firm. On the contrary, firms are strategic actors whose role is central to the process of production, and the choices exercised by firms (subject to the kind of constraints discussed below) shape markets as much as they are in turn shaped by the characteristics of markets.[25] Indeed we will see in later chapters that one of the choices open to firms is to innovate (at research, development, or marketing phases) in a way which re-draws the boundaries of markets.

Such redrawing is a creative process which transforms the effect of constraints on behaviour. A firm which is constrained by, say, a declining level of demand for mature products in a saturated market has a number of options open to it. It can at one extreme make no changes and follow a path leading to bankruptcy and exit from the industry; at the other extreme it can create new products and new markets which transform the nature of its business. In between there is an indefinite range of possibilities. Such concerns are central to any discussion of corporate strategy, and involve putting the firm at the centre of an analysis which considers what factors might explain differences in strategy observed amongst different firms facing the same apparent constraints.

The discussion earlier in this chapter of three possible types of closure strategy can help to reveal differences in firm behaviour if it can be linked to the internal characteristics of the firms. One way to do this would be to try to examine firms as systems of power in which different kinds of interests within the firm try to pursue their own closure strategies. For example, a firm dominated by technical staff within a engineering culture, as Philips was in the 1960s and 1970s, will seek to obtain a dominant position through innovation and licensing, and will tend to favour the liberalization of international trade regimes. But when faced with the erosion of its market position by the arrival of aggressive competitors, it may try to influence national governments to protect its dominant position to avoid the costs of restructuring. What is needed to further this kind of approach is comparative business history, such as a comparison of Philips and, say, Matsushita, which treats firms as evolving systems of power.[26]

It is beyond the scope of this book to pursue such themes in more than suggestive ways, which arose from a development of our original focus on government–industry relations. Having identified the firms as the actors whose role is likely to become more dominant as the scope of markets is increased, with a corresponding diminution in the role of trade associations, trade unions, and other intermediary organizations, we arrived at the conclusion that we lack useful theories to explain the way in which firms behave. What we can do, however, is to examine differences in corporate strategy from outside the firm, showing how firms seek to undermine the dominant position of other firms. The social closure approach can be usefully adapted to this end by considering the attempt by one firm to reduce the market share of another firm as a case of usurpation, which may depend on the usurping firm's capacity to subordinate in turn still weaker firms.

Closure, Exclusion, and Usurpation

Social closure is a process by which a group is formed on the basis of criteria which are employed by members of the group to exclude others who might want to join. Parkin discusses two types of criteria: *collective* and *individual*.[27] Collective criteria are those applied to a particular category of people, who may have no choice as to whether they fit into the category. Perhaps racial discrimination is the best example of exclusion according to collective criteria which are (often) unambiguous and difficult to escape. Closure of markets against 'foreign' firms is another example where collective criteria are applied.[28] Individual criteria are essentially those of achievement and certification which are more or less open to all, and commonly many if not most forms of closure in liberal democracies are of this type.

Parkin's particular contribution to the theory of social closure is to elaborate the process whereby excluded groups organize to undermine the process by which they are excluded — a process he calls usurpation. The purpose of Parkin's work is to explore an alternative model of social class to that employed in Marxist theory, and he uses the notion of usurpation to analyse the political role of the working class. Parkin suggests that the working class is itself divided according to modes of closure based on individualist criteria, so that the process of usurpation is in turn undermined by segregation within the working class according to status categories. A further aspect of this is what Parkin calls 'dual closure', whereby the group dominated by the ruling group itself excludes a lower group with even fewer economic and social privileges.[29]

The concepts of usurpation and dual closure can also be useful in the analysis of markets, whereby a dominant firm may find itself under pressure from a subordinate firm which is attempting to alter the basis on which the dominant firm can practise exclusion. Such firms may in turn exclude their own client firms—for example sub-contractors—in a process of dual closure.[30] In this context it is particularly instructive to consider the position of 'outsiders' who are excluded from a sector or market, but who attempt to usurp the economic privileges of the dominant firms. Outsider status confers several advantages on firms wishing to break down an existing pattern of exclusion. In the case where domination of a market has been achieved by success in market competition, but where an attempt is made to reproduce the pattern of domination by enforcing collective criteria, outsider status may be crucial for successful usurpation. We will see in Chapter 10 that the dominant position of old-established firms in the British consumer electronics industry was undermined by different kinds of outsider. On the one hand there was a domestic firm, Amstrad, which refused to play by the unwritten rules of the industry, and whose founder, Alan Sugar, was regarded with contempt by the established firms. On the other hand there were the incoming Japanese firms, whose usurpation strategy succeeded because they rewrote the conventional understanding of how television sets were efficiently produced. In both cases outsider status was an essential ingredient of their success.

Outsiders can present the appearance of wishing to join the existing club by accepting the existing rules, but at the same time can be engaged in a process of redefining the rules and in effect forming their own club. By presenting themseves as good corporate citizens prepared to behave as gentlemen, the Japanese firms were able to take advantage of the false sense of security that such a stance engendered among the existing firms. The latter were led into thinking that the competitive threat could be managed by encouraging the Japanese to become absorbed into the 'ethos' of the British firms. This had the decisive advantage of making relatively invisible the real threat posed by new production technologies and a commercial strategy based on quality and reliability rather than low price.

Outsiders are able to operate relatively unnoticed in such a context. Their strategies appear to conform to the rules, but in reality break the rules, which may be enforced by inertia and habit rather than by any compelling economic logic. New entrants to a market can introduce new working practices, new criteria for trade union recognition, new patterns of component procurement, new products, and new process technologies, all of which can offer substantial competitive advantages. In addition they may be actively or passively assisted by public policy. By locating new plants in regions which attract subsidies and tax holidays, as well as a particular kind of labour force, incoming firms can enjoy real advantages denied to existing firms. It is perhaps no surprise that the previously dominant firms interpret public policy as subsidizing 'unfair competition'. What may be less easy to explain is why governments appear to discriminate against their 'own' firms in this way. The suggestion developed in later chapters based on the evidence collected during our research is that governments saw incoming firms as bearers of good practice, which would rub off on the existing firms when they were forced to respond to the challenge of the usurping firms. They would then be required, not by government directly, but by the logic of competition, to follow suit and become more efficient producers. The final outcome of such policies is always indeterminate, however, and perhaps few advocates of this policy within the British government would have wished for an outcome in which *all* the significant manufacturers of consumer electronics products were to be foreign subsidiaries.

The usurpers, however, are not always foreign or domestic producers wishing to pursue a competitive strategy to undermine market share. Indeed, in markets dominated by public procurement such a strategy is ruled out a priori and a state-targeted strategy may be necessary to gain entry. When we looked at the telecommunications market, which was almost entirely closed until the deregulation pushes and pulls of the 1980s, we found that the impetus came from major customers rather than from would-be competitors. In Chapter 5 we show that a significant pressure for liberalization in the British telecommunications regime came, not from excluded producers, but from large corporate users of telecommunications. These firms, especially those in the financial sector, were concerned that the provision of new services such as data transmission was constrained by the public monopoly position of British Telecom. They provided a useful ally to a radical government seeking explicitly to undermine the entrenched position of trade union monopoly power and the cosy procurement relationship between BT and the equipment suppliers.

'Deregulation' of this kind is never, however, the substitution of a market order for a political order. It is, rather, a shift in the balance between a form of state-centred corporatist regime in which policies are bargained with privileged groups but within constraints dictated by governments, towards a system in which policy outcomes more closely reflect the market power of the dominant firms. In Weber's terminology this is a transition from a system characterized by the power of command, formally vested (by the state) in a monopoly organization (the national PTT), towards governance through power as a 'constellation of interests'.[31] No longer are customers (e.g. for customer premises equipment such as small telephone exchanges) obliged to purchase from a single supplier, but the erstwhile monopolist has such market power that the formally free choice is in reality constrained by that power. In order to prevent the exploitation of consumers, the dominant firm may be obliged to accept the enforcement of a new regulatory code. In practice, therefore, deregulation is likely always to be a form of 'reregulation' which signals a shift in the *mode* of closure. The extent to which such reregulation entails a shift in the *degree* of market closure is an important question for research, and our findings for the three countries are presented in later chapters.

A third type of power implicit in Weber is what Murphy calls the 'power to profit from', which is 'the capacity to take advantage of possibilities that are presented by others'.[32] This kind of power may not be intentional, in that the actor who profits may not have sought the state of affairs from which it profits, but nevertheless advantages accrue which enhance the power of that actor. In Weber's schema, however, disadvantages are equally stressed, and change may entail the erosion of power as an unintended consequence of social action. Thus we should always be alert to losers as well as winners in any process of reregulation, whether it be of the 'big bang' kind, or marked by a steady process of attrition. In Chapter 10 we argue that Amstrad was such a winner in consumer electronics; it reaped the benefits of the changes wrought by the competitive onslaught of the Japanese firms, but it could not by itself have produced these changes. In Chapter 11 we show how in the French case Thomson profited from the Socialist government's policy of forcing nationalized firms to return to profit, although it is unlikely that in the absence of such pressures Thomson would have behaved the way that it did. In a larger sense the response of the Japanese firms to repeated attempts to protect the European market against them opened up possibilities which the Japanese were able to exploit. Such examples suggest that firms may have some difficulty in determining where their real interests lie, and the Marxian idea of false consciousness may be more appropriately applied to capitalists than to workers.

Conclusion: From Associative Action to Strategic Partnerships

Earlier in this chapter we identified three types of closure strategy which firms might adopt in seeking to improve their competitiveness. Put simply, these are market-orientated, cartel-orientated, and state-orientated strategies. We suggested that historically the most important cartel-orientated strategy was based around trade associations, which sometimes were able to organize and defend the interests of their members through a process of collective action. These trade associations had a national basis, even where they were 'private interest governments' with considerable autonomy from the national state. But in an era when markets have extended to the global level, such organizations have become decreasingly effective in representing the collective interests of producers. As we note at various occasions in subsequent chapters, transnational firms have a broader set of interests than national governments, and increasingly orientate their actions towards transnational public authorities such as the EEC. But beyond that, firms such as Philips, Thomson, and AT&T have begun to see the market in information technology as a global one, which leads to a concern to be active producers located in and thus close to markets in the Far East, Europe, and North America.

Although there is some evidence that trade associations are themselves becoming international in scope, for example in the formation of the European Association of Consumer Electronics Manfacturers (EACEM), or the International Telecommunications User Group (INTUG), their response lags a long way behind that of the leading transnational firms. For these, closure through market-orientated strategies alone is recognized as impracticable for an industry such as IT where the range of technologies and expertise extends well beyond the traditional identification of the firm's products and markets. Even IBM, which has managed to achieve an unparalleled domination of the world's computer industry, recognizes that it lacks expertise in telecommunications, and will surely recognize the same problem in due course with respect to consumer electronics. A market-orientated response, which might involve bringing telecommunications into the scope of the firm through either organic growth or acquisition, is one possibility. But increasingly evident is a tendency for firms to create linkages with other firms in various forms of strategic partnerships.[33] Such new forms of combination, stopping short of merger, can best be analysed as a closure strategy based on a new type of associative action, but a very old principle of 'hostile brotherhood'. These alliances may have quite different objectives, for example in developing new products, or marketing existing products, or in resisting hostile take-overs, but they have in common a recognition that on its own a single firm may be hampered in maintaining or extending its competitiveness. In the terms of the transaction cost approach discussed above, firms perceive that their objectives may be reached at lower cost through partnership than by extending their hierarchy to new functions.

It should be stressed that, as with all ideal types, these forms of closure strategy always occur in combination rather than as pure types. Thus, to take the example of Philips, it is simultaneously pursuing all three modes of closure. In the first place the firm is now pursuing a market-orientated strategy by restructuring its organization, closing plants and shedding labour in order to reduce its costs and gain competitiveness. At the same time it is seeking to develop new product clusters and new markets by establishing a complex network of strategic alliances. An alliance with Sony in compact disc audio helped to create a world CD standard to avoid the expensive video format wars which had damaged Philips so badly in the early 1980s. In CD—Interactive, seen as potentially an important consumer product of the 1990s, Philips has forged partnerships with a range of software houses, publishing firms, and professional equipment suppliers in North America, Europe, and the Far East. Yet still at the same time, Philips has been pushing hard at the doors of the European Commission to introduce a specific high (19 per cent) rate of tariff in the initial phase of marketing CD-I, as was conceded by the EC for CD—Audio. Thus its overall corporate strategy contains elements of all three modes of closure, and a dynamic analysis of the firm would chart shifts in the relative importance of the different modes.

The research for this book was carried out in the period from 1985–8, and it deals mainly with the unfolding of the two chosen sectors in the period from 1973 (the first oil shock). Before 1973 closure strategies of the firms in Britain, France, and Germany were principally directed at national markets, national trade associations, and national governments. Telecommunications infrastructure and equipment procurement was outside the scope of the competition policy of the European Commission, and consumer electronics markets were largely segregated along national lines. In telecoms closure was very largely state-managed, and in consumer electronics achieved by cartel-like behaviour in Britain and West Germany, and a state-orientation among the leading firms in France.

The chapters that follow explore the factors which led to radical changes in this state of affairs, and provide a context for understanding the increasing resort to mergers and alliances in the 1980s. In Chapter 3 we provide an overview of the national frameworks of government–industry relations in the three countries, which highlights the extent to which there were important contextual variations which need to be understood in order to analyse the trajectory of the two sectors. Subsequent chapters show in considerable detail how and why these national variations have become less significant, as the European Community institutions have succeeded in extending their power at the expense of that of national governments, and even more important how the pressures of international competition, spearheaded in consumer electronics by the Japanese and in telecommunications by the Americans, have forced European firms to internationalize or perish.

These have been momentous developments, and their unfolding is far from complete. But we contend that the basic concepts of competition and collaboration which are essential to understanding markets as systems of power can be applied, with suitable refinements, at different levels from local to global. There is an important chain of causation which links these different levels. The growth of global producers in, say, video recorders is directly linked to the remorseless pressures on small independent electrical retailers in Britain which have led many to close and the market become dominated by the giant rental companies and large retail chains such as Dixons and Comet. We cannot trace all of these links in a single research project and within a single book, but we can provide a basic understanding of the process of competitive collaboration—of social closure applied to production and marketing—with which to examine them.

The empirical chapters of this book provide a detailed analysis of a chosen segment of this universe. In the final chapter we will return to the theory of social closure, and suggest, in the light of our findings about the effects of internationalization on government–industry relations, what future lines of research look most promising. To anticipate these for a moment, we will argue that everything we have discovered about the increasing importance of firms (relative to other institutions) and their new patterns of behaviour leads us to to the view that more needs to be known. Our conventional understandings inherited from orthodoxies in econ-

omic and political science tend to be a hindrance rather than a
help in this task.

Notes

1. To avoid repetition we frequently use synonyms for the terms 'competition' and 'collaboration'. Raymond Murphy, *Social Closure: The
   Theory of Monopolization and Exclusion* (Oxford: Clarendon Press,
   1988), 4, suggests that at the heart of Weber's work is a dialectic
   between constraint and creativity, but we do not wish to identify the
   tensions between competition and closure as identical with this, if
   it would then be inferred that it is competition within markets which
   produces constraints, and the principal mode of group closure is
   around shared creativity. Such *may* be the case, but equally, closure
   erodes creativity (in the long run), and the process of competition
   can lead to creative outcomes. In this book, which concentrates on
   competition and closure within economic markets, we will tend to
   be more concerned with particular forms of *economic* competition,
   and the process of closure around various forms of property. The
   dialectic between these processes is a constant leitmotiv of the book.
2. But apparently without too much effect on the mainstream of economics teaching where there is a long and distinguished dissonance
   between received wisdom and the real world. For an example, see
   J. K. Galbraith, 'How Keynes came to America', in *Economics, Peace
   and Laughter* (London: André Deutsch, 1971). On this side of the
   Atlantic, Richard Stone concluded a review of economics over the
   past three generations with the stirring cry: 'The world may be going
   to the dogs, but economics certainly is not.' ('Political Economy, Economics and Beyond', *Economic Journal*, 90 (Dec. 1980), 733.)
3. See ch. 1, pp. 7–8.
4. The most important works of this school are J. G. March and
   H. Simon, *Organizations* (New York: John Wiley and Sons, 1958),
   and R. M. Cyert and J. G. March, *A Behavioral Theory of the Firm*
   (Englewood Cliffs, N. J.: Prentice-Hall, 1963).
5. Max Weber, *Economy and Society: An Outline of Interpretive Sociology*, ed. G. Roth and C. Wittich (Berkeley, Los Angeles and London:
   University of California Press, 1978), p. 38. (This edition was first
   published by the Bedminster Press, New York, in 1968.)
6. *Economy and Society*, p. 38.
7. 'People of the same trade seldom meet together, even for merriment
   and diversion, but the conversation ends in a conspiracy against the
   public, or in some contrivance to raise prices.' Adam Smith, *The
   Wealth of Nations*, i (London: Methuen, 1950), p. 412.

8. *Economy and Society*, p. 637.
9. This is an important point, given the tendency of many critics of Weber to assume that his ideal type method allows only static forms of analysis. In reality Weber identified *processes* (in this case closure and competition, but also more general processes such as rationalization) as well as configurations of characteristics abstracted from empirical observation, and his concepts allow for diachronic analysis as well as genuinely dynamic analysis.
10. *Economy and Society*, pp. 44–5.
11. J. A. Schumpeter, *Capitalism, Socialism and Democracy* (London: Allen & Unwin, various editions from 1943), Part II.
12. Murphy, *Social Closure*, pp. 214–5 points to the growth of collective decision-making within bureaucracies, at the expense of the power wielded by individual bureaucrats, as the major change in the pattern of bureaucracy since Weber's time. It seems to us, however, that the revisions to Weber's ideal type of bureaucracy need to be more far-reaching than this.
13. In what many see as the archetype of the competitive market-place—the stock exchange—many transactions used to be settled by word of mouth alone and only later confirmed in writing, which was only possible where relations of trust were continually reproduced. The advent of computerized trading is likely to introduce new hostilities into such brotherhoods.
14. Harrison C. White, 'Where do Markets come from?', *American Journal of Sociology*, 87/3 (1981), p. 518.
15. O. Williamson, *Markets and Hierarchies* (New York: Free Press, 1975); O. Williamson, 'The Economics of Organization: The Transaction Cost Approach', *American Journal of Sociology*, 87/3 (1981), pp. 548–77.
16. *Economy and Society*, p. 947.
17. By 'active' we mean consciously sought; by 'passive' we mean protection which arises as a consequence of, for example, the adoption of incompatible technical standards. This point is made in ch. 6 in respect of the unique French television standard SECAM.
18. For recent work on private government from the perspective of corporatist theory, see W. Streeck and P. C. Schmitter (eds.), *Private Interest Government: Beyond Market and State* (London: Sage Publications, 1985).
19. *Economy and Society*, p. 342.
20. Frank Parkin, *Marxism and Class Theory: A Bourgeois Critique* (London: Tavistock, 1979).
21. J. K. Galbraith, 'Power and the Useful Economist', *American Economic Review*, 63 (1973), p. 3.

22. This is as true of some Marxist theorists as it is of those who have looked towards corporatism for precisely this reason. The point is made at greater length in A. Cawson, *Corporatism and Political Theory* (Oxford: Blackwell, 1986).

23. Galbraith, 'Power and the Useful Economist', p. 10.

24. For a discussion of these attempts, see Alan Cawson, 'Is there a Corporatist Theory of the State', in G. Duncan (ed.), *Democracy and the Capitalist State* (Cambridge: Cambridge University Press, 1989).

25. This is particularly important in the case of technical innovation where decisions about the nature of products can influence the development of markets. See the discussion of teletext in ch. 10.

26. Ronald Dore's *British Factory—Japanese Factory* (Berkeley, Los Angeles and London: University of California Press, 1973) pioneered this approach for industrial relations and work organization. What we are pointing to is the need for a similar approach which links internal organization to market development and competitive strategy.

27. Parkin, *Marxism and Class Theory*, pp. 65 ff.

28. Except that the definition of 'foreign' may not be rigorously applied (i.e. may be subject to usurpation), and 'foreign' firms may become 'British' or 'French' without any change in ownership, as Philips's subsidiary companies have done.

29. Parkin, *Marxism and Class Theory*, ch. 6.

30. This seems to have been one of the responses of the Japanese electronics majors to the appreciation of the yen; sub-contractors outside the lifetime employment system were forced to lay off workers and accept enforced lower prices.

31. *Economy and Society*, p. 943.

32. Murphy, *Social Closure*, p. 136.

33. For a useful discussion of such alliances in Europe, see Margaret Sharp and Claire Shearman, *European Technological Collaboration*, Chatham House Papers 36 (London: Royal Institute of International Affairs/Routledge & Kegan Paul, 1987).

3

National Frameworks: Britain, France, and Germany

Introduction

The differing responses of governments and two industrial sectors in three Western European countries to rather similar industrial, trading and commercial challenges form the main concern of Chapters 4–13 of this book. The analysis in those chapters will focus upon the specific characteristics of the two sectors. In this chapter the concern is with the national frameworks within which they operate.

Many of the decisions, actions, and developments considered in later chapters cannot simply be discussed as though they were the result of some sort of autonomous decision based upon an abstract judgement of rationality in a neutral environment. At the crudest level the decision to cede Thomson's telecommunications interests to CGE, discussed in chapter 6 below, cannot be understood without some appreciation of the effects of a political regime in France that could at that time loosely be described as presidential.

The aim of this chapter is to set out in comparative terms some of the aspects of the national environments that we have found to be most important for an understanding of the process of government–industry relations. The chapter will not attempt to be a summary of centuries of political and economic development in each country, nor will it be an examination of the 'industrial spirit', 'civic culture', or 'ethos' of each country. Such matters are inevitably disputable, elusive, and hard to capture. It may be that the discussion of specific sectoral cases later in this book will permit readers to draw a number of conclusions in such areas but this chapter is concerned with themes related to political and institutional arrangements.

Such themes are the stuff of textbooks on comparative politics and deserve to be dealt with at appropriate length. However, we found that certain areas came to appear crucial as our research progressed. These crucial aspects were: the nature of the constitutional and legal framework within which both government and industry act; the nature of any political consensus or conflicts around economic and industrial policy; the structure and nature of the civil service and its relationships with both industry and politicians; the nature, role, and scope of the trade unions and employers' organizations; and the structure and organization of finance and banking. In all these areas the three countries present marked differences. A final section considers the European Community framework in so far as it affects government–industry relations.

Constitutional and Legal Frameworks

Three aspects of the constitutional framework have seemed to us sufficiently germane to the way in which government industry relations are handled to warrant discussion here. They are the nature and role of the central leadership in government, the place of Parliament within the policy-making structures, and the nature and role in the field of government–industry relations of formal legal prescriptions and of the courts.

The existence of written constitutions in France and Germany may seem to give constitutional considerations more importance in the governmental life of those two countries than in the UK. Even in Britain, however, powerful constitutional conventions exist,[1] while in France what is normally called constitutional practice has come to seem at least as important as the written provisions of what is acknowledged to be an ambiguous constitution. In all three countries, however, the perceived requirements of constitutional practice do condition government activity in all fields, including relationships with industry.

The dominant style of economic and industrial policy-making in Germany has been described as concertative.[2] It is above all the organization of the German state, especially its federal character, which has imposed this more or less concertative style of government on successive central governments of the FRG. In addition to the division of powers prescribed by the Basic Law four factors help to produce considerable interdependence between the federal government and the *Länder*. The first is the representation of the *Länder* in the federal Parliament through the Bundesrat, the upper house of the legislature. Secondly, as federal ministries are in the main policy-making organizations without their own administrative apparatus, most federal legislation is actually administered by the *Länder* as their 'own concern'.[3] Thirdly, even in those areas where they do not formally have a policy-making role the *Länder* may play an active lobbying role, and they themselves are lobbied by firms and business organizations.[4] Fourthly, the Basic Law designates some policy spheres, including regional policy, as 'joint tasks' of the *Länder* and the federation. In the FRG federal industrial policy thus coexists with *Land* and local industrial policies and may be possible only on the basis of concertation between the different levels of government. A successful policy for the expansion of cable television, for example, presupposes co-operation between the federal post office, which provides the telecommunications network, and the *Länder*, which determine under what conditions, if any, and by whom radio stations or TV channels may be set up and programmes offered.

The industrial policy 'will' of the federal government is likewise generally the product of a lengthy process of internal consultation. This is a function, chiefly but not exclusively, of the fact that the federal government in Germany has, as a result of the nature of the FRG's electoral system, almost always been a coalition government and in practice the determination of the guidelines of government policy—the responsibility of the Federal Chancellor under the Basic Law—has been undertaken jointly by the coalition partners.[5] For all but seven years since the creation of the FRG, the FDP, although a small party, has been a coalition member and has almost always been able to insist upon compromises in policy. The FDP is, moreover, a particularly 'industry-friendly' party, heavily dependent on business interests.

In France too all the governments under the current (Fifth Republic) constitution, introduced in 1958, have included members from more than one political party. In other respects the contrast with the FRG is striking. Perhaps most striking is the extent of the role of the President throughout the period, with one brief exception between March 1986 and May 1988. The exact nature of the political regime in France has been the subject of debate ever since 1958. Two points are clear. A combination of constitutional provisions and political practice, some of it by almost any interpretation unconstitutional, has resulted, for most of the period, in a regime that can be called presidential. Secondly, this distribution of power is not immutably fixed. It depends upon support for the President in Parliament and by a government team headed by a Prime Minister chosen by the President from amongst his supporters. In the general election of 1986, with a Socialist President in office, a right-wing parliamentary majority was returned. The President chose the leader (Jacques Chirac) of the dominant party (the Gaullist Rassemblement pour la République) as Prime Minister. This situation, known as *cohabitation*, resulted, for the following two years, in a changed balance of power.

Apart from the period of *cohabitation* the Prime Minister has overseen government–industry relations on a day-to-day basis, but presidents have intervened decisively from time to time. Four factors assisted the President's freedom of manœuvre. Firstly, the President always presented himself to the electorate on the basis of his personal political stance, and until March 1986 was always upheld in Parliament by a majority explicitly committed to general support for that stance. The main orientations of government policy were thus clearly the President's responsibility.

Secondly, there is no real concept of the collective responsibility of the Council of Ministers. Contentious matters are likely to be settled elsewhere, in small meetings, and through the *arbitrage*—the word means umpiring—of Prime Minister or President.

Thirdly, the President has, in the Élysée, a personal staff who, before 1986, were able to be active in particular policy fields where the President was known to have an interest. The predominant political place of the President allowed his staff to undertake key roles.[6] Fourthly, other than between 1986 and 1988, although formally endorsed by the Council of Ministers, the chairmanship of the nationalized companies was clearly in the President's personal gift. The chairmen of those companies regarded themselves as responsible directly to the President for their behaviour. They were very likely to insist on going directly to the Élysée on serious matters.

In Britain the convention of the collective responsibility of the Cabinet means that while decisions are announced as being those of the ministers directly concerned they will be defended by all ministers, which implies less departmental autonomy than is the case in either Germany or France.[7] Responsibility for industrial policy is, as in Germany, widely diffused between departments. The result may be slowness to react, and conflict.[8] Certain major decisions—

Wilks cites the closure of the Invergordon smelter, and the collapse of both Laker Airways and De Lorean cars[9]—are ultimately made not on detailed knowledge but at Cabinet level on 'political' criteria. Amongst these are what Wilks has described as 'vigorous free market argument and an uncompromising parsimony from a Treasury machine that has been strengthened rather than weakened under the Thatcher government'.[10] Within the convention of collective responsibility the Prime Minister plays a key role.

In all three countries Parliament has a role to play within the policy process. In France, this role, in relation to industrial policy, is a very limited one. The constitution restricts the length of parliamentary sessions and the scope of Parliament's activity. Laws can be very brief and not particularly technical.[11] Very large areas of industrial policy require no explicit legislative backing although the budget of the Industry Ministry does have to be passed annually. While it should not be supposed that the French Parliament is uninterested in the details of legislation or totally powerless, the limitations on the scope of its deliberations, combined with the absence of an effective question time, adjournment debates, or opposition days, weaken the parliamentary preoccupations of French ministers compared with their British counterparts.

The nature of the British legal system requires laws that are highly technical and take all foreseeable contingencies into account. Parliament is thus presented with a great deal of complex detail. Yet in practice major alterations and amendments during the legislative process are rare. The role of the British Parliament is however of importance in two ways. Firstly, the fact that all ministers have emerged from its ranks and that parliamentary performance is vital to the continuation of their careers means that British ministers are likely to be very conscious of the short-term issues of political impact and presentation. Secondly, although the British Parliament is deficient in its ability to monitor, let alone control, government activity, its select committees do provide occasions where some aspects of policy are fairly publicly examined.[12]

In both France and the FRG there are important parliamentary standing committees which review and may sometimes amend legislative proposals in addition to producing their own reports. In Germany, where the powers of the committees are not subject to the same constitutional restraints as in France, Members of Parliament may specialize over a long period in the work of one committee, which thereby gains in expertise, status, and influence. Groups of MPs from the majority party may be able to exert pressure upon the government[13] although the function of such parliamentary party experts may more often be to explain the minister's policy to their colleagues than to influence that policy. The upper house of the FRG's legislature, the Bundesrat, has a veto over actual legislation which may affect the administrative, territorial, or financial interests of the *Länder* and is particularly likely to be influential when there are conflicting majorities in the two houses.

The parliaments of the three countries, while limited in the extent to which they are able to exercise oversight over governmental policy in the field of relations with industry, do impose rather different constraints upon the three governments in terms of presentation and political defence of policies and sheer weight of parliamentary business. It seems clear that in terms of the immediate preoccupations of ministers the British Parliament is more prominent than those of France or Germany. In terms of influence upon certain outcomes the German Parliament is probably the most effective.

The third important way in which constitutional and legal frameworks influence the nature of relations between government and industry is through the operation of the law and the role of the legal institutions. Here the greatest contrast is between the FRG and the other two countries. The history of Germany and the FRG'S foundation as a *Rechtstaat* based upon respect for the law and legal principles and with a Basic Law as its constitution has given adherence to the letter and spirit of legal provisions a particular importance. Moreover, the Basic Law rules out certain policy options except where they are supported by a very broad inter-party consensus. For example, privatizing the Bundespost would involve an amendment to the Basic Law and require a two-thirds majority in Parliament.

Attention to the provisions of the law by ministries and divisions is encouraged by the fact that division heads are personally and legally responsible for their section's decisions, by the role of the Federal Constitutional Court that may declare not only laws but also the actions of the federal government unconstitutional and hence invalid, and by the right of redress open to both citizens and companies through the administrative courts. Unwelcome policies and decisions, including the decisions of the Federal Cartel Office, may be challenged before the courts both by citizens—and cases against the building and operation of nuclear plants long delayed the nuclear energy programme—and by companies.[14]

In France the broader and more ambiguous nature of the constitution means that it acts as less of a specific constraint. Nevertheless, the length of time required for the introduction of legislation—and the consequent period of uncertainty—may be increased by an appeal from within the National Assembly to the Constitutional Council.[15] Beyond this, however, the courts have played a very small part in the operation of industrial policy in France. In principle government activities are subject to challenge before the administrative courts. In practice this rarely occurs.[16]

Britain is sharply distinguished from France and Germany by the absence of a specific public law system which applies to bodies that are regarded as fulfilling public functions.[17] Day-to-day activities within both the civil service and industry are normally undertaken with legal provisions figuring only as a background frame of reference. However, specific key points in the development of policy may be marked by a change in the framework—for example the 1969 Act which disestablished the Post Office as a government department or the 1982 Act which abolished the telecommunications monopoly. In the latter case the introduction of the new framework was so rapid that the translation of intent into the technical legal form did not always achieve the results the policy-makers were seeking. However, the existence of a legal provision may be used as an excuse or defence in a very narrow way, as, for example, when Post Office managers argued that the provisions of the 1969 Act included no reference to any duty in the national interest to consider the exportability of telecommunications equipment, and thus specifically exempted them from paying any attention to export potential.

To argue that constitutional and legal frameworks result in differing perceptions of the processes by which policy has to be made and implemented is not to argue any specific or necessary connection between frameworks and outcomes. What such frameworks do is to limit the range of options open to particular governments.

Political and Economic Attitudes to Industrial Policy

Amongst the factors and constraints which affect policy-making in the three countries is the nature of political attitudes to the industrial shape of the country. In Germany, for example, since the war the importance of the FRG's dependence upon international trade has been acknowledged by all the political parties except the Greens. Maintaining an internationally competitive industry and pursuing an 'offensive' industrial policy may thus be described as veritable 'national economic policy objectives'. Allied to this is the effect of German political sensitivity to issues of price stability and unemployment. Differences between the political parties are contained within the bounds of a political system that appears to require the broad-based 'people's parties' not to forsake the political middle ground. Popular perceptions of the nature of both Nazism and Communism and of the relative success of the post-war economy are crucial. Neither large-scale nationalization, nor a *laissez-faire* brand of capitalism that failed to pay adequate attention to the social consequences of industrial decisions, would be a realistic policy option within the FRG.[18]

In France the period after the Second World War saw major developments in economic attitudes, as an approach which distrusted expansion and privileged the state as the guardian of a supposedly 'natural' balance between different groups within society gave way to an emphasis on reconstruction, development, production, and growth. The (intentional) result was the emergence in France of a modern capitalist form of industrial organization. Amongst many politicians and senior civil servants there was an insistence on the possibility of consensus around technically correct objectives. Undoubtedly this was aided by the fact that although there was a major change of political regime in 1958, and shifting political fortunes amongst the parties, the period between 1944 and 1981 never saw a complete replacement of one entire governmental team by another. In the late 1960s government objectives shifted but the underlying attitude that the state has a proper and important role in economic and industrial strategies did not change. The new government objectives—an emphasis on profit rather than production, an overt encouragement of concentration in industry, and the encouragement of an awareness of France's position in international markets—which led to a 'national champions' policy, were widely accepted.

Since the period of the first oil crisis, with one brief exception,[19] French national objectives have been presented in terms of liberalism, or at least of scope for firms to maximize their endeavours, but it is still doubtful whether business would be willing to see the state abandon much of its traditionally close oversight over industrial activity. There has been much less questioning of the general legitimacy of such oversight, or of the overall competence of senior government officials in the area, than has occurred in Britain,[20] although individual actions and decisions may be contested.

British attitudes towards economic and industrial matters are shaped, amongst other factors, by deeply entrenched views, found amongst both firms and civil servants, that discriminatory policy is improper, and that governments have a duty to be even-handed. State intervention has been constrained by the unwillingness of firms to admit that the state may have a legitimate role to play in industrial strategy. Civil servants, unlike their French counterparts, are reluctant to 'pick winners' and indeed both they and a great many firms would question their competence to do so. Moreover governmental objectives in the economic and industrial fields are often described as vacillating and uncertain. This is in part the result of the alternation in government of parties with modes of discussing and presenting policy options which appear sharply contrasted, and with a habit of fierce attack upon the record and proposals of their opponents.[21] Our studies, presented in Chapters 5 and 10, demonstrate that it is too simplistic either to talk of sharp variations or to argue that in the end underlying and relatively unchanging civil service policy preferences win out over political priorities. Nevertheless, the political context is important. Many of the ideas underlying the liberalization of telecommunications were not new; but the Thatcher government after 1979 provided a propitious environment for their development.

Privatization and Nationalization

Attitudes to the issues of nationalization and privatization form major parts of general national attitudes towards government–industry relationships. The extent to which ownership and control are interrelated and whether ownership constitutes an important variable influencing relationships between industrial enterprises and the government are important themes of our case-studies to which we return in our conclusions. Here it seems appropriate to consider the patterns of nationalization and privatization within the three countries.

In West Germany, for reasons arising from the historical circumstances of the state's emergence, from negative perceptions of the effect of nationalization in state Socialist and other neighbours, and from positive perceptions of the success of post-war liberal economic policy, nationalization is kept within strict bounds. A substantial and diversified state sector exists, employing, in 1982, nearly 9 per cent of the total labour force.[22] Most of the communications infrastructure of the FRG (not only posts and telecommunications but also railways and airlines) is in public hands and the state has substantial shareholdings in companies in the steel, energy, shipbuilding, and automobile sectors (including minority shareholdings in Volkswagen). However, demands for the nationalization of further firms or whole industries are virtually 'beyond the pale'. Equally, however, proposals for privatization have made little headway and indeed there is a quite high level of state intervention in industry in the FRG.[23]

In France the period of the Liberation saw the first major wave of nationalizations.[24] The public sector thereafter included not only what were regarded as non-competitive public service monopolies, such as gas, electricity, rail, and air transport (but not water!), but also a number of companies in what is called the competitive sector, such as the oil company Elf Aquitaine and Renault cars, and more than half the banking and insurance sector. The period between 1959 and 1981 can be described as one of 'creeping nationalization'; money was put into new public and joint firms to implement major projects (such as Framatome, which builds nuclear power stations) and to aid ailing industry.[25]

The existence of a large public sector was readily accepted, until the 1980s, by all sides in France. Just how large that sector should be became a subject of political debate during the 1970s. Following the installation of a government of the Left under President Mitterrand in 1981, twelve industrial firms, thirty-six banks, and two major investment trusts were brought into the public sector. Thirteen of the twenty largest French industrial groups were thus in the public sector, and its share of industrial output rose from 17 per cent to 30 per cent if energy is included. The programme was not uncontested, for the political opposition consistently attacked it in the name of liberalism, and the legislation was hotly debated in Parliament and referred to the Constitutional Council. The President insisted upon the managerial autonomy of the newly nationalized companies, and they were not subjected to the close formal financial audit and control that is imposed upon others such as Électricité de France. From 1983 the public sector companies were given one key priority—to be making profits by 1986. The Socialist government's emphasis on autonomy, coupled with its 'rediscovery' of the virtues of the *entreprise* and the increasing adoption even by members of the government of a 'liberal' discourse, was followed, after the 1986 election, by the announcement of an ambitious programme of privatization by the Chirac government, which was halted, but not reversed, by its successor.[26] There had already been a degree of what might be called 'creeping privatization'; nationalized companies had been both selling off all or part of their subsidiaries[27] and issuing non-voting shares (*titres participatifs*) on the stock exchange.

Britain differs from France through the absence of a specific legal regime for public sector enterprises. The boundary between public and private is not clearly defined. In Britain during the period of the Thatcher governments after 1979, but especially after the 1983 election, a privatization programme came to hold a prominent place in political activity.[28] Public spending and activities, it was argued, had to be reduced to make way for increased private activities and reductions in taxation, and this must involve returning large parts of public activity to the private sector.[29] Most of the companies that were returned to the private sector before 1983 were already public limited companies, for example British Petroleum and the British National Oil Corporation, and all were in areas where they operated alongside private sector competition. This was not the case with the very large post-1983 privatizations such as British Telecom and British Gas. The privatization programme is controversial and highly political for its motivation can be seen to include the avoidance of either higher taxes or public borrowing as means of financing public expenditure,[30] and the creation of a class of small shareholders with a vested interest in returning governments opposed to renationalization.[31]

By the mid-1980s in neither France nor Britain was there the kind of very general consensus about the scope and nature of the shifting boundary between public and private sectors that had broadly existed in the 1960s and 1970s and still obtains in the

FRG. In both countries the issue of industrial ownership had become a prominent and very politicized one, used by parties to demarcate and identify themselves. There was, however, very little popular understanding and even less discussion of the issues of the relationship between ownership and control.

Structure and Nature of Government Institutions

Relationships between industry and government are continuous and take place at a multiplicity of levels. Companies are, for instance, taxpayers and employers and are thus in contact with those responsible for the collection of taxes and the enforcement of regulations relating to employment. Legislation relating to matters such as health and safety and the protection of the environment also has to be observed and enforced.[32]

Certain aspects of the machinery of government are particularly important to government–industry relations. Detailed investigation reveals the extent to which varying, contradicting, and conflicting lines of conduct may be followed both by different ministers and by their administrative staff. In the FRG the Basic Law stipulates that ministers conduct the affairs of their departments 'on their own responsibility'. In France too departments enjoy a good deal of formal autonomy.

The finding that the institutions of the state may, in their actions, be far from monolithic is scarcely new.[33] Our research has confirmed previous findings and emphasized the salience of them for government–industry relations. Amongst the key factors are: the nature and role of ministries of finance; notions of industrial sponsorship and the role of sponsoring ministries; the extent of political freedom of appointment to senior administrative posts; and the recruitment and career patterns of civil servants.

In France the ministries chiefly concerned with general industrial matters in the sectors covered by this study are the Industry Ministry and the Finance Ministry, in addition to the offices of the President and the Prime Minister. The precise machinery of government arrangements may fluctuate but divisions remain intact, usually in the same premises, and often (as in the case of Posts and Telecommunications) under a junior minister who, as is usual for French junior ministers, is characterized more by non-membership of the Council of Ministers than by a dependent relationship with a nominal chief. Central ministries in France are essentially federations of divisions (*directions*). There is no single permanent civil service head of the ministry's structure.[34] This allows a good deal of autonomy to the individual divisions, whose powerful sense of identity is reinforced by the fact that the scope of their responsibilities is laid down in legal and public form (by *arrêté*).

The French Ministry of Finance is often seen[35] as being very powerful, especially in relation to government policy towards industry. It is undoubtedly very deeply involved in many aspects of relationships between government and industry.[36] The Direction du Trésor (treasury division) administers the government's financial policy. It is linked very closely with the two major institutions which control credit and credit policy, the Bank of France and the Caisse des Dépôts et Consignations, which channels very large sums derived from the savings bank system into investment. The existence of exchange control regulations, and the treasury division's general powers of oversight over the money markets, as well as its role on the committees which administer the funds available for state subsidies and assistance to firms, give it a close knowledge not only of the general strategy but also the particular operations of individual firms. Zysman[37] has suggested that its central position in relation to credit policy allows it to implement a general industrial policy. However, our research suggests that the treasury division does not use this position to impose particular industrial strategies or develop specific policies. Rather, its views are narrow, clear, but based on purely financial criteria. Its power is essentially a veto or blocking power—but in the areas where it does act, it can do so very forcefully.

In Britain the conventions of cabinet government which are interpreted as requiring extensive consultation, combined with the co-ordinating role of the permanent secretary[38] and with civil service traditions of discretion and anonymity, mean that individual divisions play a less conspicuous role than in France and conflicts may be more muffled. Like the French Ministry of Finance the Treasury, although it has less direct influence upon credit, or subsidies, or foreign activities by firms, has a role which is greatest when the issues at stake are most clearly financial. Thus the financial intricacies and potential revenue effects of privatization have meant that the Treasury played a prominent role in the discussions leading up to the flotation of BT.[39]

In the FRG responsibility for industrial policy-making is shared between various ministries.[40] The very specific roles of both the Direction du Trésor and the Treasury do not seem to be played by the German Finance Ministry. The pre-eminent role within the West German financial system is played by the Bundesbank, which is both legally and in practice fully independent of the federal government. However, it was the Finance Ministry which, in consultation with the Economics Ministry and the Federal Chancellor's Office, made available loan guarantees as part of the rescue package for AEG-Telefunken.[41] The Finance Ministry's less prominent role in industrial policy compared with that of its British or French counterparts must partly be explained by the existence of both a separate Economics Ministry, which is much more closely concerned with industrial strategies, and a Ministry for Research and Technology, which has been a major source of subsidies for a number of industries including nuclear energy and information technology. Although the Finance Ministry acquired additional functions in 1972, as part of the deal between coalition partners by which an FDP minister took over the Economics Ministry, the FDP's crucial role in the shaping of the governing coalitions still gives the Economics Minister a powerful potential veto power.

Sponsorship and tutelle

The administration's relationships to industry were until recently described in Britain as sponsorship and in France are known as tutelle. Both words imply that an administrative department would have some kind of standing in relationship to an industrial sector. Of sponsorship Wilks observes[42] that 'the very term retains undertones of paternalism and supplication' which are a legacy of its wartime origins. Subsequently the sponsoring division's task became to ensure that its sector's interests were not overlooked and indeed were if possible forwarded both in the extensive consultations that were often a feature of the policy-formulation process within the British administration and internationally. As Leigh Hancher has pointed out, the essence of the sponsoring divisions is that they were 'industry-friendly'. However, sponsorship did not mean the formulation of strategy for sectors; rather the sponsoring divisions dealt with industrial problems as they arose.[43] In 1987 the Department of Trade and Industry abandoned the concept of sponsorship, promoting itself as the 'Department for Enterprise' and restructuring

its divisions so as to remove the notion that it had particular responsibilities for the welfare of specific sectors of industry. Both telecommunications and consumer electronics had previously been
'sponsored' by DTI divisions, although, as our case-studies reveal,
the content of the notion was never clearly fixed. Ambiguities
remain, in that ministries besides the DTI which had a sponsorshop
role continue to exercise it; for example the Department of Health
sponsors the pharmaceutical industry.

The French concept *tutelle* could be loosely translated as 'sponsorship' but the term derives from the word for guardian. It is used
not only in government–industry relations but also in other areas
of government activity[44] and carries strong overtones of supervision
and of veto powers.[45] In practice the relationship between the Direction Générale de l'Industrie and individual sectors is not so different
from 'sponsorship'. Moreover, in a move that foreshadowed the
restructuring of the British DTI, the Chirac government's Industry
Minister, Alain Madelin, reformed his ministry in 1986 so as to
remove specific responsibilities for individual sectors. Even before
that, where companies have been nationalized the emphasis upon
their managerial autonomy meant that the division's role was essentially one of negotiation, and certainly not one of control. Secondly,
the absence of an explicit concept of sponsorship of private industry
in France does not mean an absence of government–industry relations. Variations in relationships are much more likely to result
from the size, profitability and strategic position of a company than
from its status as a private or a nationalized enterprise. The Direction Générale de l'Industrie, and the Direction des Industries Électroniques et l'Informatique (DIELI) within it always had a very small
staff[46] and neither autonomous financial resources nor independent
sources of information.[47] It was very widely viewed as the mouthpiece for the sector, and especially for the big firms, within the
administrative structure. Indeed, Industry Ministry officials
regarded it as entirely natural that they should speak up for the
firms within both the French administration and the European Community.[48]

The German Economic Ministry contains sections concerned with
the various industrial sectors. These sections[49] generally have close
relationships with the industrial sectors which they monitor, and
may be seen, by other parts of the ministry, as the 'representatives'
of these sectors.[50] Since the era of Erhard, who was Economics

Minister from 1949 to 1963, the ministry has regarded itself as a 'liberal' institution. The Research and Technology Ministry, which distributes subsidies to specific products and technologies, has not, however, been immune from accusations of *dirigisme*, in the sense of giving directions to firms, or even to sectors, although its choices may largely have been a response to pressure from within industry.

Whether the formal concept involved is that of *tutelle*, as in the case of French public enterprise, or sponsorship, as in Britain, or is less clearly defined, as in the case of French private firms and of German firms, it remains true that within the administrative structures of all three countries there exists what the former German Economics Minister Lambsdorf has referred to as a 'service enterprise' for industry.

Civil Service Structures

The institutional structure of key parts of the governmental machine may have an impact upon the nature of governmental processes. The experiences and perceptions of those who staff these structures may also be important. In France, for example, civil service structure may be described as both fragmented and rigid. It is based upon a system of '*corps*', which group officials of similar functions within a career structure. The most distinguished and most prominent of these are the so-called *grands corps*, marked out by their small size and their close camaraderie. They act, amongst other things, as a reservoir of talent from which individuals can be drawn for senior and interesting posts. In its more specialized fields the *corps* of telecommunications engineers forms an important group. Its members are not only to be found in technical and managerial positions within the telecommunications system, but also, for example, provide the desk officer on telecommunications for the Direction du Trésor. The Ingénieurs des Mines, a notably cohesive and rather small *corps*, hold many of the key posts within the Industry Ministry.

Although their expertise may be of a fairly broad and general type,[51] the *grands corps* provide a reservoir of talent not just for civil service but also for senior industrial posts.[52] The phenomenon of *pantouflage* by which those who start their careers move out into public or private sector concerns, in both the industrial and financial fields, has been a marked feature of some *corps* since the

last century. A *corps* member within a ministry may well know
that the future lies with one of the companies with which the ministry
deals. There is often a more or less conscious policy of 'renvoyer
l'ascenseur'—senior members 'sending the lift back down' to the
benefit of their juniors. However, there is only very rarely movement
into civil service posts from outside.[53]

The work of co-ordination, especially political co-ordination, of
the ministerial divisions falls to the minister's personal staff, his
cabinet. Their main purpose is that of translation between the administrative concerns of the divisions and the political concerns
of the minister. A policy adviser within a *cabinet* may play at least
as influential a role as a senior member of one of the divisions.
Such advisers are recruited from amongst the members of the main
corps, from elsewhere in the public service, or from outsiders such
as journalists or academics.

This pattern of cross-cutting political and administrative loyalties
amongst a fairly small and in some respects homogeneous élite is
not found in the other countries studied. Germany resembles France
in that the party political loyalties of individual civil servants may
be known, and may be a factor in appointments to the very highest
posts in the ministries. In contrast to France, however, and in common with Britain, there is very little interchange of personnel
between the administration and industry.[54]

The role of the civil service in Germany seems to be conceived
of as vital, but fairly technical, an attitude encouraged by the tendency for civil servants to stay within one ministry, indeed often
one division, for a very large part of their careers. They see themselves as particularly concerned with making and implementing the
legal framework that will allow the economy to develop along
agreed lines. Parliament, which tends to contain a high proportion
of members with civil service backgrounds, contributes by a relatively non-adversarial approach to such regulation.

In Britain too the personal and career links between the civil
service and industry that characterize the French system do not
exist. Wilks suggests that 'the absence of a social structure in which
the discussion of restructuring and anticipatory action between busi-
nessmen, bankers and officials is possible'[55] helps to produce an
isolated and precedent-bound administration. The importance
attached to general skills and experience in 'administration' within
a neutral and secretive service, coupled with a recruitment to higher

level posts that draws from all academic disciplines or, much more than in the other two countries, from within the lower ranks of the service, may also contribute to this. It is also claimed that the short periods that British civil servants at the higher levels spend in one post mean that expertise is not built up.[56] This phenomenon is not peculiar to Britain however. While the French Direction du Trésor exhibits a good deal of continuity of staffing very few of the staff of the DIELI remained in the same post for three years or more during the decade before 1986.

The Organization and Influence of Labour

The nature of the organization and influence of labour in the three countries under study is substantially determined by the differing historical and political context of the development of trade unions in the three countries. This varying context has resulted in sharp differences in the shape and role of the unions in Britain, France, and West Germany.

The central feature of organized labour in Britain is its relationship to the Labour Party which has, however, only very seldom been translated into a secure influence on policy.[57] The essential political feature of the role of most UK unions is their commitment to the defence of their members' immediate economic interests, which often amounts to an adversarial role. The TUC, as the unions' umbrella organization, has an impressive coverage, accounting for 90 per cent of all British trade unionists. This in turn represents, by European standards, a large proportion of the workforce, for since 1974 between 48 and 54 per cent of the total workforce, including those unemployed, have been union members[58] in contrast to densities of around 36–8 per cent in West Germany and 23 per cent or less in France in the same period.

Jelle Visser's studies suggest, however, that the TUC is, compared with other European confederations, relatively weak in organizational terms; 'a seemingly monopolised and representational confederation may lack all the organizational resources and degree of concentration necessary for any control over its constituent parts'.[59]

The TUC does not have a single industrial policy committee, but maintains a range of committees dealing with individual industries, although Grant[60] suggests that these committees' relationships with individual unions are often tenuous. Since 1962 the TUC has sent six representatives to the National Economic Development Council (NEDC), but there these men tend to exercise their influence as leaders of the large industrial unions rather than as TUC representatives. Much more important has been the participation of union officials, nominated by the TUC, in the Economic Development Committees (EDCs) of the NEDC, and also in the Sector Working Parties (SWPs), such as that set up for consumer electronics in 1975. The members of these tripartite bodies are not chosen as representatives of particular interests, but the EDCs and SWPs have been means through which union officials have, for example, been able to influence inward investment policy under the Labour government to a greater extent than has been possible for their counterparts in France and the FRG.

In France union density is low[61] and the union movement itself is divided along lines stemming from historical and ideological cleavages. The largest union confederation is the Confederation Générale du Travail.[62] Its leadership is dominated by members of the Communist Party. The Confédération Française Démocratique du Travail[63] and the Force Ouvrière[64] are the other two major confederations. These organizations compete for members with each other and with the small, independent associations or unions that exist in particular branches of industry. The motivation for union activism is usually ideological commitment and a sense of working-class solidarity. Ideological goals have been pursued through political methods, with the result that advances that might elsewhere have been achieved by collective bargaining have been 'the object of politics, legislation and state regulation in France'.[65]

Between 1981 and 1986 the Mitterrand government introduced major legislation with the intention of extending workers' rights.[66] For the public sector, including the groups nationalized in 1981, the *loi sur la démocratisation du secteur public* required the election of worker representatives to company 'boards' (*conseils d'administration*). In practice this seems to have reinforced the previous situation, at least in the companies that we have examined closely, whereby the 'boards' had a largely formal and consultative non-executive role, but also increased their importance as a channel for the presentation to the workforce of parts at least of the company strategy. The changes have encouraged some greater attention to the provision of information to worker directors and the workforce, but given them no increase in real influence or control over company strategy.

At national level the French unions have consistently been 'policy community outsiders'. 'Industrial policies ... have been the subject of a bi-partite, not tripartite, corporatist relationship between government and large firms, with the trade unions conspicuous by their absence, except as far as dealing with the redundancies consequent upon industrial decisions.'[67]

In West Germany, the German Trade Union Federation (DGB) organizes about 80 per cent of all union members. Though higher than in France, union density in the FRG is not high in general European terms. The main base of the unions has historically been the skilled manual workers; white collar workers, women, and young people are much less unionized.

The DGB has no formal powers to intervene in the affairs of its seventeen member unions. The individual unions are, however, highly centralized. They represent, or seek to represent, the interests of all workers in their respective industries. In the case of consumer electronics the union concerned is the largest German union, the IG Metall. Because it organizes workers in all the engineering industries it steers clear of advocating 'sectorally egoistic' measures such as import controls, and plays a relatively passive role in relation to mergers and company rescue politics. Were it to do otherwise it might endanger its own internal cohesion.

In contrast, the Post Office Workers' Union enjoys considerable influence. It is normally consulted at an early stage in the policy-making process.[68] As officials (*Beamte*) its members benefit from legally protected security of employment, but may not legally strike. The union's influence derives from its high level of organization of Bundespost staff, its co-determination powers through the Bundespost's administrative council and its personnel councils, and the public sector monopoly status of the Bundespost. Its chief concerns are with personnel and industrial relations policy.

It is the Post Office Workers' Union's place on the Bundespost's administrative council that helps to support its influence. Indeed the integration of labour within the industrial structure is institutionalized by the systems of co-determination and worker participation which constitute the core of the 'historic compromise' reached by labour and capital in the FRG after the Second World War.[69]

Works councils, which have extensive powers in the fields of working conditions and personnel policies, do not possess a formal veto power over whether a plant is to be closed, a firm sold or merged, or a new production technology introduced. Their influence may, however, extend beyond their formal powers, and the works council of AEG-Telefunken, for example, played a major role in preventing part of the firm being sold to GEC in 1982 and in supporting demands for government intervention. Despite close links between the unions and the SPD, the SPD members of the government quickly rejected the union demands for the nationalization of AEG.

The Organization of Finance and Capital

In three major areas of their industrial and financial structures the three countries studied display variations which appear to have some salience for government–industry relations. They are in the level and nature of the concentration of business and the role of small firms; in the nature and role of the organizations representing business interests; and in the role and nature of banks and the financial sector.

In both France and the FRG the role of the small firm remains important. West German industry appears to be the least concentrated of all the three countries.[70] In the FRG small and medium-sized companies may in certain areas exercise a good deal of influence. Our research suggests that this is particularly true of the telecommunications sector. For example, there are approximately ten medium- or small-sized firms which supply the Bundespost with terminals equipment, especially telephones, and they are able to express their views (for example on the desirability of the retention by the Bundespost of the monopoly of the supply of telephone sets) through the communications technology sub-association of the ZVEI (the electrical engineering industry's central association). The small and medium-sized firms may also benefit from the fact that three of the political parties (the CDU, the FDP, and, in Bavaria where the sector is particularly strong, the CSU) are concerned to attract their vote.

Many of the smaller sub-contractor firms depend heavily for their orders on the larger companies; for example Siemens's suppliers are said to include some 32,000 small and medium-sized firms. One of the reasons why the federal and, most particularly, the *Land* governments supported the AEG-Telefunken solution in 1982 was the fear that very many small firms would also founder if AEG sank.[71] In Britain, which has the highest level of industrial concentration of the three countries (a 1978 estimate suggested that 100 firms between them produce about 70 per cent of total output) small firms are also very frequently closely tied to particular large firms, without which their existence might be in jeopardy.

Our findings on the role of the business and trade associations in all three countries emphasized the extent to which this role may differ and vary both between the peak and the sectoral associations, and between differing sectors. It is clearly inadequate simply to consider whether an employers' organization is influential in policy-making, is given a privileged status as an interlocutor of government, or, indeed, accorded powers to act in certain areas in the government's stead. All these features do apply to some degree to organizations that represent business interests, but all of them require qualification.

Confederations represent the interests of business in the three countries. In Britain some 150 employers and trade associations are members of the Confederation of British Industry which also has over 10,000 industrial companies as members. In France the main organization for business is the Conseil National du Patronat Français. The Trade Associations are federated within the CNPF. In the FRG the employers are highly organized in the industrial relations sphere through the BDA (the Federation of German Employers Associations) and manufacturing industry is represented in all other spheres through the BDI (the Federation of German Industry), which is organized by sector. In certain spheres these peak organizations are undoubtedly of great importance; for example in German industrial relations policy the role of the BDA is a major one, while in France the unemployment benefit scheme is supervised by the government but operated through a joint scheme by employers and unions. In Britain one of the main tasks of the CBI is the nomination of members to official committees, including the NEDC.

The peak organizations are important interlocutors of the government not only in the social field, but also in the discussion of broad cross-sectoral economic issues such as exchange rate policy or trade policy. Indeed our interviews confirmed Streeck's argument[72] that the German Economics Ministry attempts to mobilize the peak associations to protect it from the more particularist demands of sector associations or firms, not always successfully. On sector-specific issues, however, our research suggests that the role of the peak organizations is minimal.

Sector-specific issues are likely to be the concern of the sectoral or trade associations. Industrial sectors may constitute fairly small and specialized worlds. Contacts and discussions occur in a number of ways both formal and informal. Trade fairs and exhibitions, conferences and Christmas parties have their place alongside more formal structures such as the trade associations provide. 'Man trifft sich, man kennt sich' (we meet and know each other), said one of our German interviewees. Indeed one of the important roles of sectoral bodies may be simply to provide the arena in which key people encounter each other. The salience of their role in the affairs of their sector clearly varies. In Britain in consumer electronics the British Radio and Electronic Equipment Manufacturers Association (BREMA) is in constant touch with the Department of Trade and Industry and takes part in industry-to-industry trade talks with Far Eastern countries, although it was a NEDO initiative which launched the highly successful development of teletext.[73] In Germany the sectoral and trade associations (such as the ZVEI for electronics and electrical engineering) play a part, for example as the bodies which are consulted about technical issues. However, in areas where their members' interests may be in conflict the need to maintain internal cohesion restrains their intervention.[74] Large firms may also maintain their own offices and lobbyists in Bonn and our case-studies illustrate the growing importance of direct bilateral relationships between firms and the government.

In France the trade associations are federated within the CNPF; they may have certain legal roles as agents of the government, for example in the collection of statistics, and under certain conditions, most notoriously in the case of the pre-1980s steel industry and in agriculture, as the distributors of subsidies. Many observers[75] have concluded however that collective action is quite simply bypassed, indeed rendered redundant, by the major companies, who have their own, often personal, links into a number of different places and levels within the government machine. Our findings support this conclusion.

Zysman has argued that differences in industrial structure and performance between advanced capitalist countries may largely be accounted for by differences in the financial systems that underlie those industrial structures. There are sharp contrasts between the three countries studied, especially in three interlinked areas: the size and importance of the stock market, the role of the banks, and the role of the state.

There is a conventional wisdom that sees Britain as characterized by a 'split' between the City and industry, whereby the financial institutions have neglected to invest sufficiently in British industry. This view has recently been challenged from a number of directions.[76] However, there are features of the financial structure that are not found in France and Germany. The British stock market is much larger, in terms of volume and value of transactions, than those of the other two countries. There are very large institutional investors, such as pension funds and insurance companies, which may be important to mergers and take-overs, but do not necessarily intervene very closely in the day-to-day management of companies. The dominance of the stock market causes companies to be very conscious of the short-term effects of their actions and strategies upon their profitability and share price, and may have an inhibiting effect upon the formulation of long-term plans.

In Germany the stock market is small, and firms operate with less equity capital than their British counterparts. The French stock market is also small. In the late 1970s only 1,000 firms were quoted on it, as against 4,000 in Britain. Government schemes promoting shareholding, for example by the authorization of unit trusts, and the granting of tax concessions, were amongst the causes of a marked expansion under the Mitterrand government after 1981—the total number of transactions more than doubled between 1982 and 1984.[77] Nevertheless although profitability is a prime concern, there seemed to be agreement within the French companies we studied that their stock exchange rating was not necessarily a major preoccupation of private companies; the privatization of nationalized enterprises was thought to be of minimal significance in this respect.

The FRG is often contrasted with Britain and France in terms of the role played in industrial development and adjustment by the banks. It is certainly renowned for its system of 'universal banks'— banks, that is, that engage in the whole range of banking activities, including lending to, investing in, and participating in the management of, industrial firms. The three biggest banks, the Deutsche Bank, the Dresdner Bank and the Commerzbank, are all 'universal banks par excellence'.[78] The proportion of shares actually owned by the banks amounted to 8 per cent in 1983. This alone would not enable them to play as central a role as they appear to occupy in the industrial world. The key factor is their exercise of proxy rights on behalf of individual shareholders who deposit their shares in the banks. This enables them to be strongly represented on the supervisory boards of companies.[79] This representation, the bank's own shareholdings, their proxy powers, and their control of credit lines give the banks a potentially strong voice in the management of firms. However, they do not necessarily influence day-to-day affairs. Large and flourishing firms may in turn have their representatives on the supervisory board of the bank, and need not necessarily defer to the banks. Siemens, for example, refused pleas from the banks to help in the rescue of AEG-Telefunken. It is when firms run into problems that the role of the banks may be prominent; they then play a 'fire-fighting' role. The banks may in such circumstances act as a buffer between the industrial firms and the government and thereby stave off pressure on government to intervene directly with a rescue operation. Even when government does intervene its action may be indirect; when the federal government was negotiating the AEG-Telefunken rescue it was in fact talking to the banks. The banks are clearly potentially crucial actors;[80] opinions vary even within Germany as to the extent to which this potential is fulfilled.[81]

In France over half the banking sector was nationalized in 1945; the remaining banks were nationalized in 1982, including a number of smaller banks, some of which proved to be in financial difficulties, and were reorganized. The state banks (including those nationalized in 1982), despite fairly close relationships with the Finance Ministry, do not seem to accept instructions on lending policy outside the framework of normal monetary control.[82] Also nationalized in 1982 were the two large *banques d'affaires* (financial holding companies) Suez and Paribas. Both of these hold important share portfolios, largely accumulated in the past. It has been argued that Paribas played an important part in the industrial restructuring of the late 1960s and 1970s. Our research has led us to conclude that at least in the sectors in which we are interested the role of both banks and the financial holding companies has been minimal. It is notable in France that companies, especially the largest companies,[83] have looked to the state for financial assistance, subsidies, and loans rather than to the stock market or the banks.[84]

The role of the state within the financial sector in France is much more prominent than in Britain or the FRG for two main reasons; one is the extent of continuing state control over certain activities, for example foreign exchange and overseas acquisitions; the other is the extent to which the state is involved in some of the major credit-granting institutions, such as the Caisse de Dépôts et Consignations, in which funds from the very large mutual savings banks are deposited. The Bank of France works closely with the Direction du Trésor; its main role is executing overall monetary policy.

The Bundesbank, in contrast, is both legally and in practice fully independent of the West German government. It has always seen the maintenance of price stability as its main objective, and it possesses all the instruments of monetary policy.[85]

In Britain, as Moran has demonstrated, the government's relationship to the financial sector was in the period from the First World War until the late 1960s largely mediated through the Bank of England, which itself exercised a fairly tight control over some (but not all) parts of the financial sector. More recently the Bank of England's role as the instrument of self-regulation has weakened as monetary policy has become more central to political concerns and institutions such as the clearing banks have sought more direct contact with the government. While the Treasury has effectively become the 'sponsoring' department for the financial sector, we have found no evidence to suggest that the state plays a role that can be regarded as comparable to that of the state in France.

Zysman[86] argues that the financial system in France is credit based, with administered prices, and dominated by the state. He contrasts that with the system in Germany, which he sees as also credit based, but dominated by the banks, whereas the British system is essentially a capital-based market system. As our case-studies make clear, our research does not support some of the further conclusions that may be drawn from this broad categorization; but Zysman's formulation does point in general terms to some of the main points of contrast between the three countries.

The European Framework

In the mid-1950s, as those anxious to advance the cause of European integration sought a field for action that would regain the ground lost with the defeat of the European Defence Community in 1954, a 'Common Market' seemed to offer a particularly promising prospect. Experience in one industrial field (coal and steel) had been encouraging, increased liberalization of trade (foreshadowed by Benelux, the European Payments Union, GATT, etc.) seemed to offer prospects for growth, and all were anxious to avoid any possibility of a return to the autarchy of the 1930s. The Treaty of Rome was drafted around an economic concept of liberal capitalism.[87] In consequence the Treaty contains quite well-developed provisions for trade policy and competition policy at Community level. The intention was to set up a viable and integrated internal market, including necessary concomitant rights, such as free movement of labour and the right of establishment.

The internal market is still far from fully developed,[88] although the customs union is completely established. Trade policy is thus now largely a Community matter; the member states have no individual rights to impose external tariffs and major protectionist measures (such as the 19 per cent tariff on compact disc players and the Multi-Fibre Agreement) have to be agreed at EEC level. Moreover, in international (e.g. GATT) negotiations the EEC speaks with one voice, usually through a Commission official. However, the Commission does not have an autonomous policy-making role in this area. The negotiators can only act on the basis of instructions agreed by the governments of the member states through the Council of Ministers. It is perhaps fair to say that the existence of the Treaty forces intergovernmental action in very wide areas of trade and tariffs policy, without removing all possibility of individual national action. There are safeguard clauses which can be flexibly interpreted, and national quotas do seem still to exist, whether publicly and legally or not.[89] Nor has the existence of the EEC yet had a major impact on public procurement preferences.[90]

The Treaty was also concerned to safeguard competition within the market, and thus provided for a competition policy. The Treaty gives the Commission quite wide autonomous powers in this respect. Thus the Commission is entitled without consultation with the Council of Ministers to determine whether in its view a firm is abusing a dominant position in a market, to require it to desist, and to fine it. The firm has a right of appeal to the Court of Justice. These are of course negative powers and relate to the abuse of a position, not the acquisition of that position. There is no EEC equivalent of a monopolies and mergers commission to police take-overs, for example, but its officials have recently been active in interpreting the implications of proposed take-overs for competition policy. There have been some leading cases in the consumer electronics field,[91] but these have related to supply to retailers and sole dealerships, not directly to production or relationships to other producers. Nevertheless, the notion of the necessity for market competition within the EEC is a powerful one. In areas where major efforts in research and development are required that probably extend beyond the capacity of any one company or indeed member state the EEC has sponsored important programmes. However, the RACE programme for example is now moving forward from a period of specific research project collaboration to a second, pre-competitive, stage (ACE—Action for Communications and Electronics) where innovations require development and indeed pilot production. The Council of Ministers has been reluctant to appear to sanction what might be interpreted as anti-competitive behaviour.

Another aspect of the internal market is the issue of standardization and harmonization. Clearly, different standards can constitute major non-tariff barriers.[92] Here, however, the EEC has recently shown an increased willingness to recognize the international dimensions of the problem, and increasingly the Council of Ministers has agreed, on the basis of Commission proposals, that where standards are set in international bodies which may include non-member states (e.g. CEPT in telecoms, and CEM and CENELEC in electrical goods) these standards will be mandatory within the EEC.

In competition and trade policy the EEC thus has powers that are defined by the Treaty and by now, after two and a half decades, surrounded by legislation and court judgments. Nevertheless the legal powers of the Community are the subject of close scrutiny by member states, and the Commission is aware that it requires the political backing of all the member states as well as its legal resources if it is to act effectively. That this is well appreciated by the various interest groups and lobbies within the Community is demonstrated by the fact that even over trade policy matters firms and groups devote effort to lobbying their national governments at least as much as to direct approaches to the Community institutions.

The EEC has a common agricultural policy; it does not have

a common industrial policy. Other considerations—the agricultural policy, the monetary system, the problems of enlargement, above all questions of budgeting and resources—have all overshadowed industrial questions. In the Regional Fund some potential for industrial support and restructuring exists, but the fund is small, subject to the additionality principle (that projects must be those that would not otherwise be undertaken and must also be supported by national government funds) and available only to projects located within the designated regions.

Thus in some respects the EEC is developing into a supra-national state system, in that in certain designated areas described above, EEC institutions are either upholding, or beginning to uphold, a successful claim to the monopoly of legitimate coercion. It seems clear, however, from our case-studies which follow, that the process of internationalization is developing rather more strongly at the level of the firm, and pressures to develop further the role of EEC institutions will come in part from responses to transnational firm behaviour.

Notes

1. Some of them embodied in documents, such as the *Questions of Procedure for Ministers*. See P. Hennessy, *Cabinet* (Oxford: Basil Blackwell, 1986).
2. K. Dyson, 'West Germany: The Search for a Rationalist Consensus', in J. Richardson (ed.), *Policy Styles in Western Europe* (London: Allen & Unwin, 1982), pp. 34–5.
3. The federal government does have its own administration in some areas, such as the Post Office and Telecommunications. However, even here, where they have no formal constitutional competence, the *Länder* may seek to intervene, as they have done in the debate on privatization of the Bundespost. They are represented on the Bundespost's administrative council.
4. This occurred when the rescue plans for AEG-Telefunken were put together (see below, pp. 293–4). The Bavarian government was active at the time of the Thomson–Grundig affair in seeking a 'Bavarian solution' for the future of Grundig. See below, pp. 302–4.
5. Central control over the federal bureaucracy remains weak, despite attempts by the Social–Liberal coalition between 1969 and 1972 to undertake 'political planning' through the Federal Chancellor's Office. The Basic Law (Article 65) stipulates that ministers conduct the affairs

of their departments 'on their own responsibility', and is generally construed as ruling out detailed intervention by the Chancellor or his staff in the ministries' affairs.

6. Alain Boublil, the President's industrial adviser, certainly played an important, if backstage, role, in the Thomson–CGE telecommunications agreement. See below, p. 133.

7. A. G. Jordan, and J. J. Richardson, *British Politics and the Policy Process* (London: Allen & Unwin, 1987) pp. 119–62.

8. For a detailed account of the Westland helicopters affair, where both defence and industrial policy considerations were involved, and severe conflict occurred between ministers, see House of Commons Select Committee on Defence, *Fourth Report of the Defence Committee: Westland PLC: Government Decision-Making*, Session 1985–6, HCP 281 (London: HMSO, July 1986).

9. S. Wilks, 'Liberal State and Party Competition: Britain', in K. Dyson and S. Wilks (eds.), *Industrial Crisis: A Comparative Study of the State and Industry* (Oxford: Martin Robertson, 1983), p. 129.

10. Wilks, 'Liberal State', p. 183.

11. For example, the law of 2 July 1986, a single, brief piece of legislation, authorized the privatization of up to 65 companies. In Britain each privatization requires a separate Act of Parliament.

12. D. Coombes and S. A. Walkland (eds.), *Parliaments and Economic Affairs in Britain, France, Italy and the Netherlands* (London: Heinemann, 1981). A strking example of a select committee examination of policy is the report from the House of Lords' Select Committee on Overseas Trade chaired by Lord Aldington (Session 1984–5, House of Lords Paper 238). Unlike the parliamentary committees of France and Germany, British select committees normally have powers only to inquire, monitor, report, and recommend. Their membership may change from year to year. Only in the case of the select committees of the two Houses on European Community legislation (the so-called scrutiny committees) are legislative proposals submitted for comment to a committee before they are passed into law, and they are proposals for European Community legislation, not British domestic law.

13. K. Dyson, 'The Politics of Economic Management', in W. Paterson and G. Smith (eds.), *The West German Model: Perspectives on a Stable State* (London: Frank Cass, 1981).

14. The cost and time involved in challenging such decisions may be a deterrent. Nor should the strong sense of the importance of the law be taken to imply that firms, officials, and citizens are necessarily more law-abiding in the FRG than elsewhere.

15. In the case of the nationalization legislation of 1981–2 the Constitutional Council effectively dictated the terms on which existing share-

holders in the companies were to be compensated by rather detailed comments on the application of the constitutional right of the individual to property.

16. In 1975–6 only 1% of cases before the administrative court of appeal, the Conseil d'État, came under the heading 'commerce, industry, economy'. D. Labetoulle, 'Le Juge administratif et l'interventionnisme économique de l'état', in Institut de l'Entreprise, *Relations entre état et entreprises privées dans la CEE* (Paris: Masson, 1979), p. 75.

17. F. Dreyfus and F. D'Arcy, *Les Institutions politiques et administratives de la France* (Paris: Economica, 1985), 107, say they are distinguished by their creation as a result of a decision by a political authority, by their objectives, which are in the general interest, by their management, which is subject to control by elected political authorities, and by the application to them of specific legal rules related to administrative law.

18. It may be argued that the industrial policies of the Christian Democrat–Liberal coalition under Chancellor Kohl, which have led to a considerable increase in subsidies during its period in office, reflect a particular sensitivity to unemployment, and the resilience of the 'social democratic' consensus in the FRG. This is in strong contrast to the declared policies of the Thatcher government in Britain since 1979. See also above, n. 5.

19. Between 1981 and 1983.

20. See A. Stevens, 'The Higher Civil Service and Economic Policy-Making in France', in P. G. Cerny and M. A. Schain (eds.), *French Politics and Public Policy* (London: Frances Pinter, 1980); and E. Suleiman, *Élites in French Society* (Princeton, N. J.: Princeton University Press, 1978).

21. Some commentators attack what they perceive as a damagingly unstable climate for industry. S. Finer, *Adversary Politics and Electoral Reform* (London: Anthony Wigram, 1975), and M. Stewart, *The Jekyll and Hyde Years: Politics and Economic Policy in Britain* (London: Dent, 1977). Others allege on the contrary that civil service resistance frustrates political initiatives. See B. Sedgemore, *The Secret Constitution* (London: Hodder & Stoughton, 1980), and J. Hoskyns, 'Whitehall and Westminster: An Outsider's View', *Parliamentary Affairs* 36 (1983), pp. 137–47.

22. See H. Parris, P. Pestieau, and P. J. Saynor, *Public Enterprise in Western Europe* (London: Croom Helm, 1987), pp. 28–35 and p. 108.

23. See above n. 19. Recently quite limited proposals to reduce the federal government's holding in Lufthansa were thwarted, largely by the chairman of Lufthansa's Supervisory Board. On the other hand the Social Democratic Party, the SPD, distanced itself hastily from its own

workers' auxiliary organization's call to nationalize the steel industry in 1984.

24. The railways and the Bank of France were nationalized by the Popular Front government in 1936.

25. The most striking example was in steel, where the state forced some reconstruction and appointed government directors to the *conseils d'administration* of the new companies as it poured in money to rescue the industry. Nationalization when it came, in that case, was certainly only the legal regularization of a position that had long existed *de facto*.

26. The emphasis on managerial autonomy was supported by Pierre Dreyfus, the former head of Renault, who was Industry Minister 1981–2 and remained a close adviser of the President. Dreyfus's successor, Jean-Pierre Chevènement, took a much more interventionist approach; complaints by the heads of the nationalized companies, allegedly expressed, for instance, at a dinner with Mitterrand early in 1983, preceded his departure later that year. M. Bauer and B. Bertin-Mourot, 'Entreprises publiques et mouvement patronal: Le Cas français', unpublished paper for colloquium, The Politics of Private Business and Public Enterprises, European University Institute, Florence, 1986. On privatization see Mairi Macdonald, 'The Future of Privatisation in France: A Crisis of Confidence', *Modern and Contemporary France*, 31 (October 1987), pp. 1–9.

27. The legality of this was dubious. There was one test case, brought by the unions and relating to the sale of the Renault subsidiary Renix, but no judgement had been given before the 1986 election. A *loi sur la respiration du secteur public* to regularize the practice was under discussion before the election.

28. Privatization is a broad and often ill-defined concept; it can mean contracting out of services previously undertaken in-house by central or local government, but in the context of industrial policy the sale of nationalized companies is its most significant aspect. While this has, in Britain, been a particularly marked feature of the period of the Mrs Thatcher's governments, especially since 1983, the government of her Labour predecessor, James Callaghan, sold off 17% of British Petroleum in 1977.

29. P. Hall, *Governing the Economy: The Politics of State Intervention in Britain and France* (Cambridge: Polity Press, 1986), p. 100.

30. The idiosyncrasies of British public accounting which includes the borrowing of public sector companies in the public sector borrowing requirement (PSBR), meant that removing companies from the public sector had an immediately beneficial effect on the level of the PSBR, which is held to be an important indicator of governmental success

in achieving a healthy economy. The PSBR is the measure of government indebtedness. It is not the practice in France to include public sector borrowing in such computations — indeed French observers are bemused by this convention. There is, for example, almost no concern about the huge debts of Électricité de France.

31. The Conservative Party purchased lists of British Telecom shareholders as a basis for direct mailings to potential supporters at the time of the 1987 election.

32. It was argued by interviewees in France that one of the less desirable effects of nationalization was not the imposition of new controls but the realization by a number of ministries that here were large firms to whose practices special attention should be paid, since the government as a shareholder should be sure that they were exemplary in all respects. The Service des Entreprises Nationalisés of the Industry Ministry then felt that part of its responsibility was to protect the firms against what it felt to be undue interference by bodies such as, for example, the Ministry of Youth and Sports concerned about employees' recreational facilities.

33. In 1978 Suleiman spoke of the differing approaches to be found amongst members of apparently rather cohesive *corps* within the French civil service, depending upon the role within the administration that the *corps* member was at that time fulfilling. In 1980 Grant Jordan described cleavages within a single ministry where divisions were sponsoring sectors with conflicting interests. E. N. Suleiman, *Politics, Power and Bureaucracy in France* (Princeton, N. J.: Princeton University Press, 1974); A. G. Jordan, 'Iron Triangles, Woolly Corporatism and Elastic Nets: Images of the Policy Process', *Journal of Public Policy*, 1 (1981).

34. The abolition of the post of Secretary-General in the PTT Ministry in the early 1970s coincided with the complete separation of the postal and telecommunications sides of the ministry into two *directions générales*. Previously there had been a number of common service departments within the ministry. This marked the achievement by the DGT of complete functional autonomy.

35. D. Green, 'Strategic Management and the State: France', in Dyson and Wilks, *Industrial Crisis*; J. Saint Geours, *Pouvoir et finance* (Paris: Fayard, 1979); and X. Beauchamps, *Un état dans l'état?: Le Ministère de l'économie et des finances* (Paris: Bordas, 1976).

36. Amongst the major *directions* are the budget division, which between 1978 and 1981 formed the nucleus of a separate budget ministry, and is chiefly concerned to limit public expenditure. The Ministry of Finances also possesses an economic analysis unit, the Direction de la Prévision (forecasting division), which tends to take a fairly wide

and long-term view. It may be seen as having interests in common with those of the planning commission, but by comparison with the Trésor has a more marginal role.

37. J. Zysman, *Governments, Markets and Growth* (Berkeley and Los Angeles: University of California Press, 1983).

38. The Department of Trade and Industry was first formed under the Heath government in 1970, and was split into separate departments of Trade and of Industry in 1974, apparently to limit Tony Benn's power. The department was reunited in 1983, but retained two permanent secretaries for the first few years.

39. Similarly the Department of Industry found itself in conflict with the Treasury over the scale of funds required for telecommunications developments, since the financing of such developments affects the public sector borrowing requirement.

40. The federal government's attempt during 1983–4 to promote information technology involved negotiating agreements with no fewer than six central ministries. How difficult the attainment of a compromise between the participating ministries was is revealed by the fact that what emerged from the consultation process was not the integrated programme which the government had pledged but rather a much more vague and non-binding 'conception'.

41. The Finance Ministry also has its own, strictly fiscal, attitude to Bundespost privatization, which would turn the Bundespost into a normal tax-paying enterprise. At present the Bundespost pays no VAT but rather a levy of 10% of its turnover directly to the Finance Ministry. A half or more of 'normal' tax revenues would go to *Land* or local governments.

42. S. Wilks, *Industrial Policy and the Motor Industry* (Manchester: Manchester University Press, 1984), p. 193.

43. Before they were abolished in 1987, sponsoring divisions had minimal resources and were not staffed at a level that would allow them a major role. In 1986 the consumer electronics industry was 'sponsored' by one principal and half of the time of a higher executive officer.

44. For example in relations between central government and local authorities.

45. It is used to describe the relationship between a public sector enterprise and the ministry which has primary responsibility for it. The concept of *tutelle* cannot, however, extend to private industrial enterprises. This distinction is a legal and formal one. In the case of the companies nationalized in 1982 the primary responsibility was allocated to the Direction Générale de l'Industrie: the official civil service list gave a list of the companies for which its Service des Entreprises Nationalisés

was held to have official responsibility as part of the formal description of the division's activities and scope.

46. From the staff lists in the annual editions of the *Bottin administrative* it appears that there was little continuity of staffing, and below the level of division head the officials mostly came from relatively low-status or marginal, if technical, corps.

47. The DIELI did have a very small branch concerned with economic studies—before 1984 the Economic and Financial Service, thereafter the Industrial Strategy and Market Study branch. But it was heavily dependent upon the firms for the information available to it. Only after 1984 did the DIELI have a branch dealing specifically with 'audio-visual communication and consumer electronics' with three desk officers. Before that there was no formal allocation of responsibility for consumer electronics within what was then the Electronics and Space Branch.

48. A. Cawson, P. Holmes, and A. Stevens, 'The Interaction Between Firms and the State in France: The Case of Telecommunications and Consumer Electronics', in S. Wilks and M. Wright (eds.), *Comparative Government Industry Relations: Western Europe, the United States, and Japan* (Oxford: Clarendon Press, 1987), p. 14.

49. The sectoral sections are grouped in Division Four of the ministry.

50. Interview with Federal Ministry of Economics official, Feb. 1968. This position brings them into conflict with other divisions, such as that responsible for European Community policy or, particularly, Division One of the ministry which is the division for general policy principles. This division, which 'cuts across' the other divisions, has a general attitude, to some extent shared throughout the ministry, which strongly favours the market economy.

51. Suleiman, *Élites in French Society.*

52. We interviewed a number of people in such posts who could ascribe their positions to their *corps* membership. An explanation advanced several times was that in French conditions industry itself did not seem to provide a suitable pool of people with the talent, training, and experience needed for such posts. (Conversely, it is also true that people with such talents and ambitions will look to the *corps* as their starting-point.)

53. Those who have not commenced their careers within the public service (there is no provision for 'late entry' recruitment) can legally only fill temporary posts, or the very highest posts where the minister has absolute discretion. In principle a former official may return after a period in industry; in practice this virtually never happens. Remuneration in nationalized industry is said to exceed that of comparable levels within the civil service by about 200%.

54. Lohr, the head of SEL, came from the Bundespost, as did a board member of TN Telenorma, Wigand, but such cases are unusual.
55. Wilks, 'Liberal State', p. 141.
56. In 1977 the English Committee cited an average of three years. House of Commons, Select Committee on Expenditure, *Eleventh Report*, Session 1976–77 HCP 535-I-II-III.
57. In 1974–5, in the early phase of the social contract, economic policy was quite largely determined by the agreements arrived at between the party and the TUC. But the TUC was unable to maintain its position.
58. Figures from J. Visser, 'Dimensions of Union Growth in Postwar Western Europe', European University Institute, Working Paper No. 89 (Florence: EUI, Feb. 1984).
59. J. Visser, 'The Positions of Central Confederations in the National Union Movement: A Ten-Country Comparison', European University Institute, Working Paper No. 102 (Florence: EUI, May 1984), 72.
60. W. Grant, *The Political Economy of Industrial Policy* (London: Butterworths, 1982), p. 42.
61. The absence of reliable figures makes it extraordinarily difficult to calculate French trade union density with any degree of accuracy.
62. 1.3m. members in 1981. Visser, 'Dimensions of Union Growth'.
63. 0.75m. members in 1981. Ibid. It was formerly the CFTC, of which a rump still exists. The CFDT severed its links with the Catholic Church in 1964.
64. 0.67m. members in 1981. Ibid.
65. G. Ross, 'The Perils of Politics: French Unions and the Crisis of the 1970s', in P. Lange, G. Ross, and M. Vannicelli, *Unions, Change and Crisis: French and Italian Union Strategy and the Political Economy* (London: Allen & Unwin, 1982), p. 7.
66. D. Gallie, 'The *Lois Auroux*: The Reform of French Industrial Relations', in H. Machin and V. Wright (eds.), *Economic Policy and Policy-Making under the Mitterrand Presidency 1981–1984* (London: Frances Pinter, 1985).
67. J. E. S. Hayward, *The State and the Market Economy: Industrial Patriotism and Economic Intervention in France* (Brighton: Wheatsheaf Books, 1986), pp. 63–4.
68. D. Webber, 'The Politics of Telecommunications Deregulation in the Federal Republic of Germany', Working Paper Series on Government–Industry Relations, No. 3 (University of Sussex, 1986), p. 7.
69. The most advanced system of co-determination applies only to the iron and steel and coal industries. Other firms with more than 2,000 employees must have a supervisory board (*Aufsichtsrat*) with equal representation from both 'labour' (including some union nominees and

also at least one managerial employee) and 'capital', who provide the chairman who has a casting vote. A third system covers most other firms. In all firms of more than 5 employees shop-floor level participation is provided for by works councils (*Betriebsräte*).

70. The following table shows enterprises by number of employees:

	France 1980		FRG 1970		UK 1972	
	enterprises (%)	employees (%)	enterprises (%)	employees (%)	enterprises (%)	employees (%)
1–9	84.7	14.1	85.9	22.9		
10–49	11.9	20.1	11.1	20.9		
50–499	3.1	26.2	2.7	32.4		
over 500	0.3	39.6	0.2	24.6		
1–19					83.5	11.3
20–499					14.0	20.4
over 500					2.5	68.3

Source: Banque Nationale de Paris, *Guide statistique 1983: La France devant le monde* (Paris: BNP, 1983).

71. The Hesse government implemented a special programme for small and medium-sized firms to alleviate the repercussions of AEG's financial problems on them.

72. We are indebted to Professor Wolfgang Streeck for this insight. See D. Webber, 'The Framework of Government–Industry Relations and Industrial Policy-Making in the Federal Republic of Germany', Working Paper Series on Government–Industry Relations, No. 1 (University of Sussex, 1986), p. 31.

73. See A. Cawson, 'The Teletext Initiative in Britain: Anatomy of Successful Neo-corporatist Policy-Making', Economic and Social Research Council, *Corporatism and Accountability Newsletter* (1986), 1–3. Equally, the work of Grant, Paterson, and Whitston has demonstrated the major role of the Chemical Industry Association in that sector. W. Grant, W. Paterson, and C. Whitston, 'Government–Industry Relations in the Chemical Industry: An Anglo-German Comparison', in Wilks and Wright (eds.), *Comparative Government–Industry Relations*.

74. For example, over the voluntary export restraint agreement for VCRs.

75. S. Berger, 'Lame Ducks and National Champions: Industrial Policy in the Fifth Republic', in W. Andrews and S. Hoffman (eds.), *The Fifth Republic at Twenty* (Albany N.J.: State University of New York Press, 1979); E. Friedberg, 'Administration et entreprises', in M. Crozier (ed.), *Où va l'administration française?* (Paris: Éditions Ouvrières, 1974); Bauer and Bertin-Mourot, 'Entreprises publiques et mouvement patronal'.

76. For example by the Wilson Committee—Committee to Review the Functioning of Financial Institutions, *Report and Appendices*, House

of Commons Session 1979–80, Cmnd. 7937, 2 vols. (London: HMSO, 1980) and by Scott and Griff's work on interlocking directorates; J. Scott and C. Griff, *Directors of Industry: The British Corporate Network* (Oxford: Martin Robertson, 1983).

77. Le Monde, *Dossiers et documents: Bilan économique 1984* (Paris: Le Monde, 1985).

78. B. Bayliss and A. Butt-Phillip, *Capital Markets and Industrial Investment in Germany and France* (London: Saxon House, 1980).

79. Of the 400 top companies some 318 are said to have had bankers on their boards. Banks occupied about 15% of the seats on the supervisory boards of the 100 biggest German joint-stock companies in 1974 and in 1978 a fifth of all the chairmen of these firms' boards were bankers.

80. As our case-study in ch. 12 below reveals, *Der Spiegel*'s claim that it was the Deutsche Bank that prevented the take-over of Grundig by Thomson is somewhat wide of the mark. The banks' role seems to have been largely that of urging that the company be sold, without strong views as to the identity of the eventual purchaser.

81. Bankers interviewed tended to play down their role, while industrialists were more inclined to see them as the 'mafia' of German business.

82. One economics professor nominated as the government representative on a bank's *conseil d'administration* said he had never received any instructions as to his behaviour. The banks fiercely resisted government pressure in 1981–2 to put money into a *Fonds Industrielle de Modernisation* for industrial investment, and the attempt has not been repeated.

83. In Lacorne's phrase, the most effective 'bounty hunters', *chasseurs des primes*. See D. Lacorne, 'La Politique Giscardienne des exportations ou le Colbertisme dans les moyens en vue du libéralisme comme fin', in M.-C. Smouts (ed.), *La Politique extérieure de Valéry Giscard d'Estaing* (Paris: Presses Universitaires de France, 1985).

84. One of the arguments for nationalization in 1982 in France was that since shareholders were unwilling or unable to play their proper role, the state must undertake this instead. The first two years of nationalization saw capital subventions of 12.5m. fr. and 12.8m. fr. respectively from the government to the newly nationalized companies.

85. For example, determination of minimum reserve ratios, interest rates, and, especially since the advent of floating exchange rates, the determination of the exchange rate through intervention in the currency markets.

86. Zysman, *Governments, Markets and Growth*.

87. This is perhaps not surprising given the influence of Jean Monnet who was so attached to a notion of entrepreneurial capitalism within a framework of concertation.

88. The Single European Act now commits the member states to substantial advances towards a common internal market by 1992. For an analysis of the costs and benefits of the single market, see P. Cecchini, *The European Challenge: 1992* (Aldershot: Wildwood House, 1988).

89. Some countries, notably France and Italy, still require certificates of origin, as they did before the creation of the EEC, and the persistence of this system permits the continued defence of segmented markets.

90. Indeed in certain areas public procurement is exempt. There is a Commission recommendation that 10% of tenders for telecommunications equipment should be advertised in Community member states other than the originating member state, but this does not mean that orders are placed abroad.

91. For example, *Consten and Grundig* v. *EEC Commission* [1966] CMLR 418.

92. However the view that one of the objects of making all VCRs enter France through Poitiers was to check that the instructions were, in accordance with the French government's pro-francophone linguistic policy, in French, should not be taken too seriously.

4

Telecommunications: Politics, Technologies, and Markets

Telecommunications occupies a very special place in the spectrum of government–industry relations. Along with defence and agriculture it has enjoyed privileged treatment from the state in practically every capitalist country, with the result that the telecom 'market' has been highly insulated from competitive processes. The specificity of telecommunications stems from two distinctive institutional features:

1. the service side has long been controlled by a public monopoly, usually a government department known as the Post, Telegraph and Telephone authority (PTT), or else a public corporation; and
2. the equipment side has been dominated by a small ring of private manufacturers and these have been protected against both domestic and foreign competition by the chauvinistic purchasing policies of the public service monopoly, their chief customer.

In this traditional model the PTT and the suppliers formed what we might call a *telecom club* which, for all practical purposes, was effectively closed to new entrants on either side. The rationale for this abnormal institutional arrangement rested on two factors so far as the service side was concerned. The first, a technical justification, was that the telecommunications network comprised a *natural monopoly*, that is, an activity where economies of scale are so substantial that costs are supposed to be minimized by relying on a sole supplier.[1] The second, a socio-political justification, was that a public monopoly provided the best means for delivering a uniform service irrespective of cost, which meant that high density routes subsidized low density routes. This position was buttressed by the fear that if new entrants were admitted into the service sector they would 'cream off' the more lucrative routes, thus eroding the public monopoly's ability to subsidize less profitable routes.

On the equipment side entry was restricted for a number of reasons, the most important being large economies of scale in production and the need for close R. & D. collaboration between the PTT and its suppliers because of nationally specific standards and network features. Whatever the actual merit of these technical claims the fact is that they neatly coincided with three political goals: protecting a market for domestic producers, ensuring security of supply in a strategically sensitive industry, and preserving employment.

That this model went unchallenged for so long is a tribute to the tenacity of the telecom club and its political allies, governments and unions in particular. But in retrospect the model was also contingent on a number of other conditions, namely, a stable pattern of technological change, the viability of the national market, a concentration of technical expertise in the hands of the public monopoly and a political commitment to the status quo. It is worth elaborating on each of these in turn.

1. *Technological Change.* Over the past decade in particular the pace of technological change has been increasing faster than ever before. This has made a deep impression on each of the three main segments of the telecommunications network—switching (i.e. telephone exchanges), transmission (copper or optical fibre cables, satellites, and microwave) and terminals (equipment normally located on the customer's premises, which includes everything from telephones to highly sophisticated PABXs, or Private Automatic Branch Exchanges). For example, in the case of switching, the largest single capital item in the network, the main change has been the transition from semi-electronic analogue exchanges to fully electronic digital systems.

When combined with digital transmission, this lays the basis for the *digitalization* of the network, the most important trend in telecommunications.[2] This allows all forms of information—voice, data, text, and image—to be converted into the binary code of the computer, with the result that more information can be transmitted, at greater speed and higher quality. Digitalization also means that telecommunications, computing, and consumer electronics are converging into a new hybrid information technology or telematics sector, which has already spawned a wide array of new services way beyond traditional telephony.[3] This in turn lays the basis for firms from different industries to invade each other's territory. In short the digital era heralds what Schumpeter once referred to as a 'gale of creative destruction'.[4]

2. *Internationalization.* Under the traditional model a combination of chauvinistic PTT purchasing policies and a thicket of nationally specific technical standards meant that the equipment industry addressed itself to protected national markets, hence international trade and foreign direct investment played a relatively minor role, unlike the semiconductor or consumer electronics industries. However, national markets are slowly being prised open, albeit unevenly, as a result of liberalization on the one hand and burgeoning development costs on the other. Public switching systems provide the best illustration of the pressure of burgeoning costs. The cost of developing a digital public exchange is estimated at over $1 billion and, to be economically viable, this requires some 8 per cent of the world market. However, since no EEC member country individually accounts for more than 6 per cent of the world telecom market the limits of the national market become all too obvious.[5]

3. *Rival Expertise.* Telecommunications has always been an extremely complex technological field, so much so that there were few sources of expertise that could challenge the PTT in its knowledge of network idiosyncrasies and traditional analogue technology. However, two developments began to erode this near monopoly of technical expertise. The first was the advent of digital technology, which gave computing firms a head start over the 'priesthood' of the PTTs, versed as it was in traditional analogue technology. Secondly, and ultimately more important, the diffusion of information technology into the corporate user population has created a powerful body of technical expertise outside the PTTs.

The requirements of these large corporate users are no longer confined to basic telephony, nor are they likely to be met by standardized solutions. On the contrary, in many large corporations the demand for non-voice (data, information, text) communication services has increased rapidly, up to 40 per cent per annum from the leading users. For such corporate users telecommunications is not a 'utility' but a critical competitive weapon, hence their struggle to liberate themselves from PTT regulatory controls, the aim being to have as much control over their telecommunications activities as possible within the confines of the regulatory system. However, the main point here is that as their telecom needs have grown so has their in-house technical expertise, and this is increasingly being deployed to restrict the power of the PTTs.[6]

4. *Deregulation*. The political commitment to the traditional model in telecommunications first began to be challenged in the US, where the model was in any case different in that a regulated private company, American Telephone and Telegraph (AT&T), fulfilled the function of the PTT. In response to the combined pressure of large corporate users and aspiring new suppliers AT&T was eventually divested of its twenty-two Bell Operating Companies (BOCs) in 1984 and most segments of the US market were opened up to competitive entry.[7] Two important political repercussions followed.

First the US government stepped up its efforts to create a 'level playing field' in the international telecom market, using access to the US market as a lever to gain reciprocity elsewhere. Second the US experience had an enormously important demonstration effect for other pro-liberal governments, and the UK and Japan were the first to add their weight to this deregulatory momentum. Even without their actions, however, the traditional model was by no means secure. Indeed, deregulation in the US alone was enough to send an electric shock through the international system. For example, since large US business users were the first to reap the gains of liberalization—in the form of lower telecom charges and greater regulatory freedom—their rivals in other countries felt themselves to be at a competitive disadvantage unless they too had access to these benefits.

Thus the US experience induced corporate users in Europe to agitate for deregulation. Once the UK joined the liberal camp it improved its traditional position as a European 'telecom hub', that is, a cheap location in which to base corporate communication centres or else an attractive place through which to route traffic between the US and Europe. As we shall see, this put enormous pressure on those continental PTTs that were less disposed to join the liberal camp because, if they wished to avoid losing revenue to the UK, they were obliged to reduce their transatlantic tariffs. In these ways traditional PTTs have had to respond to deregulatory trends outside their borders.

Taken together these changes signify that a new 'game' has emerged in telecommunications, one in which the actors are having to adjust to a radically new set of rules. Turning first to the PTTs,

TABLE 4.1. *How the PTTs compared in 1982*

	BT (UK)	DGT (France)	DBP (FRG)
Revenues ($bn)	10.3	8.0	11.7
Capital investment ($bn)	2.6	4.0	4.7
Employees (000)	246	164	203
Subscriber lines (m.)	19.4	19.5	23.0
Employees per 1000 subscriber lines	127	84	88
Revenue per employee ($)	4,200	4,900	5,764
Capital investment per subscriber line ($)	133	205	204
Private leased lines (000)	115	93.7	2.5
Data terminals on public networks (000)	93.3	26.9	51.3
PTT's share of domestic production (1980, %)	75	60	59

Sources: Financial Times (27 September 1983); OECD (1983); ITU Yearbook (Annual).

it is evident from Table 4.1 that their performance has been decidedly uneven.[8]

The most striking feature to emerge from Table 4.1, a snapshot of performance at the time of BT's privatization in 1982, is the relatively poor record of British Telecom in terms of capital investment and productivity. With roughly the same number of subscriber lines as its French counterpart, BT nevertheless had 82,000 more employees on its payroll than the DGT, while the comparison with the Bundespost is even less flattering to BT. Table 4.1 also tells us something about the specificity of the UK network. Firstly, even before the privatization of BT the UK had the most liberal policy on private leased lines, i.e. capacity leased to corporate users for their private needs, and here the UK presents a stark contrast with the Bundespost, which practises an extremely tight leased line regime. The UK again stands out with respect to the number of data terminals attached to the public telephone network, an indication that the UK business user population outstrips the French and German populations in the use of data communications.[9] This is an important point because data-intensive users, like financial institutions and multinationals, are often the leading proponents of liberalization. In this respect BT had to contend with more sophisticated business users than the DGT and the Bundespost.

From Table 4.1 we can also see how important the PTTs have

TABLE 4.2. *Employment in telecommunications 1976–1986*

	1976	1986	% change
BT	240,000	224,427	– 6.5
UK equipment industry	75,291	38,837	– 48.4
DGT	134,937	165,198	22.4
French equipment industry	75,000	63,000	– 16.0
DBP	177,000	214,349	21.1
FRG equipment industry	94,030	104,730	11.4

Sources: BT; EITB; DGT; DBP.

been as a customer for their indigenous telecom industries, taking 75 per cent of domestic production in the UK, 60 per cent in France, and 59 per cent in the FRG. This means that the telecom market was quite unlike other electronics market segments, where there has been no monopsony, i.e. a single buyer which dominates the market. The monopsonistic structure of the telecom market was paralleled by a high degree of concentration on the supply side, with the result that over 75 per cent of total output was supplied by just four firms in each of the three countries. Whatever the benefits of this arrangement the costs were to be found in relatively high price differentials between Europe and North America; indeed, European prices for switching equipment were 60-100 per cent higher, while transmission equipment prices were some 40 per cent higher.[10]

Given the protected nature of this market there was relatively little pressure on these firms to bring their prices down to the level of their lower-cost North American 'competitors'. Faced with growing competitive pressures and labour-saving technological change, the first effects of the new 'game' have been felt on employment, as we can see from Table 4.2.

Although telecommunications is generally perceived to be one of the modern 'high tech' growth sectors Table 4.2 shows that it is more accurate to speak of *jobless* growth, that is, output growth combined with declining employment.[11] Here we see that employment has been falling on both the services and the equipment sides. What stands out above all else is the massive decline in the UK equipment industry, where employment fell by nearly 50 per cent in the decade to 1986. This can be attributed to the UK's poorer trade performance in telecoms and to the fact that the UK industry was exposed to the chill winds of competition long before its French

TABLE 4.3. *Telecommunications trade balances (m.ECU)*

	Extra-EEC			Intra-EEC		
	1983	1984	1985	1983	1984	1985
FRG	+ 712	+ 761	+ 692	+ 257	+ 252	+ 326
France	+ 746	+ 716	+ 761	+ 20	− 15	+ 47
UK	− 36	− 211	− 329	− 120	− 97	− 131

Source: European Research Associates (1986).

and German rivals. In fact those countries which liberalized first are more likely to suffer trade deficits because they have yet to gain reciprocal access to protected foreign markets.

The case of the US is instructive here. Despite being a world leader in telecommunications the US recorded a telecom deficit of nearly $2 billion in 1986, and this has been attributed to its open market.[12] The UK has found itself in a similar position, with a trade deficit growing as liberalization quickened. Indeed, of the three countries the UK is the only one to have a negative trade balance on its internal and external EEC account, as Table 4.3 illustrates.

What emerges from this brief introduction is that the changes under way in telecommunications in no way amount to a positive-sum 'game'. The changed rules involve a new configuration of winners and losers, so much so that governments have to weigh up the costs against the benefits if and when they pursue the deregulatory path. As we shall see in the following three chapters, the same actors can command very different political weight, so that broadly similar pressures have produced *dissimilar* results. This should not be as surprising as it seems because, contrary to what economic determinists would have us believe, political discretion accompanies the most radical changes in markets and technology.

The following three chapters show that technological change has been negotiated in different ways in each of the three countries, and the same is true of the process of liberalization. The main reason for this is that the constellation of political forces, especially as between government, producers, and users, has been quite different in each of the three countries. For example, there are a number of features which differentiate the UK from its two continental neighbours. First, even though all three countries have been governed by conservative administrations in recent years, the continental variants proved to be far more cautious and pragmatic about instigating radical political change. The Thatcher government was more willing and more able to embark on a course of radical political surgery: on the one hand because the British 'telecom club' had less to show for its privileged (i.e. protected) position than those in France and Germany and, on the other, because there were fewer constitutional constraints on central government in the UK.

Secondly, telecom producer interests enjoyed much more political support in France and the FRG than they did in the UK. There are at least two reasons for this: (1) UK producer interests had lost what political capital they might have enjoyed because of a poor record in delivering digital technology and in exploiting export markets and (2) the Thatcher government accorded a higher priority to promoting the interests of large business users, rather than those of the indigenous telecom supply industry, the converse of the situation in France and the FRG.

Thirdly, business user interests were more advanced and better organized in the UK than in either France or the FRG. The structure of the business user population in the UK has a greater bias towards large, multi-site plants and offices than those of France and the FRG, and these companies tend to be more intensive users of telecommunications services. Within the business user population the most advanced users are to be found in the banking and financial services sector, and it is worth noting that France and the FRG had no equivalent to the City of London in their business user populations. User interests could be used as a lever to support the neoliberal programme of usurping producer interests. As we shall see, part of the rationale behind liberalization and privatization in the UK was the government's belief that the traditional telecom monopoly threatened the City's position as a leading international financial centre. It is perhaps more than a coincidence that the three leading deregulating countries— the US, Britain, and Japan—are also the three premier centres of international finance.

Thus while technological pressures may have been broadly similar in Britain, France, and the FRG, these pressures were handled differently because the balance of power between producers and users was different and this, in turn, manifested itself in divergent political priorities.

In the following three chapters we will focus on three themes: (1) the changing regulatory regime for telecommunications, i.e.

liberalization; (2) the extent to which liberalization (and privatization in the UK) has affected government–industry relations in the telecom sector; and (3) the ways in which the three countries have negotiated the challenge of digital technology. As regards the digital challenge we have chosen to look at the public switching segment (i.e. telephone exchanges) because, traditionally at least, this has been the largest single item in the telecommunications network as well as the flagship product of the telecom industry.

Notes

1. The evidence for natural monopoly was, and continues to be, strongest with respect to the basic network of switching and transmission. There appears to be little or no evidence of natural monopoly tendencies with respect to customer premises equipment (CPE) markets or value added network services (VANS) markets. For an evaluation of the evidence see H. Ergas, *Regulation, Monopoly and Competition in the Telecommunications Infrastructure* (Paris: OECD, 1986).
2. Digitalization is also perhaps the most important technological trend in consumer electronics, discussed in ch. 8 below.
3. Despite all the attention devoted to new services it is worth reminding ourselves that telephony still accounts for 85–90% of all telecommunications service revenue in the EEC. See Commission of the European Communities, *Green Paper on the Development of the Common Market for Telecommunications Services and Equipment*, Com (87) 290 Final (Brussels, 1987).
4. 'The opening up of new markets, foreign or domestic, and the organizational development from the craft shop and factory to such concerns as US Steel . . . incessantly revolutionizes the economic structure *from within*, incessantly destroying the old one, incessantly creating a new one. This process of Creative Destruction is the essential fact about capitalism.' J. A. Schumpeter, *Capitalism, Socialism and Democracy*, 4th edn. (London: Allen & Unwin, 1954), p. 83.
5. Commission of the European Communities, *Green Paper*, 1987.
6. Roundtable of European Industrialists, *Clearing the Lines: A User's View on Business Communications in Europe* (Brussels, 1986).
7. P. Huber, *The Geodesic Network: 1987 Report on Competition in the Telephone Industry* (Washington, DC: US Department of Justice, Anti-Trust Division, 1987).
8. We use the term PTT here merely for the sake of convenience because, strictly speaking, BT has been a public corporation since 1969. The DGT and the Bundespost are still government departments, with the

latter responsible for both posts and telecommunications, though the comparison in Table 4.1 refers only to the telecommunications side of the Bundespost.

9. Eurodata Foundation, *Data Communications in Western Europe in the 1980s* (London, 1980); K. Sauvant, *International Transactions in Services: The Politics of Transborder Data Flows* (Boulder, Colo., and London: Westview Press, 1986).

10. Organization for Economic Co-operation and Development, *Telecommunications: Pressures and Policies for Change* (Paris: OECD, 1983).

11. K. Morgan and A. Sayer, *Microcircuits of Capital: 'Sunrise' Industry and Uneven Development* (Cambridge: Polity Press, 1988).

12. Federal Communications Commission, *Regulatory Policies and International Telecommunications*, Docket No. 86–494 (Washington, D.C.: FCC, 1987).

5

Breaching the Monopoly:
The Neo-liberal Offensive in Britain

Few organizations had the potential to make a more important contribution to economy and society in Britain than the Post Office. Through its postal and telecom divisions it directly controlled two of the major forms of communications, touching the lives of virtually everyone and thus making it somewhat unique among the nationalized industries. With the exception of central government it was the largest employer in the country, with close to half a million employees. Apart from the Ministry of Defence it housed the largest R. & D. facility for advanced technology in the public sector. The investment programme of its telecom division was the major single source of public purchasing in the civilian electronics industry, and here it had untold potential for sponsoring innovation and for promoting exports.

For all this the relationship between the Post Office and successive governments was ill defined and left much to be desired on both sides. At times the Post Office seemed to be an empire unto itself, deeply resistant to public scrutiny; while governments, for their part, frequently subordinated the Post Office's tariff and investment plans to the exigencies of the moment. An ill-defined relationship was also the source of a good deal of confusion and acrimony between the Post Office and its private equipment suppliers, one reason why the telecom club in Britain had a less than illustrious record. Indeed, this record made the British club more vulnerable than the continental telecom clubs because the Thatcher government seized upon it as evidence of the 'dead hand' of the state in the telecommunications sector.

Re-making the Telecom Regime: Towards Liberalization and Privatization

Prior to 1969 the Post Office was a revenue-earning department of government, internally governed by cumbersome civil service conventions and externally subject to detailed Treasury and parliamentary interventions. Its reputation for being a somewhat ponderous organization, poorly equipped to respond to the challenges of the 'white heat' of the technological revolution prompted the Labour government to convert it into a public corporation in 1969.[1] This, it was hoped, would provide the Post Office with more autonomy from central government and allow it to become a more innovative organization.

As a public corporation the general duty of the Post Office was to exercise its powers so as to meet 'the social, industrial and commercial needs of the British Islands'.[2] To fulfil this duty it was given powers to diversify into manufacturing to supply its own needs and to acquire subsidiaries. It was also given an 'exclusive privilege' to run the telecommunications network, and here it had the right to specify what types of equipment users could attach to the network as well as the right to supply, install and maintain all this equipment. The Post Office justified this monopoly—or 'integral network policy' as it preferred to call it—on two grounds. Firstly, it was said to guarantee the technical integrity of the network, which was 'complex and idiosyncratic'. Secondly, the technologies of switching, transmission and customer apparatus were said to be increasingly interdependent, there was thus a growing need to think in terms of overall system development. In other words technological trends demanded more, rather than less, emphasis on this 'integral network policy' so far as the Post Office was concerned.[3] In short, the 1969 Act had conferred a monopoly regime that was as comprehensive as anything in Western Europe.[4] Indeed, some critics have claimed that under this regime the UK telecom market was 'the most closed within the OECD'.[5]

The major actors within this monopoly regime were:

1. The government, or rather the Department of Industry (D.o.I.), which had sponsorship responsibility for the Post Office and the (private) suppliers, and the Treasury, from which the D.o.I. had to seek approval for telecom investment because this was classified as part of the public sector borrowing requirement. As the 'voice' of its two charges within government the D.o.I. not infrequently found itself in conflict with the Treasury over the scale of funds necessary for the development of the telecommunications network.

2. The Post Office, consisting of the telecom division and its Board, the latter also being responsible for posts, giro, and data processing. This unitary structure increasingly came under fire from the Board itself: the Board felt that the telecom and posts divisions ought to be separated because the two were diverging in terms of both technology and skills. As we shall see, conflicts between the Board and its telecom division were such that one cannot speak of the 'Post Office' as though it was a homogeneous actor

3. The Post Office unions, which between them organized 90 per cent of the total workforce. In all there were eight different unions, the two major ones being the Post Office Engineering Union (POEU), responsible for technical and engineering staff, and the Union of Post Office Workers (UPW), which represented postal workers and telephonists. Because these two unions were well-organized and powerful actors the Post Office was anxious to maintain harmonious relations with them: so much so that it did not feel able to 'exert greater pressure on the unions to change practices which obstruct its policies'.[6] However, these two unions diverged on one major issue: the POEU was all for separating posts and telecoms for reasons similar to those advanced by the Board, while the UPW remained passionately opposed to the notion, fearing that posts would be left to wither on the vine.

4. The equipment suppliers, who had been part of a telecom club with the Post Office since the 1920s. The most palpable expressions of this cartel-like arrangement were the Bulk Supply Agreements: these effectively locked the Post Office into an agreement to buy its equipment from an agreed 'ring' of domestic suppliers. These private suppliers (principally GEC, Plessey, and STC) were able to marshal formidable economic and political resources to defend and advance their positions under the monopoly regime.

5. Finally, there were the users, formally represented by the Post Office Users' National Council (POUNC), which had the difficult task of representing both residential and business users. Although the Post Office was obliged to consult with POUNC it had no obligation to act on POUNC's proposals. Apart from POUNC the other major user groups were the Telecommunications Managers' Association (TMA), composed of the telecom managers of large companies, and the smaller Telephone Users' Association (TUA). The Post Office, however, had no statutory obligation to consult with these 'outsider' organizations.

Public corporation status was supposed to give the Post Office greater operating autonomy; this was the intent of the 1969 Act. However, this hope was quickly dashed by a series of unprecedented interventions on the part of the newly elected Heath government. By far the most important of these were (1) the sacking of the Post Office chairman for trying to insist on the commercial freedom which had recently been granted to the Post Office and (2) the refusal to allow telecommunications tariffs to keep abreast of inflation, proof that the Post Office was being used as a macro-economic tool to contain inflation.[7] As a result of price restraint, Post Office finances deteriorated badly: in each of the three years to 1975 its telecom division recorded mounting deficits. To compensate for three years of price restraint several major tariff hikes occurred in 1975 to restore the Post Office's profitability, provoking widespread criticism from both residential and business users.

In addition to price restraint the Post Office also had to contend with sudden cuts in its capital investment programme, as in 1973, when the government imposed a cut of 20 per cent without any prior consultation. These interventions contributed to the Post Office's inability to satisfy residential and business demand. But external factors alone cannot account for this situation. Among the main internal shortcomings the most important was the Post Office's archaic approach to marketing, a problem which the POEU rightly ascribed to the dominance of the 'civil service mentality'.[8] This, it argued, was ultimately responsible for the failure to raise telephone density and the difficulties which the Post Office had experienced in identifying and supplying the advanced equipment which business users were increasingly demanding.

Growing unease over tariff hikes and poor service provision persuaded the new Labour government to set up a major review of the Post Office in 1975, with a brief to consider what changes, if any, were required to enable the Post Office to execute its functions more efficiently. The review found that the Post Office was 'significantly less efficient than the best of its overseas competitors' and, on the marketing side, it found that the Post Office 'knows too little about its customers'.[9]

The review exposed three other problems. First, there was a thoroughly confused relationship between government and the Post Office, with no clear agreement as to their respective roles in policy formation. This was compounded by the fact that the D.o.I. was heavily dependent on information which the Post Office chose to supply, hence it had no independent knowledge of the telecommunications business. In this situation the formal powers of the D.o.I. were severely compromised and, although the review refrained from saying so, there are strong grounds for thinking that the D.o.I. had been 'captured' by the Post Office.

Alarmed by the Post Office's lack of accountability, and by the dearth of information available to interested parties, the review proposed that a Council on Post Office and Telecommunications Affairs be set up, composed of all the interested actors, with the task of supplying independent advice to the Secretary of State for Industry.

The second problem concerned the unitary structure of the Post Office, which had led to over-centralization, poor delegation, and slow decision-making, and this in turn had inhibited 'sound strategic thinking'.[10] To remedy the situation the review recommended that posts and telecoms be split into two separate businesses. As regards the third problem—the Post Office monopoly—the review was 'not convinced that the balance of advantage to the community favours the continuation of the present monopoly situation in the UK'.[11] Drawing on US experience, which showed that customer-provided equipment did not harm the network, the review called for a trial liberalization with small PABXs. But, anxious to protect domestic producers, the review said that liberalization should only be introduced 'at a rate which would allow British manufacturers to become competitive in the home market'.[12]

The significance of the review lies not in its immediate political impact—indeed there was none, because the Labour government proved unable or unwilling to act on the proposals—but in the light it shed on the plight of the UK telecom regime. It also showed that some of the changes introduced by the Thatcher government were not entirely novel. However, in the final year of the Labour government, in 1979, the POEU solemnly took note of a 'growing chorus of voices against the monopoly'.[13]

It was difficult to imagine a less propitious time for the defence of the monopoly. The advent of a Thatcher government was sufficient of a threat in itself; in opposition the Conservatives had warned that the abolition of the customer apparatus monopoly would be one of the earliest acts of a future Conservative government. What made matters worse was the fact that a huge log-jam of equipment and service had built up, partly as a result of the severe cuts imposed on the Post Office in the wake of the IMF crisis of 1976. As a result complaints from both residential and business users were escalating. For instance, POUNC recorded that complaints about excessive delays in the provision of service had virtually doubled between 1978 and 1979, and doubled again in the following year.[14] On top of this there was mounting concern about the pedestrian performance of the UK telecom manufacturers, a problem which the Conservatives attributed to an atrophied telecom club, which was closed to potential domestic and foreign entrants.

Thus the situation was tailor-made for radical political reform from the Right, because it lent itself to a credible critique which claimed that 'consumers' should be liberated from the 'dead hand of state controls'.[15] The incoming Thatcher government lost no time in adapting this situation to its neo-liberal project.

Radical change presented the D.o.I. with a major dilemma. Hitherto it had been almost totally dependent on the Post Office for information and advice on telecommunications. Well aware of the power associated with a virtual monopoly of technical expertise, the Post Office astutely used this power to further its own interests. Most of the managers in the Post Office, especially those who were former civil servants, had little appetite for the changes on the horizon.[16] Under new political masters, the posts and telecom division of the D.o.I. was ordererd to flesh out a new telecom regime. But it could no longer rely upon the 'neutral' advice of the Post Office: the traditional network between the D.o.I. and the Post Office 'worked' only so long as the latter's interests were not seriously threatened. Clearly this was no longer the case.

The D.o.I. was well aware that liberalization of customer apparatus was not especially contentious in the wake of the 1977 review. But the same could not be said for licensing a private competitor to BT (as the telecom business was christened after the separation from posts in 1981) or for the privatization of BT itself. However, the D.o.I. set about mobilizing a rival body of expert opinion which was independent of, and often opposed to, BT's dominant position. Corporate users formed the core of this rival body of informed (and partisan) expertise, and the D.o.I. sought to utilize their knowledge of the network as a counterweight to BT's own expertise. Having had little access to either government or the Post Office in the past, the TMA suddenly found itself after 1979 with an open invitation into the corridors of power. In the light of later changes it is significant that the TMA and the TUA never actually demanded that BT's basic network should be broken or that BT should be privatized in the manner in which it was. Indeed, in its proposals for liberalization (of customer apparatus), the TUA accepted that BT's basic network monopoly should remain inviolate![17]

Led by Keith Joseph, the political team at the D.o.I. pushed for a more radical reorganization. In July 1980 the D.o.I. commissioned MDA, a small private consultancy, to examine the feasibility of a rival, privately run telecommunications network. The MDA report was drafted in such a way as to appeal to its neo-liberal sponsors and, not surprisingly, it concluded that a rival private network was not only urgently needed, but was technically and politically feasible. In reaching this conclusion MDA warned of the particular threat to the City, where the inefficiency of the monopoly threatened 'to weaken London's strength as an international centre of commerce'.[18]

It also argued that monopoly abuses would occur in other quarters because 'much effective power lies with the trades unions, and the POEU fully recognizes the increasing leverage it can exert in a monopoly'.[19] Fully aware of the provocative nature of its proposals, MDA said it would be necessary for the 'capitalist network to have an acceptable face'. Its solution was for the government to allow a single bid from a broad-based private consortium of users and operators, so that the network could be seen to be in responsible hands. The proposed owners included the clearing banks, BP, ICI and Cable and Wireless. The MDA report—produced in only ten days—fortified politicians and pro-liberal civil servants at the D.o.I.; it gave them more confidence to overrule the Post Office's view that the basic network was a 'natural monopoly'.

In June 1981 a consortium of Cable and Wireless, Barclays Bank, and BP announced a plan to build a rival network, to be run by Mercury. However, one can hardly describe this as an unsolicited bid.[20]

Remaking the telecom regime was undoubtedly a top political priority of the Thatcher governments: the first phase of liberalization had been announced in July 1980 and the decision to privatize BT was announced exactly two years later. The government's declared aims for the new telecom regime were nothing if not ambitious.

This can be seen in the 'general duties' imposed on Oftel, the new regulatory agency set up to police the UK telecom scene. The major duties are to:

1. secure the provision of services throughout the UK, in so far as this is reasonably practical, and to ensure that the service supplier is able to finance these services;
2. promote the interests of consumers, purchasers, and other users in the UK;
3. maintain and promote effective competition between suppliers of telecommunications;
4. encourage major overseas users of telecommunications to locate in the UK;
5. enable UK telecom producers to compete effectively within and outside the UK.[21]

Here we have the formal agenda of aims, and even on this level it is clear that there is a good deal of conflict between some of them; as, for example, between sponsoring the interests of consumers and producers at one and the same time. Something which was conspicuously absent from this agenda, however, was the government's desire to break the power of the unions; the abolition of the monopoly and the privatization of BT were both means to this end.

Liberalization, which must be distinguished from privatization, has been introduced into each of the three main segments of the UK telecom market, albeit unevenly. The customer apparatus market has been completely liberalized, at least in principle.[22] At the network level itself liberalization has been more partial: only two national public networks (BT and Mercury) are to be licensed before 1990 in what is called 'basic conveyance'. However, the government was more liberal with networks serving specialized markets: here it has licensed two rival consortia (BT and Racal) to operate cellular mobile telephone networks, and eleven cable TV consortia, each of which is permitted to carry data and voice traffic, providing the latter is carried in conjunction with either BT or Mercury. In the value added network services segment the government has licensed over 600 VANS, but it stopped short of allowing 'simple resale' of BT capacity until 1989.

Liberalizing VANS involved the government in a regulatory nightmare, which was compounded by the haste and contradictory nature of its telecom policy. The problem, in short, stemmed from a conceptual confusion as to the borderline between VANS and the basic telephone network, the sphere of 'basic conveyance', where the government had committed itself to the BT–Mercury duopoly until 1990. Eventually the VANS category had to be abandoned in favour of VADS—value added and data services—and these were defined in the negative, i.e. to include everything that was not telephony or telex.[23] In all three segments, however, liberalization has been qualified by the *de facto* market power of BT.

Privatization was no part of the government's original liberalization programme. It seems to have emerged as a serious option in late 1981, prompted by three factors. In the first place experience to date had proved that BT could frustrate the liberalization process and that civil servants were no match for BT's near-monopoly of technical expertise. Secondly, privatization seemed to offer a solution to the problem of BT's borrowing limits: as a public sector company BT's borrowing counted against the PSBR and the government saw tight control over the PSBR as a vital weapon in the fight against inflation. Thirdly, a publicly owned BT was thought to have too few incentives to enhance internal efficiency; privatization, it was argued, would force BT into better shape and this, in turn, would yield better service and more stable prices.[24]

Faced with the task of privatizing BT—then the biggest stock market flotation in the world—the D.o.I. once again felt it necessary to enlist outside technical expertise. Throughout the campaign the government became extremely dependent on City institutions, especially Kleinwort Benson, financial advisors to the government and one of the underwriters of the issue. As one senior civil servant put it:

The underwriters were seen as a source of legitimate expertise. Civil servants did not constitute an equal counterweight to them. If it flopped Kleinwort Benson would be able to say 'we told you so'. Consequently, we had to keep the City warm throughout the privatization period.[25]

However, in view of the *de facto* power which BT would yield as a private company the government was implored (by liberal MPs, prospective competitors, and user groups like the TMA) to break it up along the lines of AT&T.

This would obviously have been the solution most compatible

with the logic of liberalization, which was to promote competition. But the 'break-up' option was abandoned for a number of reasons. For one thing BT lobbied furiously against this option, deploying skilful arguments to the effect that this would render the company less able to compete with overseas IT giants; this in turn would devalue the attractions of the sale itself; and a broken BT would have less purchasing power to sustain domestic equipment suppliers. To cap it all BT's chairman threatened to resign over the issue. Equally important was the poor state of BT's internal accounts, which made it difficult if not impossible to assess the profitability of BT's constituent businesses: so if BT was to be broken up the sale would have had to be delayed. Anxious to proceed as quickly as possible, and conscious of its need for BT's co-operation, the government abandoned the 'break-up' option.[26]

Apart from the Labour Party and the trade unions the main opposition to privatization came from the domestic equipment manufacturers. One of their main criticisms was that a private monopoly in all but name was being substituted for a public monopoly. They feared that a private BT would be freer to squeeze them, first as a competitor and second as the major domestic customer. They attacked the government for allowing BT to extend itself into new markets, like cellular mobile radio and cable TV. Finally, they tried—unsuccessfully—to persuade the government to restrict BT's share of the customer apparatus market to 25 per cent and to veto BT's entry into direct manufacturing.[27] But such was the government's contempt for the suppliers' performance that it never fully consulted with these firms during the privatization process.[28]

The unions fared no better with their main aim, namely, the defeat of the 1984 Telecommunications Bill. When they finally realized that this privatization bill would succeed their bottom line was to prevent BT from being broken up, a line on which they were at one with their senior management. Overall, the unions felt that they had salvaged all that was possible in the circumstances: not only was BT to remain intact, but they had helped to force some amendments to the original bill which offered greater protection for rural areas and the socially disadvantaged.[29]

In the event the sale of 51 per cent of BT shares in November 1984 proved to be the world's largest single share issue, raising nearly £3.9 billion for the UK Treasury. Even so, an all-party parliamentary committee had serious misgivings about the manner of the sale. For instance, it argued that the issue was under-priced, the share price having increased by 33 per cent on the first day of dealing, with the result that the taxpayer had lost out. And, secondly, it attacked the size of the commissions paid to the underwriters which, with other items, put the total costs of the sale at £263 million.[30]

On the shareholding front the government wanted the widest possible form of ownership, in the belief that this constituted the best deterrent against public ownership in the future. However, BT's list of shareholders had shrunk from 2.3 million in November 1984 to 1.49 million at the end of 1986. Of these, the proportion of shares owned by individual investors had fallen to less than 12 per cent, signs of a growing concentration of ownership in the hands of institutional investors.[31]

The new regulatory regime is nothing if not fluid, and much will depend on what happens when the ban on 'simple resale' and the basic network duopoly are reviewed in 1989 and 1990 respectively. Thus far the new regulatory watchdog, Oftel, has had mixed results in policing BT. Its major success to date has been the imposition of terms under which Mercury 'interconnects' with the BT network, terms which were very favourable to Mercury.[32] Yet, as we shall see, Oftel appeared to be powerless when it tried to influence BT's new procurement policy. However, as mixed as its record may be, there is no sense in which Oftel has been 'captured' by those whom it seeks to regulate. Overall the new telecom regime has fashioned a radically different configuration of winners and losers, a point we return to later.

Breaking the Telecom Club: The New Era of Government–Industry Relations

From the 1920s through to the 1960s the relationship between the Post Office and the equipment suppliers was governed by the Bulk Supply Agreements. The Agreements arose in the first place out of the need for standardized equipment and because they eased the pooling of R. & D. between the Post Office and its suppliers. These Agreements obliged the Post Office to buy the bulk of its equipment from a 'ring' of privileged suppliers and the latter divided the orders among themselves. However, with few penalties for poor performance and little or no scope for new entrants, there was no great incentive for these firms to innovate and prices within the 'ring' were often well above those on the outside market. Not surprisingly, these Agreements attracted mounting opposition, especially in the 1960s when the Post Office faced a supply-side crisis, with the result that a Labour government abolished the final Agreement in 1969.[33]

The termination of the Agreements may have ended the least defensible features of the telecom club but it did not spell the end of the club itself. The latter continued to exist until BT was privatized, although it was under considerable strain before then. As we show in the following section, a number of attempts were made to reorganize the supply industry, but these efforts came to nothing. They foundered on the fact that neither the Post Office nor the D.o.I. was prepared to challenge the sovereignty of the private firms in the club. These firms, it seemed, possessed an inalienable right to a share in the Post Office investment programme. It is for this reason that we can speak of the club persisting long after the Bulk Supply Agreements had ended. It was precisely this fact which caused one senior Post Office manager to rue that 'the Post Office was unable to do what it wanted in its own house'.[34]

As a monopsonist with a large in-house R. & D. facility the Post Office undoubtedly possessed enormous formal power *vis-à-vis* its suppliers. But apart from the design and development spheres, where it did indeed exercise its authority, its real power as a customer was heavily circumscribed. Having no manufacturing capability the Post Office was wholly dependent on its private suppliers and political 'patriotism' on the part of successive governments made it virtually impossible for the Post Office to extricate itself from GEC, Plessey, and STC, the main suppliers. Here we have a perfect illustration of the reciprocal nature of power relations.[35]

The telecom club could not long survive the twin challenges of liberalization and privatization: the first exposed BT to competition, the second allowed it to pursue a more aggressive commercial strategy. In this new context BT felt it could no longer afford a paternalistic relationship with these suppliers and, as we shall see later, the Thatcher government's 'cold shower' strategy was designed to have this knock-on effect. Nothing better illustrates BT's new found aggression than: (1) the rationalization of the System X programme, which is examined in the following section; (2) the introduction

of Thorn-Ericsson as a rival to GEC and Plessey; and (3) the acquisition of Mitel. These last two episodes also provide an insight
into the contradictory character of the government's pro-competitive policy: indeed, since they encapsulate many of the new trade-
offs that have to be made under the new regime, each deserves
to be examined.

The Thorn-Ericsson Controversy

BT began seeking an alternative supplier of digital exchanges as
early as 1982 and it would have acted sooner but the DTI 'invited'
it to suspend its controversial decision until after the election and
after BT had been privatized. The reasons why BT felt it necessary
to have an alternative supplier were twofold: it wanted security
of delivery for its huge modernization programme and it wanted
to introduce a 'pacing horse' to ensure that GEC and Plessey, the
sole suppliers of System X, improved upon their lacklustre performance. In short, BT was trying to usurp the closure strategy of its
suppliers. Having invited tenders from eight suppliers at the end
of 1984, BT short-listed three: AT&T-Philips, Northern Telecom,
and Thorn-Ericsson.[36] In the event the last was selected because
it offered the best financial package, it promised the earliest delivery
date, and, although it was based on Swedish technology, it was
51 per cent UK-owned with existing facilities in the UK.[37]

BT's decision to go 'foreign' provoked a storm of protest from
the traditional suppliers, their unions, and from an all-party group
of MPs, on the grounds that this would reduce the home market
for System X and reduce employment. They appealed to Oftel to
overrule the decision.

The Thorn-Ericsson affair seemed to offer an important test of
how Oftel would juggle with its conflicting responsibilities. But Oftel
was in no doubt as to where its priorities lay. Its Director-General
argued that if he opposed BT's decision, which was taken to be
pro-competitive and in the consumer interest, he would be falling
foul of the 'primary rationale of the regulatory regime in telecommunications'.[38] But, aware of his secondary responsibility to the UK
industry, he was concerned that too rapid a shift towards System
Y (Thorn-Ericsson's exchange) might give GEC and Plessey too
little time to adjust to the new competitive era. In addition to this

adjustment issue he was also alive to the fact that the UK had opened its market without gaining reciprocal benefits abroad. In view of these two factors he recommended that BT should not buy more than 20 per cent of its exchange needs from Thorn-Ericsson for three years from 1987. However, BT lost no time in rejecting this limitation, leaving Oftel looking foolish and powerless.[39]

Two further points are worth making about the Oftel inquiry. First, Oftel made it clear that it was not obliged to attach any great significance to the employment dimension. Even so, it judged that the net effect on jobs would be marginal because losses at GEC and Plessey would be offset by gains at Thorn-Ericsson's plant. Second, Oftel expressed concern about the viability of the UK telecom industry, acknowledging that 'market forces, if allowed completely free play, may bring about a situation in which technological skills are not maintained in the UK'.[40] To alleviate this problem Oftel floated the idea of a collaborative research organization. Yet here it conceded that BT's immediate commercial interests may now 'tell against substantial involvement in basic long-term research'.[41] Oftel has been silent on these issues ever since.

The final twist to the Thorn-Ericsson controversy came when the joint venture unravelled in 1988. The roots of the divorce on Thorn's side lay in the financial crisis which swept the firm in 1985, the response to which was a huge divestment programme. The joint venture with Ericsson was an obvious contender for divestment because Thorn's new corporate philosophy was to develop those activities that were already well-established international businesses. The joint venture failed to meet this criterion because it was set up specifically to address the UK market. Although much was made of Thorn-Ericsson being a 'British' company, by virtue of Thorn's 51 per cent shareholding, the latter was always the junior partner in the marriage since it was totally dependent on Ericsson technology. A more important reason for the divorce, however, was that the joint venture had outlived its usefulness to Ericsson, because its main purpose had been to enable the Swedish firm to gain entry to the UK market. Indeed, during the tendering period for the System Y contract the link with Thorn was one of the chief reasons why Ericsson won out over the competition. However, it is a sign of how open the UK market had become and how much weaker the unions were, that this divorce passed off without attracting any comment.

The Mitel affair

Here was another test of conflicting claims under the new regulatory regime. In 1985 BT reached a tentative take-over agreement with Mitel, a Canadian supplier of PABXs which had been supplying BT and which had run into severe financial difficulties. However, widespread concern from both competitors and users resulted in the merger being referred to the Monopolies and Mergers Commission (MMC). The concern of the UK suppliers was understandable. The three UK companies, GEC, Plessey, and TMC, were more dependent on BT for the distribution of their PABXs than was Mitel; in 1984, for example, BT accounted for 81 per cent of their combined sales. Moreover, BT was itself becoming more aggressive in PABXs, having stalled the liberalization process in order to 'churn' the PABX market in its favour, as a result of which it had pushed up its share of distribution from 65 per cent of the total value in 1981 to 74 per cent in 1984.[42] The proposed merger also alarmed the independent distributors because Mitel had supplied 50 per cent of their total requirements and, since the BT–Mitel accord, their relationship with the latter had deteriorated.

BT portrayed the merger as vital to its ambitions in international IT markets, down-playing the domestic implications. Playing on the government's Achilles' heel, BT added that it would be failing its shareholders if it did not diversify in the face of growing competition.

The proposed merger provoked divisions within the regulatory authorities. The MMC was itself split, with a majority in favour of the merger providing stringent measures were enforced, like a three-year ban on BT's sales of Mitel products in the UK. It was led to this conclusion because it felt that the merger was 'likely to operate seriously to reduce the growth of competition in the market with adverse effects on telecommunications users who may expect reduced choice and higher prices'.[43] For its part Oftel wanted the MMC to consider a modification of BT's licence to strengthen the pro-competitive mechanisms. In the end however, the DTI approved the merger with conditions that were considerably weaker than either of those envisaged by Oftel and the MMC. This decision can be explained by the fact that, within the DTI, competition was not the primary issue. As one official conceded:

there was enormous political pressure on us to allow it to go through from those wishing to see BT establish itself in the US. But more important was the pressure from the Welsh Office: the Welsh Secretary went to the PM and simply said that Mitel would close its plant in Wales if the deal did not go through. That clinched it.

In contrast to the pro-competitive outcome of the Thorn-Ericsson controversy, some critics saw the Mitel affair as evidence of the weakness of the UK's regulatory regime and its poor commitment to pro-competitive practices.[44] But it would be closer to the truth to interpret it as a comment on the contradictory character of public policy, with the government torn between liberalization on the one hand and covert industrial and regional policies on the other.

The acquisition of Mitel is just one of a whole series of take-overs and joint ventures which BT has launched in an attempt to become a broader-based IT company. To complement these external initiatives BT is now busily reorganizing its internal structures and practices, designed to equip itself with the requisite commercial skills and to shed surplus labour. The latter aim is already well advanced, with 20,000 jobs lost in the four years to 1986 and a further 24,000 redundancies planned between 1986 and 1990. In an attempt to become 'leaner and fitter' BT has launched an offensive against organized labour, the aim being to de-unionize middle management, to extract more flexible work practices from all parts of its workforce, and to abolish centralized bargaining.[45]

Yet for all its grand ambitions to become a broad-based IT company, BT's traditional role as a telephone network operator dwarfs all its other activities. For example, in 1984 the public switched telephone network accounted for 60 per cent of BT's turnover, 80 per cent of its total assets, and 67 per cent of its pre-tax profits.[46] Despite being much larger than its new competitor Mercury, BT was genuinely worried by the threat of competition because of its imbalanced revenue base. The imbalance stems from the fact that some 75 per cent of BT's trunk revenues are generated by business users and, of these, the top 300 customers account for around 20 per cent of trunk revenue even though they represent less than 1 per cent of all BT's business installations. As the business sector is more profitable than the residential sector, and since trunk and international traffic was used to subsidize local traffic, BT has thrown itself into rebalancing its tariff structure. The broad thrust has been to increase local charges, which BT considers to have been 'uneconomic', and to reduce trunk and international charges, where BT expects to face growing competition from Mercury.

Such rebalancing has proved to be politically contentious, since residential customers feel that they are losing out to large business users. Under its licence BT is obliged to limit a weighted average of price changes to three percentage points below the rate of inflation, the so-called 'RPI-3' formula. Although Oftel found that BT's rebalancing had complied with this formula, it also acknowledged that 'many people felt a sense of outrage because BT was already making profits that the complainants regarded as extremely high'.[47] Indeed, Oftel itself agreed that BT's rate of return exceeded the minimum acceptable level in competitive markets, but it decided against intervening so soon after BT's shares had been sold under the existing licence. As a result of BT's rebalancing, local charges are now among the highest in the OECD, while international call charges are among the cheapest.[48] Overall, BT can be well satisfied with its position: with very few exceptions it has won all its regulatory battles.[49]

BT may, however, find itself facing a more stringent regulatory regime in the future because throughout 1987 its quality of service was found to be extraordinarily poor. One report after another, including one from the National Consumer Council, indicted BT for its record, particularly as regards public call boxes, up to 25 per cent of which were said to be out of order. Faced with a collapse of public confidence in its performance, BT has made some progress in rehabilitating itself and, for the time being at least, its grand ambitions in the IT field have been subordinated to the task of 'cleaning up its act' as a provider of basic telephone service.

For BT's traditional suppliers the new rules of the game contain a strong zero-sum element; they feel that BT's gains have been their losses. The two major suppliers, GEC and Plessey, together accounted for a third of BT's total orders in 1984–5, but this was less than it had been and their share was expected to decline further in the future. What makes matters worse is that these firms are not strong actors by international standards: their volumes are low, export performance has been poor, and their *combined* spending on R. & D. in telecoms is less than that of Ericsson of Sweden. Indeed, the only index which shows GEC and Plessey in the top ten suppliers of electronic capital equipment is operating profit as a percentage of sales.[50] Both companies believe this to be the all-important index however, even though it leads to short-term horizons. As one manager put it: 'if one did not submit to this philosophy then the City would force your share-price down'.

Faced with an increasingly competitive market at home and abroad the leading UK firms have had to rethink their strategies. The main thrust of Plessey's strategy has been to try to establish itself in the US market, the first step being the acquisition of Stromberg-Carlson in 1982. Within Europe the main leg of its strategy is to exploit the collaborative R. & D. programmes sponsored by the EEC. GEC has been less adventurous: it has effectively written off the US market as too competitive, and it is more reliant than Plessey on licensing products from other firms (e.g. Northern Telecom and NEC). Like Plessey however, it is an avid participant in the EEC's R. & D. programmes. The main plank of GEC's strategy consisted of trying to win Plessey's agreement to some form of joint-venture in telecoms. With no prospect of an agreement in sight GEC decided to force the issue at the end of 1985 by launching a take-over bid for Plessey, signalling the most important corporate battle in the recent history of the UK electronics sector.

The GEC–Plessey merger battle

This take-over battle was by no means a purely telecom affair, a factor which ultimately proved to be decisive. Between them GEC and Plessey accounted for 25–30 per cent of UK output for electronic capital equipment. GEC's challenge was originally prompted by its urge to rationalize their two System X activities, even though combined sales of System X accounted for a mere 5 per cent of the aggregated turnover of the two companies. However, GEC's core argument was that the merger would provide the economies of scale necessary for the new group to 'fight off foreign competitors at home and abroad'.[51] GEC had been encouraged to make its bid by positive soundings from the DTI and by the fact that BT was known to be in favour of a rationalization of System X production.[52]

In its response Plessey disputed that size was the critical factor, adding that GEC's philosophy of short-term accounting and cash accumulation was 'fundamentally unsuited to running a high technology business'.[53] But its key argument was that a total merger would create massive market dominance in the UK, especially in the defence sector. Here Plessey was knocking on an open door so far as the M.o.D. was concerned. In recent years the M.o.D. had been moving towards a more competitive procurement policy, and it was horrified at the potential lobbying power of a combined company which would have nearly 25 per cent of its £7.8 billion equipment budget. As a result the M.o.D. strenuously opposed the merger because the 'certain loss of competition would be more harmful than the speculative gains from larger size'.[54] The main lobby within government in favour of the merger was the DTI, but its support was not forcefully expressed and the best it could do was to speak of the 'possible benefits of the proposed merger'.[55]

Considerable forces were aligned against the merger. Oftel thought that the only justification for a merger was in the sphere of System X. Moreover, since Plessey had warned of the threat to direct and indirect employment, the majority of the unions also came out against GEC's bid. In the event the MMC judged that the merger could be expected to 'operate against the public interest', except in the case of System X. With one dissenting voice the MMC had been unable to establish a direct link between company size and performance in the electronics sector. However, the dissenting voice maintained that the merger could 'strengthen competition if it is seen in an international context'.[56] Overall it seems that the national context was the main arena in which the potential effects of the merger were assessed, a reverse situation to the US, where anti-trust regulations are being relaxed to allow US firms to become stronger international actors. Above all else, however, the outcome was one more reminder of the increasingly powerful role which the M.o.D. plays in the UK electronics sector.

If the merger battle accentuated the intense rivalry between GEC and Plessey it should not obscure the shared sense of outrage which the *traditional* suppliers feel towards the government's 'cold shower' industrial policies.[57] Their main complaint was that BT had been privatized in one piece, which meant that the suppliers could not be 'too aggressive in the market for fear of annoying an all-powerful patron'.[58] More generally, however, they fear that they are being squeezed by unilateral liberalization on one side, and by the government's strong commitment to inward investment on the other, which they perceive to be both unpatriotic and a false economy, because inward investment in particular displaces indigenous output. Summing up their attitude the chairman of GEC declared that 'it is impossible to imagine any of our foreign competitors being so disadvantaged by their own people'.[59] In charging 'their' government with unpatriotic behaviour the traditional suppliers do not fully appreciate that what matters in the neo-liberal scenario is not so much the *nationality* of capital, but its *competitive* capability.

The Thatcher government makes little or no distinction between British-owned and British-based firms, other than to hope that inward investors operate as 'tutors' or exemplars for the traditional UK firms.[60] In the government's view the corporatist policies of the past had made little impression on state-dependent firms like GEC and Plessey, largely because they placed too few demands on the firms. This reinforced the government's inclination to substitute market forces for political pressure because, of the two, the former appeared to carry a more credible threat to state-dependent firms.

While there is some evidence to support this view—as we shall see in the case of System X—the fact remains that the neo-liberal strategy is a high-risk strategy, as Oftel's Director-General implied when he argued, 'if everyone dies on the road it is not much help pointing out that the road leads to Utopia'.[61] So far as the traditional telecom firms are concerned they are now among the least sheltered in Western Europe and, in terms of its telecom trade balance, the UK has become the major deficit country in the EEC. Whatever the benefits of liberalization on the business user side, the costs lie in a deteriorating trade balance, greater dependence on foreign technology, and a domestic industry which is exposed to an open market at home, without having reciprocal access abroad. It is clearly one thing to liberalize a telecom market in which indigenous producers are strong, as in the US, it is quite another to do so in a market, like the UK, where domestic producers are relatively weak. Thus the capacity of the UK firms to maintain effective closure after the demise of the 'club' was much less than that of their French or German counterparts.

Going Digital: The Politics of Public Switching

Public switching equipment is the largest single item of capital invest-ment in the telecommunications network. The long lead times involved in designing and producing switching equipment were the main rationale for the close ties between the Post Office and the privileged ring of suppliers. Since 1956 the two sides of the telecom club had pooled their development efforts in the Joint Electronic Research Committee. But this joint forum was dissolved in 1968, when the Post Office briefly flirted with competitive development, a period which turned out to be something of a nightmare.[62] Even then, however, not all ties were severed because the Post Office and its suppliers began to collaborate in a new forum, the Advisory Group on System Definition, which was created in 1968 to specify the digital switching needs of the future.

In the mean time the Post Office wanted its interim switching requirements to be filled by the semi-electronic TXE4 technology, because it felt that its network was dominated to an embarrassing extent by electro-mechanical exchanges. Yet two years elapsed before this plan was approved by the (Conservative) government in 1973, largely because of the opposition mounted against the plan by GEC and Plessey. These firms had large sunk costs in the rival, electro-mechanical Crossbar technology and they were anxious to recoup these costs. Having lost their case before the Post Office they appealed to the government, stressing the greater export potential of Crossbar and 'threatening the government with massive unemployment in depressed areas plus the disruption of the strategically important telephone manufacturing industry'.[63] In the event they succeeded in modifying the original plan, although the TXE4 was still to be the main interim technology.[64] This episode gave an early indication of the political resources which the suppliers were able to muster when their perceived interests ran counter to Post Office requirements.

As it happened this episode also proved to be the first of many delays which dogged the Post Office's modernization strategy. Although the AGSD was wound up in 1973, having specified the outlines of a digital system, the main development contracts were not signed until 1977! This delay can be ascribed to three different obstacles, each of which merits some attention.

Commercial rivalry

Here the two main issues concerned which firms were to be admitted into the System X programme and what balance should be struck between collaboration and competition. From the outset the Post Office Board was intent on a new supply-side arrangement. The three firms—GEC, Plessey, and STC—had evolved from the electro-mechanical era and the Board saw the digital era as an ideal opportunity to wring more competitive practices from these firms. To this end the Board wanted to introduce a fourth supplier in the form of Pye-TMC, a UK-based subsidiary of Philips, which was able to draw on its parent's electronics expertise. However, this proposal met with furious opposition from the three traditional suppliers, resulting in a long and bitter dispute. Once again, the suppliers sought to circumvent the Board's authority by lobbying the D.o.I., where a newly elected Labour government proved to be sympathetic to their case.

As it turned out the Post Office was itself divided on the issue, since the telecom division was opposed to another entrant: the telecom fraternity felt that there were already too many actors without a fourth supplier adding to the problems of overcrowding and excess capacity. In the end, however, this dispute was settled *not* by any decisive action on the parts of the Post Office or the D.o.I., but by the collective action of the 'insider' firms. In a classic example of *closure*, they simply refused to co-operate with Pye-TMC and even threatened to break off discussions with the Post Office itself. Realizing that it had been shut out, Pye-TMC abandoned its System X ambitions. But the main casualty here was the System X programme because this affair had absorbed the better part of two years.

The second problem arose over the Board's desire for collaborative development followed by competitive procurement. This made the Board reluctant to give the suppliers any firm guarantee on future orders for System X exchanges. Anxious to make up for lost time, however, the telecom division was again totally opposed to its Board's stance. However, the Board felt that if the telecom division had its way the Post Office would be committing itself in advance to the suppliers, thus removing its bargaining power. As one senior member of the Board put it:

Why should the Post Office give the firms a guarantee which would make us beholden to them? After all, System X was our thing—we were the sponsors, we gave the directions and we wanted to decide how it was used. It was for us to control and take responsibility.

The dilemma stemmed from having to move from collaborative development to competitive supply, a problem which never arose in France and the FRG because in these countries a single firm was responsible for both development and supply. Eventually, the Board was forced to relax its position because the suppliers refused to treat System X as a manufacturing project until they had received firm orders. Consequently, it was not until 1977 that the first orders were made, with the result that the suppliers only then began to commit engineering resources to the project, a further source of delay.

Project management

Although System X was a collaborative effort the Post Office made it abundantly clear that as it was funding the programme it would be assuming the main authority in the design and leadership of the project. This was not the only model available. It could have followed M.o.D. practice, where project management was delegated to the principal contractor, a model which had three advantages over the System X set up: (1) it ensured that the roles of customer and supplier were well defined; (2) it meant that the task of specifying was kept separate from the task of meeting specifications, and (3) it gave the customer a clearer idea of where blame could be allotted in the event of slippage. Why did the Post Office eschew this model? At the time the Post Office was profoundly unhappy with the performance of its suppliers and this made it reluctant to cede control to any one of them. However, a confidential audit carried out for the D.o.I. claimed that such was the inertia within the Post Office that it was 'unfortunate that circumstances encouraged the Post Office to take on the project management role— a role which does not suit its organization and ethos'.[65]

As a result of its financial and technical dominance the Post Office tended towards rigid and over-elaborate specifications, thus adding to the delays because development contracts took longer to negotiate and longer to engineer. And, once under way, the decision-making process became retarded by a complex bureaucracy, in which minor details had to be authorized at high levels within the Post Office. For these reasons the Post Office review committee had the 'gravest misgivings' about the Post Office's project management role. However, the review also noted that the three manufacturers were in no way a 'natural team' and it bemoaned the fact that these 'jealously independent manufacturers' made the project management task more difficult.[66] Overall, the main drawback of this collaborative model was that the Post Office was not well placed to exert its full customer power over its suppliers because it was itself part of the team. In contrast, the DGT in France and DBP in the FRG were better placed in this respect because, being outside the development process, they were able to bargain more forcefully with their suppliers. Moreover, the fact that the UK had four actors developing System X, with at least two sites per actor, made the development process more complicated than it was in France and the FRG.

The engineering challenge

Once under way the major issues revolved around how to forge a common engineering culture, how to accelerate design and production cycles, and how to reduce costs. One of the most intractable problems here was the lack of a common equipment base, a problem compounded by the divergent working practices of the three firms. The Post Office quickly realized that it was not enough to win over the engineering teams because:

After we had got all the engineers from the firms to agree on the need for common equipment and common working practices, these would be unable to deliver. The reason for this was that their commercial superiors refused to write-off existing equipment and this made it very difficult to get going on the engineering side.

Another bottle-neck arose from a lack of investment on the part of the firms in both production capacity and new process technology. To its horror the Post Office gradually discovered that its own cost-plus contract arrangements contributed to this problem because:

The firms got richer by minimizing capital employed: that way they were able to convert the 13 per cent return on cost, allowed by the Treasury formula for cost-plus contracts, into a higher return on capital employed. It provided no incentive to invest, to innovate, or to raise efficiency.

To overcome this problem the Post Office was eventually driven to finance new production capacity as well as supplying each of the firms with common Computer Aided Design systems. However, there was an additional reason for the firms' lack of investment in System X facilities, namely the absence of any strong commercial pressure at a time when the firms were beginning the manufacturing phase of the interim TXE4 system, which was a more lucrative contract than System X!

Finally, there was the issue of how to reduce the excessive cost of System X. The collaborative nature of the project was itself a factor in raising costs in both R. & D. and production. Collaboration involved a good deal of duplication, which was 'doubly unfortunate in that the duplication occurs in those areas where there is a shortage of staff anyway'.[67] On the R. & D. side the Post Office became deeply worried about the cost and lack of power of the central processor for which GEC was responsible. This had fallen way behind schedule, partly because of GEC's lack of expertise, partly because the specifications kept changing. In the end the Post Office took the extraordinary step of requiring GEC to subcontract the processor to a Californian design company, and this led to a staggering improvement in its price–performance ratio.

On the production side the Post Office had been aware from the outset that three firms would be too many for the manufacturing requirements of System X. This was identified as one of the main problems by the Post Office chairman in a comparison of the UK and US situations. Western Electric, he said, had the capacity to produce nearly 1 million lines of electronic switching in each of its five factories. In contrast, the UK had the capacity to produce just 1 million lines, but this was 'dispersed over nine towns—not factories but towns'.[68] Clearly, the UK supply industry cried out for rationalization.

In 1978 a major effort was launched to rationalize the industry, sponsored by the D.o.I. and the National Enterprise Board (NEB). It arose out of the D.o.I.'s concern over the viability of System X, especially on the export front. Throughout the System X programme the D.o.I. had little or no independent information about what was actually going on; here again it was totally dependent on the Post Office and the latter resented its interference.[69] In a confidential audit carried out for the D.o.I., the NEB recommended that the number of suppliers should be reduced from three to two, and it suggested that Plessey and STC should merge their telecom facilities. However, each firm insisted upon its 'right' as a sovereign supplier. Indeed, when the Post Office tried to ease STC out in 1979, the firm appealed to the D.o.I. and succeeded in winning political support to remain in the System X programme. STC was able to marshal two important resources here. As one of its managers argued: 'First, many locations were in development areas and we realized that this was a raw political nerve. Secondly, there were legal contracts and, if the Post Office threatened to unilaterally tear these up, we could take to the courts.' Significantly, however, the D.o.I. was at no time inclined to force the issue because, as one Labour minister frankly conceded, 'the D.o.I. would only intervene if the industry wanted intervention'!

Yet the D.o.I. did keep up its pressure to improve the export potential of System X. The Post Office had not paid any serious attention to export potential until very late in the day.[70] The same was true of the firms themselves; so much so that the NEB had been 'taken aback by the lack of resources devoted to overseas marketing efforts'.[71] Only after intense political pressure did the four parties agree to set up a joint export company, BTS, in 1979. But BTS proved to be a short-lived and unhappy venture, torn by corporate rivalry: for instance, while STC was prepared to loss-lead in order to break into new export markets, GEC resisted this, arguing for state export aid. Indeed, it was not entirely clear if the firms saw exporting as such a crucial issue because, as one of their number admitted, 'even if we do not sell a single line abroad, System X will be profitable for us'.

Paradoxically, while the Labour government was loath to intervene, the Thatcher administration was more intolerant of the existing situation. Taking advantage of a BTS request for export aid the D.o.I. decided to make financial support conditional on an agreement to restructure the supply-side arrangements. Once it became clear that the three firms were again unable to rationalize themselves, the D.o.I. allowed BT to force the issue to a head. In May 1982 BT made its move. Without warning, it announced its intention of placing all System X orders with a *single* company and, equally shocking, it said it would be offering around 30 per cent of its switching business to international tender. This 'bombshell' was not as unexpected as is often thought. Plessey was well prepared for the news because, in November 1981, it had met privately with the D.o.I. and BT to promote such a course of action!

Having studied each company's performance over the previous three years, BT ranked Plessey first, STC second, and GEC last; on this basis, Plessey was recommended to the D.o.I. as the chosen contractor. However, this proved to be too radical for the government, and so the Cabinet pressed for a less contentious solution.

Following furious lobbying on the part of GEC it was finally decided that Plessey should be made prime contractor, with GEC the sub-contractor. STC was eventually bought out on highly favourable terms, namely, an exclusive right to supply BT with an updated version of the TXE4, estimated to be worth some £100 million annually for five years.[72]

This long overdue rationalization closed one chapter in the saga of System X, but other daunting challenges lay ahead for the two remaining suppliers. As we have seen, BT is now pressing each of them hard on cost, quality, and delivery and they have to compete on a fully competitive basis with Ericsson. From a national perspective the most disturbing part of the saga is that System X has won few export orders. But without such orders it would be difficult, if not impossible, for the UK market to sustain three independent suppliers: further rationalization or collaboration was thus inevitable.

That rationalization took so long to materialize was due almost entirely to the tenacious rivalry between GEC and Plessey at board-room level. Nevertheless, this impasse was broken in 1988, when the two companies finally agreed to merge their respective telecom businesses into GEC-Plessey Telecoms (GPT). However, such was the fragility of this joint venture that eight months after its birth in April 1988, GEC formed an alliance with Siemens in order to launch a hostile bid for Plessey. The aim behind this Anglo-German alliance was to gain sufficient scale to compete with the larger US and Japanese telecom firms in the European market-place, and also to share the burgeoning development costs of the next generation of digital public switches. If this bid proves successful it will signal the end of an independent British presence in this high technology sector. Even if the bid fails, however, the chances of GPT being able to chart an independent course are slim, such are the pressures to amalgamate along international lines.

Conclusion

Of the three countries studied here the UK undoubtedly represents the most radical break with the past in the telecommunications sector. It has liberalized its market to a greater extent than any other country in Europe. It has privatized its national carrier (BT) and broken the latter's monopoly by licensing a rival carrier

(Mercury). And, as regards government–industry relations, the Thatcher government has been less concerned than other European governments about protecting domestic telecom producers. Indeed it has overridden traditional producer interests in the name of greater freedom of choice for *business users*.

Given its fervent ideological commitment to market-based solutions, the Thatcher government was far less tolerant of the extent of market closure achieved by the producers than was the previous Labour government. Corporate closure reached its heights in the UK when the traditional suppliers collectively succeeded in keeping a new entrant, Pye, out of the Post Office market for a new generation of switching technology. However, the closure of the UK telecom market had manifestly failed to create a successful telecom industry, hence the traditional suppliers had few achievements to justify their privileges. Acutely conscious of Labour's failure to reform the telecom club, particularly with respect to the System X programme, the Thatcher government effectively undermined the club by means of liberalization and privatization.

So far as producers are concerned, the only ones to have benefited from the neo-liberal offensive in the UK are the new entrants and, as we have seen, many of these are foreign firms. Unlike its opposite numbers in France and the FRG, the Thatcher government is not concerned about the nationality of capital, hence the UK seems likely to become one of the main platforms from which US and Japanese firms launch themselves into Europe. In Chapter 8 we shall see that this policy is causing some concern in the European Community because it undermines the attempt to create a more coherent European identity in this strategic industrial sector.

Notes

1. For a first-hand account of the archaic structures and practices of the Post Office see Tony Benn, *Out of the Wilderness: Diaries 1963–67* (London: Arrow Books, 1988). On becoming Postmaster General in 1964 Benn found this office to be something akin to the Duchy of Lancaster, an honorific post, while the Post Office itself appeared as a veritable museum, dominated at the top by ex-military personnel and profoundly resistant to new management techniques.
2. Department of Industry, *Report of the Post Office Review Committee*, Cmnd. 6850 (London: HMSO, 1977).

3. Post Office, *Evidence to the Post Office Review Committee*, Appendix to Cmnd. 6850, 1976.

4. There were some exceptions to the Post Office supply monopoly, the chief one being that business users could purchase large PABXs direct from the supplier—subject to Post Office approval—because these were often tailor-made for particular user requirements.

5. J. Solomon, 'Telecommunications Evolution in the UK', *Telecommunications Policy* (Sept. 1986).

6. *Report of the Post Office Review Committee*, p. 53.

7. D.o.I., *Evidence to the Review Committee*; D. Pitt, *The Telecommunications Function in the British Post Office* (Farnborough: Saxon House, 1980).

8. Post Office Engineering Union, *Evidence to the Post Office Review Committee*, Appendix to Cmnd. 6850.

9. *Report of the Post Office Review Committee*, p. 42.

10. *Report of the Post Office Review Committee*.

11. *Report of the Post Office Review Committee*, p. 108.

12. *Report of the Post Office Review Committee*, p. 108.

13. POEU, *The Modernisation of Telecommunications* (London: POEU, 1979), p. 88.

14. Post Office Users National Council, *Annual Reports for 1979–80 and 1980–81* (London: POUNC, 1980, 1981).

15. Department of Trade and Industry, *The Future of Telecommunications: Government Policy Explained* (London: HMSO, 1983).

16. For a fuller discussion of these points, see K. Morgan, 'Breaching the Monopoly: Telecommunications and the State in Britain', Working Paper Series on Government–Industry Relations No. 7 (University of Sussex, 1987).

17. Microelectronics Design Associates, *Independent Telecommunications Networks: Report to the D.o.I.* (London, 1980).

18. *Independent Telecommunications Networks*, p. 9.

19. *Independent Telecommunications Networks*, p. 16.

20. The D.o.I. commissioned a number of (pro-liberal) feasibility studies, the most prominent being the Beesley Report, published in 1981. The conclusions of this report turned out to be rather too radical for the government, especially the central conclusion that 'in the home market there should be no restriction on the freedom to offer services to third parties over BT's network' (M. Beesley, *Liberalisation of the Use of the British Telecommunications Network*, (London: HMSO, 1981), p. 36). In other words, Beesley argued in favour of allowing competitors to lease transmission capacity from BT in order to resell this to third parties, as was the practice in the US. In the face of massive opposition from BT the government came down against 'simple resale'

of BT capacity. Instead competitors would be allowed to resell capacity only where the service contained a substantial addition to the basic network facility, hence the designation value-added network services (VANS).

21. Oftel, *Annual Report for 1985* (London, 1986).
22. Severe barriers to entry continue to exist in the testing and approval of customer apparatus, which can be both costly and protracted. For instance, Ferranti-GTE claims it incurred £200,000 in costs just to get interim approval for a small PABX. Although Oftel wishes to reduce this barrier, by making some tests voluntary instead of mandatory, it has been forced to backtrack on this issue in the face of concerted opposition from BT, Mercury, and the established UK equipment suppliers.
23. Department of Trade and Industry, *Revised Government Proposals for the Future Licensing of Value Added and Data Services* (London: HMSO, 1986).
24. Department of Industry, *The Future of Telecommunications in Britain*, Cmnd. 8610 (London: HMSO, 1982); J. Hills, *Deregulating Telecoms: Competition and Control in the US, Japan and Britain* (London: Frances Pinter, 1986).
25. The influence of these financial advisers was both subtle and compelling. They informed the government, for example, that the City would not accept (i.e. underwrite) a situation in which a private BT was still directly subject to government influence, as was the case in Japan after the privatization of NTT. It was also said that the City would be more 'comfortable' with the government having a 49% rather than a 51% stake in BT. And it was the financial advisers who persuaded the government to allow overseas interests to participate in the sale.
26. What seems astonishing is that BT appears not to have been informed, let alone consulted, about the government's decision to privatize: it first heard the news in the form of a public announcement in July 1982. Even so, most of its senior management were quickly persuaded of the benefits of private status, like freedom from government interference, greater remuneration, and the ability to be more assertive with suppliers.
27. Lord Weinstock in *House of Lords Debates*, Cols. 859–63, 16 Jan. 1984.
28. Morgan, 'Breaching the Monopoly'.
29. British Telecom Unions Committee, *The Battle for British Telecom* (London, 1984).
30. House of Commons, Public Accounts Committee, *Sale of Government Shareholding in British Telecommunications*, HC 35 (London: HMSO, 1985).

31. M. Cassell, 'Labour Raps Claim that BT is Public', *Financial Times*, 31 Dec. 1986.

32. J. Hills, *Deregulating Telecoms*.

33. Post Office Engineering Union, *The Telephone Ring: It's Time to Investigate* (London: POEU, 1962); House of Commons, Select Committee on Nationalized Industries, *The Post Office* (London: HMSO, 1967). For all the rhetoric of 'going for growth' in the 1960s the Postmaster General was privately told that the Post Office dared not advertise the telephone service because of critical supply-side constraints. This crisis of supply stemmed from the Post Office's failure to anticipate the surge in telephone demand in the early 1960s. But the core of the supply-side problem lay in a deep conflict of interests within the club. To meet the surge in demand the Post Office wanted an immediate expansion of traditional Strowger exchange equipment. But the suppliers, fearing that this equipment would shortly become obsolete, were reluctant to expand their facilities. R. Caves and Associates, *Britain's Economic Prospects* (London: Allen & Unwin, 1968).

34. Although the Post Office was in principle free to manufacture for its own needs this freedom was never used, partly because of opposition from the privately owned equipment manufacturers.

35. A. Giddens, *Central Problems in Sociological Theory* (London: Macmillan, 1979).

36. Even the short-list proved to be controversial because it contained no company from the EEC. The French felt deeply aggrieved, having made great efforts to get BT to agree to a reciprocal opening of UK and French markets, a policy in line with that of the EEC. On French reaction see J. Dondoux, 'Towards a European Telecommunications Market', address to the *Financial Times* World Telecommunications Conference, London, 11–12 Dec. 1984.

37. What was also significant was that Thorn-Ericsson's chairman, Sir William Barlow, a former chairman of the Post Office and well connected with the BT Board, was in a unique position to brief Thorn-Ericsson on BT's requirements.

38. Oftel, *BT's Procurement of Digital Exchanges* (London, 1985), p. 9.

39. As it stood Oftel's recommendation was unenforceable. The main course of action open to it, had it felt sufficiently determined, would have been to try to amend BT's licence. But this would have created severe embarrassment to the government, coming so soon after BT had been privatized on terms which promised minimum regulatory interference.

40. Oftel, *BT's Procurement of Digital Exchanges*, p. 36.

41. Oftel, *BT's Procurement of Digital Exchanges*, p. 38.

42. Monopolies and Mergers Commission, *British Telecommunications plc and Mitel Corporation* (London: HMSO, 1986).
43. *BT and Mitel*, p. 73.
44. P. Gist and S. Meadowcroft, 'Regulating for Competition: The Newly Liberalised Market for Private Branch Exchanges', *Fiscal Studies*, 7/3 (1986), pp. 41–86.
45. POEU, *Making the Future Work: The Broad Strategy* (London: POEU, 1984); C. Leadbeater, 'BT's Strategy May Weaken Unions', *Financial Times*, 4 June 1987. BT's offensive led the National Communications Union (formerly the POEU) to declare a strike in the early part of 1987 over pay and working practices. However, since this had little disruptive effect, the strike collapsed after two weeks.
46. De Zoete and Bevan, *British Telecom* (London, 1984).
47. Oftel, *Annual Report for 1985*.
48. BT's policy of lowering its international tariffs has another aim besides that of pre-empting domestic competition from Mercury. In the context of an international price war, it is trying to maintain the UK's status as the major transatlantic hub for telecom traffic between Europe and North America. Currently, a third of all multinational companies in Western Europe route their traffic through London, and the UK accounts for around 50% of the transatlantic telephone market. See R. Bruce, J. Cunard, and M. Director, *From Telecommunications to Electronic Services* (London: Butterworths, 1986), and M. Sauvant, *International Transactions in Services: The Politics of Transborder Data Flows* (Boulder, Color.: Westview Press, 1986).
49. The two main exceptions were the government's refusal to allow BT and IBM to form a joint venture to provide a managed data network, and BT's failure to prevent Mercury from gaining favourable 'interconnection' terms.
50. MMC, *The General Electric Company plc and the Plessey Company plc* (London: HMSO, 1986).
51. GEC, *Annual Report and Accounts* (1985).
52. In 1984 a junior Minister at the DTI (Lord Lucas) had publicly spoken of the logic for a merger between GEC and Plessey because, he said, they were both too small to compete on their own.
53. *Reject the GEC Bid* (London: Plessey, 1986).
55. *GEC plc and Plessey plc*, p. 66.
55. *GEC plc and Plessey plc*, p. 70. Strictly speaking the full weight of the DTI was never brought to bear in favour of the merger: the pro-merger faction consisted only of those DTI divisions which had sponsorship responsibility for the telecom and electronics sectors. As the Secretary of State for Trade and Industry was supposed to have the final say on the MMC inquiry it was thought inappropriate for him

to combine the roles of witness and judge. This undoubtedly weakened the pro-merger faction because the DTI divisions were no match for the powerful M.o.D.

56. *GEC plc and Plessey plc*, p. 135.

57. We emphasize traditional suppliers because there is a deep conflict of interest between these and the newly emerging, smaller suppliers organized in the Telecommunications Industry Association. The latter owe their birth or growth to liberalization and they are therefore anxious to distinguish themselves from the 'old guard' of GEC and Co.

58. A. Weinstock, *House of Lords Debates*, 16 Jan. 1984; J. Clark, evidence to the House of Lords, Select Committee on Overseas Trade, HC 238–11, pp. 264–74.

59. GEC, *Offer for Plessey* (1985). Nothing better illustrates the new era than the unconventional political tactics which Lord Weinstock of GEC has been forced to adopt. In the past Weinstock had lobbied via private pressure, frequently at Prime Ministerial level, rather than through public protest. During the privatization debate, however, he was forced into open opposition to the government in the House of Lords for what he had previously failed to secure through private discussions in Whitehall. P. Riddell, 'Lord Weinstock's Public Protest', *Financial Times*, 28 Mar. 1984; Morgan, *Breaching the Monopoly*.

60. K. Morgan and A. Sayer, *Microcircuits of Capital: 'Sunrise' Industry and Uneven Development* (Cambridge: Polity Press, 1988).

61. Quoted in J. Crisp, 'The Problems of Policing an Industry with New-Found Freedoms', *Financial Times*, 26 July 1985.

62. The origins of the problem lay in the premature decision (made in the late 1940s or early 1950s) to leap from the electro-mechanical Strowger exchange to a fully electronic digital exchange. This strategy came to grief in 1962 when an experimental electronic exchange failed, forcing the Post Office to turn to the Crossbar technology which it had consistently eschewed. Desperately in need of a stop-gap exchange, it swallowed its antipathy towards systems which it had no hand in designing and accepted two proprietary Crossbar systems, one from Plessey and GEC, the other from STC. The results were disastrous: higher costs, poor quality, and late delivery forced the Post Office to resort to obsolete, but reliable, Strowger technology.

63. *New Scientist*, Vol. 58, 7 June 1973, p. 617.

64. J. Hills, *Information Technology and Industrial Policy* (London: Croom Helm, 1984).

65. National Enterprise Board, 'Report on Telecommunications', unpublished (London: NEB, 1978).

66. D.o.I., *Report of the Post Office Review Committee*.

67. NEB, *Report on Telecommunications*.
68. W. Ryland, *Life and Letters: The Sixth STC Communication Lecture* (London, 1976).
69. There was a small faction within the D.o.I. which pressed for a more stringent audit of System X, but the dominant attitude was against 'rocking the boat' because too many resources had already been committed. This was the classic Whitehall response to big projects, according to one member of the Carter review committee, who also felt that the D.o.I. and the Carter team should have demanded a radical reorganization of System X in the late 1970s.
70. On the export issue the Post Office always took refuge in the letter of the 1969 Act. This Act laid no explicit duty on the Post Office to promote exports or to take exporting into consideration when specifying equipment.
71. National Enterprise Board, 'Report on Telecommunications', unpublished (London: NEB, 1978).
72. The main reason why STC was asked to withdraw was not because it was a subsidiary of ITT—indeed STC was about to become an independent UK company as ITT had decided to disinvest—but because its share of System X had been substantially less than that of the other two, it having devoted its main switching resources to the TXE4 and TXE4A interim exchanges. It was also the case that during 1982 STC had run into such difficulties on its System X contracts that BT threatened to reallocate them to Plessey.

6

France: The Rise and Fall of *Dirigisme*

Telecommunications is often seen as one of the great success stories of post-war economic development in France. In Chapter 3 we argued that the most successful industrial strategies in France have been in those sectors deemed to be critical either to national security (e.g. defence and energy) or to national economic development (e.g. mass transport and telecommunications). Here the state itself constitutes much of the market and thus these sectors lend themselves to the '*grand projet*' type of intervention. That is to say the French state has displayed an extraordinary capacity to marshal large resources so as to accomplish a national 'mission'.[1] This mode of intervention, however, appears to be less viable where markets are open to strong international competition, and where the state is less of a force as regards public procurement. Indeed, the French telecommunications sector provides a perfect illustration of the scope of, and the limits to, the industrial power of the French state.

In Search of a Flexible Telecom Regime

Up until the 1970s the French telephone network was appallingly backward. As a result of financial neglect and political indifference France then had one of the lowest telephone densities amongst the OECD countries. Modernization of the network pre-supposed a new balance of power within the state and between the state and the equipment industry. Although the power relationships between them have changed over time, the following are the main actors within the French telecom system:

1. Within the state itself there is, first and foremost, the Ministry of Finance: until the late 1960s this ministry had forced the Direction Générale des Télécommunications (the DGT, now renamed France Télécom) to finance most telecom investment from internally generated funds, the major single obstacle to modernization. Secondly,

there is the Ministère des Postes, des Télécommunications et de Télédiffusion (the PTT Ministry). A single administrative entity, it has a small ministerial staff presiding over two substantially autonomous units, the DGT, itself composed of different actors, and the DGP (Direction Générale de la Poste). At times the PTT Minister has been formally subordinate to the Industry Minister, whose department shares certain responsibilities for the electronics industry.

2. The equipment suppliers have been a major force in certain conjunctures. Unlike in Britain or Germany, the suppliers in France have changed dramatically over the years, as a cosy cartel of CGE (CIT-Alcatel),[2] ITT, and Ericsson was first replaced by CGE and Thomson, with the restructured Alcatel NV finally sharing the business with a newly re-entered Ericsson (in alliance with Matra as MET).

3. The trade unions are, by French standards, well represented in the telecom sector, where Force Ouvrière is the main union. The Association des Ingénieurs des Télécommunications (AIT) is the lobby for senior engineers within the civil service, and the latter belongs to the Corps des Ingénieurs de Télécommunications. While the manual unions within the DGT are fervently committed to its public service status, the AIT is above all committed to the DGT's autonomy.

4. There are also a number of user groups, the largest being the Association Française des Utilisateurs du Téléphone et des Télécommunications (AFUTT), which represents both residential and business customers. Overall, however, French business users are less well organized and less vocal than their UK counterparts, partly because of the belated development of the French network.

The impetus for the modernization of the network stemmed largely from forces within the state. The origins of this pressure can be traced back to the formation of the Centre National d'Études des Télécommunications (CNET) in 1944. Although nominally just an R. & D. centre, the CNET gradually assumed enormous powers over procurement and industrial policy in telecoms.[3] The CNET was the main source for what became a powerful technical stratum within the state system, and its lobbying contributed to a heightened political sensitivity towards the 'crise du telephone'. Although the major advances occurred under Giscard's presidency, three important institutional innovations were realized before 1974. First the Caisse Nationale des Télécommunications was created in 1967, through which the DGT was able to borrow money from international capital markets, and the creation of other CNT-like entities gradually eased the DGT's borrowing limits.[4] Secondly, the PTT Ministry was reorganized in 1971 to give more autonomy to the DGT and the VIth plan (1970–5) announced that telecoms would henceforth be a major priority.

The real sea change, however, must be located in a new balance of power which began to emerge in 1974. The 'modern era' of French telecommunications was intimately associated with Gerard Théry, who was appointed by Giscard as the new head of the DGT in 1974.[5] A very close political relationship between Théry and Giscard further enhanced the political profile of telecommunications. Accordingly, in the VIIth plan (1976–80) telecoms was defined as a Priority Action Programme, and telecoms alone accounted for over 50 per cent of the total 200 billion fr. budget allocated to all such programmes. So far as the DGT was concerned the major concession which it had wrung from the Ministry of Finance was a five-year period of budgetary freedom, replacing annually controlled budgets.

Théry realized that the goal of bringing France up to the best network standards in Europe could not be accomplished without major internal reforms. Within the constraints of a civil service culture the new leadership set about transforming the DGT into a more commercially minded organization. Among the most important reforms were: (1) breaking the traditional power of the CNET and reducing its functions to those befitting an R. & D. centre; (2) decentralizing managerial responsibility to regional directors, who were obliged to submit a *monthly* progress report; (3) the recruitment of a new breed of commercial manager; and (4) the introduction of financial incentives to engineers. The net effect of these reforms was that the DGT began to earn itself a rather dynamic reputation, to some it was 'an enterprise disguised as an administration'.[6] Without these internal reforms it is doubtful if the modernization plan would have yielded such spectacular results. On most counts the goals of the VIIth plan were realized: by the early 1980s France's telephone density was comparable with that of Britain and Germany; average waiting times for equipment had been considerably reduced; tariffs had increased by less than the rate of inflation;

and the DGT had one of the best productivity records among national telecom operators.

The success of the modernization plan greatly enhanced the power and prestige of the DGT and Théry, its Director-General, carried more weight with the President than the sequence of PTT Ministers who were nominally in charge. Even so, the DGT knew that its newly acquired stature depended upon a large, but diminishing, investment programme. With the ambition of becoming an independent public corporation, along the lines of Électricité de France, the DGT leadership sought to increase its autonomy by capitalizing on the 'telematics revolution', a resonant issue in France given the widely acclaimed Nora–Minc report.[7] Exploiting this receptive political climate the DGT proposed a Plan Télématique, which received official blessing from the government at the end of 1978. What emerged was a whole series of new initiatives, orchestrated by the DGT, to develop telematic services in such fields as videotext, teletext, facsimile, and broadband cable systems.[8] As well as trying to provide French suppliers with new product markets, the DGT set up its own subsidiaries under *private* commercial law, like Transpac in data transmission. Through this innovative mechanism the DGT had found a more autonomous, thus more flexible, means of providing new telematic services. Without these 'private' subsidiaries the development of advanced services would have been much slower given the problems of recruiting commercial skills in a public administration.[9]

The Plan Télématique involved the DGT in a new 'game', in which it became clear that there were a number of important differences between developing the network and promoting telematics. For one thing there was less uncertainty about technology and demand with the former. Equally important, while the first task fell clearly within its mandate, the second involved the DGT in a division of labour with equipment suppliers and information vendors (like the press) which was ambiguous and a potential source of conflict.[10] The DGT paid too little attention to these differences. Consequently, while some of the initiatives proved successful— videotext, for example—others had to be abandoned because of poor demand. Apart from the mixed commercial results, the DGT's new self-defined role in telematics began to attract severe criticism. Politicians from all sides of the political spectrum accused the DGT of authoritarian behaviour and questioned the impact of telematics on individual liberty, while the unions criticized the DGT for acting as an unaccountable 'state within a state'.[11] Indeed, one DGT official summed the situation up in this way:

Prior to 1981 there could be no doubt that the DGT was immensely powerful. This was partly because of the close political relationship that existed between Théry and Giscard and because the PTT was only a paper Ministry. Under the Théry regime the DGT considered itself more of an autonomous private company than a public administration.[12]

The prominent role which the DGT had won for itself under Giscard meant that it was politically exposed when the Socialists assumed office in 1981. Indeed, two changes were introduced immediately: Théry was replaced by Jacques Dondoux, who was closely identified with the 'fallen' CNET establishment, and the PTT Ministry strove to reassert its control over the DGT, emphasizing that the latter was a *public* administration. Under the Socialists the DGT became subordinated to the wider aims of the government. For example:

1. The DGT lost its financial autonomy and it was forced to subsidize the general budget. Since the DGT was not subject to value added tax, the government resorted to an unofficial tax which increased year by year, rising from 2.8 b. fr. in 1982 to 16.7 b. fr. in 1986. On top of this the Finance Ministry ordered a 25 per cent increase in telephone tariffs in 1984, provoking fierce protests from the DGT because this violated the 'management charter' which it had signed with the Council of Ministers for the 1983–6 period.

2. The DGT was obliged to manage and finance the Plan de la Filière Électronique, an ambitious five-year plan, launched in 1982, to boost the French electronics sector. A large part of these funds was used to subsidize loss-making nationalized firms.

3. The DGT's interests were subordinated to those of its newly nationalized equipment suppliers, a theme examined in the following section.

In each case the DGT's autonomy was severely reduced, but it was far from powerless. It still managed to win approval for another major state initiative (the Plan Câble) and it faced none of the deregulatory pressure which was then engulfing its British counterpart. Indeed, the Plan Câble could be interpreted as an attempt by certain elements within the DGT actually to extend the DGT's monopoly over the French network. At an estimated cost of between 45–60

b. fr. the Plan Câble envisaged cabling some six million homes by 1992, and a further one million homes a year thereafter.[13] Significantly, the sponsors of the Plan Câble were almost entirely drawn from within the French administration. External actors, like potential suppliers, played little or no sponsorship role.[14] The primary sponsors were the CNET, the PTT Ministry, and the Élysée. However, elements within the DGT, including the Director-General, had been sceptical about the project from the start, and, over time, these gained the upper hand as the huge costs of the Plan Câble became apparent. Hence well before the advent of a right-wing government the DGT had already began to backtrack on the grand ambitions of the Plan Câble.[15]

The burgeoning cost was not the only reason for the DGT's growing caution over the Plan Câble. It became concerned that its enhanced profile in the network would induce a political backlash against its monopoly if the Right won power in the 1986 election. Although the DGT's monopoly was secure under the Socialists, the DGT was nevertheless becoming anxious about the external threats of deregulation in the US and the UK. In the belief that there was no ineluctable pressure for all countries to adopt the same regime, the Director-General none the less stressed the need for more flexibility:

The rules of the monopoly must surely be moderated. Its management must be adapted to radically new missions. But the French style public service can reconcile the need for liberalization and the need for coherence. A national telecommunications network must take account not only of market criteria but also of its own contribution to wider economic and social objectives, such as regional development ... We still think the best way of reconciling these objectives is management of the network by a national telecommunications department, which implies maintaining a monopoly over the basic service.[16]

As the DGT saw it, the fact that there had been less pressure for deregulation in France was attributable to a combination of strengths and weaknesses. On the positive side three factors were at work: (1) the DGT's excellent record in modernizing the network; (2) a long-established liberal policy with respect to customer equipment, which meant that the French monopoly was never as absolute as in the UK or the FRG; and (3) the high productivity record of the DGT. On the negative side there were two factors: (1) the fact that the DGT was not sufficiently equipped with the commercial expertise to operate in a more competitive market; and (2) the fact that the French equipment industry was not yet strong enough to meet international competition. So, in the DGT's eyes, its own record had forestalled pressures for deregulation, while the weaknesses were so many reasons for 'delaying entry into a new world'.[17]

The relative absence of a (public) debate on deregulation until 1986 was also due to the fact that France had a very different government from that in Britain. However, what also distinguishes the two countries is that France did not have such powerful actors on the business user side. The French business user population had no equivalent of the 'City', for instance. More generally, such users were less critical of the DGT partly because they had less cause to be compared to their British counterparts, but also because they are less well organized and less conscious of telecommunications costs.[18]

However, well before the Chirac government came to power the DGT had already begun to adjust to what it saw as the 'imported' effects of deregulation overseas. For example, in an attempt to pre-empt loss of custom on its lucrative North American route, occasioned by an international price war among operators, the DGT lowered its tariffs. To compensate, it also began to reassess its entire tariff structure, with the aim of increasing local tariffs. So despite being a public monopoly the DGT still felt that France could not immunize itself from deregulation abroad. Further pressures for change came from *within* the DGT, in particular from the influential AIT. Escalating political interference under the Socialists was the root grievance. The AIT was especially aggrieved at the 'milking' of DGT revenue for the purposes of subsidizing the unprofitable post and nationalized firm sectors. Hence the AIT demanded that posts and telecoms be separated and that the DGT be given more autonomy from government.[19] Such festering internal discontent was one reason why the PTT Minister began to consider reforming the DGT in the last year of the Socialist government.[20] But this initiative was eventually overtaken by the general election of March 1986, when a new right-wing government arrived in office.

Despite radical postures the new coalition government was far more cautious than its Conservative counterpart in Britain. For one thing it was torn between the pragmatism of Chirac (who was fearful of antagonizing the DGT's unions before the 1988 presidential elections) and the radical liberalism of Madelin and Longuet, the Ministers of Industry and the PTT respectively.[21] The result was a *pragmatic liberalism*, one sign of which was that Longuet's draft law on telecommunications had not been passed by the time of the 1988 general election. In the mean time it announced that value added network services (VANS) were to be fully liberalized, although the planned opening date was not met. The most tangible reform was the creation of a new regulatory watchdog, the Commission Nationale des Communications et Libertés (CNCL), which was modelled on the American FCC and which took over regulatory responsibility for telecoms and broadcasting. However, the pace of reform has slowed down sharply since the election of a new Socialist government. The CNCL is to be replaced by a Conseil Supérieur de l'Audiovisuel, with no telecom responsibility. The EEC's liberalization programme requires that a new regulatory regime be instituted in which the regulation of the network is separated from its operation. A new law has been promised and it will be very hard to brush aside the question of the DGT's status at this point.[22]

Once fearful of losing its monopoly the DGT perceives certain advantages in deregulation. Given the choice between the status quo and a deregulation which would enable it to compete in basic and advanced services, even at the cost of a French Mercury, the DGT's leadership would prefer the latter. Indeed, many managers yearn to emulate BT's position. However, the accent is very much on caution in changing the DGT's status. The Right was fearful of antagonizing the DGT unions, and the Left has a residual belief in state control. There are other obstacles too, like the lack of enthusiasm on the part of the Finance Ministry, which is anxious not to lose a valuable source of revenue from the DGT. A more liberal telecom regime may emerge in France, but it will be one in which the DGT remains firmly within the public sector.

The Tortuous Restructuring of the French Telecom Industry

The perennial poverty of the PTT Ministry helps to explain why a market controlled by the state on the demand side was for so long dominated by foreign firms on the supply side. Indeed, ITT and Ericsson dominated the 'French' equipment industry right up until 1975. It seems remarkable in retrospect that there was no telecom lobby, apart from the CNET, to protest at the absence of French firms in this industry. It was in this context that the CNET, animated by Gaullist ambitions, took it upon itself to fill the vacuum created by a weak PTT Ministry so as to promote the interests of indigenous industry. As we have seen, the CNET was much more than a conventional R. & D. centre; as the main centre of telecom expertise it was given tasks way beyond its true remit, like control over procurement contracts. At the behest of the CNET, the PTT Ministry established two telecom clubs for pooling patents and sharing orders: Sotélec, for transmission equipment, was formed in 1947, and Socotel, for switching systems, emerged in 1958. These were created as independent legal entities in which suppliers and the DGT both participated.[23] In effect they were telecom cartels, much like the R. & D. and market-sharing arrangements in the Britain. One major difference, however, was that the CNET tried to use them to reallocate market shares away from ITT towards French firms, though this was only partially successful. As foreign firms it was difficult for ITT and Ericsson publicly to resist this state-backed strategy of usurping their position.

As in Britain these cartels attracted a barrage of criticism in the late 1960s. Prices were inflated because entry was restricted and because production was too fragmented to permit economies of scale. Moreover, with the embarrassing exception of ITT, the French industry had a poor export record. As a result, the CNET was accused by aspiring elements in the DGT of having mishandled its responsibilities by eliminating competition, neglecting exports, and pursuing technological goals at the expense of commercial efficiency. At the same time CGE, the main French firm in the sector, was indicted for not having made a genuine commitment in telecommunications.[24]

As we have seen, a new balance of power was beginning to emerge in the telecom establishment. Until then the CNET's power had been directly related to the weakness of the DGT. With the appointment of an aggressive chief at the DGT, the roles which the CNET had once filled by default were suddenly contested. The result was a series of bold political manœuvres between 1974 and 1976. Firstly, the CNET was unceremoniously stripped of all industrial policy functions apart from R. & D., and these were transferred to the DAII, a newly created unit within the DGT, whose head was made personally responsible to Théry.[25] Secondly, in an attempt to 'de-colonize' the industry the DGT arranged for Thomson to acquire the main subsidiaries of ITT and Ericsson, a classic example of *dirigisme* which is examined in the following section.

Throughout the network modernization programme the DGT enjoyed extensive autonomy. But, as we have seen, its ambitions were not confined to being a simple network operator. In fact the Plan Télématique was another example of the DGT's *dirigiste* approach, only here it strove to pioneer new markets for a domestic industry which had been encouraged to boost capacity to cater for the (temporary) needs of the DGT. Without production facilities of its own the DGT realized that its own ambitions were directly linked to the success of its suppliers. It hoped that a strong domestic market for telematic products would compensate for the saturating market for basic network equipment, and that the former would serve as a platform from which its suppliers could capture export markets. Hence the DGT entered into a whole series of bilateral negotiations with traditional and new suppliers with the aim of purchasing low-cost terminals. By and large the suppliers themselves assumed a relatively passive role, rather like simple sub-contractors to a powerful domestic customer. Some found it difficult, if not impossible, to manufacture terminals as cheaply as the DGT had specified.[26] Although the French videotext terminal—'Minitel'—was far more successful than its British counterpart, this success was achieved at home rather than abroad. Overall the DGT's industrial policy in telematics fell well short of its goals, partly because export markets were less susceptible to a state-led diffusion strategy.[27]

Ironically, by the time the Socialists arrived in power the halcyon days of domestic expansion were over and, over the next five years, France underwent a series of bewildering changes in government–industry relations. Some of the changes were induced by design, others were the product of implacable circumstance. Here we intend to focus first on the nationalizations and second on the subsequent restructuring of the telecommunications industry.

Of the fifty entities nationalized in 1981–2, twelve were industrial firms, including Thomson, CGE, Bull, and ITT's subsidiary CGCT. With the sole exception of CGE these electronics firms were all recording losses in 1981. Indeed, one of the putative reasons for nationalization was to inject capital into these firms so that they would constitute 'une force de frappe industrielle', as Mitterrand so grandly put it. The issue as to whether public control or capital injections required full-scale nationalization was hotly contested;

some Socialists (like Rocard and Delors) favoured a 51 per cent stake, but others (including Mitterrand) successfully pushed for 100 per cent state ownership.[28] In the context of a general reflation the nationalized electronics firms were expected to pioneer new strategies in keeping with the Plan Filière Électronique.[29] In reality, however, this grand plan never commanded much support in government beyond Chevènement, the highly *dirigiste* Industry Minister. Nevertheless, Chevènement continued to impose political pressure on the nationalized firms in an effort to bend them into serving wider national goals. But he lacked the political strength to be more than an irritant to the heads of the nationalized firms, and the latter circumvented his authority by appealing directly to the Élysée, where they found a receptive audience in the President's industrial advisers. After less than a year in office Chevènement was forced to resign in March 1983. Any prospect of realizing his *dirigiste* aims had vanished with the reversal of macro-economic policy in 1982. From March 1983 onwards, the profitability of the nationalized firms became the over-riding goal for Fabius, the new Industry Minister.[30]

The nationalization of Thomson, CGE, and CGCT meant that the bulk of the French telecommunications industry fell within the public sector. Initially, the government introduced the principle that in industries which had a good record (like telecoms) two competing national champions would be maintained. But, in less successful industries (like computers and consumer electronics), a single natio-nal champion was deemed more appropriate because state aid could be concentrated in such firms. In telecoms the government wished to maintain Thomson and CGE's subsidiary, CIT-Alcatel, a decision which left CGCT out in the cold. Indeed, it seems that the main reason for nationalizing CGCT was ideological disgust at ITT's role in Chile. In fact, Dondoux, the pro-Socialist head of the DGT, had actually campaigned against the nationalization of CGCT because the costs outweighed the benefits. The price of acquiring CGCT proved to be high given the fact that it had been recording heavy losses since 1976.

The relationship between the government and the nationalized firms was meant to be resolved via the *contrat de plan* ('planning contract'), supposedly a mutually binding pact. It has been claimed that these are an excellent means of resolving the potential conflict between corporate autonomy and the wider claims of industrial

TABLE 6.1 *Companies' net profits (m. fr.)*

	1981	1982	1983	1984
GCE	586	638	662	797
Thomson	- 167	- 2207	- 1251	- 35
CGCT	- 29	- 345	- 555	- 997

Source: Industry Ministry.

policy.[31] But the public firms had very different conceptions of the value of these contracts. One official at the Commissariat Général au Plan claimed that the use of the term 'contract' was positively fraudulent! Thomson, he argued, had little or no group strategy when it signed its *contrat de plan*. In contrast, CGE adopted a much more positive approach here, because it felt that it could exploit the *contrat de plan* for its own ends. For CGE the contract was perceived as a '*garde-fous*', an umbrella, to shield it from political criticism, and as a means of limiting any interventions that had not been agreed in the contract. Overall, however, the degree of control which the Industry Ministry was able to exert over the firms was ultimately limited by the fact that it was almost wholly dependent on information from the firms, with little internal expertise to challenge the reliability of this information. In practice the relationship turned out to be very different from what was originally intended by the more radical elements in the government. One senior Socialist official, an adviser to both the Industry Minister and the DGT, argued:

Before 1981 firms like Thomson and CGE lacked cash and they had no means of imposing their will on the government. The nationalizations had one, and only one, major effect: the firms received the cash they so desperately wanted. But the government had no real means of imposing its will on the firms, especially after 1983 when its top priority was to make these firms profitable. This inadvertently gave the firms new power: thereafter they said to government 'unless you give us money our results will be poor and the Right will discredit nationalization'. Paradoxically, these firms became more powerful under the Socialists once the goal of profit came to dominate all others.[32]

There was no better illustration of this new found power than the manœuvres of 1983, which culminated in Alcatel acquiring Thomson's civil telecom business. CGE had never reconciled itself to Thomson's politically inspired entry into telecoms in 1976. Under

its former chairman, Roux, CGE had earned a formidable reputation for penetrating public sector markets. After 1976 it had been
Roux's ambition to eliminate competition from the telecom sector,
and this inevitably meant displacing Thomson. For its part Thomson, in a desperate financial situation in 1982–3, realized that it
could no longer remain a major actor in consumer electronics, semiconductors, defence, telecoms, and medical equipment. Initially it
chose to withdraw from the latter business, by selling out to a US
firm, a decision vetoed by an alliance between Chevènement and
the Minister of Health, at that time a Communist. In view of CGE's
ambitions it finally decided to dispose of its telecom business.

At the time when the first *contrats de plan* were signed, in February 1983, the DGT had strongly opposed any merger as a solution
to Thomson's financial crisis, and the contracts made no mention
of such a possibility. Fully aware of the opposition the heads of
CGE and Thomson—Pebereau and Gomez, both appointed by the
Socialists—resorted to private negotiations. Taking advantage of
the new political climate, with its stress on profit and corporate
autonomy, the two chiefs presented the Ministry of Industry with
their proposals in September 1983. The main proposal was an asset
swap, whereby Alcatel would take over Thomson's telecom business, while the latter would acquire CGE's interests in consumer
electronics, components, and military equipment.[33] The DGT and
the Ministry of Finance were the main opponents of the merger,
because it reduced the former's bargaining power. However, Pebereau and Gomez succeeded in outflanking this opposition. They took
their proposal direct to Fabius—who had recently been given Cabinet responsibility for the PTT Ministry—having already elicited the
support of the President's industrial adviser, Boublil, a close associate of Pebereau. The Industry Minister consented to the merger
almost immediately, as did the President, even though no audit
had been conducted as to the likely effects. The merger was rationalized in terms of allowing Alcatel to gain economies of scale, reducing duplication and stemming Thomson's financial losses. In fact
the deal involved a complex financial arrangement, in which the
government provided additional capital to 'buy' shares in an enterprise it already owned, so that neither firm would have to carry
Thomson's telecom losses.[34]

Whatever else it achieved the merger destroyed the DGT's cherished goal of having two competing suppliers for bargaining

purposes. During the modernization programme (1975-80) the DGT had been quite successful in obtaining progressively lower prices from its suppliers. After 1983, however, this became more difficult with one politically strong supplier. Although Fabius presented the merger as a grand step towards making France the 'third electronic nation in the world', the reality was more prosaic. Far from being an exercise in *dirigiste* industrial policy, it was, rather, an example of 'industrialists' policy'. The government's earlier preference for two telecom suppliers was discreetly forgotten, so in this sense the merger was a defeat masquerading as a victory.

Faced with a monopoly supplier for a large part of its equipment needs the DGT was anxious to find a second supplier. Initially it hoped to reach an agreement with the British, but BT rejected the DGT's overtures.[35] After this the DGT seems to have encouraged CGE to look for potential partners. This is precisely what CGE was doing anyway. With designs on the US market Pebereau was intent on reaching an accord with AT&T and, after protracted negotiations, the two signed a memorandum of understanding in June 1985. Under the terms of the understanding AT&T (in alliance with Philips) would acquire CGCT's 16 per cent share of the French public switching market. In return AT&T would provide technical assistance for Alcatel's efforts in the US, while Philips would set up a joint venture with CGE in microwave transmission equipment, under CGE's control. The most fascinating aspect of this proposed deal was that CGE acted as though it had the power to dispose of CGCT's share of the French market. One DGT executive ascribed this incredible situation to the 'special political problem of Pebereau', who had:

projected himself to AT&T in a way that implied that he was the boss of the French market. This was both incredible and paradoxical. It was paradoxical because his power had actually increased under the Socialist government. Throughout this period he made life very difficult for the DGT and there was little we could do to prevent him acting in this way.[36]

The DGT, the Industry Ministry, and the Finance Ministry had little idea of what CGE was really up to in the negotiations with AT&T. Nor was the government aware that Pebereau was simultaneously involved in private negotiations with ITT. So when CGE announced, in July 1986, that it was merging its telecom activities with those of ITT to create the largest telecom entity in Europe, the deal apparently came as a surprise to both the DGT and the Industry and Finance Ministries.[37]

Although the Chirac government eventually endorsed the CGE–ITT merger, it was unable to decide what to do about CGCT. Playing for time, it invited Siemens and Ericsson to submit alternative bids to AT&T. Coming when it did, the ITT deal had introduced a new complication into the politics of the CGCT affair, since ITT's most illustrious subsidiary, the German-based SEL, was a major supplier to the Bundespost. Indeed, the German PTT intimated that if SEL was to prosper in the FRG, then Siemens should be admitted into France. This in turn prompted the US government to exert more political pressure, to the extent that the FCC threatened to prohibit the Bell Operating Companies from purchasing Siemens equipment in the US.[38] An affair which had lasted for nearly *two years* was finally settled in April 1987, when it was announced that Ericsson and Matra in a new alliance would take over CGCT to form Matra-Ericsson Telecommunications (MET)—a political compromise designed to limit any retaliatory action had either AT&T or Siemens won.[39] The new MET grouping provides the DGT with a potentially strong bargaining counter *vis-à-vis* CGE, exactly what it had been seeking since 1983. Liberalization will further enhance the DGT's power in this respect. Indeed, the DGT's purchasing policy is already beginning to change; it is now placing more emphasis on cost and quality factors and it is expanding the range of its suppliers. As a result of these changes the traditional suppliers will find the domestic market less hospitable than in the past. Above all, this new conjuncture will make it more difficult for Alcatel to practise the kind of closure strategy it has successfully pursued in the French public sector market.

The Chirac government had all along announced its intention to privatize CGE along with the rest of the 'competitive' private sector. The painful realization that state ownership did not mean state control meant that privatization stirred up little controversy except over the share prices (which ended up being much closer to market values than in Britain), and the nature of the controlling interests. The Chirac government was accused of placing strategic holdings in the hands of its political allies. In fact CGE was privatized in May 1987 with no controlling bloc. Instead it built up an alliance of cross-share holdings with the privatized Société Générale bank, a position that has been (so far unsuccessfully) challenged by manœuvres led by Pebereau backed by the new Socialist government in 1988.

CGE hopes that its new multinational profile and 'manager-controlled' status will make it less exposed to the competitive winds at home. But, with 60 per cent of its turnover coming from telecommunications, and with competitive pressures increasing in the world-wide telecom arena, a multinational profile guarantees nothing, as ITT ultimately discovered. On the national scale France currently enjoys a trade surplus in telecoms—unlike the UK—but this will be more difficult to sustain in the future *if* the liberal pretensions of the government are given practical effect.

The *Grand Projet* in Digital Switching: A Qualified Success

One of the proudest claims of the French telecom establishment is that France was the first country in the world to have a digital exchange in its network. Here we examine the reasons for this success, showing how France was able to avoid some of the problems which Britain faced in going digital. On the other hand the French equipment industry was not able to sustain its early commercial lead in digital switching, hence our emphasis on the *qualified* success of this *grand projet*.

The digital challenge was eminently suited to a *grand projet* approach because the state was the main market, the crucial ingredient. In itself, however, this was no guarantee of success as the British experience testifies. As we have seen, the technical expertise of the telecom establishment developed so much later in France than in Britain and this is enormously significant when comparing the different trajectories of the two countries. In fact the under-developed state of the French network bequeathed certain advantages, since France was able to benefit from being a 'late-starter'. At least three advantages can be identified here: (1) the DGT may have had to rely on foreign technology but the ITT and Ericsson Crossbar systems were tried and tested; (2) the traditionally weak position of the French equipment industry induced a determined effort to forge a new government–industry alliance for the digital era; and (3) the early experiment in digital switching was far more modest than was the case in Britain so the latter provided the French with some valuable lessons in how *not* to proceed.[40]

One of the CNET's most cherished ambitions was to develop

indigenous technology in co-operation with genuinely French firms. Having first built up its expertise in transmission technology the CNET turned its attention to switching systems in 1957.[41] The body primarily responsible for the digital switching initiative was the CNET laboratory at Lannion, Brittany. As a result of a fact-finding mission to the UK in the early 1960s, French engineers apprised themselves of two of the main problems behind the High-gate Wood fiasco, in which the first British prototype digital exchange failed. First, they became conscious of the hazards of proceeding too quickly with digital switching until semiconductor technology was more advanced. Second, they realized the problems which could occur when one had too many actors, all scattered over different locations, engaged in the development process. To alleviate the first problem the CNET decided to concentrate its efforts on a small digital exchange; and it hoped to overcome the second problem by persuading CGE to establish a subsidiary in close proximity to its Lannion R. & D. laboratory.

The basic R. & D. work for what later became known as the E10 digital exchange was carried out by the CNET, in association with SLE-Citerel, a joint subsidiary of Ericsson and Alcatel.[42] The project was eventually transferred to Alcatel for further commercial development, the bulk of which was funded by the DGT. The task of technology transfer was greatly facilitated by 'donor' and 'recipient' being in such close physical proximity and, equally important, by the fact that the CNET engineers were themselves transferred to Alcatel. Thus one of the most important ingredients for successful technology transfer was preserved, namely, continuity.

The fact that an E10 was installed as early as 1970 gave the French an enormous cachet, especially in export markets. However, as a small subscriber exchange, designed for low density rural networks, the E10 was not able to service the switching needs of large urban centres. A larger version (the E12) was later developed, but because of problems with the mainframe computer, designed by CII-Honeywell-Bull, controlled at the time by Thomson,[43] this larger version was not very successful, indeed it was abandoned in the early 1980s.

A fundamental consideration in the DGT's procurement policy was to have two competing switching systems, thus creating a degree of *technological* competition on the supply side which rarely existed in Britain. During the Crossbar era it had used Ericsson's CP 400 and ITT's Pentaconta switching systems. At the dawn of the modernization programme, in 1975, the DGT was intent on preserving this element of technical rivalry when it invited tenders for the switching systems that would be used in addition to the E10. Ostensibly just a technical selection process, the DGT used this opportunity to 'de-colonize' the switching industry. Although it eventually selected Ericsson's AXE and ITT's Metaconta systems, thereby assuring each firm of potentially large royalty payments, it made its decision contingent on them selling their major French subsidiaries to Thomson. Reluctantly, the two firms agreed, with the result that Thomson emerged as France's leading switching supplier, its share increasing from zero to 40 per cent virtually overnight.[44] Thomson had been trying to break into telecoms for some time and its ambitions neatly coincided with the DGT's desire to have two (French) suppliers. What also facilitated Thomson's entry was its strong political association with the Giscard camp, a sharp contrast with CGE, whose chairman had been a vigorous supporter of Giscard's presidential opponent Chaban-Delmas in 1974.[45]

The original DGT plan was to have Alcatel supplying digital exchanges, with Thomson supplying semi-electronic (analogue) exchanges under licence. The rationale was that French digital technology was not sufficiently developed to form the basis of a huge modernization programme. Equally important, the DGT did not wish to rely on Alcatel alone because this would have reduced its bargaining power. Indeed, at that time the DGT was decidedly unhappy with the quality of the E10.[46] However, within two years this original plan had been overturned by the DGT's decision to accelerate its digital ordering programme from 1978. Initially sceptical about its own E10 the DGT became much more optimistic about the future of electronic switching, and Alcatel were spurred into enthusiasm on the E10 by Thomson's discovery in 1976[47] that it had acquired plans for a digital exchange along with its acquisitions from ITT. The DGT decided to accelerate its digital ordering on the basis of competition between Alcatel and Thomson, who launched a crash development programme with the aim of completing their new 'MT20' exchange by 1980, at the same time as having to supply the AXE and Metaconta systems!

Compared to the slow and fractious System X set-up, however, the French development effort had a number of advantages besides those already mentioned. First, the locus of responsibility for developing the E10 and the MT20 lay entirely within a single firm, so the French never had the technical and commercial problems associated with inter-firm collaboration (apart from Alcatel's dependence on CII). Second, the customer–supplier relationship was better defined in France, since the DGT had more of an arm's length relationship with its suppliers, unlike the Post Office. Not being directly involved in development the DGT felt it could exert more pressure on its suppliers. Moreover, with two suppliers producing different digital systems it was able to play one off against the other to exact better terms and, during the late 1970s especially, the degree of competition appears to have increased considerably.[48] Third, the DGT allowed its suppliers far more autonomy in design and development, so that Alcatel and Thomson never laboured under 'battleship' specifications to nearly the same extent as their British counterparts. Finally, the French launched a large professional training programme to equip its engineers with the requisite electronics skills, another important contrast with Britain.[49]

While the British tended to strive after technological sophistication, with the idiosyncratic needs of the Post Office in the forefront, the French placed infinitely more emphasis on commercializing their digital systems in overseas markets. The fact that France had two digital systems to support made it all the more important to have a concerted export drive. Whereas the Post Office was unsure about its export promotion role until it was well into the System X programme, the DGT saw export promotion as one of its most critical tasks from the start. So much so that it began establishing a network of overseas marketing offices, especially in developing countries, to support the efforts of its two suppliers. To increase the incentive to export the DGT paid its suppliers bonus payments on each export order. Moreover, the French were better equipped to succeed in developing country markets than the British, for two reasons. In the first place Alcatel and Thomson were far more willing to accept a loss-lead pricing strategy so as to make the initial breakthrough into these markets. Secondly, since these markets invariably involved some political bargaining, the French government was more than willing to facilitate export sales by assembling a package of aid, soft loans, and even military equipment. In fact French export success owed as much if not more to the mercantilist *élan* of the French government as it did to technical merit. Indeed, in the case of the large Egyptian contract which Thomson won in alliance with

Siemens in 1979, Thomson's digital exchange malfunctioned, so that it was forced to install ITT's older Metaconta system!

Below the surface, however, the prospects for Thomson and Alcatel were far from encouraging. Thomson had originally hoped to have its new digital system fully operational by 1980, a goal it failed to meet largely because it had run into severe technical problems on the software front. The heavy R. & D. cost of its crash digital programme turned out to be one of the main reasons for Thomson's desperate financial plight in the early 1980s, thus prompting the merger with Alcatel. The *technical* logic for merging the telecom activities of the two national champions was compelling enough, at least on paper. However, Thomson and CGE had a long history of bitter corporate rivalry, and this added to the technical problems of rationalization. What also compounded matters was that decision-making power had shifted from the operational level at CIT-Alcatel to the parent holding company, CGE, since Pebereau had assumed control of the latter in 1982. This may have been responsible for the charge that product rationalization owed more to corporate chauvinism than to technical considerations. For example, CGE decided to retain Thomson's MT20 and Alcatel's E10 for large and small capacity systems respectively, even though the DGT felt that Thomson's smaller exchange (the MT35) was technically superior to the E10.

All in all the merger was not well managed and, in the words of one CNET official, the amalgamation was 'less than the sum of its parts'.[50] This was amply illustrated on the export front, where foreign orders fell to such an extent that joint sales in the following two years were no higher than what Alcatel had itself achieved in 1983. In part this was due to uncertainty on the part of foreign customers as to what the future product lines would be, a problem exacerbated by rumours that Pebereau eventually intended to discontinue the entire Thomson product line in the future. On the domestic front the most palpable effect of the merger was the loss of some 7,000 jobs, 5,000 from Thomson, which provoked large-scale industrial unrest.[51]

Apart from the difficulty of digesting Thomson's telecom activities, CGE had other problems with which to contend. Pebereau's main goal on assuming power was to break into the huge US market, then in a state of flux as a result of deregulation and the impending divestiture of AT&T. In 1984 Pebereau suddenly decided that

Alcatel might do better in the US if it offered a new version of the E10, the E10-S. Adapting a European public switching system to US standards can cost anything between $200 million and $300 million. To offset these costs CGE appealed to the PTT Ministry for financial support but, on the advice of the DGT, the PTT Ministry refused. The DGT was opposed to this new product strategy because it felt that CGE was subordinating the needs of the domestic network to the perceived needs of the US market, hence it favoured staying with the E10 and MT20 systems.[52]

The failure to make much headway in the US confirmed Pebereau in his belief that Alcatel was still vulnerable, both financially and technically. In fact the basic design of the E10 now began to look rudimentary compared to the more advanced systems of AT&T, Northern Telecom, Siemens, and Ericsson. In international circles the E10 was perceived to be short on memory capacity and processing power. This meant that it was more difficult for the E10 to accommodate advanced features, like Centrex, which were essential in the more sophisticated US market. These financial and technical limitations encouraged CGE to look to collaboration or merger. As we have seen, CGE initially hoped that AT&T would provide 'inside' help for the E10 in the US, as part of a quid pro quo for AT&T's entry into France. But when this proposed deal became embroiled in a time-consuming political controversy, CGE consoled itself with a more radical solution in the shape of a merger with ITT. The Chirac government had no grounds for opposition, but were so annoyed at Pebereau's pre-privatization manœuvres that in the run-up to the 1987 sell-off Pebereau was replaced by his deputy, P. Suard, who, however, carried on with identical policies.

For CGE the attractions of the link-up with ITT have been three-fold: (1) it provided immediate access to hitherto closed markets in Western Europe, which accounted for 75 per cent of ITT's activities; (2) in the field of public switching it meant that Alcatel's turn-over was comparable to that of AT&T; and (3) it gave Alcatel access to ITT's advanced System 12 digital exchange. However, this merger raises as many questions as it answers. First there is the problem of having three different switching systems: the E10, MT20, and System 12. If all are retained then the scope for econo-mies of scale will be much less than Alcatel's size would suggest. A second question is whether, and at what cost, Alcatel can rectify the technical problems with the System 12 design: its fully distributed processing design apparently makes it 'overload' in large switching configurations.[53] As a result of these technical problems ITT had fallen behind in delivering System 12 to a number of PTTs well before the merger. Naturally enough, CGE maintains that it can resolve all these technical problems and it is devoting an enormous amount of time and effort into this project. Indeed, what it seems to fear most is that it will be unable to finance the necessary upgrading of its older systems![54] If so, this would be a reversal for the DGT which originally saw System 12 as an export-only system.[55] Considerable question marks hang over the fate of the privatized CGE, majority shareholder in Alcatel NV, which is registered in Holland and headquartered in Brussels. Ostensibly a European not a French multinational, and diversifying into North America (buying Ericsson's US cabling interests), Alcatel NV and its parent CGE remain heavily dependent on public policy.

Ironically, France has come full circle. Having 'de-colonized' the industry by banishing Ericsson and ITT, the former has been reintroduced by the government, while the latter has been acquired in the hope that it can give CGE a technological lead in the international switching arena. In the light of the CNET's long-standing goal of developing indigenous technology this can hardly be counted a resounding success.

Overall, the French *grand projet* in switching is more chequered than is often realized. An early commercial lead in digital technology, underpinned by the DGT's huge domestic ordering programme, enabled France to construct a modern telephone network which is among the most digitalized in the world.[56] Herein lies the main success of the *grand projet*. Thanks to a formidable mercantilist export drive, over fifty countries have selected Alcatel's E10 system, although these markets have largely been in developing countries, where state-to-state bargaining is often the decisive factor.

Yet for all this the two national champions were in a precarious position by the early 1980s, and this raises a question about the efficacy of French industrial policy. Why, for instance, was Alcatel not able to sustain its early commercial lead in digital switching? One answer, much favoured by the 'old guard' of the CNET, is that Alcatel's lead had been inadvertently retarded by the political decision to invite Thomson into telecoms, thus diluting the support which Alcatel would otherwise have received.[57] While this is partially true, the Théry camp defends its decision in two ways. First, the capacity limits of the E10, together with the problems of the larger E12, made it necessary to resort to interim technology. Second, the poor quality of the early E10 meant that a rival (digital) supplier was deemed essential to force Alcatel to improve its performance.[58] Another explanation, though not mutually exclusive, is that Alcatel's R. & D. expenditure had been too low to sustain its initial technological advantage.[59] In part this is attributable to the DGT's success in driving down prices in the 1970s and to slender profit margins in export markets, the latter exacerbated by the tendency to loss-lead for the sake of a market share. Furthermore, although Alcatel was a relatively small company by international standards, it prided itself on being able to supply a wide range of telecom equipment, hence R. & D. resources had to be spread over a number of fronts besides public switching. These internal limitations, combined with more rapid advances among foreign suppliers, help to explain why Alcatel lost its early lead.

Conclusion

The post-war development of French telecommunications illustrates both the power and the limits of the French state. Unlike the British Post Office, the DGT was both able and willing to use its formidable procurement power to achieve certain national goals, namely, the rapid modernization of the network and the creation of a domestic industry in which French firms played the dominant role. There are two main reasons why the DGT was able to act in this way, at least in the 1974–81 period: first, because the backward state of the French network was seen as a national scandal, calling for a radical political initiative, and, second, because of a close political alliance between the President (Giscard) and the Head of the DGT (Théry). As a result Théry was effectively liberated from the control of the Finance Ministry and given a free hand to reorganize the French telecom sector. No such autonomy was ever bestowed on the British Post Office.

The modernization of the network allowed the DGT to pursue an effective closure strategy which privileged certain domestic firms because it was willing to use its power as the chief customer. The DGT's later plans, for telematics and cable, can also be interpreted in terms of the pre-conditions for effective closure. For example the Plan Télématique may have been stimulated by the desire to find new markets for the French equipment industry, but it was also the case that the DGT saw this as a way of preventing IBM from dominating the telematic services market in France. However, as we have seen, telematics presented far more difficulties than network modernization in privileging selected firms and through them dictating the pace of market development.

With the arrival of the Socialists in 1981 the DGT began to lose power within the state system and *vis-à-vis* its suppliers. The best illustration of its diminished capacity to influence its suppliers was its failure to prevent CGE and Thomson merging their telecom businesses, a merger wich reduced the DGT's freedom of choice. Indeed, this episode was also a defeat for the government's chosen policy of maintaining two competing suppliers because of the particular conjuncture in which the industry found itself. The merger was presented as the best way of stemming the heavy financial losses at Thomson (see Table 6.1 above).

Although nationalization was designed to give the government more control over its major firms, this aim was subverted as soon as profitability became the dominant criterion for the nationalized sector. The result of this new emphasis was, quite simply, that the firms became more autonomous and the Socialist government found itself with ownership but not control! The planning paraphernalia, like the *contrat de plan*, should not obscure the fact that the nationalized firms pursued a closure strategy against the Socialist government with respect to information and corporate planning, and this was rendered that much easier once profitability became the major yardstick. It was in this context that CGE was able to negotiate the biggest merger in the history of European telecommunications, namely, the merger between Alcatel and ITT, a deal about which the French government had very little knowledge.

The power of CGE, the leading French telecom firm, has, however, been tempered by the liberalization of the French market on the one hand, and by the emergence of a potentially strong competitor, MET, on the other. The pace of liberalization has lagged behind that in the UK and this illustrates the critically important role of national governments. We saw how the Chirac government, although ostensibly committed to the same kind of liberalization programme as the Thatcher government, was in practice much more cautious, anxious as it was not to offend organized labour in the telecommunications industry. However, the modest liberalization set in train by the Chirac government was checked by its Socialist successor. As we shall see in Chapter 8, this Socialist government has been the major force pushing for a more modest degree of liberalization than is desired by the European Commission at the Community level. This suggests that the French government is intent on pursuing a form of closure strategy at the supra-national level.

Notes

1. Organization for Economic Co-operation and Development, *Review of Innovation Policies* (Paris: OECD, 1986).
2. The Compagnie Générale d'Electricite has since the 1920s had a controlling interest in the telecommunications equipment producer, Alcatel, known in the past variously as, SIT, CIT, CIT-Alcatel. For our purposes the labels are interchangeable.
3. C. Bertho, *Télégraphes et Téléphones de Valmy au microprocesseur* (Paris: Livre de Poche, 1981).
4. A former head of the DGT described the CNT as one of the single most important steps towards modernization; it was an early example of the 'privatization of the financing of telecoms, rather than the privatization of the telecom carrier'. This helped the DGT to avoid the financial shackles which limited the British Post Office's room for manœuvre.
5. The appointment of Théry represented a radical break in the traditional power network within the DGT. Hitherto it had been an accepted practice that the head of the CNET succeeded to the post of Director-General of the DGT. Théry was meant to symbolize a new commercial ethos at the DGT.
6. E. Cohen and M. Bauer, *Les Grandes Manœuvres industrielles* (Paris: Belfond, 1985).
7. The Nora–Minc report, *L'Informatisation de la société*, appeared in 1978, having been commissioned by Giscard in 1976. This report had alerted France to the threat to sovereignty which was embodied in telematics (i.e. the convergence of telecommunications and computing) and it recommended a nationally co-ordinated response with the DGT playing a leading role. It stressed, however, that the DGT would have to become more like IBM, the telematic giant. This in turn meant that the DGT should be allowed more autonomy from government.
8. G. Dang Nguyen, 'Telecommunications; A Challenge to the Old Order', in M. Sharp (ed.), *Europe and the New Technologies* (London: Frances Pinter, 1985).

9. Arthur D. Little, Inc., *World Telecommunications Information Program: France* (Cambridge, Mass.: Arthur D. Little, 1985).

10. H. Ergas, *Regulation, Monopoly and Competition in the Telecommunications Infrastructure* (Paris: OECD, 1986).

11. J.-H. Lorenzi and E. Le Boucher, *Mémoires volés* (Paris: Ramsay, 1979); H. Pigéat and L. Virol, *Du téléphone au télématique* (Paris: Documentation Française/Commissariat au Plan, 1980).

12. Interview.

13. Interview.

14. E. Brenac, B. Jobert, P. Mallein, G. Payen, and Y. Toussaint, *La DGT et le Plan Câble* (CEPS/CERAT, University of Grenoble II, 1986).

15. The DGT's gradual disenchantment with the Plan Câble produced a bizarre bout of in-fighting between the DGT and the PTT Minister, who saw the original Plan Câble as an ideal platform for the equipment suppliers to launch themselves into new cable-related product markets. There were other conflicts too, as some municipalities challenged the initial emphasis on high-cost optical fibre technology, instead of the cheaper co-axial technology. J.-F. Lacan, 'Le Ministère des PTT contre la DGT', *Le Monde*, 13 Feb. 1986; J.-F. Lacan, 'La Fin du Plan Câble', *Le Monde*, 13 Jan. 1987.

16. J. Dondoux, 'L'Impact de la déréglementation internationale: Le Point de vue français', *Financial Times* World Telecommunications Conference, London, 4 Dec. 1985.

17. ibid.

18. According to INTUG, the international user group, France lags the UK by at least 5 years in the number of professional telecom managers in its business user population—personal communication. Significantly though, in the field of data communications, where corporate user pressure is often strong, the DGT prudently set up a user group—Utipac—for its Transpac data network and these users were persuaded to take a shareholding in the DGT's private Transpac subsidiary.

19. Association des Ingénieurs des Télécommunications, unpublished internal policy memorandum, 1985.

20. J. Villeneuve, 'PTT: Les Télécommunications veulent changer d'adresse', *Libération*, 27 Nov. 1986.

21. Despite the PTT Ministry's attempts to force the pace of liberalization, Chirac apparently gave an assurance to Force Ouvrière that there would be no major changes in the DGT until after the 1988 elections.

22. *Le Monde*, 15 Oct. 1988.

23. Bertho, *Télégraphes et téléphones*.

24. J.-F. Ruges, *Le Téléphone pour tous* (Paris: Seuil, 1970).

25. To ensure that the transfer of power from the CNET to the DAII

was more than a paper exercise, Théry appointed an outsider as the head of the DAII. Significantly, he was not a member of the AIT. Senior managers within the DGT saw this as an important innovation because it broke the traditional social network within the DGT, where engineers had great loyalty to both the AIT and the CNET. This internal reorganization provoked intense institutional rivalry between the CNET establishment and the new DGT leadership.

26. Dang Nguyen, 'Telecommunications'.
27. At the beginning of 1987 there were 2.3 million minitel terminals linked to the French videotext network, far more than in either the UK or the FRG. Part of this success is attributable to the DGT's policy of giving these terminals away free of charge, on the grounds that the extra traffic generated would offset the price of the terminal.
28. T. Pfister, *La Vie quotidienne à Matignon au temps de l'union de la Gauche* (Paris: Hachette, 1985).
29. A. Farnoux, *Rapport de la mission de la Filière Électronique* (Paris: Ministry of Research and Technology, 1982).
30. Chevènement's period as Industry Minister (June 1982–Mar. 1983) was highly problematic, since his *dirigiste* posture was totally contradicted by the Finance Ministry's austerity regime, which began in June 1982. Under his successor, Fabius, the policies of the Industry Ministry were at least consistent with those of the Finance Ministry. Continuity was rendered all the more difficult by the fact that France had five different Industry Ministers in six years!
31. C. Stoffaes, 'The Nationalisations 1981–4: An Initial Assessment', in H. Machin and V. Wright, (eds.), *Economic Policy and Policy-Making under the Mitterrand Presidency 1981–1984* (London: Frances Pinter, 1985).
32. Interview.
33. P. Betts, 'The struggle to Keep up with the Leaders', *Financial Times*, 4 Oct. 1983.
34. J.-M. Quatrepoint, *Histoire secrète des dossiers noirs de la Gauche* (Paris: Alain Moreau, 1987).
35. As a step towards the reciprocal opening of public markets in the EEC, the DGT proposed that France and the UK should each supply part of the other's market. After negotiations in 1983 and 1984 the DGT felt humiliated when BT refused to consider CGE as a short-list candidate for the System Y tender. BT spurned the French offer for two reasons: (1) it felt that Alcatel's switching system, the E10, was technically obsolete; and (2) George Jefferson, the BT chairman, refused to have any dealings with Pebereau of CGE, because of bad experiences between the two when Jefferson was with British Aerospace.

36. Interview.
37. Significantly, Pebereau was dismissed soon after the merger with ITT had been announced. His penchant for empire-building and political intrigue had won him few allies and the dismissal was a signal that CGE's days as a wayward empire were over. For an insider account of the power which accrued to the heads of the nationalized firms see P. Gabriel, *L'État patron c'est moi* (Paris: Flammanion, 1985).
38. T. Dodsworth, 'US Promotes AT&T Move into France', *Financial Times*, 3 Nov. 1986.
39. The CGCT affair provoked deep divisions within the government, one reason why it took so long to resolve. Although loyalties tended to change over time, especially within the DGT, a strong lobby eventually emerged in favour of AT&T, composed of the DGT, the PTT Ministry, and the Industry Ministry. However, Chirac inclined towards a European solution. Late in the day the suitors had to rearrange their bids to take account of new privatization rules, which placed a 20% ceiling on foreign stakes in newly privatized French concerns. Since CGCT was about to be privatized each suitor had to ally itself with a French consortium. Ericsson's position improved considerably towards the end because it proposed an additional joint effort (MET) with Matra to exploit the European market for digital mobile telephones. Even so, political diplomacy rather than technical merit was the decisive factor in the end.
40. L.-J. Libois, *Le Genèse et croissance des télécommunications* (Paris: Masson/CNET, 1983).
41. This was not the first time that the CNET had tried to develop an indigenous switching system. Back in the late 1940s it developed its own electro-mechanical exchange which it hoped would launch CGE into the home market. Unfortunately, this so-called L43 exchange burst into flames when it was installed, thus persuading CGE to stick to producing under licence.
42. Libois, *Le Genèse*.
43. A. Le Diberder, *La Production de réseau de télécommunications* (Paris: Economica, 1983).
44. Bertho, *Télégraphes et téléphones*.
45. Lorenzi and Le Boucher, *Mémoires volés*; Cohen and Bauer, *Les Grandes Manœuvres industrielles*.
46. Interview.
47. Bertho, *Télégraphes et téléphones*.
48. M. Texier, *La Stratégie des commandes publiques dans le secteur des télécommunications 1966–1980* (Paris: DGT, 1981).
49. J. Corré, 'Formation professionelle en commutation électronique', *Revue française des télécommunications*, 21 (1976), pp. 28–9.

50. Interview.
51. Quatrepoint, *Histoire secrète*.
52. Interview. We emphasize the *perceived* needs of the US because it soon became clear that US customers were not at all interested in the E10-S because of its technical and capacity limitations. This reinforced the DGT's suspicions about CGE's weak marketing of the product, which was done from Paris rather than at first hand in the US itself.
53. J. Rippeteau, 'The ITT–CGE Deal: A Hole in the System's Heart', *Financial Times*, 28 July 1986.
54. We are grateful to Elie Cohen for drawing our attention to this dilemma.
55. Interview.
56. J. Dondoux, 'France: Fast Network Digitization', *Telephony*, 24 Feb. 1986.
57. Cohen and Bauer, *Les Grandes Manœuvres industrielles*.
58. Interview.
59. Interview.

7

Germany: Defending the Monopoly

Introduction

The history of government–industry relations in the FRG is predominantly the history of the relationship between the Bundespost, the publicly owned network and service monopolist, and Siemens, which, by the 1920s, had assumed the dominant position among the Bundespost's suppliers. For a period of several decades, the Bundespost's monopoly formed a windbreak which protected Siemens and a small group of other German or German-based equipment manufacturers from the stiff breezes of competition. The first major disturbance in this cosy relationship occurred in the late 1970s, when a Siemens-led consortium failed to deliver a Bundespost order for a computer-controlled long-distance telephone exchange.

This chapter begins with an analysis of the German telecommunications regime and the principal actors in it. The following sections explore the general character of government–industry relations, and the problems created in the procurement of the new generation of exchanges. It shows that, even in a political conjuncture which was most unfavourable for Siemens, the nature of this regime and the firm's dominant position in the German industry so constrained the decision-making process that it was impossible, at least in the short term, for the Bundespost to bypass Siemens. The final section demonstrates how institutional and political factors—particularly constitutional provisions, the fragmentation of telecommunications policy-making competences among several ministries, the policy of co-determination powers of state governments, and the high level of mobilization and political influence of the Post Office Workers' Union—have strongly moderated the process of telecommunications deregulation in the FRG, which has worked to the advantage of the Bundespost's 'court suppliers' (*Hoflieferanten*). This breathing space was used in particular by Siemens to launch a bold strategy of investment, joint ventures, and take-overs to try to

cement its position as one of the world's leading telecom multinationals. This strategy involved its acquiescing in a partial opening of
the German market (which it could not prevent anyway), but not
at the expense of a complete abandonment of its close ties with
the Bundespost, whose network monopoly it hoped would continue
to guarantee its status as the flagship of the German telecommunications industry.

The Telecom Regime

The Post Ministry and the Bundespost

As recently as 1989, the Federal Republic of Germany exhibited
all the main trade marks of a traditional European telecommunications system. The Bundespost is a state-owned telecommunications
administration (as opposed to independent public corporation).
This administration still united the (profit-making) telecommunications and (loss-making) postal services. It possessed a legally backed
monopoly of the telecommunications network, of the provision of
telecommunications services, and of the supply of simple telephone
sets, though not of other terminal equipment. In its self-conception
(as in law), it was an organization which provided a public service
in which distributional policy objectives had priority over the maximization of efficiency and profit, although it was highly profitable.
According to the law under which it was constituted it was obliged
to act in conformity with the federal government's economic, financial, and transport policies. The state ownership of the Bundespost
was protected by the Basic Law, which can be changed only with
a two-thirds majority in the Bundestag.

The Bundespost was headed by the federal Minister of Post and
Telecommunications, a member of the federal cabinet, and his
rather small ministry, which has a staff of some 1,300, of whom
no more than 400 worked in the telecommunications divisions.
On telecommunications issues the ministry's principal intra-state
source of policy advice is the FTZ, which employs 2,700 staff.
The FTZ implemented telecommunications policy, together with
the eighteen regional post offices, or indeed made it according to
guidelines laid down by the ministry. A separate organization, the
ZZF, which licensed telecommunication equipment, had been hived
off from the FTZ under political pressure in 1982, but was still

formally subordinate to the Post Ministry. The Bundespost itself possessed only very modest R. & D. facilities at the FTZ, and did not manufacture equipment. In the early 1980s it satisfied almost its entire demand for equipment from the domestic market, although not necessarily from German-owned firms.

The Bundespost was overseen by an administrative council (*Verwaltungsrat*). In practice the council concerned itself mainly with the Bundespost's budget and charges. Of the council's twenty-four members, five were nominated by business organizations, seven by the Bundespost staff and trade unions, five by the state (*Land*) governments, and five by the parties in the Bundestag. The minister nominated two further members, one an expert in telecommunications, who invariably came from Siemens, the other an expert in financial affairs, always from one of the banks. The council rarely rejected the Post Minister's proposals. If it did, the minister could request the Cabinet to overthrow the council's decision. However, the position of a minister who had to do this regularly would probably soon have become untenable. The minister had therefore to take some account of the likely majority opinion in the council, even if it is fair to say that its influence generally was 'weak'.

The Bundespost is unlikely to be privatized, since no government would find the two-thirds majority needed in the Bundestag to change the Basic Law provision that the Bundespost must be state-owned. Moreover, despite numerous inquiries and proposals over the past three decades, and major changes in the status of PTTs in other countries, the Bundespost has not been radically reorganized. The stability of the West German telecommunications regime is not, however, to be equated with a lack of changes in telecommunications *policy*. These changes have been made with the more or less explicit objective of accommodating the Bundespost's critics so that the regime itself can be kept intact. However, they have not prevented the Bundespost, its structure, and its monopoly powers—which are not constitutionally protected, but can be amended by ordinary laws or ministerial decree—from becoming increasingly contested during the 1980s.

The telecommunications policies of the Post Ministry are constrained by legal provisions which concede the federal Interior, Finance, and Economics Ministries important powers of policy co-determination. The Interior Ministry, as the ministry responsible for the regulation of employment conditions in the public service, would have to give its consent if the Bundespost wanted to employ any staff outside the normal salary scales. It has never done so—despite Post Ministry pleas motivated by the desire to ease engineering recruitment problems. The Finance Ministry must approve the Bundespost's budget and borrowing on the capital market. In practice, its primary concern is to restrain the Bundespost's personnel expenditure. It has no official views on the Bundespost's investment or technology policies. The Finance Ministry benefits from existing telecommunications law in so far as 10 per cent of the Bundespost's annual revenue is paid into the federal budget in lieu of VAT, a sum which in 1985 totalled 4.6 billion DM. As a privatized enterprise or an independent public corporation the Bundespost would be required instead to pay VAT, 57 per cent of which flows to *Land* and local governments. As the Finance Ministry would, in its view, 'never be compensated' for this revenue loss, it defended the status quo in the telecom deregulation debate.

The Economics Ministry—the 'guardian' of the social market economy in West Germany—must approve all telecommunications charges. In practice this provision grants the ministry a veto power over the conditions in which new telecommunications services are introduced—one which it has frequently used to curb the monopolistic aspirations of the Bundespost. As recent technological changes have created opportunities for new telecommunications services the introduction of each new service has been marked by a conflict between the Post Ministry and the Economics Ministry over Bundespost participation in the terminals market. The Economics Ministry has since 1973 been in the hands of ministers from the Liberal Party (the FDP) (see below).

In contrast to the Economics Ministry, the Research and Technology Ministry has long cherished ambitions to pursue an industrial policy for telecommunications, but its competence in telecommunications is confined to promoting a limited range of research and development projects.

The Federal Cartel Office (BKA), the administrative arm of government competition policy, has the promotion of competition as part of its *raison d'être* and has indeed had an impact upon the Bundespost's equipment purchasing, for example through a decision not to allow the prolongation of a long-standing co-axial copper cable production cartel. Moreover it has a brief to prevent the Bundespost from abusing its monopoly *buying* power, although ironically its intervention in respect of public switching equipment (see below) had the effect of braking any radical change in the distribution of Bundespost orders in the short term. But the Bundespost as a *supplier* is exempt from competition law and in this role therefore beyond the BKA's reach.

Parliament, the parties, and organized labour

The role of the Bundestag in the formulation of telecommunications policy in the FRG is extremely limited. It cannot exert any direct influence on the Bundespost's budget and the role of its postal and telecommunications committee is confined to questioning the minister and holding (extremely rare) hearings on policy issues.

There is also wide scope for policy to be changed without changing laws. The telecom policy specialists of the governing parliamentary parties (who are themselves sometimes members of the Bundespost's administrative council) have some potential influence on telecommunications policy, in so far as the Post Minister seeks their approval of proposals he is to put before the council. However, the predominant role of the parliamentary party specialists is more often to impress the Post Ministry's priorities on the parliamentary party than vice versa.

This of course still leaves open the question as to whether the Post Minister can instrumentalize the Bundespost for the telecommunications policy objectives of his party or the governing parties. During the post-war period, the telecommunications regime portrayed above has generally been supported by a broad inter-party consensus. Neither the major political parties not the trade unions nor the equipment manufacturing industry wanted to make radical changes to the status quo. Changes in the political complexion of the federal government were not followed by radical changes in telecommunications policy. The adage was coined that 'whether black [i.e. CDU] or red [i.e. SPD] at the outset, within three months all Post Ministers are yellow' (i.e. the colour of the Bundespost). In other words, the Post Minister was always captured by the bureaucracy. The continuity of the telecom regime could just as easily be explained, however, by the lack of demand for radical change from any relevant political grouping or constituency, domestic or foreign. This situation was to change, however, in the 1980s.

Arguably the most ardent supporters of the Bundespost as a *public administration* combining the telecommunications and postal services, and a powerful constraint on the freedom of manœuvre of the Post Minister, are the Bundespost trade unions, of which only one, the DPG, has any significance. Even under a Centre-Right federal government, such as that which has been in office in the FRG since 1982, there are politicians 'right the way up to the Federal Chancellor' who prefer to avoid a conflict with the DPG.

Roughly three-quarters of the Bundespost's staff of over 500,000, including many middle and senior management, are organized in the DPG. This high level of union organization, the representation of labour in the administrative council, and the co-determination rights of the union-dominated staff councils (*Personalräte*) combine to make the DPG a force to be reckoned with by every FRG Post Minister and government. It is well informed about the policy plans of the ministry and can intervene in the decision-making process at an early stage. However, the union's influence is much greater on the Bundespost's personnel and social policies than, for example, on its investment policies. It is the most ardent defender of the existing telecommunications regime, on the grounds that changes would result in a decline in employment (and hence in its membership) and worsened working conditions for the staff.

Telecommunications users

Every firm in the FRG is a *user* of telecommunications services and therefore a customer of the Bundespost.[1] However, the interests of different groups of business users are difficult to reconcile and the articulation of such interests in German telecommunications politics is low. German telecommunications users are said in any case to be 'docile'.

The principal channels for the representation of business users' interests are the peak business organizations, the BDI and the DIHT. Both these organizations aspire to represent simultaneously the telecommunications interests of both the users and the equipment manufacturers. However, the BDI has been obliged to maintain a low profile on telecommunications issues by conflicts between two of its member trade associations, the ZVEI in which the classical telecommunications equipment manufacturers predominate, and the VDMA where the newcomers, such as IBM, have a voice. Nor has the DIHT, which complains about being consulted too little and too late by the Post Ministry, proved a powerful lobby. Although their representatative on the government telecommunications commission voted in favour of an extensive reorganization of the Bundespost and the liberalization of telecommunications, the banks have not been a motor for change in the same way that they have been in Britain (see Chapter 5), which has been argued to stem from their close ties to the big telecom manufacturers such as Siemens and Bosch.[2]

Firms also now dominate the membership of the small association of Bundespost users, the VPB, which began as a 'citizens' initiative' protesting against the inefficiency of the Bundespost's service in the early 1970s. It has no institutionalized access to policy-making, however, and acts mainly through the threat or actual undertaking of legal action.

The equipment suppliers

The central business actors in telecommunications politics are to be found within the equipment manufacturing industry. But not all actual or potential equipment manufacturing firms can be said to belong to the favoured group known in telecom circles as the 'court suppliers'. The most decisive criterion for admission to the status of 'court supplier' is the maintenance of manufacturing facilities in the FRG—this is a pre-condition of admission to the relevant bodies of the ZVEI which discuss equipment standards with the Bundespost and of obtaining Bundespost orders. Newcomers to telecommunications equipment manufacture, in particular firms such as Nixdorf and IBM, which have traditionally manufactured computers but are trying to diversify their product range as computer and telecommunications technologies increasingly merge, have typically experienced great difficulty obtaining entry to the 'court'. The combination of the Bundespost's network monopoly and trade association policy 'closed off' the bulk of the German equipment market to foreign competitors—unless the latter were prepared to invest in the FRG without being certain in advance as to whether they would obtain Bundespost orders.

The number of traditional German-owned or -based manufacturers of telecommunications is small in absolute terms, though not as small as in France or Britain. In particular they include some twenty manufacturers of telephone sets and telecommunications cable which are heavily dependent on the Bundespost for orders and mostly lack the distribution and sales networks which they would need to survive in a de-monopolized market.[3] Within the ZVEI sub-association for information and communication technology the small and medium-sized firms have organized as a faction and claim thus to have bolstered their influence *vis-à-vis* the big telecommunications manufacturers.

The telecommunications industry in the FRG, however, consists first and foremost of some seven firms or divisions or subsidiaries of conglomerate enterprises which together account for more than 80 per cent of the production capacity in the German industry.[4] These firms or parts of firms are Siemens, SEL (Standard Elektrik Lorenz), PKI (Philips Kommunikations Industrie), TN Telenorma and ANT Nachrichtentechnik, AEG-Telefunken, and Detewe. Siemens employs well over 30,000 staff in its telecommunications division and produces virtually the whole range of telecommunications equipment. SEL, which has a telecommunications staff of about 18,000, is the German subsidiary of ITT acquired by Alcatel in 1987. PKI is Philips's German telecommunications subsidiary, with a staff of some 3,800. AEG-Telefunken still has a telecommunications division staff of some 9,300, but its foothold in the sector was weakened by its sale of majority shareholdings in TN Telenorma (estimated telecommunications staff 13,500) and ANT Nachrichtentechnik (workforce of 6,200) to the electronics conglomerate Bosch. Through a large indirect shareholding Siemens exercises a strong influence over the remaining firm, Detewe.[5] Together these firms picked up around 60 per cent of the Bundespost's telecommunications equipment orders in the mid-1980s.

These firms maintain very intensive contacts with the Bundespost, with the ministry on general policy issues, and with the FTZ on technical and purchasing issues. The statement of a member of TN Telenorma's executive board that 'I am very often at the Post Ministry' and that people from the Bundespost 'often' come to TN Telenorma may safely be assumed to be true for the other major equipment manufacturing firms. Conversely, the Bundespost's relations with the 'industry' are predominantly with these firms—they constitute the majority of the 'six to ten' firms which the FTZ, guided by its perceptions of the 'technological prowess', consults about telecommunications technology and equipment specifications. They provide half of the members of the Post Minister's technical advisory council.[6] These firms predominate amongst those consulted by the Economics Ministry's section for the information and communications technology industry, and they also provide a majority of the executive board members of the ZVEI's information and communication technology sub-association. Despite the increased organization and weight of the small and medium-sized firms in the sub-association and the fact that such firms actually constitute a majority of the sub-association's members, the big firms determine the 'substantive work' the association does and the direction it takes. The share which these firms take of the Bundespost's orders and the intensity of their relations with the Bundespost justify categorizing them as core actors in German telecommunications politics. Accusations sometimes made that the Bundespost's equipment specifications reflect the technologies or products of particular firms point to a clear link between the intensity of the relationship and the share of orders.

Relations between the Bundespost and the equipment manufacturing firms are institutionalized in various ways. At annual 'talks with the industry' the Post Minister explains the Bundespost's telecommunications policies for the past year and for the next. His technical advisory council consists of board chairmen or members of equipment manufacturing firms. Its establishment was motivated by the minister's desire to draw 'not only on the technical knowledge of the Bundespost, but also that of the industry'. At its regular meetings, fundamental issues of telecommunications policy are discussed. The manufacturers are also represented in the service-related 'working groups' attached to the ministry and the FTZ. The Bundespost was probably pressed into setting up these groups by the manufacturers, in particular by those who did not already belong to the Bundespost's 'court suppliers'. The Siemens telecommunications head's membership of the Bundespost administrative council also provides the manufacturers with a—weighty—voice in the 'Parliament' of telecommunications policy. Finally, contacts are also institutionalized in the 'working groups' which link the FTZ and the ZVEI sub-association and its member firms and discuss telecommunications standards and specifications for equipment to be ordered by the Bundespost (see above).

In most cases, however, these institutions may represent no more than the façade of relations between the Bundespost and the telecommunications equipment manufacturing industry. The 'technical advisory council' has an exclusively consultative function and does not concern itself with purchasing decisions. The service-related 'working groups' composed of manufacturers and major users may have a predominantly 'alibi' function. Where they proffer advice or make demands contradicting the Bundespost's own position, they are likely to find them rejected. Even the administrative council takes none of the decisions—such as those about which firms are to get orders or which technologies are going to be adopted for the network—which would be of particular relevance to a firm such as Siemens.

The Bundespost–industry contacts which matter are predominantly of an *informal* and *bilateral* nature, bypassing the trade associations and sub-associations. Thus, in a period in which major decisions affecting the future of the telecommunications system were made, the head of the Post Ministry's telecommunications division had 'practically no contacts' with the trade association, the ZVEI. Conversely, for Siemens, for example, the trade association is not an important vehicle of political interest-representation. The association may fulfil a more important interest-representation role for its small and medium-sized firms, but they, too, maintain their own, direct lines of political communication with the Bundespost. Where the firms' own interests are at stake, their political strategies are hardly influenced by the ZVEI and there are, in any event, many issues on which the trade association, constrained by the divergent interests of its members, does not take a stance. The section responsible for monitoring the Bundespost at the federal Economics Ministry maintains more intensive relations with peak business organizations. Its role in telecommunications politics, however, is largely reactive. The ministry's section for the industry has more to do with the manufacturing firms, especially the large ones, both multilaterally through the ZVEI and bilaterally. As by far the biggest equipment exporter, Siemens also cultivates close contacts with the federal Development Aid Ministry, which subsidizes its telecommunications sales to Third World states.[7]

The involvement of the trade association(s) in the discussion and determination of telecommunications standards and equipment specifications is, however, a crucial incentive for firms to be members.[8] All the significant German-owned or German-based telecommunications equipment manufacturers do in fact belong to the ZVEI and its communication and information technology sub-association.

Membership in the relevant ZVEI product-related sub-committees and commissions enables firms to obtain information about the thinking of the Bundespost on standards and specifications issues and, since the Bundespost's formal decisions never depart from the recommendations formulated in the talks between the FTZ and the sub-committees, to influence standards and specifications in their favour.[9] The limitation of membership of these sub-committees to firms which produce equipment in Germany constitutes an indirect form of protection of German, or German-based, manufacturers. In the case of PABXs, this precipitated a fierce conflict between the ZVEI, whose stand was conditioned above all by Siemens and SEL, and the VDMA, behind which stood IBM and Ericsson (which belongs to both trade associations, but threatened to resign from the ZVEI if it were not admitted to its PABX sub-committee). The conflict culminated—after the VDMA had threatened to call in the BKA to right the discriminatory consultative practices of the Bundespost—in the formation of a joint ZVEI–VDMA committee to discuss PABX technology with the Bundespost. Such incidents tag the ZVEI as a 'typical German closed shop', although firms which manufacture in the FRG can legally enforce their right to membership of the association.

The relations *between* the 'court suppliers' are by no means relations between equals. Of Siemens, it is said in the German industry that 'you can do a lot with it, a bit without it, but nothing against it'. This statement starkly expresses the dominant position which Siemens is perceived to occupy in the German industry, although Siemens itself regards the reality as being 'more differentiated'. The representation of the Siemens telecommunications division head on the Bundespost's administrative council *symbolizes* the leading role of Siemens within the industry, but it is not its foundation. The level at which Siemens exerts influence upon the Bundespost is rather that of the FTZ. Between the Bundespost engineers and Siemens— and the other big equipment manufacturers—there has been a close exchange of views on telecommunications technologies 'for decades'.

The dominant position of Siemens within this network of relations rests on three main, and interrelated, factors. Firstly, the German market has been kept closed to imported foreign equipment, with the exception of some kinds of terminal equipment—a policy legitimated by reference to the obstacles to the export of German telecommunications equipment to other states. Second, Siemens's expertise and knowhow, in its range at least, is superior to that of any other firm in the German industry. The third factor is the entrenchment of Siemens's technological dominance or leadership through the 'single technology' (*Einheitstechnik*) policy practised over decades by the Bundespost. The fact that the Bundespost used only a single type of switching or transmission equipment in its telecommunication network, that this technology was developed by Siemens, and that other suppliers produced equipment under Siemens's licences could not but give Siemens an advantage over its 'competitors'.[10]

The Post Ministry's decisions in the early 1980s to abandon the 'single technology' concept first for switching and then for transmission equipment had potentially revolutionary implications for German telecommunications politics and for the relations of power both within the industry and between the industry and the state. These decisions can only be understood in the light of the experiences of the Bundespost as a new generation of switching equipment was developed for it in the 1970s. We analyse this saga and its repercussions in the following section.

The Politics of Switching Technology Choices in the FRG: *Plus ça change, plus c'est la même* Siemens

From the turn of the century until 1985, the switching technology used by the Bundespost (and its predecessor, the Reichspost) had always originated from Siemens. It supplied the equipment which permitted the introduction of direct dialling in the local network in Germany in 1908 and then the *Wahlsystem 22*, which began to be introduced in the 1920s. Although the Reichspost wanted to have just the one (Siemens's) type of switching equipment, it did not want to be dependent on a single supplier. It therefore insisted that Siemens grant production licences to two other firms, SEL and Detewe, in exchange for guaranteeing Siemens a minimum volume of orders.[11] The Bundespost's and its predecessor's desire to avoid dependence on a single supplier of equipment, while retaining the single technology policy, is a thread which runs through the history of German switching equipment politics. What originated in the switching industry in the 1920s was not a state-licensed monopoly, but a state-licensed oligopoly, albeit under Siemens's leadership.

For a period after the war, in which a large part of the German telecommunications infrastructure was destroyed, there was a chronic surplus of demand over supply, and the Bundespost took switching equipment from whichever firm could supply it, irrespective of the implications for market shares. This situation of excess demand was in fact to continue until the early 1970s. However, with the introduction of a new switching technology, the EMD (*Edelmetall-Motor-Drehwahler*), from the late 1950s onwards, a similar market-sharing agreement was reached, with the exception that now a fourth firm, TN Telenorma, which had threatened to mobilize the BKA to break open the supply 'cartel', was admitted to the circle of equipment suppliers.[12] The division of the Bundespost's orders was agreed by the firms in so-called 'heads of agreement' under which Siemens granted licences to the other three firms. The Bundespost was not a formal party to the agreements, but nevertheless respected them. Siemens received about 46 per cent of the orders, SEL 30 per cent, Detewe 14 per cent, and TN Telenorma 10 per cent.[13] Under the 'heads of agreement', the ability of the latter three firms to export switching equipment was tightly limited. This was the price Siemens demanded in exchange for the other firms using its patents.

The introduction of EMD switching equipment began in the late 1950s and had been completed by 1970. The Bundespost's investments in the new equipment were heavy. In 1986, some 95 per cent of all telephone calls in the FRG were still being switched by this equipment, which, at the beginning of the 1970s, is said to have performed as well as any electronic switching system. It was well maintained and is said still to be in excellent condition. With it, the FRG became the second country in the world, after Switzerland, to achieve 100 per cent direct local dialling (1966), and 100 per cent direct long-distance dialling was achieved in 1972.[14]

The EWS-A débâcle

In 1966 the FTZ launched an initiative to develop a new, computer-controlled analogue switching equipment generation, which was to form a bridge between analogue and digital technologies. The plan then was that the equipment should be ready for introduction in the network beginning in 1973. According to one source, the impetus for this project came from Siemens.

A number of factors led to long delays in the development of the technology and the eventual abandonment of plans to develop, produce, and introduce long-distance exchanges based on the EWS-A (*elektronisches Wahlsystem—analog*) technology.

The problems encountered in developing the new switching technology included some of a technical nature. This was the first computer-controlled switching system the industry was (or was not) to produce—the development work therefore involved a 'learning process' for all participants. The development consortium (see below) ran into problems developing the software for the new system. Other factors which delayed the project's completion and the abandonment of part of it were rooted, however, in the organization of the project, the relations between the Bundespost and the industry, and the respective interest-situations of the Bundespost and the industry, particularly of Siemens.

The EWS technology was to be developed not by Siemens alone, as the EMD switching system had been, but by a Siemens-led consortium of the four switching equipment manufacturers. Apparently, Siemens considered the project too big for it to tackle it by itself. The collaboration between the consortium members proved, however, to be 'very bad'. The Post Ministry's impression was that, since the firms were otherwise competitors, 'no real exchange of views' or ideas took place between them.

Since the Bundespost had stuck with the concept of the single technology, the fact that the firms were not competing with each other for orders for the new equipment reduced the pressure on them to develop the new equipment quickly. As three of the firms could not in any case export the new system and Siemens—up to the mid-1970s—continued to export the EMD system, developments on the world market did not put the firms under pressure to develop the new system rapidly.

Further delays were caused by the behaviour of the Bundespost itself—which regularly came up with requests for modifications to the equipment specifications which had originally been agreed, so that the specifications became 'too complex'. According to the then head of the Post Ministry's telecommunications division, the Bundespost was such an important customer for the firms that they did not dare to contradict it when it came along to them with new wishes. The firms' acquiescence in the Bundespost's demands must also have been conditioned, however, by their expectation that they could sell their entire output to the Bundespost—at a price which would enable them comfortably to recover the research and development investments which they (not the Bundespost) had made in the equipment. Moreover, since the EMD exchanges were still in such good condition, the Bundespost itself had little reason to twist the firms' arms by setting a rigid delivery date.

The first EWS-A local exchanges were delivered to the Bundespost in 1978, five years after the initially envisaged completion date. Meanwhile, technological progress in telecommunications had begun to make the computer-controlled analogue switching technology seem increasingly outmoded. In fact, the trends towards the digitalization of switching equipment had started emerging not long after the EWS-A project had started. This trend had not gone unnoticed at Siemens, which had been carrying out research and development work into digital exchanges parallel to that on the EWS-A system right through the 1970s. Increasingly, it began to get the message from its overseas clients, notably the Finnish, South African, and Austrian telecommunications administrations, that digital rather than computer-controlled switching technology was the order of the day. By this time, Ericsson already had a cheaper, digital system on the market. For Siemens, which (unlike the other members of the development consortium) sold around half of its switching equipment abroad, the probability that it was now too late to sell the EWS-A system abroad was an important consideration. Siemens' thinking may also have been influenced by its not having had enough research and development personnel to carry on work simultaneously on the EWS-A and digital systems.[15] Against these considerations, Siemens in particular had, however, to weigh up the damage that could be done to its image if the EWS-A project were to be suspended before its completion.

The Bundespost's growing doubts as to whether it was going to get equipment which 'corresponded to the international trend' showed that it, too, was conscious of the movement towards digital switching technology. In 1978, the new head of the Post Ministry's telecommunications division made a trip to the United States and returned convinced that the time for introducing an analogue system in the FRG was now past, that the Bundespost would be saddled with an out-of-date technology, and that the German industry would not be able to sell it on the world market. Shortly after his return from the US, the telecommunications division head spoke to a Siemens executive who, contrary to the line the firm had hitherto presented, admitted doubts about the EWS-A system and its market prospects. It may have been this meeting which motivated Siemens shortly afterwards to approach the Bundespost with a formal request for the suspension of the work on the EWS-A long-distance exchange. Waiting to be approached by Siemens to call off the project was advantageous for the Bundespost, in so far as it might otherwise have been liable to refund the firms' research and development outlays for a project for which it had invited tenders. What was abundantly clear was that the credibility of the German club was severely tarnished by the EWS-A débâcle, which began to raise questions as to the legitimacy of closure in telecommuncations.

In abandoning the EWS-A long-distance exchange project, the firms involved were forced to write off considerable research and development investments, although these may not have been nearly as vast as was speculated at the time in the media.[16] Moreover the speed with which both firms got digital equipment on to the market suggested that the work on the EWS-A exchange was relevant for the digital exchanges subsequently brought out by Siemens and SEL. So far as the Post Ministry was concerned, the costs involved in giving up the EWS-A project were, according to one source, 'minimal'. The dominant view in both Siemens and the Bundespost seems to have been that the costs of continuing the project would have been greater than its abandonment. In having the project suspended, Siemens is reputed to have left its fellow consortium members standing. But, although they appear to have played no role in the formulation of the decision, the two smaller firms in the consortium, TN Telenorma and Detewe, arguably had a no less strong interest in giving up the project than Siemens, since they would have been less able than Siemens to sustain the financial burden involved. As for SEL, it detected a chance in the abandonment of the EWS-A project to challenge Siemens's hitherto dominant position in the German switching equipment market. Opinion within the Bundespost, on the other hand, was divided. The FTZ favoured carrying on with the EWS-A project, but was overruled by the leadership of the Post Ministry, where the head of the telecommunications division was in the process of wresting control of telecommunications policy away from the FTZ.

Farewell to the 'single technology' policy

The fiasco with the EWS-A long-distance exchange was a major embarrassment for the Bundespost and Siemens as the consortium leader. It shook the hitherto cosy relationship between the Bundespost and the supply industry. Combined with the trend towards digitalization, which made it easier to contemplate the coexistence of multiple switching technologies in the same network, it made Siemens's dominant position in the equipment industry suddenly appear vulnerable. Could the Bundespost depart from the single technology policy for the new generation of switching equipment? Could competition be introduced into the purchasing process? Could foreign manufacturers obtain a slice of the pie—if they wanted to bid for it? These were the issues now on the telecom policy agenda.

On the prompting of the firms, and drawing a lesson from its experiences with the EWS-A project, the Post Ministry decided to keep the specifications for the new digital equipment to a minimum and base them on international (CCITT) recommendations. In deciding to set such specifications for digital equipment, the Post Ministry was motivated by the recognition that it had a 'macroeconomic responsibility' to order equipment which the firms could sell abroad and not just one which satisfied first and foremost the operational requirements of the Bundespost, especially since the demand for telephones in the FRG was approaching saturation level.

The Post Ministry also anticipated that the more equipment the firms exported and the bigger therefore their production runs, the cheaper would be the prices the firms demanded for their equipment from the Bundespost. The specifications for new digital equipment were entirely functional, requiring the systems offered only to be safe and compatible with existing equipment, and the supplier firms played little part in these decisions. Nothing was written into them, according to the FTZ, which the firms could not meet. According to SEL, for example, the specifications were relatively straightforward, and it was able to fulfil them without difficulty.

In the end there had been widespread agreement between the Post Ministry and the industry concerning the abandonment of the EWS-A long-distance exchange project and the simplification and world-market orientation of specifications for new digital equipment. The EWS-A fiasco nevertheless shook the Post Ministry's confidence in the hitherto sacred principle of the 'single technology'. This policy none the less had formidable backers. At the FTZ, majority opinion, especially among the engineering staff, was for the retention of the single technology—having two systems meant for the Bundespost's technical staff more work, training, planning, technical supervision, and so on. This view was shared by the DPG, which insisted that if the single technology policy were to be abandoned at all, then no more than two systems should be introduced. Since they could not develop their own digital switching technologies, the smaller suppliers, TN Telenorma and Detewe, are likely to have wanted to maintain the single technology policy. TN Telenorma feared that it might be eliminated from the switching equipment market altogether. These firms' best chances of keeping among the Bundespost orders lay in the barriers which competition and anti-monopoly law erected to the Bundespost's making sudden changes in the distribution of orders (see below).

The attitude which Siemens took over the single technology policy is disputed. The most plausible view is that Siemens pushed strongly for the single technology policy so as to safeguard its technological domination of the German supply industry and was 'shocked' by its abandonment, through which it also feared that its prestige and business abroad would be damaged. It is supported by Siemens's behaviour—by its approach to SEL at around this time, offering SEL co-operation with Siemens in developing new digital equipment. By drawing SEL into its own boat, Siemens may have hoped to deprive the Bundespost of an effective choice between competing digital technologies, given that the only other firm permitted and able to offer a digital system to the Bundespost (Philips) had no previous experience of manufacturing switching equipment for the German market and would be hard pressed to meet the Bundespost's delivery deadline (see below). Also, a joint venture with SEL could have saved Siemens financial and manpower resources.

SEL, however, rejected Siemens's offer. It had worked hard on the Bundespost to convince it that the future was digital and, having considered the alternatives of co-operating once again with Siemens, co-operating with a foreign firm such as Ericsson or Northern Telecom, or of developing a new system with the other ITT subsidiaries, it opted for the latter and pressed for the abandonment of the single technology. Going it alone technologically against Siemens was, in SEL's view, 'much more risky' than co-operating with it.

However, the ITT family had long seen the trend towards digitalization and had its new System 12 'at hand'—a system which it was convinced was or would be better than Siemens's. Pursuing a policy of technological independence from Siemens was also perceived as enhancing the firm's long-term commercial prospects and its scope for exporting switching equipment and thereby recovering the high research and development investments involved in digital technology. Constrained by the 'heads of agreement' with Siemens, SEL had hitherto exported EMD switching equipment to just two countries—Greece and Iran.

However the procurement divisions of both the FTZ and the ministry (where, in 1973, responsibility for purchasing had been transferred from the telecommunications to the finance division) argued that there had been 'no sensible' price competition among suppliers under the single technology set-up and that price competition could only be secured if there were to be two systems. More significantly, the view that the time had come to put the single technology policy on the line was also held by the senior civil servants in the Post Ministry (the permanent secretary and the telecommunications division head). The experience with the EWS-A had convinced the ministerial leadership that, at the level of the people actually carrying out the development work, the relations between the Bundespost and the firms had grown too close.

The 'contest' for digital switching equipment orders

The decision to abandon the Bundespost's single technology policy was, according to Post Ministry sources, taken without an 'excited debate' and in a 'relatively short time'. Equally new and revolutionary was the policy—expressly wished by the firms—of ordering a system or systems which were to be developed for the world market and then adapted for the Bundespost's network. Neither of these two policies could have been introduced had it not been for the EWS-A project débâcle. In addition the Post Ministry insisted that before it gave any orders for new digital equipment, the tendering firms should submit their product to a year-long operational trial by the Bundespost. Some firms are said to have been 'deeply shocked' about the delivery date imposed for the systems for testing by the Bundespost. The date had been set, however, after the Bundespost had consulted 'the industry' and been assured that long-distance digital exchanges would be ready by 1982. Moreover, as is borne out by the ease with which SEL reportedly fulfilled them, nothing was written into the specifications which 'the firms' (or at least Siemens and SEL) could not fulfil. The fact that Siemens supplied South Africa with digital switching equipment as early as 1980 indicates that it can hardly have been greatly stretched to present a system for trial by the Bundespost's deadline.

The Bundespost also stipulated in advance that orders would be given only to firms which developed and manufactured their equipment 'predominantly' in the FRG,[17] a condition motivated by employment considerations.[18] It referred to the 'necessity' of an industrial nation such as the FRG having its own switching technology and pointed to the nationalistic purchasing policies of other telecommunications administrations, but the former head of the ministry's telecommunications division admitted that this policy was also conditioned by more overtly political considerations. He argued that the step from having a single switching technology, developed and manufactured in Germany, to having a foreign technology would have been much too difficult and, despite the EWS-A débâcle, 'politically impossible ... No-one would have been able to see through such a conflict.'[19] In fact, the firms in the German industry exercised an effective veto over the Bundespost's purchasing digital switching equipment abroad.[20]

Potential suppliers were thus limited to the four existing suppliers and to one newcomer, Philips's German telecommunications subsidiary PKI, which had hitherto been one of the Bundespost's main suppliers in the now declining transmission equipment market. As neither TN Telenorma nor Detewe could conceivably have developed its own digital exchange, the number of possible suppliers was, in practice, limited to three—the maximum number of systems which the Bundespost declared it would test in its year-long trials.

Siemens and SEL had supplied, and therefore were much better acquainted with, the Bundespost's existing switching equipment, with which the new digital technologies had to be compatible, and this gave them a considerable advantage over the third competitor, Philips, which started off with a research and development team of just 10 persons, compared with teams of 500 and 600, according to PKI's estimates, at Siemens and SEL respectively. Within the Post Ministry, there was scepticism from the outset concerning the likelihood of PKI being able to meet the delivery deadline for the system trials. This scepticism, which was based on PKI's not having participated in the EWS-A development consortium, proved to be justified. The firm did not come up with a functioning system by the delivery deadline and had to be satisfied with its system being tested, and found to function, by the Bundespost six months later.

Siemens contends that it had to convince the Bundespost through 'performance' and that it had 'not been at all certain' that it would get an order. Within the upper echelons of the Post Ministry, however, the situation was viewed somewhat differently. While it was not certain that Siemens would meet the delivery date, the telecommunications division head, for example, thought that if Siemens did not meet it, then neither would the other two firms. Siemens had had the best starting position. It had been the consortium leader for the EWS-A system and had therefore possessed greater system know-how than its competitors. It had (like SEL in this case) begun work on a digital system already. And it undoubtedly had the money to finance the development work.

According to *Der Spiegel*, Siemens used the 'employment card', the threat of staff redundancies, to try to ensure that it would be among the recipients of the contracts for digital switching equipment—it told the Post Minister and his top officials that some 20,000 jobs depended on Siemens being retained as a Bundespost supplier.[21] The reality, according to Siemens, was 'somewhat more nuanced and complex'. Siemens met the Bundespost deadline and presumably did not therefore need to play the jobs card. The decisive advantage which it enjoyed over Philips in particular, but also over SEL, was its superior technical knowledge based on its design and manufacture of the Bundespost's existing switching technology, with which the digital equipment had to be compatible, and on its leadership of the EWS-A consortium. In the FRG's transition to digital switching technology, Siemens was thus the beneficiary of the Bundespost's past decisions, which had bestowed on it a dominant position on the supply side of the market.

SEL, with its System 12 technology, also met the Bundespost's deadline. Whether one or two systems were to be bought and installed by the Bundespost, and, if only one, which one, depended officially on the systems' performance in the trial and their cost. As a result of the trials, the FTZ came to different judgements concerning particular attributes of the two systems, but overall found them equally satisfactory. This, and the prices offered by the two firms, 'permitted' the Bundespost to adopt both technologies.[22] It may be doubted, however, whether, even if there had been significant differences in the technical performance and price competitiveness of the two firms' systems, the Bundespost would have opted for a single system manufactured by a single firm, as, at the end of its new competitive purchasing procedure, it would thus have established precisely the kind of (albeit temporary) supply-side monopoly which in the past it had gone to great lengths to avert.

It was left to decide how the Bundespost's orders were to be shared out between Siemens and SEL, and whether any piece of the cake would be set aside for the two firms TN Telenorma and Detewe. Here the Bundespost aimed to introduce a much higher level of price competition between suppliers. A first move in this direction had been made in 1974 for electro-mechanical switching equipment, but the additional share of orders allocated to the firm submitting the lowest bid had been limited to just 2 per cent.

If the Bundespost had entertained any ideas about awarding contracts for new digital exchanges to the lowest respective bidder, these were nipped in the bud by the BKA, whose responsibilities include preventing any abuse of market power by *demand* monopolists—i.e., in the market for telecommunications switching equipment, the Bundespost. The Cartel Office told the Bundespost that it had to heed the 'particular market structure' that existed for switching equipment. A firm could be excluded from orders over a transitional period, but not suddenly from one year to another—something which presumably could only happen in a market which was dominated by one buyer. This ruling obliged the Bundespost to carry on giving orders to Detewe and TN Telenorma. The two smaller suppliers negotiated manufacturing licences from Siemens and carried out some development work on the EWS-D system, enabling Siemens to spread the research and development burden over a broader basis.

Despite the BKA's intervention, the Bundespost was able to increase the share of its orders allocated in free competition from 2 to 30 per cent. Under this regime, the annual fluctuations in market shares as between Siemens and SEL have been much more pronounced than in the pre-digital era. Siemens expected that its share of Bundespost orders in the period from 1985 to 1987 would be somewhat smaller than previously. Similarly, SEL reported that its market share had 'not necessarily improved' under the Bundes-post's purchasing regime for digital exchanges.[23] In fact, the distribu-tion of orders in 1986 suggested that Siemens (marginally) and SEL (appreciably) increased their respective shares of the order at the expense of their two smaller counterparts.[24]

The Bundespost's new policies have resulted in price competition, described by SEL as 'very intense'. Within the Bundespost the price level established for digital exchanges is regarded as 'sensible'. In the international price league table for digital equipment, the FRG occupies, in the Post Ministry's view, a 'very good position'. This may, in turn, be related to Siemens's and SEL's success in winning export orders for digital equipment, thus securing longer production runs and greater economies of scale. By 1986, Siemens had won digital contracts from 49 telecommunications companies in 25 states.[25] System 12 exchanges, not all of them manufactured, how-ever, by SEL, had been sold in 21 states.[26] At the margins, at least, the success of Siemens's export drive with its EWS-D system has been facilitated by, or even based on, government subsidies made available in the form of soft loans to the buying (Third World) state and funded by the Development Aid Ministry.[27] Also, it cannot be excluded that the prices offered by the firms for digital exchanges both for the Bundespost and foreign customers are subsidized from the firms' more profitable sales of pre-digital switching equipment to the Bundespost.[28] In 1987 digital exchanges accounted for little more than one-third of the Bundespost's switching equipment orders.

Aftermath of the switching story

The Bundespost's misadventure with the EWS-A switching techno-logy in the 1970s relegated the FRG to the stragglers among the advanced industrial states in terms of the digitalization of telephone switching. Thanks to the high quality performance of existing elec-tro-mechanical switching equipment, the FRG's backwardness in digitalization did not necessarily have any negative consequences for telephone users.

The EWS-A débâcle shook the confidence of the Bundespost in the industry and, in particular, in the hitherto dominant supplier, Siemens. The Bundespost broke with long-established practices and principles in its technology and procurement policies. For the new generation of digital switching equipment, the hitherto sacred policy of having a single technology was abandoned, price competition between suppliers was increased, a strict delivery date for the delivery of trial equipment was laid down, contracts were made dependent on the performance of the equipment in trials, and equipment specifications were simplified and tailored to the dictates of the world market. The Bundespost suppliers' strategy of closing the market to (potential) competitors by means of the maintenance of a state-sanctioned cartel had reached the end of the road. Neither the Bundespost (or at least the dominant coalition within it) nor at least one of the erstwhile members of the cartel wanted it to be extended into the digital equipment generation. The switching equipment manufacturers had to revert to other means to try to safeguard their domination of the German market. In the event, the changes in the Bundespost's switching technology and procurement policies did not lead to a dramatic reshuffling of the cards on the supply side of the market.

In practice, the freedom of the Bundespost to allocate orders for new digital switching equipment was tightly circumscribed. Irrespective of the firms' co-responsibility for the EWS-A débâcle, labour market considerations dictated that orders be confined again to German or German-based manufacturers. The political obstacles—that is, the firms' and their works councils' opposition—to bringing in a foreign supplier or foreign suppliers would have been insurmountable. Also, the Cartel Office stood in the way of a sudden and major redistribution of market shares between the established suppliers and helped to conserve the status quo. The established suppliers in any event enjoyed a major advantage over the sole new would-be supplier by virtue of the new technologies having to be compatible with the existing equipment which they had developed and manufactured. The Bundespost's past decisions greatly reduced the likelihood that its future ones would hurt the established suppliers, least of all Siemens.

Indeed, it is possible to argue that, with the Post Ministry's explicit acceptance in the late 1970s of a responsibility to look not just to the Bundespost's needs, but also to those of the German telecommunications industry, the Bundespost became more sensitive than it had been hitherto to the long-term interests of the equipment manufacturing industry. This happened, however, by the Bundespost changing its procurement policies so as to help, or force, the firms to export. The Bundespost's increased concern to promote the export trade of the German industry was motivated by the growing saturation of the demand for telephones in the FRG, as a consequence of which the Bundespost in future could not absorb as great a share of the firms' production capacity. This concern manifested itself in the decision to tailor the specifications for digital switching equipment according to world market requirements. This strategy of forcing German switching equipment exports—which was backed up by the Development Aid Ministry with soft loans to Third World purchasers—also promised rewards for the Bundespost in the form of lower prices. The more equipment the firms exported and the higher their output, the lower became their unit production costs and the lower the prices at which they could sell to the Bundespost. The firms' interest in turnover and profit maximization and that of the Bundespost in low equipment prices could be reconciled by expansion into foreign markets. That, at least, is the theory, but the reality is somewhat different. Despite the export success of the German industry it seems that the Bundespost pays much higher prices for its digital equipment than British Telecom.[29]

Conclusion

An additional motive for the changes in the Bundespost's purchasing policy for switching equipment had been to deflect growing attacks on the Bundespost monopoly and allegations that the monopoly was inimical to technological progress. Changes in policy for procuring other types of telecommunications equipment followed. Competitive purchasing was introduced for transmission equipment and the number of suppliers increased from four to eight—according to one source as a result of political pressure from a group of small and medium-sized firms exercised through the federal Economics Ministry. The Bundespost's stance was also decisive for the termination by the Federal Cartel Office (BKA) of the long-existing suppliers' cartel for telecommunications cable. For some firms, life as a supplier to the Bundespost in the 1980s undoubtedly became more uncomfortable and uncertain, although the circle of suppliers was still largely confined in practice to German or German-based companies.

However, these steps did not suffice to prevent the telecommunications regime becoming increasingly contested in the FRG as in other West European states during the 1980s. The growing deregulation and privatization debate was fuelled by a variety of factors, both international and domestic, ideological, political, and technical. Deregulation and privatization measures in other states, especially in Britain and the USA, prompted the question, raised initially by right-wing intellectuals: why not also in the FRG? Following the break-up of AT&T and the increased exposure of the American equipment industry to foreign competition, American firms and the US government began to lobby foreign governments, particularly the German, to follow suit. The domestic political conjuncture changed with the coming to power of a coalition government of the CDU–CSU and FDP in 1982. The new Christian Democratic Post Minister had been a strong critic of the Bundespost monopoly while in opposition, and his coalition partner, the FDP, far from being a moderating influence in this sphere, had placed itself in the vanguard of the deregulation and privatization campaign. All these changes occurred against a background of a growing confluence of classical telecommunications and computer technology—which created vast opportunities for new telecommunications services, products, and markets, and which more and more firms from outside the traditional telecommunications industry wanted to exploit.

The telecommunications reform strategy pursued by the new government was notable, however, for its gradualness and caution.[30] The government had been in office for more than two years before the Post Minister appointed the Witte Commission, including representatives of the opposition, the DPG, and the equipment industry, to formulate recommendations for reorganizing the Bundespost and liberalizing telecommunications. The commission's brief explicitly ruled out the option of privatizing the Bundespost, and the Post Minister stressed that employment and income-distribution objectives limited the extent to which the Bundespost's existing responsibilities could be hived off to the private sector and telecommunications charges strictly orientated to costs. In its report,[31] released in autumn 1987, the commission recommended that the Bundespost should by and large retain its network and telephone services monopoly. Competition should be allowed for value added services and for all kinds of terminal equipment, but the Bundespost should be permitted to compete with private enterprise. The separation of the postal and telecommunications services,

and of the regulatory and entrepreneurial functions of the Bundespost (involving the creation of a public corporation, 'Telekom',
which would have its own executive board similar to the Geman
Federal Railways), was also proposed. The commission's recommendations were very similar to those made by the European Commission in its telecommunications 'Green Paper' of 1987.

The ensuing Bundespost reform bill closely followed the commission's report (large parts of which, according to one source, were
written in the Post Ministry), but was less ambitious, in so far
as it foresaw the continued cross-subsidization of the postal branch
of the Bundespost by the telecommunications services. Opposition
to the Post Minister's plans was nevertheless so strong that the adoption of the bill was delayed by several months and it was still possible
that it would be substantially amended. The focal points of this
opposition were other federal ministries, the state governments, and
the DPG. The Interior Ministry tried to block the proposed new
corporation's being empowered to hire staff other than at public
service pay rates and so maintain uniform pay and working conditions for public servants. The Finance Ministry fought against
the abolition of the Bundespost turnover levy and the imposition
of normal VAT on postal and telecommunications services—which
would have brought about a reduction in revenues for the federal
budget (see above). The state governments were concerned most
of all to prevent the separation of the postal and telecommunications
services—for fear that in the longer term 'Telekom' would evade
its cross-subsidization obligations and that, left to its own devices,
the postal branch would not be able to maintain existing services
to outlying areas. Since the reform required the consent of the Bundesrat, the states' chamber in the federal Parliament, the majority
of the state governments' opposition could lead to the bill's defeat.
Within the federal coalition, the labour wing of the CDU and, more
importantly, the Bavarian CSU, which could coalesce with the SPD-
governed states in the Bundesrat to vote down the bill, had strong
reservations concerning the bill. In the case of the CSU, they had
to do not only with the possible impact of the separation of the
postal and telecommunications services on the postal service infrastructure, but also with the relaxation of the Bundespost's network
monopoly. Its stance on the latter issue could be attributed in no
small measure to its concern with the well-being of Siemens, whose
main production and R. & D. facilities are located in Bavaria.

By the late 1980s the major equipment manufacturing firms in the FRG had ceased to defend the existing telecommunications regime and were equipping themselves to try to survive in a much more internationalized and competitive market environment. The issues which concerned the Bundespost's traditional small and medium-sized suppliers—such as the maintenance of the Bundespost's monopoly of the first telephone set—were of no consequence to firms such as Siemens. The latter felt that it could produce cheaply enough and avail itself of a sufficiently extensive sales and service network to be able to hold its own in liberalized terminal equipment markets. It could also hope to establish itself as a supplier in the value added services markets—in which its main concern was that standards be harmonized to prevent IBM imposing its own. A limited opening of the German market was acknowledged as the quid pro quo of (continued or improved) access to foreign markets, especially the American, which accounts for a third of the entire world market, and is the technological trend setter (see Chapter 8). Access to foreign markets was indispensable if Siemens was to recover its R. & D. investments and remain a world telecommunications player.

The key issue for Siemens in the German deregulation conflict related to the network monopoly, where the bulk of Siemens's business with the Bundepost lay. Any loss of orders through a relaxation of the network monopoly could have adverse knock-on effects on Siemens's export business, given the Bundespost's important role as a 'reference market' for foreign customers, and, in so far as the Bundespost's orders subsidized its foreign sales, prejudice its price competitiveness abroad. As long as the Bundespost retained the telephone service monopoly, in practice as well as in law, it could continue to finance a comprehensive network modernization scheme (ISDN); so long as it retained the network monopoly and bought primarily on the German market, Siemens could reckon on getting a substantial slice of the order pie.

If the retention of the strongest possible home base was one pillar of Siemens's telecommunications strategy, the second was the penetration of key foreign markets through a network of strategic alliances and take-overs. In the late 1980s, Siemens embarked on an unparalleled shopping and 'joint venture' expedition in the telecommunications industry. Among other moves, in the USA it acquired the foreign telecom business of GTE, and the IBM subsidiary Rolm. In Europe it sought to team up with GEC to acquire Plessey, having failed in its bid to take over CGCT. While SEL was absorbed into the empire of the French CGE, Siemens's other main competitor on the German market, Bosch, also sought to strengthen its presence abroad. In so far as they were still independent, 'internationalization' was the battle cry of the major German equipment firms. This also meant that the attractions of a nationally based closure strategy were less powerful than they had been in the past.

The imminent liberalization of the terminal equipment markets jeopardized the survival, at the other end of the German industry, of the Bundespost's traditional small and medium-sized suppliers. Faced with competition from low-priced Far Eastern equipment imported by German retail chains, these firms, with their high unit production costs and without their own sales networks, could go to the wall unless the Bundespost retained its dominant position on the liberalized telephone set market and continued to buy German. In the deregulation debate, this group of firms split into two factions on the issue of liberalization. Coupled with US and EEC pressures, and the indifference of the big firms, it was clear that the campaign to preserve a 100 per cent monopoly was doomed. The government's bill, however, did allow for phasing out the monopoly over eighteen months to give the firms some breathing space for adjustment to foreign competition.

Long before the government's bill reached its parliamentary stage, the most strident critics of the Bundespost in the electronics industry, the computer firms IBM and Nixdorf, had suspended any frontal attacks on its network monopoly. In part, this reflected their increased success in winning Bundespost orders (IBM, for example, won the contract for the central exchange of the German videotext service), but it also was a recognition that for the time being at least the political obstacles to such a move were insuperable. Beyond the short term the key question would be whether, in the light of technological change and the advent of ISDN, in whose conception Siemens had played a leading role, and which may be understood as a network monopolist's preferred network monopolization strategy, the protection of the Bundespost's telephone service monopoly would remain technically feasible. The *practical* undermining of the telephone service monopoly would in turn threaten the Bundespost's capacity to finance network investments, the network monopoly itself, and Siemens's privileged position as the leading supplier of network equipment on the German market.

To this extent, the future character of the German telecommunications regime remained open, despite the measures foreseen in the Christian–Liberal government's reform bill. The course and outcome of the deregulation debate underlined, however, that the demand for a radical change in the direction of telecommunications policy was considerably more limited in the FRG than in Britain, and that the political, institutional, and legal obstacles to the government's implementing a change of direction in telecommunications policy are greater than in Britain. If the Bundespost's traditional 'court suppliers' were not necessarily the main sources of resistance to deregulation, this was because they hoped to be among its principal beneficiaries. Compared to their British counterparts they thus had more *time* to equip themselves to survive in a much more internationalized industry and market.

Notes

Note: Unless specifically cited quotations in this chapter are taken from interviews conducted for this project.

1. Conversely, some 35% of the Bundespost's telephone revenues, according to information supplied by the DIHT, comes from firms.
2. Boy Luthje, 'Regulierungskrise in Telekommunikationssektor in der BRD', unpublished manuscript (Frankfurt-on-Main, 1986), pp. 21–2.
3. There are some eight small and medium-sized manufacturers of telephone sets in the FRG, and they receive about 65% of the Bundespost's orders.
4. Our calculation based on employment figures in company reports. It assumes roughly equal productivity among the firms.
5. 'Langer Abschied von der Mutter in den USA', *Manager-Magazin*, No. 3 (Mar. 1985).
6. 'Manager und Markte', *Die Zeit*, 21 Oct. 1983.
7. The West German Green Party published the text of a letter from the executive chairman of Siemens to the (Bavarian CSU) Development Aid Minister, which read as follows: '... Unfortunately, ... I could not take part in your and the Federal Chancellor's visit to Pakistan after the trip to China ...

    I am all the more grateful to you that you intervened in such an outstanding way on behalf of our firm ...

    I use this opportunity, dear Minister, to thank you and your staff

very cordially for the positive attitude of your ministry . . .'
8. According to one ZVEI official, the high level of organization of firms in the industry is also attributable to the opportunity which membership gives to firms to exercise political influence, as well as to the range of services which it offers to members, including information on customs law and tariffs, foreign trade and statistics. The level of organization of firms in other industries—both in employers' and trade associations—is also very high.
9. Where equipment is manufactured by only a few firms, the FTZ talks to the firms directly. The role of the ZVEI in this process is that of an 'intermediary', bringing the FTZ and the firms together. Standards and specifications are discussed between the FTZ and the representatives of the firms rather than of the FTZ.
10. K. Hoffman, 'Digitale Fernsprechvermittlungstechnik bei der Deutschen Bundespost—Das Präsentationasverfahren', offprint from *Jahrbuche der Deutschen Bundespost*, (Bad Windsheim, 1984), 20. Some 47% of the Bundespost's telecommunications investments in 1982 was in switching and transmission equipment.
11. Ibid. 60–1.
12. Ibid. 63.
13. M. Reinhard, L. Scholz, and B. Thanner, *Gesamtwirtschaftliche und sektorale Perspektiven der Telekommunikation in der Bundesrepublik Deutschland* (Munich, 1983), pp. 147–8.
14. Hoffman, 'Digitale . . .', p. 12.
15. Interview with Siemens official.
16. Some reports suggested that the EWS-A project had lost the consortium members as much as 1bn. DM. The former telecommunications division head in the Post Ministry estimates that the losses for Siemens or SEL were no more than about 50 m. DM.
17. Hoffman, 'Digitale . . .', p. 23.
18. This policy was reiterated by the Bundespost to Ericsson in 1986. The Swedish firm was told in unequivocal terms that it would not buy any switching system which had not been produced by German labour.
19. Interviewed in Sept. 1986.
20. The Bundespost accepted the pledges of the firms which offered systems for trial that their equipment had been developed 'predominantly' in the FRG, although in the case of the ITT System 12, the proportions claimed by German, Spanish, and Belgian subsidiaries came to more than 100%. However, the credibility of the firms' claims could be assessed roughly by their employment levels in the FRG.
21. *Der Spiegel*, 5 Mar. 1979 and 10 Sept. 1979.
22. Bundesministerium für das Post- und Fernmeldewesen, 'Schwarz-

Schilling setzt auf digitale Telefon- Vermittlungstechnik', press release, 21 Oct. 1983.
23. According to *Der Spiegel* (6 Oct. 1986), two-thirds of the Bundespost's orders for digital exchanges were then for Siemens's EWS-D system (supplied partly by Detewe and TN Telenorma), and one-third for SEL's System 12. Other estimates from SEL itself and the FTZ were similar.
24. Siemens claimed to have 43% of the Bundespost's switching equipment orders in 1988—3% less than in the pre-digital era (*Frankfurter Rundschau*, 6 July 1988).
25. *Handelsblatt*, 30 Sept. 1986.
26. *Frankfurter Rundschau*, 14 Mar. 1986.
27. Siemens estimates between 10 and 15% of its business abroad carries such subsidies.
28. A Siemens spokesman claimed that Siemens was even losing money on its public procurement orders due to the competitive regime and the high costs of R. & D. for digital exchanges.
29. The comparison of prices is complicated by the fact that BT paid for the R. & D. on System X, whereas the Bundespost did not do so for the EWS-D exchange. Even allowing for this difference, however, it seems that the price of digital lines is still lower in the UK.
30. The debate and conflict over telecommunications deregulation in the FRG are analysed in much greater detail in Douglas Webber, 'Die ausbleibende Wende bei der Deutschen Bundespost: Zur Regulierung des Telekommunikationswesens in der Bundesrepublik Deutschland', *Politische Vierteljahresschrift*, 27 Apr. 1986, 397–414, and Kevin Morgan and Douglas Webber, 'Divergent Paths: Political Strategies for Telecommunications in Britain, France and the Federal Republic of Germany', *West European Politics*, 9 Apr. 1986, pp. 56–79.
31. E. Witte, *Neuordnung der Telekommunikation: Bericht der Regierungskommission Fernmeldewesen* (Heidelberg, 1987).

Telecom Strategies in Europe: The End of Parochialism?

The development of telecommunications in Britain, France and Germany has been sufficiently different, as regards regulatory regimes and government–industry relations, for us to speak of the continued existence of distinctive national telecom regimes. The fact that liberalization is beginning to emerge on the continent does not mean that national specificities are no longer of any account, only that the differences are in some respects becoming less stark. The interesting question from a comparative standpoint is this: why should regulatory regimes and government–industry relations differ so much when each country appears to have encountered broadly similar pressures? This issue is addressed in Chapter 14. Divergent national paths carry enormous opportunity costs from a supra-national European perspective: different regulatory regimes, incompatible technical standards, duplicative R. & D. efforts and chauvinistic procurement policies all conspire to the same end, namely an uncommon market in which European firms are denied the economies of scale available to their US and Japanese competitors.

In recent years the European Commission has tried to reduce these opportunity costs by promoting a European strategy for telecommunications, the hope being that supra-national regulations will eventually replace country-specific norms. A Europe balkanized by fragmented national markets is less likely to be able to follow an independent path *vis-à-vis* Japan and the US than a Europe which can aggregate its collective resources. This is the reasoning behind the European Commission's strategy for telecommunications, a sector whose strategic importance is deemed to be so great that 'Europe must stake its all on a Community response'.[1]

As a bloc the European Community accounts for 19 per cent of the world market for telecom equipment, compared to 38 per cent for the US and 9 per cent for Japan. The European share of this market, however, appears to be declining. The Community's trade surplus, which shrank from 1.5 billion ECUs in 1984 to 1.2 billion ECUs in 1986, is derived from smaller countries; by contrast, the Community runs a growing deficit with the US and Japan.[2] This is a particularly disturbing trend because telecoms was the one information technology sector in which the Community appeared to be holding its own against the US and Japan. Europe's weakness in the basic technologies of information technology (i.e. micro-electronics and data processing) has long been a cause for concern; indeed, the Community imports some 80 per cent of the micro-electronic components which will increasingly be used for telecom equipment.

The case for greater European collaboration is helped by the fact that national-based strategies are patently no longer viable. As we saw in Chapter 4, the national market is no longer large enough for firms to amortize product development costs; they are thus obliged to look further afield. This search is reinforced by trends in the political market-place, as deregulation makes it more difficult for domestic telecom firms to reserve their home markets to themselves. More generally, the move to create a single European Community market by 1992 'signals a definitive end to national soft options'.[3]

Trends in technology, markets, and regulation point to the limits of the nation-state as a commercial and political arena. It is hardly surprising then that large firms have been trying to develop their 'brotherhood' at the European level, in supra-national trade associations, user groups, technology clubs, and new lobbying organizations. Perhaps the most powerful supra-national lobbying organization is the European 'Round Table', which represents Europe's leading information technology firms: Siemens, Nixdorf, and AEG of West Germany; CGE, Thomson, and Bull of France; GEC, Plessey, and STC-ICL of the UK; Olivetti and Stet of Italy; and Philips of the Netherlands. Formed in the late 1970s the 'Round Table' was in part the brainchild of the former EEC Industry Commissioner, Viscount Étienne Davignon, who felt a growing despair about Europe's loss of technological and industrial competitiveness to the US and Japan.[4]

The 'Round Table' has been one of the major industrial 'clubs' pressing for a European industrial strategy in information technology. Its main demands are for a co-ordinated liberalization of telecom regulations throughout the Community, Euro-wide tele-communication standards, and an extension of the Community's pre-competitive R. & D. programmes to cover projects closer to the market. However, the 'Round Table' firms are becoming very nervous about the European Commission's more robust competition policy, which could effectively block cross-border mergers and acquisitions which involve sales of more than 1 billion ECUs (£650 million). The 'Round Table' feels that restrictions on European mergers should be lifted because US and Japanese firms will provide sufficient competition. As we shall see, this is but one example of the tension between *pro-competitive* and *pro-industrial* pressures within the European Commission itself.[5]

The 'Round Table' group, which represents the European producer interest, is only one of a number of stakeholders pushing its agenda at the Community level. The other major corporate stakeholders are (1) foreign equipment suppliers, especially American firms like IBM and AT&T, as well as Japanese firms like NEC; (2) value added network service (VANS) suppliers, who are demanding better access to the public networks throughout Europe; (3) telecom administrations like BT, France Télécom, and the DBP, all of which belong to the PTT 'club', the Conference of European Post and Telecommunications Administrations (CEPT), which represents twenty-six European telecom administrations; and (4) major corporate user groups, like the International Telecommunications User Group (INTUG). Clearly, the interests of these stakeholders are to some extent mutually exclusive, and the European Commission will have to tread a delicate path if it is to sustain its strategy. Although the producer interest has traditionally been the strongest in the telecom sector, the European Commission is acutely aware that, in numerical terms, the corporate user interest is far more important. For example, the European Commission estimates that by the end of the century some 7 per cent of Community GDP will result from telecommunications, as against 2 per cent today, and more than 60 per cent of Community employment will be dependent on telecommunications.[6]

One further stakeholder should be mentioned here, the US government, which has been among the most powerful external pressures on European governments. The US government has singled out telecommunications as one of its primary targets in the Uruguay round of GATT negotiations, which began in 1986. Its longer-term objective here is to create market openings for American equipment and service suppliers, and to enhance the competitive position of American firms (such as American Express and Citicorp) which are intensive users of telecommunications. As we shall see, telecoms now contains all the ingredients for a major trade war between the US and the Community.

The European Commission's strategy for telecommunications raises a number of crucial questions. To what extent will national governments cede control over their industrial affairs to supra-national institutions? Is corporate collaboration among European firms a substitute for, or a complement to, alliances with US and Japanese firms? What balance should be drawn between pro-competitive policies, designed to enhance the position of European telecom users, and pro-industrial policies, designed to ensure a viable European supply industry? These are some of the questions that will be addressed in this chapter.

The Commission's telecom strategy

Although the European Commission had been concerned about Europe's position in the 'telematics' sector back in the 1970s, it was not until 1983 that a serious strategy for telecoms began to emerge. Two factors in particular help to explain why telecoms was propelled to the top of its agenda. The first was the external threat from the US: in 1982 the US had taken the momentous decision to break up AT&T, and the European Commission saw this leading to a new, more intense phase of competition in global telecom markets. The second was the opportunity offered by new technologies, such as digitalization, optical fibres, and new cable and satellite links, which were eroding the sectoral boundaries between telecoms, data processing, and audio-visual media.

In response to a combination of external threats and internal opportunities the European Commission developed an Action Programme for Telecommunications in 1984, which consisted of six interrelated threads:

1. concerted programmes to promote future network development in the areas of ISDN, mobile communications, and broadband communications;
2. the promotion of European-wide open standards;

3. the promotion of industrial co-operation, especially in the field of pre-competitive research;
4. the creation of a Community-wide telecommunications market;
5. the promotion of advanced communications in the peripheral regions of the Community; and
6. building common European positions on telecom issues *vis-à-vis* the Community's external trading partners.

This Action Programme took on a new sense of urgency in the light of the European White Paper on the Internal Market, which identified 1992 as the date for the creation of a common internal market for telecom services and equipment.[7] In an attempt to force the pace of change, and indeed to enhance its own role in this process, the European Commission published a Green Paper on telecommunications in June 1987.[8] Compared to past proposals the Green Paper was a radical document, designed to 'initiate a common thinking process regarding the fundamental adjustment of the institutional and regulatory conditions which the telecommunications sector now faces'.[9]

Faced with the need to win as broad a consensus as possible, and to avoid alienating the more regulation-conscious member states, the European Commission tried to allay fears that it was aping US-style deregulation. To this end it endorsed an earlier resolution by the European Parliament which called for a process of 'reregulation'. Decoded, this meant a rejection of the US model of deregulation in favour of a European path which would combine as much competition as possible with a recognition of the 'vital public service obligations of telecom administrations'.[10] However, the European Commission's proposals involve contradictory demands. On the one hand it argues for the sphere of competition to be expanded in both equipment and service markets, but at the same time it wants the financial viability of the telecom administrations to be assured, because only they are deemed to be able to afford the massive front-loaded investments needed for new generations of infrastructure. This is the basic conundrum in a deregulated telecom environment.

In the light of the Green Paper it is worth examining what progress has been made in parts of the European Commission's Action Programme.

Future Network Development. The main focus here has been placed on co-ordinating the introduction of ISDN, developing a pan-European digital mobile communications network, and, longer term, laying the basis for an integrated broadband communications (IBC) network which is expected to come on stream in the mid-1990s. The great attraction of the ISDN is that it dispenses with the need to have separate networks for different types of traffic, since it permits voice, data, text, and simple video to be carried in digital form on a single network.[11] The European Commission attaches great significance to ISDN because it is seen as a necessary step on the road to the IBC network, as well as creating an opportunity for advanced terminal equipment and a new generation of Community-wide services. Although the Green Paper set certain objectives for a co-ordinated introduction of ISDN, the reality is much less promising. Indeed, in its own audit of ISDN in 1986 the European Commission was forced to conclude that 'only the general concept of ISDN is common'.[12] Dates for the introduction of new services, even the definition of these services, differ significantly from one country to another. While this is partly due to the uneven development of telecom facilities within the Community, it also reflects different commercial pressures on the telecom administrations. France Télécom and the Bundespost are by far the most committed to ISDN, while British Telecom, because of its privatized status, feels less inclined to undertake infrastructural investments ahead of market signals.

The acid test as to whether the Community countries can successfully collaborate together is the pan-European mobile communications project, which is scheduled to be in operation by 1991. This project also includes Sweden, so that in all there are thirteen European countries involved. Initial conflicts centred on the choice of technology—whether it should be narrowband or broadband—with France and the FRG alone holding out for the latter option. In the event they reluctantly agreed to support the majority choice because it was felt that the sooner the project got under way, the sooner the European industry could tool up to supply the equipment, thus reducing the threat from US and Japanese suppliers. Perhaps a reflection of the shape of things to come, a consortium of firms, rather than 'national champions', has emerged as the most likely suppliers. For example, Ericsson, Siemens, Matra, and

Orbitel (a joint venture between Plessey and Racal) are in one group; Alcatel, Nokia, and AEG are in another.

Conflicts of interest have threatened to derail the ambitious schedule for this project. The most important of these is a dispute between the network operators and the manufacturers over intellectual property rights. The operators have insisted that they be given the ownership rights to the patents. For their part the manufacturers object to giving the operators the patents free of charge, and they also fear that the operators could pass on the patents to foreign competitors. At bottom the issue reflects the operators' wish to be as independent as possible from their suppliers, hence they have made tenders conditional on the free availability of interface specifications. Because interface points are mandatory, operators can choose different suppliers for each segment of the network (telephone exchange, base station, and telephones), and indeed change suppliers as they wish. The project's schedule made little allowance for conflicts of this kind and, if the project fails to live up to its original promise, the credibility of European collaboration will have been severely devalued.

Open Standards. The European Commission has been rightly concerned to make open standards a priority issue. Liberalized markets will remain liberal in name only if customers are effectively locked into proprietary standards, the best example of which is IBM's Systems Network Architecture (SNA), which dominates the global computer market. To overcome this threat the European Commission is unequivocally committed to the Open Systems Interconnection (OSI) standard. Up until now uneven standards have been at the heart of the uncommon telecom market in the Community and the major non-tariff barrier to intra-Community trade. By and large neither suppliers nor users have had much influence on the standards-setting process. This arcane process has been dominated by the telecom administrations, and by their collective organization, CEPT; but the latter was painfully under-resourced, lacking even its own office! As a result standards have taken an inordinately long time to emerge, and even then there was sufficient discretion at national level for inter-working to be difficult if not impossible. One of the main demands of manufacturers and users alike has been to open up the standards-setting process in Europe. Pro-competitive elements in the Commission believe that open standards are the surest way of preventing firms and governments from engaging in national closure strategies.

The European Commission's key innovation in this field was its proposal for a new European Telecom Standards Institute (ETSI). That ETSI was established less than a year after being proposed was something of a miracle in the pedestrian world of European standards-setting. ETSI is open to a wide body of members, including users and manufacturers, and the latter hope that it will be independent of the telecom administrations. However, it may be premature to think that ETSI will have the standards turf to itself. Indeed, CEPT, which has now been revamped, will not meekly surrender its powers, certainly not if the national telecom administrations have their way. In fact one of CEPT's most important functions—the setting of mandatory standards—will not be transferred to ETSI. These mandatory standards, known as Normes Européennes de Télécommunications (NET), will have binding legal force in the Community. If ETSI's standards are to attain the same stature as NET's, they have to be approved by CEPT. This has been interpreted to mean that the telecom administrations, led by the Bundespost, are using CEPT to stem any loss of power on the standards front.[13] However, real progress has been made on this front, not just with ETSI but with concepts such as mutual recognition, which allows each country's equipment approval procedures to be recognized in other member countries.

Industrial Collaboration. The emphasis here has been placed on pre-competitive R. & D. work, the only activity that is exempted *en bloc* from the EEC's competition policy. The incentives for firms to participate in these collective projects are twofold: first, to get a 'window' on emerging technologies, and second, to get access to R. & D. subsidies since most R. & D. projects are funded on the basis of a 50 per cent contribution from the EEC. The second aim is especially strong in the UK, where the Thatcher government has reduced its national R. & D. budget on the grounds that UK firms can get access to EEC funds; hence the latter is seen as a substitute for, rather than a complement to, national support. This may help to explain why GEC is represented in more projects than any other European firm.[14]

These programmes are the most explicitly designed to foster a stronger telecom supply industry within the Community. Two of the most important are ESPRIT (information technology) and

RACE (broadband communications). The latter is by far the most ambitious and, at around 1 billion ECU overall, the most expensive of the EEC's initiatives in telecommunications (apart from the STAR programme designed to promote telecom-related development in the less-favoured regions of the Community). The thrust of RACE, which began in 1986 and is scheduled to run at least until 1992, is 'to establish on the world market a strong, if not leading, position of the Community telecom manufacturing and service industries in broadband communications'.[15] In addition to this industrial policy goal, RACE aims to provide the Community with an integrated broadband communications network by 1995, a network that will be capable of handling very high speed communications, including high definition television (HDTV), neither of which can be accommodated on narrowband ISDN. In all 109 organizations have participated in the definition phase of RACE, drawn from the supply industry, the telecom administrations, the broadcasting industry, and academia. Forging co-operative linkages of this sort is critically important because RACE is far more 'systems-driven' than the EEC's other R. & D. projects.

However, RACE raises a number of troublesome issues. First, it is not at all clear if the requisite demand will materialize for broadband services, since many services will be accessible through narrowband ISDN. A greater involvement of the user community would have helped to overcome this problem. As it is, this 'chicken and egg' dilemma will probably mean that BT, which is more exposed to competition than its continental counterparts, will hold back until it can 'see the future' so to speak. This may explain why the UK manufacturers criticize BT for its lack of enthusiasm on RACE, which they ascribe to BT's new short-termism. Second, although an IBC network technically dissolves the distinction between telecoms and broadcasting, the national regulatory regimes are still quite separate, as though boundary erosion did not exist. The third issue, which applies to the R. & D. programmes in general, is this: to what extent is R. & D. at the heart of the supply industry's problems? The evidence suggests that Community firms' R. & D. spending per unit of output is comparable to that of their US and Japanese competitors. The major difference, however, is that the return on R. & D. investment is too low, partly because of a poor track record in commercializing the R. & D. effort.[16]

Market Opening. The three foregoing action lines are all pre-conditions for more liberalized markets, but they do not directly prise open the dozen national telecom markets in the Community. As a result the European Commission is now prepared to use the full force of its Treaty of Rome powers to ensure that regulatory barriers are removed in both equipment and service markets. Treaty of Rome obligations require the Commission to control the behaviour of any body, public or private, to which the member states give 'exclusive or special rights', a situation which abounds in the telecom market.[17] As regards equipment (which is divided into terminal and network segments) the regulatory conditions are very uneven, as Figure 8.1 shows for the terminal market. As we can see, all except the UK and France reserve the supply of the first telephone to the national telecom administration. This picture would have been more biased towards monopoly supply had the European Commission not intervened to prevent the Bundespost and others from trying to extend their monopoly to modems. Resorting to a rarely used power—Article 90 of the Treaty of Rome, which enables the Commission to force member states to comply with its directives—the Commission issued a directive in April 1988, obliging member states to open up their terminal equipment markets.

The network equipment market, covering public switching and transmission equipment, is a much larger market, accounting as it does for some 70 per cent of the Community's 17.5 billion ECUs telecom market. However, this is a far more intractable market to prise open than terminals, because national telecom administrations' procurement policies dominate the market, which makes the sector attractive as a conduit for industrial policy goals. But, as the European Commission never tires of repeating, the objective basis for 'national champion' policies here is fading fast, because a new digital public switching system requires 8 per cent of the world market to be viable, yet no single national market in the Community accounts for more than 6 per cent of the world market. Chauvinistic procurement policy led to five switching systems being developed in the Community, with a price per line ranging between $225 and $500, compared with $100 in the US. The European Commission estimates that with open tendering the European price would fall to around $150 and, with completely open markets, there would be space for just two switch manufacturers.[18]

The European Commission would like to see the supply industry

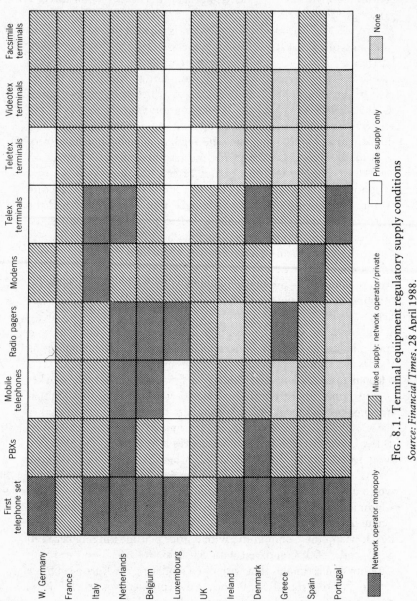

FIG. 8.1. Terminal equipment regulatory supply conditions
Source: Financial Times, 28 April 1988.

reorganize itself on a European basis, the main ingredient for which, it argues, is an open and transparent Europe-wide procurement policy. To this end it aims to launch a directive requiring member states to move towards fully open tendering by 1992. If this is indeed achieved we are likely to see a rash of new alliances and mergers in this industry, something that would already have occurred were it not for the market closure effects of regulatory barriers. Moves to open up this network equipment market will probably induce a battle royal between the Commission and member governments, or those governments that are concerned to have a national presence in this industry.

The opening up of the telecom services market will also be a formidably difficult task. Indeed it is already proving to be a highly contentious affair, partly because service provision is inextricably linked with social policy. The European Commission concedes that no natural or stable distinction can be made between basic services and value added services (VANS). Hence the relevant distinction, according to the Commission, should be between 'services for which exclusive provision by the telecom administrations continues to be acceptable for the time being ("reserved services") and all other services open to competition ("competitive services")'.[19]

As to what should be defined as a 'reserved service' the European Commission claimed that voice telephony was the only obvious candidate. Voice telephony still accounts for between 85 and 90 per cent of the Community's 63 billion ECU telecom services market, and the Commission had two reasons for reserving this service for monopoly provision. First, most member states are deeply opposed to any breaching of the public monopoly on voice telephony, with the major exception of the UK, where competition already exists in the shape of a duopoly. Second, the Commission itself is concerned to protect the financial viability of the telecom administrations, otherwise the large-scale investments needed for ISDN and IBC networks might not be forthcoming. These factors, potential opposition and operator viability, may also explain why the Green Paper did not demand a complete liberalization of two-way satellite services, which would have allowed for the bypassing of the public telephone network.

If private satellite facilities are anathema to the telecom administrations, the latter may well acquire a strong distaste for Open Network Provision (ONP), the Commission's key concept for opening up the services market. ONP is designed to allow both users and private operators access to the public network on reasonable terms and conditions (i.e. technical interfaces, usage conditions, and tariff principles). If the US experience with a comparable concept, Open Network Architecture, is any guide, ONP will provoke a new set of political conflicts in and around the network. In fact these strains have already begun to emerge: corporate users complain that they are being excluded from the ONP definition process, while potential competitors remain unconvinced about the efficacy of ONP as a regulatory concept, precisely the situation in the US.[20] It was to allay such fears that the Green Paper demanded a complete separation of the regulatory and operational functions of the telecom administrations, so that the latter were not both referee and player.

Finally, it is worth noting that the European Commission was realistic enough to appreciate that 'substantial differences will continue to exist between member states', but that these had to be accommodated.[21] In other words, convergence, not uniformity, was the goal. So despite the current diversity of national situations, the Commission took comfort from a number of convergent regulatory trends towards (1) opening of the terminal market to competition; (2) a competitive VANS market; (3) separation of regulatory and operational functions; (4) a more cost-based tariff structure; and (5) maintenance of exclusive rights for the provision of the network infrastructure, i.e. preserving the public monopoly for basic or 'reserved' services. European convergence on this fifth point shows that the UK path, of breaching the public monopoly on basic service, has been decisively rejected elsewhere in the Community. Other member states also show little appetite for privatizing their telecom administrations.

After the Green Paper: early reactions and skirmishes

The Community is still on the political foothills as regards the implementation of the European Commission's telecom strategy, a strategy which culminated with the Green Paper. Thus far, the official response has been mixed. At a crucial meeting of Community PTT Ministers, in June 1988, the broad thrust of the Green Paper was endorsed, but it proved impossible to reach a consensus on what services should be opened to competition. A majority group, led by France, resolved that a number of services, like voice telephony, telex, and public data communications, should be reserved for exclusive provision by the telecom administrations. This group was motivated by the desire to maintain some national control over the sector, and by a wish to be able to subsidize unprofitable but vital services in remote areas. The main opposition to France came from the UK, supported by Denmark and the Netherlands, which advocated competition in all services, including basic voice service. At bottom, this conflict is all about the French government attempting to pursue a closure strategy in which 'reserved services' are defined as broadly as possible.

The other main issue of contention is the Commission's use of Article 90 of the Treaty of Rome to liberalize the terminal equipment market. Article 90 gives the Commission the responsibility for ensuring that state undertakings comply with EEC competition policy; it 'shall, where necessary, address appropriate directives or decisions to member states'. This means bypassing the normal protracted process requiring legislation to be approved by the Council of Ministers and the European Parliament. The European Commission feels that it is justified in using this rather sweeping article, which has seldom been invoked, because any alternative would have been too time-consuming, given the imminence of 1992: direct action was 'necessary'. However, with the exception of the Netherlands, member states have objected to what they consider to be an 'authoritarian' procedure, and opposition to the Commission has been orchestrated by an unholy alliance composed of Britain, France, and Germany. France, for instance, has decided to take the Commission to the European Court of Justice over the use of Article 90, because it wishes to preserve the prerogative of the Council of Ministers in this sensitive field. However, the European Commission feels that it is on legally safe terrain, arguing that the terminal equipment problem falls directly under Article 90 and so it does not need Council approval for the directive—a position previously upheld by the Court of Justice in another case.

This issue, which has united the extremes in the Community's regulatory spectrum, is all about procedure and precedent; it has nothing to do with the substance of the Commission's telecom strategy. To avoid the substance of its policy being side-tracked by procedural issues the Commission felt obliged to make some small concessions. For example, it dropped a clause, contained in the original version of the Article 90 directive on terminals, which would have enforced the implementation of the directive a year after member states had issued their plans for opening this market. Whether such concessions will be enough to placate member states remains to be seen. Whatever happens, this will certainly not be the last skirmish between national governments and Brussels.

But the national versus the supra-national is not the only form of conflict involved here. In fact the European Commission itself seems to be divided over the implementation of the Green Paper. The directorates which are most intimately involved with these issues are DG IV (Competition Policy) and DG XIII (Telecommunications, Information Industries, and Innovation), and these seem to have somewhat different agendas. DG IV's primary aim is to ensure that the telecom market is fully subject to the pro-competitive powers of the Treaty of Rome. It sees no difference between telecoms and any other industry, and it therefore believes that competition can and should be applied to virtually every segment. In this view the overriding objective of the Green Paper is to open the telecom market so as to 'provide European users with a greater variety of telecommunications services, of better quality and at a lower cost'.[22] The main support for DG IV's position within the Community comes from the UK government and corporate user groups such as INTUG while, externally, the main body of support comes from the US government and US pressure groups, of which the most important is the US Council for International Business.

Although DG XIII does not officially dissociate itself from DG IV's view that European users ought to be the principal beneficiaries of the European Commission telecom strategy, it is concerned to promote the interests of the Community's equipment and services industry as well. DG XIII feels that it is important to accept the telecom administrations' monopoly in voice telephony, for instance. It also seems more inclined to accept that certain grey areas, like telex and public data communications, might likewise fall into the category of reserved services, at least for the time being. As the directorate responsible for telecommunications, DG XIII feels obliged to play an industrial policy role, hence its initiatives in the field of R. & D. collaboration.

It is also concerned that a rapid move towards open markets may well rebound to the benefit of US and Japanese firms, a view supported by member states like France and Germany. Privately it is worried by DG IV's apparent indifference to the need for an industrial policy other than exposure to the market. Not surprisingly, the telecom producer interest feels more affinity with DG XIII than DG IV. And, because the former tends to be the 'voice' of the telecom industry within the Commission, the dominant manufacturers look to DG XIII to protect their interests in the run up to 1992. DG XIII fervently believes in the need to create a 'European telecommunications space in order to ensure that the European actors will have fair access to a future European-wide telecom market'.[23] In DG XIII's scenario a strategy for the European telecom industry will have to be based primarily on developing the European market. The aim here is to provide these firms with a strong Community base from which to negotiate as equal partners in future collaborative deals with their US and Japanese counterparts. But is there a corporate basis for this quasi-political strategy?

The New Industrial Alliances: From National Champions to Global Actors?

Because of the special institutional features of telecommunications, which we outlined in Chapter 4, the telecom industry has been the most nationally based of all the electronics sectors. Although this is still true, the fact is that since the early 1980s telecom firms throughout the Community have been among the most active in terms of mergers and in searching out new alliances, the nature of which ranges from joint ventures to looser forms of licensing agreements and information sharing. Collaborative arrangements of this kind are also proliferating in the US, where they are said to constitute new ways in which international business is conducted, so much so that 'competition seems to be occurring less at the *firm* level, than at the *network* level, with a pivotal firm anchoring each network'.[24] Such activity is not of course confined to telecoms, though the European Commission finds a tendency for joint ventures and the like to be increasingly concentrated in high technology sectors.

The reasons for such alliances vary from deal to deal but, generally speaking, we can say that the main ones are often (1) to share the burden of development costs; (2) to reduce duplicated production facilities; (3) to penetrate new geographical markets; and (4) to gain access to new technology or new products in existing or adjacent markets. Thus the Alcatel–Thomson and GEC–Plessey mergers were mainly driven by a combination of (1) and (2), and these can be thought of as a form of defensive rationalization at the national level. However, the most significant merger to date at the supra-national level, CGE's take-over of ITT's telecom business, is a case in which all four factors played a part.

It is still too early to know whether, and to what extent, a supra-national European telecom industry will be established. While DG XIII struggles to play a midwifery role here, the firms themselves are caught between a European logic (i.e. tapping the potential of a Euro-wide market) and a global logic (i.e. pursuing world-wide markets). The European logic is attractive because the EEC provides a useful source of R. & D. subsidies and the Community is a potentially large market. But R. & D. projects count for nothing unless they are commercially exploited, and it is still premature to know if a supra-national European industry will grow out of an R. & D. cradle. What DG XIII found particularly disturbing was the fact that extra-European alliances tend to have outweighed intra-European alliances, as can be seen in Appendix 8.1.

What emerges from Appendix 8.1 is that the UK heads the Community league in terms of extra-European alliances, followed by France. However, what distinguishes the two is that the UK list appears to be more biased towards licensing deals, in which firms license foreign technology to develop it for the domestic UK market. GEC seems to be particularly prone to such alliances. Generally speaking, the intra-European alliances are biased towards R. & D. co-operation (ESPRIT, RACE, etc.), while extra-European alliances, with US and Japanese firms, are biased towards actual products. To this extent they may be said to be compatible with each other. But, over time, this imbalance could lead to the Europeans becoming the weaker partner unless they can exploit their R. & D. results in the market. Thus if the aim is to break into the US or Japanese markets, or gain immediate access to technology in commercialized form, a supra-national European alliance is not a surrogate for an alliance with US or Japanese partners.[25]

At the commercial level the major European telecom firms seem to have been loath to co-operate with one another, and this is partly due to the fact that their (traditional) product lines are similar and competitive rather different and complementary. They thus perceive each other as *hostile* brothers. This may help to explain why some of the most significant telecom alliances have been struck between

European and North American firms, e.g. Philips and AT&T, STC and Northern Telecom, and Siemens and GTE. Admittedly, Philips did try to interest Ericsson first, with whom it had collaborated in the past, but the latter spurned the offer, which proves the point being made here. However, this may be changing if the GEC-Siemens bid for Plessey is any indication.

AT&T and Northern Telecom, the two most dominant firms in the US, have recently turned their focus to Europe and, given their size and their knowledge of more feature-rich networks, they will be formidable long-term competitors in Europe. Of the two AT&T is further along with its European strategy, the linchpin of which was the 50:50 joint venture with Philips, signed in 1983. Thus far however the alliance has disappointed both sides, with the result that AT&T has increased its equity stake to 60 per cent, giving it full control. The initial rationale for this alliance was to marry AT&T's technology with Philips's marketing and political networks in Europe. However, there were two problems with this rationale. First, although Philips transferred most of its public telecom business into the joint venture, its French and German segments remained with the Dutch group's local subsidiaries, TRT and Te Ka De respectively. Second, AT&T did not sufficiently appreciate the extent to which Europe's telecom market was balkanized along national lines, which meant that one alliance was not enough. Indeed, this is precisely what led AT&T to bid, unsuccessfully, for CGCT of France. Bloodied, but undeterred, AT&T is now making overtures to other European firms, and in 1989 it struck a very important joint venture agreement with Italtel, the flagship of the Italian telecom industry.

North American and Japanese firms are busily positioning themselves to make greater inroads into the emerging single European market, and this is a radically new variable for the indigenous firms. What is disturbing from the European view is the asymmetry in global or inter-continental competition. This lies in the fact that few, if any, European firms have made much headway in Japan, where domestic suppliers have maintained the lion's share of the market despite the liberalization of the regime and the privatization of NTT. Even in the US, where regulatory barriers to entry appear to be the lowest in the world, only one Community firm, Siemens, has made much of an impression.[26]

Siemens, the largest of the Community's telecom firms after

Alcatel, considers itself a global rather than a European player, and the fact that it has made the biggest commitment to the US is the surest sign of this global ambition. Although most formal regulatory barriers are low in the US, the competitive barriers to entry are among the most formidable in the world. In addition to which the cost of adjusting to US network standards and specifications for digital public switches involves European firms in some 20–30 per cent of additional development expenditure, i.e. between $200 million and $300 million.[27] However, Siemens is fully prepared to incur these entry costs and more because the US market is not only the largest in the world but, equally significant, the most advanced. Siemens feels that exposure to the US market, where networks are more feature-rich than in Europe, gives it an earlier opportunity to meet sophisticated customer needs, and this expertise can then be applied to other markets, including Europe.

This was part of the reasoning which led Siemens, in May 1988, to transfer its entire ISDN terminal development operation to the US. Having a major base in the US was deemed essential because 'the beach is littered with the bones of overseas manufacturers who have attempted to penetrate the US market from manufacturing facilities located overseas'.[28] Sophisticated telecom equipment, like digital public switches and PABXs, is software-intensive and needs to be constantly updated or enhanced, hence these markets depend on close user–supplier relations. This is the reason why a home-based export strategy, with its arm's length relationship, is completely inappropriate in such markets.[29] That Siemens is able to mount a more ambitious US strategy than its British counterpart, GPT, is not just due to its longer-term operating horizon. It is also helped by the fact that it can charge the Bundespost between $450 and $500 per electronic exchange line, which is reported to be twice as much as GPT gets from BT.[30]

Within Europe itself regulatory uncertainty is compounded by a new composition of the telecom market. For example, public switching equipment, for long the flagship in the telecom product line, is declining relative to fast-growing segments like mobile communications equipment (cellular radio) and data communications equipment.[31] However, the great hope of the traditional public switching firms, especially in France and the FRG, is that ISDN will revamp the public telecom market. But much depends on the manner in which ISDN is implemented.

Two scenarios are possible here, based on whether the 'intelligence' (i.e. the software) is located in the public network or in customer premises equipment (PABXs, smart terminals, etc.). If the first, then the most important customer will be the network operator, the PTT, and the market would tend to consist of a limited range of standardized products, thus favouring a small number of large firms. Not surprisingly, this is the option favoured by the dominant suppliers and classical PTTs. On the other hand, if the 'intelligence' is placed in customer premises equipment, then the market will be biased towards private terminal users. This would be a more varied market with more scope for new, and not necessarily large, suppliers. The choice of location is essentially a political not a technical decision, depending on the role which the PTT is expected to play in the economy.[32]

However, if ISDN is to take off it will have to be service-driven, rather than technology-driven, otherwise large corporate users, the PTTs' major revenue base, will boycott it in favour of their in-house private networks. In an attempt to hold on to these large customers Europe's PTTs are desperately trying to offer a new generation of enhanced business services (e.g. Centrex, Freephone 800 services, and a variety of intelligent database services). These were first developed in the US and AT&T and Northern Telecom were the first switch vendors to offer them in Europe, with BT and Mercury being the first European operators to use them. The dilemma for the continental PTTs is whether to wait for their traditional suppliers to develop these enhanced service capabilities, or to buy the readily available product from the North American suppliers.

The dilemma for the traditional telecom suppliers stems from the fact that the 'intelligent' equipment, on which these enhanced services are based, depends increasingly on smart database technology, and this lies not in the telecom industry but in the data processing industry, with the likes of IBM and DEC. This means that Alcatel, Siemens, and GPT will either have to develop this in-house, which seems unlikely, or enter into alliances with the data processing community.

Because public telecom equipment markets are no longer the growth markets they were, overcrowding will undoubtedly lead to further mergers and alliances in Europe. To offset this problem the European firms are now trying to exploit new growth markets, like mobile communications equipment. As we have seen, the main stimulus here is the European Commission's pan-European mobile communications project. However, the main expertise in this area lies with Ericsson of Sweden and Motorola of the US, and these firms are likely to form the poles around which Community firms will coalesce. As well as trying to exploit new equipment markets the European firms are now turning their attention to the fast-growing service side of telecoms, yet another example of what we have referred to as boundary erosion. Indeed, the network already generates much more money than the equipment bought to run it, and the gap appears to be widening.[33] Herein lies a powerful incentive for traditional 'hardware' suppliers to diversify into the service side of the business. Although these plans are still in their early stages, they are clear enough. CGE, for example, is already planning to diversify into cable TV, publishing, and broadcasting in an effort to turn 'media services', as it calls them, into a third principal sector alongside its traditional telecom and engineering activities. GPT now sees its main opportunities in Europe lying, not with System X, but in derived services or evolved networks, i.e. mobile communications services and VANS. Both CGE and GPT are opting for alliances with firms that have some experience in these fields, thereby avoiding the need to build up expertise from scratch. This signals a new trend towards the verticalization of the telecommunications market.

Finally, we must not forget the PTTs themselves, because these too are beginning to forge new collaborative alliances. Since it is a private company, BT is obviously under more pressure to forge new links in equipment and services markets, as we saw in Chapter 5. However, one of the main fears of the European PTTs, BT included, is that the explosive growth of corporate data communications in Europe will be captured in the main by US computer services companies, like IBM, DEC, EDS and Geisco. Hence a battle for the European data communications market has commenced between these two rival groups. The main PTT response, organized under the auspices of CEPT, has been a radical proposal to develop a Managed Data Network Services (MDNS) project. MDNS is essentially a package of services, ranging from 'one-stop shopping' for data communications services to sophisticated network management capabilities, to be offered on a pan-European basis. Theoretically this would allow multinational customers to order and pay for all their data requirements at a single point, rather than dealing with a plethora of organizations as at present. Their goal is to make MDNS as universal as the telephone service.

However, some PTTs favour setting up a separate and collectively owned company for this purpose, while others want to market MDNS in their respective countries. Time-consuming wrangles of this kind have been compounded by the fact that some PTTs have already struck separate commercial deals with the 'enemy', like the DGT's agreement with Computer Science Corporation of the US, and Telefonica's deal with EDS, also of the US. If the PTTs are to stand any chance in this extremely important market they will have to shed some of the weight of the past because, in regulatory, operational, and skill terms, their traditional mission renders them ill equipped to compete with the US computer firms.

Telecoms and Trade: Europe versus the US

The prospect of a trade war in telecoms seemed unlikely a decade ago because most national markets were insulated against foreign competition and international trade accounted for a small share of total output. However, in an attempt to rectify the negative trade effects of deregulation and divestiture, the US has adopted a much more aggressive stance towards its trading partners, so much so that the Community has found itself responding to initiatives and events outside its control. In a somewhat frenetic fashion, the US has gone on to the offensive at three different political levels, each of which deserves some attention:

1. At the domestic level the US has drawn up its most assertive trade legislation since the Second World War, in the form of the Omnibus Trade and Competitiveness Act of 1988. This legislation requires the Administration to identify 'unfair practices', especially in the telecom field, and calls on it to negotiate these away under the threat of sanctions. On top of this the FCC is trying to mobilize domestic support for an 'international model', which would establish the US regulatory situation as a bench-mark for determining the degree to which foreign markets were open; the implication being that companies from 'violating' countries would be denied access to the US market.[34]

2. At the international level the US government, in close collaboration with US multinationals, has done its utmost to get telecoms,

especially telecom services, subjected to the General Agreement on Tariffs and Trade (GATT). However, this is an exceedingly difficult task because GATT has not embraced telecoms until now, at least not in any definitive way. Furthermore, the global rules and regulations for telecoms are normally set by the International Telecommunications Union (ITU), a forum dominated by PTTs. The US, supported by the UK, is opposed to what it sees as the pro-regulatory bias of the ITU and it would therefore like to transfer as much regulatory power as possible from the ITU to the GATT.[35]

3. Because multilateral negotiations are so labyrinthine and time-consuming, the US has tried to secure its objectives by a quicker route, namely, bilateral deals. Most of these have taken the form of Market Access Fact Finding (MAFF) talks, targeted at countries which the US considers to have the least liberal telecom regimes. Not surprisingly, the first country which the US pressured into holding MAFF talks was Germany. These talks, held in 1985, revolved around the US charge that (a) the Bundespost was unduly restrictive in the range of equipment which it allowed to be connected to the public network; (b) it discriminated against non-German equipment suppliers; and (c) its tariffs, particularly those for private leased lines, were politically determined and bore little relation to cost. The US followed this up with MAFF talks with France, Spain, and Italy in 1986. In contrast, the US sees Britain as its main ally in Europe, and these two countries signed a bilateral deal in 1988 which liberalized international value added network services between the US and the UK.

The European Commission is deeply concerned about these US initiatives, particularly (1) and (3) above, because it sees them as steps towards protectionism and international bilateralism. In an attempt to assert its own voice in the trade arena the Commission has already cautioned individual member states against engaging in bilateral MAFF talks with the US, arguing that such negotiations should be handled at the Community level.

However, it is the new US trade legislation with which the Commission is most concerned. The Commission objects most strenuously to those aspects of the legislation which would allow the US to (1) unilaterally reinterpret international trade agreements, such as retaliation against trading partners for so called 'unfair practices'; and (2) demand equal access for US telecom firms, a provision which the Commission says replaces the GATT principle of overall trade reciprocity with sectoral reciprocity in areas like telecoms.

In the Commission's view the US is misdirected in assailing the Community on the telecom trade issue because 'it is a myth that US deregulation has led to an invasion of the US market by European telecom products'.[36] In fact the Commission has gone to great lengths to emphasize that the Community's share of US imports has been on a declining trend. In 1984, for example, the Community share of US telecom imports was 3.6 per cent, compared to a 51 per cent share for Japan, an 11.3 per cent share for Taiwan, and a 7.3 per cent share for Hong Kong. On top of this the US has enjoyed a steadily increasing telecom trade surplus with the Community during the 1990s, a surplus that would be larger still if computer equipment were added to the picture, and the Commission argues that it should be included given the convergence between the two sectors. Thus the Commission's response has been to argue that the US is firing indiscriminately at all its trading partners when, in reality, the source of the US trade problem is the Pacific Basin.

The Commission has also gone on to the attack in charging that the US telecom market is not as open as it appears. As we saw earlier, the substance of this charge lies in the fact that the task of complying with US standards for network equipment (switching and transmission) is 'burdensome, onerous and long'.[37] Further barriers to entry in the US stem from the fact that some major network operators, like AT&T and GTE, actually manufacture their own equipment, and such vertical integration, which does not exist in the Community, is a far cry from an open market.

These rival claims will most certainly intensify in the run up to the single internal market in 1992. Indeed, '1992' constitutes an issue in itself. Here the US is deeply worried that the elimination of the Community's internal barriers will induce a form of 'single-market protectionism'.[38] This is a legitimate fear because even though the Commission publicly disavows any connection between 1992 and a 'Fortress Europe' approach, the Community is itself wracked by internal divisions with respect to its external trade policy. Some member states (like the UK) are committed to a liberal external trade policy, while others (like France) fear that such a stance will rebound to the benefit of non-Community firms. Although it is still too soon to know the shape of the Community's external trade policy, the majority view in the Commission seems to be that entry to a barrier-free Community market should be used as a negotiating lever to extract reciprocal trade concessions from third country partners.

An indication of the possible shape of things to come on the trade front was the hard-line stance which the Commission adopted in its directive on public procurement. The two main features of the directive, issued in October 1988, are (1) that 70 per cent of public procurement contracts must be open to competitive tender by 1990 and 100 per cent open from 1992 onwards; and (2) that telecom administrations can reject any bid if the value of at least half the products and services comes from outside the Community. Even if a bid meets the 50 per cent requirement, the directive states, bids by European companies shall be preferred as long as they are deemed to be equivalent. Exceptions for external trading partners would depend on whether satisfactory reciprocal agreements could be reached. The idea behind the directive is to try to break down internal Community trade barriers without exposing European producers to too much external competition. The passage of a tough US trade bill, which Community officials see as protectionist, helped to sway the Commission into taking a hard-line stance here. This directive indicates that a degree of closure is being imposed within the more general trend towards liberalization.

Clearly, the conflicts over trade in telecoms have only just begun, particularly in the field of telecom services, where there are as yet no internationally agreed rules and regulations. Unless multilateral agreement is reached then the future may well see a proliferation of bilateral deals between like-minded countries, such as that between the US and the UK in international VANS. Indeed, this pact shows the UK to be politically more attuned to the US than to its Community 'partners'. Such divisions will need to be resolved before the Community can genuinely speak with one voice on the future regulation of telecommunications.

Appendix 8.1

Inter-company Co-operation by European Telecommunications Companies since 1980

The following information is divided into two tables. The first details intra-European agreements. The second covers agreements and important contacts in telecommunications and related sectors between European firms and third country partners. Agreements concluded since the beginning of 1986 are marked with an asterisk to distinguish them from older agreements.

TABLE 8.1 *Intra-European co-operation agreements in the telecommunications industry*

Firm	Firm	Nature of agreement
CGE SGB	→ ITT	*CGE of France takes over European and overseas telecom activities of ITT. CGE incorporates its own and ITT's former telecom operations in Alcatel NV, creating Europe's biggest telecom firm in co-operation with the Société Générale de Belgique.
Philips (NL) Telefonica (SP) British Aerospace (UK) Olivetti (I) Bull (F) Brown-Boveri (CH) Saab Scania (S)	→ European Silicon Structures (ES2)	*Seven major European IT firms to co-operate in venture to produce custom-built integrated circuits for the European market
CIT-Alcatel (F)	↔ Philips (NL)	Co-operation in research and manufacturing in cellular radio-telephone
CIT-Alcatel (F)	→ Olivetti (I)	Shareholding of 10% (office equipment)
CIT-Alcatel (F)	↔ Siemens/Italtel/ Plessey	Agreement to make components and subsystems for digital exchanges

TABLE 8.1 (*continued*)

Firm	Firm	Nature of agreement
CIT-Alcatel (F)	↔ Sel (D)	Co-operation in Franco-German cellular radio consortium (with AEG)
Matra (F)	↔ British Aerospace	Co-operation in satellites
Matra (F)	↔ Bosch (D)	Negotiations on co-operation in mobile telephones
Matra-Harris (F)	↔ SGS (I)	Agreement on R. & D. and production of integrated circuits
Bull (F)	↔ Siemens (D) ↔ ICL (UK)	Foundation of a joint research institute in Germany (1984) in the field of information technology/art. intell./computer techn.
Thomson (F)	↔ Philips (NL)	Joint development of common standard for a direct broadcasting system
CGE (F)	↔ Philips (NL)	Negotiations on microwave systems production, incl. possible take-over by CGE of Philips subsidiary TRT
Jeumont-Schneider (F)	↔ Telettra (FIAT) (I)	Link-up in PABX
CGE (Thomson) (F)	↔ GEC (UK)	*Letter of intent on joint development of customs chips
Thomson (F)	↔ SGS (I)	*Merger of semiconductor activities
CGCT (F)	↔ Hermes (CH) (Olivetti group)	*Agreement on joint development of Teletext equipment
CGCT (F)	← Ericsson (S)	*Ericsson, associated with Matra, gains control of CGCT
Matra (F)	↔ Nokia-Mobira (SF)	*Joint venture on mobile phones
Philips (NL)	→ Grundig (FRG)	Take-over
Philips (NL)	↔ Siemens (FRG)	Joint R. & D. on semiconductors, CAD, and speech recognition (long term)
Philips (NL)	↔ Bull (F)	Joint manufacturing of memory cards
Bosch/ANT (D)	↔ Telettra (I) (Fiat) Matra (F) Ericsson (S)	*Co-operation in developing digital cellular radio systems
Bosch (D)	↔ Philips (NL)	*Co-operation in production of TV studio equipment

Tᴀʙʟᴇ 8.1   *(continued)*

Firm	Firm	Nature of agreement
Telenorma (D) (Bosch group)	↔ Jeumont-Schneider (F)	*Co-operation on R. & D., marketing, and export of private telephone equipment
SEL (D)	→ REL (I)	*VCR production in Italy through new joint subsidiary Vidital
Plessey-Office systems (UK)	→ Telenokia (Fin)	Supply of digital phone technology
Plessey (UK)	→ Olivetti (I)	Licence of PABX
Italtel (I)	↔ Sesa (F)	Joint venture in private packet switching networks
Italtel (I)	↔ CIT-Alcatel (F)	Joint venture in videotext
Stet (I)	↔ Ericsson (S)	Negotiations on co-operation in telecom and space communications
Olivetti (I)	→ Logabax (F)	*Take-over by Olivetti
Olivetti (I)	↔ Bull (F)	*Agreement to develop automatic bank tellers and cash dispensers
Olivetti (I)	→ Triumph-Adler(D)	*Take-over by Olivetti
Olivetti (I)	→ Pelikan (CH)	*Olivetti takes minority stake in Swiss Office equipment group
Olivetti (I)	→ Dafsa (F)	De Benedetti group (through CERUS) gains control of French firm
Ericsson (S)	→ Hassler (CH)	Building under licence of digital switching system
Ericsson (S)	→ Intelsa (E)	*Ericsson takes over Telefonica stake in Intelsa
Ericsson (S)	↔ Siemens (D)	*Co-operation in developing cellular radio
Acec (B)	← Soc. Gén. (B)/CGE (F)	Société Gén. and CGE buy out Westinghouse stake in ACEC

TABLE 8.2   *Co-operation agreement in the telecommunications industry between European firms and Non-EEC Partners*

European firm	American/Japanese firm	Nature of agreement
1. The Netherlands		
Philips	↔ AT&T (USA)	Joint venture in development and marketing of switching of exchanges outside the US
Philips	↔ Control Data (USA)	Joint production of digital optical recorders
Philips	↔ Intel (USA)	Technology exchange (semiconductors)
Philips	← Concord Data Systems (USA)	Licence of local area network technology
Philips	↔ Du Pont (USA)	*Agreement to co-operate in optical disks
PTT	↔ Western Union (USA)	*Link to offer transatlantic telemessage service
2. France		
CIT-Alcatel	← Corning Glass (USA)	Production under licence of optical fibres
Thomson	↔ Xerox (USA)	Joint corporation (Fortune Systems Corp.) for digital optical disks
Thomson	↔ Hughes (USA)	Joint efforts in satellites
Thomson	↔ DEC (USA)	Agreement to develop office communications systems using Thomson PABX
Thomson/Saint Gobain	↔ Corning Glass (USA)	Joint factory in France (Fibres Optiques Industries; 40% owned by Corning)
CIT-Alcatel (Telic)	→ Sonitrol (USA)	Purchase of 20% stake to increase presence in the US market (distribution)
CIT-Alcatel	→ Honeywell (USA)	Marketing of videotext system
Matra	↔ Tymshare (USA)	Joint efforts in videotext
Matra	↔ Boeing Aerospace Company (USA)	Production and commercialization of small satellites
Pechiney	← Mitsui (Jap.)	Negotiations on licensing agreement to use Mitsui technology to make printed circuits in France

TABLE 8.2 *(continued)*

European firm	American/Japanese firm	Nature of agreement
Câbles de Lyon (CGE group)	→ Celwave technologies (USA)	Take-over by French firm
Sem/Metra/Paribas	← IBM (USA)	*Draft agreement to co-operate on providing VANS in France
Bull	← GE (USA)	*Idem
CGE (Thomson)	→ GTE (USA)	*Successful joint bid to sell RITA military communications system to US Defense Dept.
CGE	→ United Technologies (USA)	*CGE (Thomson) takes over advanced chip-making operations of US subsidiary Mostek
CGE	→ Lynch Communications Systems (USA)	*CGE acquires majority control and combines with Celwave (see above)
Alcatel	↔ Wang (USA)	*Negotiations for joint initiative to penetrate UK Telecom Market
Bull	→ Honeywell (USA) NEC (Jap.)	*Joint venture on information systems
Thomson (CGE group)	→ Comark communications (USA)	*Acquisition of US company
3. Belgium		
RTT	↔ MCI (USA)	Agreement on transatlantic electronic mail service and transit rights through Belgium for MCI
Coditel	→ Cellular Corp. (USA)	*Belgian firm takes 6% stake in cellular telephone operation
4. United Kingdom		
Ferranti	↔ GTE (USA)	Joint venture: manufacture and sales of subscriber telephone equipment for UK
GEC	↔ Mitsubishi (Jap.)	Marketing of satellite earth stations
GEC	← Norther Tel. (Can.)	Production under licence of large PABX
GEC-Marconi	← NEC (Jap.)	Production under licence of radio telephone equipment
Plessey	→ Stromberg-Carlson (Un. Tech.) (USA)	Acquisition (£33 million)

TABLE 8.2 (*continued*)

European firm	American/Japanese firm	Nature of agreement
Plessey	→ Sc. Atlanta (USA)	12% purchase (satellite and cable)
Plessey	↔ Corning Glass (US)	Co-operation in fibre optics
British Cable	↔ Corning Glass (USA)	Joint fibre production plant in Wales
BT	↔ IBM (USA)	Joint manufacturing (in UK) of cashless shopping systems
BT BT	→ Mitel (Can.) ⎤ → CGT (Can.) ⎦	*BT has acquired controlling stake in each firm
BT	→ AT&T (USA) KDD (Jap.)	*Letter of intent for international high speed data transmission system
BT	↔ Macdonnell-Douglas (USA)	*Agreement to co-operate on developing business communications systems
BT	↔ Dupont (USA)	*Joint venture in opto-electronics
Reuters	→ Instinet (USA) ⎤ Rich (USA) ⎦	*Reuters acquires interests in two electronic financial/Business data suppliers
Reuters	→ I. P. Sharp Associates (Can.)	*Reuters acquires control of Canadian computing services company
BT + Cable & Wireless	→ Teleglobe (Can.)	*Each UK firm has submitted a bid for a stake in Canada's state-run telecom utility which is being privatized. ITT of the US is another bidder
BT	→ ITT (USA)	*BT signed letter of intent to acquire Dialcom, ITT's electronic mail unit
Cable & Wireless	↔ Pacific Telesis (USA) General Motors (USA) Toyota (Jap.) C. Itoh (Jap.)	*Planned joint venture to offer int. telecom services
Cable & Wireless	↔ Nynex (USA)	*Agreement on optic-cable joint venture
BT	→ Mitsui (Jap.)	*Mitsui to market BT city business systems in Japan

TABLE 8.2 *(continued)*

European firm	American/Japanese firm	Nature of agreement
Air Call	← Bellsouth (USA)	*Bellsouth acquires UK radio comm. firms
Plessey	↔ Burroughs (USA)	*Links to develop Telecom/Computer Interface
Plessey	↔ Westinghouse (USA)	*Joint venture on military early warning radar system
ICL	↔ Geisco (USA)	*Joint venture on business information services
STC	← Norther Telecom (Can.)	*28% acquisition
5. Germany		
AEG	↔ Mostek (USA)	Joint venture electr. components
Siemens	→ Gould (USA)	Purchase of distribution and control division
Siemens	↔ Xerox (USA)	Co-operation in PABX
Siemens	↔ Corning Glass (US)	Joint venture (Siecor) in US and Germany
Siemens	↔ Toshiba (Jap.)	Co-operation in production of integrated circuits
Wacker Chemitronic	← Sumitomo (Jap.)	Licensing and patent deal to use Japanese fibre optic technology
Siemens	↔ GTE (USA)	*Joint venture to develop switches and to improve Siemens's access to US common carrier market
Siemens	→ Siemens-Allis (USA)	*Siemens buys outstanding 12% in former joint venture from Allis-Chalmers
Siemens	→ Potter-Brumfield (USA)	*Siemens buys USA relay maker
SEL	↔ Hewlett Packard (USA)	*Co-operation on the integration of computers and peripherals
Siemens	→ Telecom Plus (USA)	*Siemens raises stake from 35% to 100%
Siemens	↔ IBM (USA)	*Co-operation in ISDN
6. Italy		
Olivetti	← AT&T (USA)	Minimal acquisition of 25%

TABLE 8.2 (*continued*)

European firm	American/Japanese firm	Nature of agreement
Olivetti	→ Toshiba (Jap.)	Olivetti sells 20% of Jap. subsidiary to Toshiba
Olivetti	→ Xerox (US)	Marketing agreement where Xerox sells Olivetti PCs in US
Olivetti	→ Allen-Bradley (USA)	Agreement to market Olivetti automated production systems in US
Pirelli	← Corning Glass (USA)	Licence in fibre optics
SGS	↔ AT&T (USA)	*Agreement to co-produce bipolar integrated circuits
FIAT	↔ IBM (USA)	*Negotiations on possible co-operation on VANS in Italy
FIAT	↔ IBM (USA)	*Creation of joint subsidiary Intesa, offering communications network for stock control
Olivetti	← Canon (Jap.)	*Agreement on developing photocopies, fax machines
Olivetti + Stet	↔ Microsoft (USA)	*Joint venture on development, manufacturing, marketing of optical disks in Europe
7. Spain		
CTNE (Telefonica)	← AT&T (USA)	*Agreement on semiconductor production in Spain
CTNE	↔ Fujitsu (Jap.)	*Agreement to co-operate on telematics production. Creation of joint subsidiary
CTNE	↔ Pacific Telesis (USA)	*Agreement to design, build, and co-manage CTNE R. & D. centre in Madrid

Source: European Commission.

Notes

1. Commission of the European Communities, *Communication from The Commission to the Council on Telecommunications*, Com (84) 277 (Brussels: CEC, 1984), p. 9.

2. Paolo Cecchini, *The European Challenge: 1992* (Aldershot: Wildwood House, 1988).

3. Cecchini, *The European Challenge*, p. xx.

4. The 'Round Table' of twelve information technology firms is not to be confused with the wider-ranging Roundtable of European Industrialists.

5. Gareth Locksley, '1992, the European Commission and Strategies for Telecommunications', Paper presented at MIT Conference on World Telecommunications, June 1988.

6. Commission of the European Communities, *Towards a Competitive Community-Wide Telecom Market in 1992*, Com (88) 48 (Brussels: CEC, 1988).

7. Commission of the European Communities, *Completing The Internal Market* (Brussels: CEC, 1986).

8. Commission of the European Communities, *Towards A Dynamic European Economy*, Green Paper on the Development of the Common Market for Telecommunications Services and Equipment, DG XIII/ 195 (87) Draft Version.

9. Ibid., 10.

10. European Parliament, *Report of the European Parliament on Telecommunications in the Community*, Doc. 1–477/3 (1984).

11. One of the great unknowns is the level of demand for ISDN offerings. Much, however, will depend on the tariff structure.

12. Commission of the European Communities, *On the Coordinated Introduction of ISDN in the European Community*, Com (86) 205 (Brussels: CEC, 1986), p. 7.

13. Transborder Data Reporting Service, *Confidential Monthly Memo* (Oct. 1987).

14. Rob Van Tulder and Gerd Junne, *European Multinationals in Core Technologies* (Chichester: Wiley, 1988).

15. Commission of the European Communities, *Report of the Commission to the Council on R&D Requirements in Telecommunications Technologies as Contribution to the Preparation of the R&D programme RACE*, Com (85) 145 (Brussels: CEC, 1985).

16. Henry Ergas, 'Exploding the Myth About What's Wrong', *Financial Times*, 26 June 1985.

17. Peter Sutherland, Commissioner for Competition Policy, 'The Commission's Responsibility for Fair and Open Competition in European

Telecommunications', *Eurostrategies Telecommunications Forum* (Brussels, 25 Feb. 1988).

18. Cecchini, *The European Challenge*.

19. *Towards a Dynamic European Economy* (Green Paper), p. 65.

20. Denis Gilhooly, 'Unlocking The Network', *Communications Week International* (July 1988), p. 4.

21. *Towards a Dynamic European Economy* (Green Paper), p. 15.

22. Sutherland, 'The Commission's Responsibility', p. 10.

23. Hubert Ungerer, 'The European Community's Telecommunications Policy: A Global Approach', in N. Garnham (ed.), *Telecommunications: National Policies in an International Context* (Communications Policy Research Conference, Windsor, 1986), pp. 171–85.

24. David Teece, 'Joint Ventures and Collaborative Arrangements in the Telecommunications Equipment Industry', in David Mowery (ed.), *International Collaborative Ventures in US Manufacturing* (Cambridge, Mass.: Ballinger, 1988).

25. Van Tulder and Junne, *European Multinationals*.

26. Ericsson, a non-Community firm, is also making a determined effort to break into the US market, as is Alcatel, but neither of them have had the same degree of success as Siemens. GPT also has a presence in the US, in the shape of a subsidiary, Stromberg-Carlson, but this has a niche strategy, selling not System X, but a small switch developed by Stromberg.

27. Commission of the European Communities, *Telecommunications in the US: Report of the EC Fact-Finding Mission, 16–27 June 1986* (Brussels: CEC, 1987).

28. 'Siemens Moves ISDN Unit To US', *Communications Week*, 30 May 1988.

29. Kevin Morgan and Andrew Sayer, *Microcircuits of Capital: 'Sunrise' Industry and Uneven Development* (Cambridge: Polity Press, 1988).

30. McKinsey & Co Inc., *Performance and Competitive Success: Strengthening Competitiveness in UK Electronics*, report prepared for the National Economic Development Council's Electronics Industry Sector Group (London: NEDC, 1988).

31. 'End of an Era as Public Switching Faces Decline', *Communications Systems Worldwide* (Sept. 1987), pp. 75–83.

32. Ann Reid, *The ISDN: A Presentation of Related Policy Issues* (Paris: OECD, 1986).

33. *Communications Systems Worldwide*.

34. K. Morgan and D. Pitt, 'America Against Itself: Re-regulating Telecommunications in the US', Berkeley Roundtable on the International Economy Monograph, University of California (Berkeley, 1989).

35. The battle over the future regulation of international telecoms was

expected to come to a head at the ITU's World Administrative Telephone and Telegraph Conference (WATTC) in Nov. 1988. See D. Gilhooly, 'WATTC 88—Keeping the Luddites at Bay', *Telecommunications* (International Edition) (Jan. 1988), p. 9.

36. M. Carpentier, 'The Inter-Relationship Between Telecom Policy Reform and International Trade Policy: An EEC View', Address to the *Financial Times* World Telecom Conference, London, 1 Dec. 1987.

37. Commission of the European Communities, *Telecommunications in the US*.

38. S. Fleming, 'US Warns EC On Single-Market Protectionism', *Financial Times*, 5 Aug. 1988.

9

Consumer Electronics:
Politics, Technologies, and Markets

Introduction

The major difference between the consumer electronics industry, and that of telecommunications which has been analysed in the last five chapters, is in the extent of regulation and government intervention in equipment supply and service provision. The final consumers of the products of the industry are households and not monopoly organizations, and, with the exception of France, national governments have not singled out the consumer electronics industry as a means of achieving their industrial policy goals. These factors have led to power in the market-place as the major determinant of outcomes. The story of European consumer electronics from the 1960s is one of successful *usurpation* of the market position of the European firms by Japanese firms. The Japanese firms' strategies have been centred around improvements in manufacturing processes and product quality, perfected against a large home market and successful exports to the US, coupled with aggressive bids for market share. European firms have adopted a variety of responses. Some have simply rolled over, whereas others have sought to match Japanese best practice. Almost all, alone, in combination with other firms, and through industry associations, have lobbied vociferously for trade policies which are intended to blunt the competitive edge of the Japanese. A major feature of the 1970s and 1980s has been a shift in the determination of these policies from national capitals to Brussels. Protectionist pressures have forced the location of a large number of Japanese and some Korean plants in the EEC, and these are beginning to emerge as important actors in the *European* industry.

The result of these processes of usurpation and counter-strategies of closure has been a major series of changes in the structure of the industry, and the emergence of three major multinational groups. The relentless pace of innovation dictated by the Japanese electronics companies has ensured that the present structure is unlikely to be a stable one. Firm strategies, in consumer electronics as in telecoms, have increasingly featured alliances and joint ventures, promoted actively amongst European firms by the European Commission. Government–industry relations have been dominated by bilateral links between major firms and national governments and the EEC, with trade associations playing a relatively minor role, largely as 'cover' for the self-interest of the dominant European producers, Philips and Thomson.

This chapter serves as an introduction to the industry, its products and the main technological trends. The three country chapters which follow trace the shift of government–industry relations from the national level to the international level: European and global. They serve to document the process referred to above, whereby the national specificities of the industry have become blurred through a process of internationalization at firm level, and also at the level of the determination of public policy. In Chapter 13 this process is analysed in terms of the pattern of technological change in the industry, which reinforces the trends set in motion by the adjustment of European firms to competition in the present generation of products.

The Industry and the Major Firms

The consumer electronics industry produces a range of audio-visual equipment (often referred to as 'brown goods' to distinguish them from household electrical appliances—'white goods'). The principal products manufactured by the European industry are colour televisions (CTVs), car radios and tape players, hi-fi equipment, video cassette recorders (VCRs), and recently compact disc players (CDs). Less significant products are radios, tape recorders, electronic watches, and TV games.

The growth of the consumer electronics industry in the Far East, initially in Japan but later in Korea, Taiwan, Hong Kong, and elsewhere, initiated a period of fierce competition which led European manufacturers to retreat from the production of low-cost items such as transistor radios, tape recorders, and monochrome TVs.

It can be seen from Table 9.1, which compares the major items produced in Britain, France, and West Germany, that CTV

TABLE 9.1 *Consumer electronics production in Britain, France and West Germany 1985 ($M.)*

	Britain	France	West Germany
Colour television	629	500	986
Monochrome television	13	23	—
Video tape recorders	187	19	538
TV games	—	11	—
Audio products	70	137	450
Other[a]	26	126	204
TOTAL	925	805	2,178

[a] Including electronic watches, but excluding home computers

Source: *Mackintosh Yearbook of West European Electronics Data 1987* (London: Benn Publications, 1986).

TABLE 9.2 *The EEC consumer electronics market 1981–1986 ($M at 1986 prices)*

	1981	1986
Colour television	5,458	8,044
Video cassette recorders	1,627	4,229
Audio systems	4,340	3,329
Compact disc players	—	599
Portable/personal audio equipment	2,585	2,456
Video camcorders	—	708
Other	116	718
TOTAL VALUE	14,126	20,083

Source: BIS Mackintosh.

represents by far the most important single product, although VCR production has grown rapidly in the period 1979–85, and the application of digital technologies to sound reproduction in the form of compact disc and digital audio tape (DAT) is leading to a renaissance in the audio market. Table 9.2 shows the development of the market for a range of consumer electronics products between 1981 and 1986, which shows continued growth in CTVs and VCRs, as well as new products such as CD players and camcorders.

The industry is highly concentrated, and a series of rationalizations and mergers in the last few years, which are analysed in the following chapters, has led to a situation dominated by the three leading European firms, Philips, Thomson, and Nokia, facing the Japanese majors such as Matsushita, Hitachi, and Toshiba, all of whom have now established manufacturing facilities in the EEC. The European firms have managed to hold their own in CTV production, and have retained a major slice of VCR production, albeit using technology licensed from Japan. In newer products such as digital audio and camcorders the Japanese have an important technological lead, with only Philips amongst the Europeans able to maintain a stake through its development of the compact disc. The strength of the European firms in CTV production is likely to be challenged by the Japanese firms with developments in digital TV technology, and flat-screen alternatives to the cathode ray tube.

Table 9.3 shows the major CTV producers in Western Europe, and illustrates the leading position of Philips-Grundig and Thomson. Philips is now the world's largest CTV producer, and it controls almost one-third of European production with plants in seven countries. Thomson now accounts for almost a fifth of production, with plants in four countries, and together the two firms control over half of European production. Japanese firms are steadily increasing their output of CTVs in their European plants, and have now been joined by the Korean firms Samsung and Daewoo with plants in the UK, and Goldstar, which set up a factory in West Germany respectively. It is unlikely that the process of rationalization among existing producers has run its course.

The European VCR industry shows a much stronger presence of Japanese firms: as Table 9.4 shows, in 1986 they accounted for nearly 40 per cent of production, compared to 14 per cent in CTVs. Here too Korean firms are entering the industry in Europe. Unlike in CTV joint ventures between European and Japanese producers have been an important factor: the JVC–Thomson company (J2T) is the largest, producing 750,000 machines per year in West Germany, and has been joined by Matsushita–Bosch and Amstrad–Funai. The failed joint ventures in CTV were politically inspired and enforced, whereas those in VCRs are more engineering- and market-driven, and are thus likely to be more enduring.

The European Association of Consumer Electronics Manufacturers (EACEM) represents the interests of European firms, and is based around a loose confederation of national associations, with a revolving secretariat. Despite this, and despite not having firms in direct membership, EACEM nevertheless is dominated by the major firms, and especially Philips. Anti-dumping complaints made to the EEC in the name of EACEM are compiled directly by the

TABLE 9.3 *Western European colour television production 1986*

Firm	Production (000s)	%
Philips	3,100	20.4
Thomson	2,000	13.2
Grundig	1,950	12.8
ITT	1,305	8.6
Thorn-EMI-Ferguson	800	5.3
Salora/Luxor	680	4.5
Blaupunkt	600	4.0
Sony	535	3.5
Sanyo	410	2.7
Hitachi	370	2.4
Toshiba	310	2.0
Matsushita	310	2.0
Other Japanese	130	0.9
Other Far East	410	2.7
Other European	2,295	15.1
TOTAL JAPANESE	2,065	13.6
TOTAL FAR EAST	2,475	16.3
TOTAL	15,205	

Note: Philips assumed managerial control of Grundig in 1985 and Thomson acquired Thorn-EMI-Ferguson in 1987. These two major firms thus control 33.2 per cent and 18.5 per cent respectively of total European production.

Source: BIS-Mackintosh based on industry estimates.

TABLE 9.4 *Western European video cassete recorder production 1986*

Firm	Production (000s)	%
Philips	800	19.0
Grundig	750	17.9
J2T	750	17.9
Hitachi	450	10.7
Matsushita–Bosch	335	8.0
Sanyo–Fisher	240	5.7
Mitsubishi	165	3.9
Sharp	160	3.8
Toshiba	160	3.8
ITT	150	3.6
Others	240	5.7
TOTAL EUROPEAN	2,605	62.0
TOTAL JAPANESE	1,595	38.0
TOTAL	4,200	

Source: BIS-Mackintosh based on industry estimates.

firms. It adopts a relatively low key stance, concentrating on trade policy issues rather than research and product development, and is handicapped by a degree of distrust between its member associations. Some of its constituent associations include Japanese firms as members (e.g. the British Radio and Electronic Equipment Manufacturers' Association), whereas others (e.g. the German Zentralverband der Elektrotechnischen Industrie) exclude Japanese participation. The Japanese firms are members of the Electronic Industries Association of Japan, which has maintained a European office in Düsseldorf since 1962.

Consumer Electronics Products

In this section we will outline the most significant developments in the staple products of the consumer electronics industry, colour television and video recorders, and briefly outline the importance of new and emergent products such as compact disc and digital audio tape. The general picture which emerges is one where the pace of product innovation is quickening, where, with the partial exception of compact disc, European firms have lost their technological lead, and where the mass production of staple video products, in the same way as happened earlier with staple audio products such as radios and tape recorders, is shifting to the newly industrializing Asian countries such as Korea, Taiwan, and Hong Kong.

Colour television

Colour television was developed during the 1950s in the United States, and a transmission standard (NTSC) was adopted by the National Television System Committee. The Japanese industry adopted this standard, and its manufacturers built up very high levels of production through developing the home market and exporting sets to the United States. The Europeans declined to adopt the NTSC system, and a struggle ensued between two rival systems, both of which were technically superior to the NTSC system. The PAL (Phase Alternation by Line) standard was developed by Telefunken and cross-licensed to Thorn, and was adopted by most of Western Europe in the late 1960s and early 1970s. The rival French SECAM (Séquence à Mémoire) system was adopted by France and later Greece alone in Western Europe, but given away to the Soviet Union and Eastern European countries.

The consequence of the failure to agree on a single technical standard in Europe was to segment the market, and in effect if not in intention to insulate the French market from international competition, at least until dual PAL–SECAM sets were produced at little extra cost in the 1980s. The importance of transmission licensing in general was to offer a substantial degree of protection to the European industry against Japanese competition, which was not present in other consumer electronics products such as radios, tape recorders, and hi-fi systems.

The PAL licences were initially refused to Japanese producers by Telefunken and Thorn, but when the Japanese threatened to disrupt the market by exporting inferior but very low-cost 300-line sets, Telefunken gave way and allowed licences for smaller-screen sets, subject to restrictions on the volume of exports to Europe. The Europeans felt secure that there was relatively little demand for small-screen sets, but they failed to predict the substantial growth of a market for second sets, and for use in conjunction with home computers and video games. Japanese producers who located in Europe were permitted to make large-screen sets, but were prevented from exporting more than 50 per cent of their production, thus restricting their ability to serve the whole European market from a single base. This restriction encouraged the Japanese to locate in those EEC countries with the largest domestic market, Britain and Germany.

The success of Japanese firms in the 1970s in exporting to Europe despite the PAL–SECAM barrier was not built on superior product technology, but rather on more efficient manufacturing processes based on the widespread use of automatic insertion of components, and on higher standards of quality and reliability which in part derived from the use of far fewer components. The European industry was fragmented into a large number of plants with relatively small production volumes serving segmented markets; the Japanese firms had the advantage of the large combined NTSC markets in Japan and the United States in which to exploit scale economies. The European firms which stayed in the industry after the upheavals of the 1970s and early 1980s were forced to modernize their production processes to remain competitive. In the medium to long term, however, competition in the television industry will increasingly develop around product innovations, as has happened with VCRs. In this new phase the European firms may not be so well placed as in the last, unless they can once more reap the benefits of incompatible transmission standards.

The PAL patents began to expire in the late 1970s, and are now no longer a significant barrier to trade. The race is now on to develop the next generation of high-definition (over 1,000 lines to the picture compared to today's 625) television technologies. A consortium of European firms led by Philips is collaborating to produce a standard in competition with the Japanese industry. A proposal to adopt the prototype Japanese system at a 1986 conference of the international standards body CCIR was defeated, and the Europeans have the chance to come up with their own working system by 1990. Success would re-erect a set of technical barriers such as those which had protected the industry in the 1970s. The implications of the battle over HDTV for the European industry are examined in Chapter 13.

In the mean time there is considerable confusion over standards to be adopted for Direct Broadcast Satellites (DBS) despite the decision in June 1986 by the EEC to adopt the MAC (Multiplexed Analogue Components) family of standards. Within this Britain was pressing for the adoption of C-MAC, but has settled for D-MAC, whereas France and Germany favour a D2-MAC variant which would be more suited to feeding into existing cable television networks. In the same way as happened with the PAL–SECAM split, the adoption of different versions of MAC for DBS transmissions would fragment the European market and add to manufacturers' costs.

Perhaps more significant in the long run is the radical change in television technology attendant on the development of alternatives to the cathode ray tube. Japanese companies have been investing heavily in liquid crystal display (LCD) technology, and have very small-screen (up to 5″) models on the market. They also have demonstrated a 14″ model, and are working rapidly towards larger models with the objective of producing totally flat wall-mounted televisions.

Video cassette recorders and disc players

Despite Philips having developed the first VCR suitable for domestic use in 1972, all VCRs now produced in Europe use proprietary Japanese technology, and innovation in video technology is dominated by the Japanese industry. Unlike the case of television systems discussed above, where governments were involved in the adoption of broadcasting standards, a single VCR technology emerged out of a competitive struggle in the market-place in which there have been Japanese as well as European losers. The dominant format world-wide is the VHS system, developed by the Japan Victor Company (JVC), a subsidiary of the world's largest consumer electronics company, Matsushita. A rival format, Beta, was independently developed at the same time by the Sony Corporation, and both formats were in competition on the European market with a succession of formats introduced by Philips (the N1500 and N1700) and Philips–Grundig (the V2000). At present the VHS system is being challenged by Sony's 8mm. format, and a new Super-VHS format has been developed. The Europeans have opted out of the struggle.

In comparison with VHS and Beta models, the early Philips machines were bulky, expensive, unreliable, and restricted to short recording times. When the Japanese firms began to ship large numbers of VCRs to Europe in 1978 and 1979 they quickly achieved significant levels of market penetration. JVC had signed agreements with the major competitor to Philips and Grundig in the three largest European markets: with Thorn-EMI in the UK, Telefunken in Germany, and Thomson in France, so that their machines would appear under European brand names, and be marketed through existing channels. The 1977 agreements also included the provision for the eventual development of a joint manufacturing operation. By the time that Philips and Grundig were seeking co-operation from other manufacturers for their new V2000 system, introduced in 1981, their European competitors were firmly ensconced in the VHS 'camp'.

At the same time, European, American, and Japanese companies were attempting to develop video disc players as mass consumer products. Philips were ahead of the competition, with the first launch of their domestic LaserVision in the UK in 1982, followed by RCA's Selectavision introduced in collaboration with Hitachi and GEC. Neither product was able to rival the popularity of VCRs, and JVC-Thorn decided to market their VHD system for industrial and educational use only. Philips had adopted a strategy of promoting both V2000 and LaserVision as complementary purchases, in the belief that consumers would buy a VCR for recording off-air and a disc player to show pre-recorded software. Thus in introducing the V2000 Philips underestimated the importance of software availability, and overestimated the willingness of consumers to spend heavily to achieve marginal increases in playback quality. Video disc players failed as a consumer product, although the Laser-Vision system has found a niche in commercial and industrial applications.

In 1981 the only manufacturers of VCRs with a base inside the EEC were Grundig, accounting for under 10 per cent of total EEC sales of 2 million VCRs, although the following year Philips opened a second VCR factory in West Germany, in addition to their existing plant in Austria. The failure of their attempt to establish wider support for the V2000 system was signalled in 1982 with the agreement between JVC and its European partners to manufacture VCRs in a joint venture, initially J3T, but in the end J2T (JVC–Thorn–Telefunken) when the French government vetoed Thomson's participation in the venture. In response to their failure to secure backing for the V2000, and facing a cost difference of some 40 per cent between V2000 machines and VCRs imported from Japan, Philips and Grundig initiated an anti-dumping suit which led to the voluntary export restraint agreement negotiated between the EEC and Japan, which is discussed in the following chapters. By the time the agreement was signed the V2000 format was effectively finished, and Philips–Grundig moved into the VHS camp. The most significant recent development in VCR technology has been the combined camera-recorder, where another format war is being fought between JVC's VHS and Sony's 8mm. systems. This product is growing rapidly just as VCR markets are reaching saturation point, and sales are expected to increase annually by 20 per cent up to 1991. At present no camcorders are manufactured in Europe, but it is likely that Philips and some of the Japanese firms in Europe will begin to manufacture them in the near future.

Compact disc

Unlike video disc players, where there were rival formats and competition from VCRs, compact disc has developed with a single world-wide format from the beginning. CD was invented by Philips in the 1970s, but in the later stages of development Philips collaborated with Sony and the two companies agreed a final standard for the product which was introduced in 1981. Again unlike CTV and VCR, Philips centralized its entire production of CD players in a single factory in Belgium, and it succeeded in persuading the EEC to introduce a special tariff of 19 per cent, reducing to 14 per cent over three years.

Despite this Philips as the major European producer is competing against all the major Japanese companies, as well as those from other Asian countries. Sony, Aiwa, and Akai have begun to manufacture players in Europe, and in mid-1987 the EEC Commission estimated that the Europeans' share of the CD market had fallen from one-half in 1984 to one-third, against the background of sharply rising sales. The total market for CD players was estimated at $600 million in 1986, and is expected to rise to $3 billion by 1991. The rapid penetration of CD followed the equal emphasis given to hardware and software in its promotion. The strength of the European music industry has so far hindered the introduction of yet another audio product, digital audio tape (DAT), which has been developed by the Japanese industry. A similar struggle is likely to emerge in the future over erasable CDs, which the French Thomson company as well as some Japanese firms claim to have nearly perfected.

In addition to its role in audio products, compact disc technology has other applications as a data storage medium for computers (CD-ROM), and as the basis for a new kind of home computer which permits high quality sound, graphics and text to be used simultaneously for educational and entertainment purposes (CD-Interactive or CD-I). Acutely aware of the standards problem, and the requirement to co-ordinate hardware and software in the launch of this product, Philips has gone the joint venture route examined in Chapter 13.

Patterns of International Trade in Consumer Electronics

The 1970s witnessed a rising trend in imports in Britain, France, and West Germany, coupled with very low levels of exports from Britain and France. The West German industry has been by far the strongest of the three in terms of production and export performance, but from 1980 onwards Germany moved into a deficit in trade in consumer electronics products as VCRs began to form a significant slice of the market. The long-standing Japanese producers in the UK, Sony, Matsushita, and Hitachi, have achieved significant export volumes to other EEC countries which gave Britain, for the first time for many years, a small export surplus in CTVs in 1987. The following year, however, a flood of imports of small-screen CTVs from China and Hong Kong reversed the position, and prompted an anti-dumping suit by the European firms.

The world consumer electronics industry is dominated by Japan, which in 1984 accounted for 44 per cent of world production of $50 billion. In that year Japan supplied 86 per cent of world demand for VCRs, and European production of consumer electronics products accounted for 58 per cent of needs. The share of the United States and Japanese markets held by European exports was around 1 per cent in each case. The trade deficit between the EEC and Japan amounted to $3.6 billion in consumer electronics products. In the five years from 1977 to 1982 the EEC's deficit in VCRs alone increased from 32 million to 1,937 million ECUs.

Japanese Investment in Europe

Japanese investment in manufacturing plants in Europe for consumer electronics products began as early as 1974 when Sony established its first factory in Wales. It was not, however, until the late 1970s and early 1980s that the pace of investment accelerated, largely in response to increasing pressure on the EEC to adopt protectionist measures which culminated in the voluntary restraint agreement for VCRs signed in 1983. In 1984 there were 20 Japanese plants in the EEC, but by 1987 the number had increased to 37. In addition there are one Taiwanese and one Chinese factory in the UK, and Korean-owned plants in both the UK and Germany.

Table 9.5 shows the distribution of Japanese investments by product in 1987 for Britain, France, and West Germany. Most of the Japanese investments have been made in these three countries, but Spain and Portugal have also been chosen as additional sites within the EEC. It can be seen that television production has been concentrated in the UK, with no factories in France and only two in Germany, compared to nine in the UK. By contrast France has been the favoured location for audio investments, but, despite a shift in policy in 1982 towards welcoming inward investment, has attracted few of the new VCR plants established in response to mounting trade frictions.

TABLE 9.5 *Japanese consumer electronics investments in Britain, France, and West Germany, 1988*

	Britain	France	W. Germany
CTV	Sony Matsushita Hitachi Toshiba Mitsubishi Sanyo Orion NEC JVC		Sony Hitachi
VCR	JVC Sanyo Mitsubishi Toshiba Sharp Hitachi Orion NEC Funai	Akai Matsushita	Sony JVC Hitachi Matsushita Sanyo Toshiba
Hi-fi	Aiwa Matsushita	Akai Trio-Kenwood Pioneer JVC	
CD	Aiwa	Akai Sony	
Car Audio		Trio-Kenwood Clarion	Sony Matsushita

The most favoured route into Europe for the Japanese has been through building new factories on greenfield sites, but under pressure they have entered into short-lived joint ventures in television production in Britain. In VCRs the joint venture route has been more common, as in the cases of MB Video in Germany, a joint venture between Matsushita and Bosch, and J2T which brought together JVC, Telefunken, and Thorn-EMI. Recently two British firms, Amstrad and Hinari, have announced joint ventures with the Japanese firms that had been supplying them with own-branded machines to produce VCRs at plants in Britain. A further recent move is the investment by Japanese component manufacturers, particularly to supply the growing VCR industry. There are now three such plants in Britain, and if pressure from the European firms on the EEC is conceded to require 60 per cent local value added in order to qualify for 'made in the EEC' status, it is probable that investment by Far Eastern components manufacturers will quickly increase.

Although the European Commission has taken the lead in determining trade policy issues, through common tariffs and the voluntary export restraint agreement, and more recently its more aggressive stance towards alleged dumping in components as well as in finished products, policies towards and incentives to promote inward investment in Europe tend to be the preserve of national governments. Indeed in recent years there has developed a significant degree of competition between European national governments to attract such plants into their countries. The rationale for this appears to be that if they are going to set up in Europe anyway the damage which will be caused to existing firms by their presence is at least offset to some extent by a reduction in imports and a slower rate of contraction of employment.

The implications of the Single European Act which envisages the creation of a single market by 1992 has accelerated a trend amongst the Japanese companies towards strengthening the intra-European links between their subsidiaries. Sony, Matsushita, and Hitachi have all formed European companies to replace some of the direct relationships between branch plants and their Japanese head offices, and are set to exploit the single market to the full. The beginnings of European R. & D. centres are evident, and a combination of political pressure and the particular demands of new products is likely to accelerate this trend.

The National Case-Studies

The next three chapters highlight some of the national differences in government–industry relations in our three chosen countries. The most important difference between France and the other two, is that French public policy has directly and indirectly insulated the French industry from some of the pressures which led to radical changes in industry structure in Britain and Germany. A pro-active industrial policy for the industry in Britain was frustrated by the election of the Thatcher government; in Germany demands for such policies were sporadic and shrugged off by the federal government. France is the only country of the three in which there was a stable pattern of firms in the 1970s; it is the only one with a nationalized consumer electronics producer (Thomson); and it is the only host country for a European multinational firm (Thomson). The British industry is now dominated by Japanese firms and the German by Dutch and French. In the following chapters we show how these outcomes occurred as a result of the particular blend of sectoral and national effects set against the context of the globalization of the industry and the impact of innovative consumer products.

Although each chapter can be read independently as a national case-study, the full picture only emerges when the different pieces are put together to show the impact of market integration and the stirrings of a concerted political response at the European level.

10

Britain: Arrival and Departure

Introduction

The 'British' consumer electronics industry is now almost entirely Japanese-owned. In the space of twenty years from 1967—the first year of colour television broadcasting in Britain—the industry was transformed. Of the ten manufacturers of CTVs in 1967, eight were British-owned, and the remaining two were subsidiaries of Dutch and American multinational companies (Philips and ITT respectively). At the close of 1988 there were eleven CTV producers in Britain: eight Japanese, and one firm each from France, Taiwan, and the People's Republic of China. Figure 10.1 charts this astonishing transformation of the industry. With respect to the other main products of the industry—VCR and CD—the position is equally stark: only one British firm has a stake in VCR manufacture with a Japanese partner, but eight of the ten other producers are Japanese; there is only one—Japanese—plant in the UK making compact disc players.

This chapter analyses this transformation of the British industry as a process of usurpation by Japanese firms of the privileges which had been gained by the British firms as a consequence of the introduction of colour television. First we examine the achievement of closure around the 'passive protection' of incompatible technical standards and segmented national markets. This cartel-like behaviour was organized through the trade association, and resulted in high prices and low quality. The Japanese successfully eroded the domestic market share of the UK firms by following a strategy of usurpation based on superior product and process technologies: they had learned how to make a better television set more efficiently. The chapter then examines the response of the British firms, trade association, and government, which was an attempt first to exclude the Japanese and, when this proved impossible, to enlist the support of government in a tripartite modernization strategy. Following the election of the Thatcher government in 1979, an explicitly market-

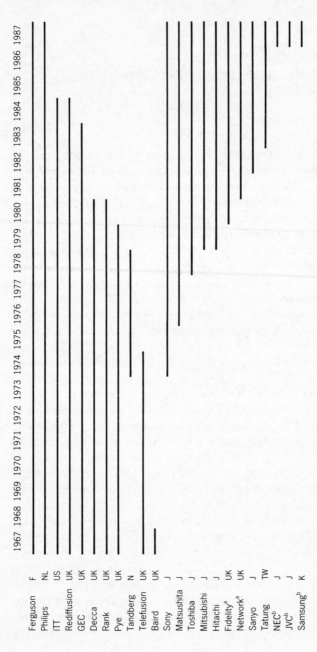

Key: F=French; NL=Dutch; US=American; N=Norwegian; J=Japanese;
UK=British; TW=Taiwanese; K=Korean

Notes   [a] Network ceased production of TVs in 1987 and Fidelity in 1988.
         [b] NEC, JVC and Samsung announced that they would begin CTV production in 1988

[a] Network ceased production of TVs in 1987 and Fidelity in 1988.
[b] NEC, JVC, and Samsung announced that they would begin CTV production in 1988.

FIG. 10.1. Television manufacturers in Britain 1967–1987

led strategy of further encouraging inward investment by the Japanese was imposed on the British industry. The technical lead achieved by the Japanese in VCR technology reinforced their dominant position as VCRs replaced CTVs as the most important segment of the consumer electronics market. In seeking to resist the competitive pressure of the Japanese firms, the rump of the British industry joined Philips in supporting a succession of European-level initiatives to restrict Japanese exports. The complete failure of this strategy was signalled by the sale of the last major British firm—Thorn-EMI-Ferguson—to the French Thomson company in 1987, and the decision by Philips to close its last remaining CTV factory in the UK in December 1988. In Japanese hands, however, the industry is thriving and investment, employment, and output levels are rising.

The Actors

The firms

The introduction of colour television in 1967 heralded the beginning of a golden era for television manufacturers in Britain, spoiled only by the uncertainties created by the restrictions on consumer spending as a consequence of government economic policies of 'fine tuning' in demand management. From 1968 until 1974 demand for CTVs outstripped the capacity of the British firms to supply them, and imports of sets, especially from Japan, began to increase rapidly, reaching 8.8 per cent of the British market in 1972. In the single year 1973 the number of Japanese sets sold in Britain doubled. The collapse of the Heath government's 'dash for growth' in 1974 was fully reflected in the CTV market, which contracted from 2.7 million to 1.6 million in a single year, leaving British firms with idle capacity of up to 50 per cent.[1]

The television industry in the early 1970s comprised ten firms producing almost exclusively for the British domestic market. In the peak year of 1973 some 2 million sets were manufactured, but only 2 per cent of the output was exported.[2] At this time Thorn's share of UK production was some 30 per cent, Philips-Pye had 20 per cent, Rank and GEC around 12 per cent each, and the remaining 25 per cent was divided between five firms.[3] The major firms were either subsidiaries of multinational companies, or diversified electronics firms for which television manufacturing was an important, although not essential, part of their business. These firms were all members of the trade association, the British Radio and Electronic Equipment Manufacturers' Association (BREMA), and although Philips and ITT were foreign-owned, they were admitted to BREMA, regarded themselves as 'British', and were so regarded by the other firms.

The industry in the late 1980s consists almost entirely of the subsidiaries of major multinational electronics companies, mainly Japanese-owned. The one British firm of significance, Amstrad, sources the bulk of its consumer electronics products in the Far East, although it has now begun to assemble VCRs in Britain in a joint venture with the small Japanese firm Funai. Most of these firms manufacture both CTVs and VCRs in the UK, together with associated products such as microwave ovens and electronic typewriters (see Table 10.1). In the early days of British operations the UK Japanese subsidiaries were tightly controlled from their headquarters and kept a very low profile in the industry by striving to be seen as 'good corporate citizens'. Unlike the British firms they replaced, the Japanese used their UK plants as a base from which to export to other EEC countries. Since 1987 many of them have begun to reorganize their European operations to prepare for the completion of the internal market, by establishing European headquarters and developing lines of communication between their subsidiaries which do not run through Japan. There are also signs that some functions, such as product development and even R. & D., are beginning to be decentralized from Japan as the firms in practice as well as in appearance seek to be identified by the EEC as 'insider firms' in the event of measures which seek to protect the single market from what are seen as unfair trading practices by outsiders.

Trade associations

BREMA is a small organization, with only four full-time officials who service the major committees—Commercial, Economics and Statistics, and Technical—which comprise managers from member firms. Only firms which manufacture electronic consumer goods in the UK are eligible for membership, which has closely mirrored the CTV industry structure shown in Figure 10.1. After a certain amount of soul-searching BREMA accepted Japanese firms as full

TABLE 10.1 *Consumer electronics firms in Britain 1988*

	CTV	VCR	Hi-fi	CD
Aiwa			×	×
Daewoo		×[a]		
Ferguson	×	×[b]		
Funai–Amstrad		×		
Hitachi	×	×		
JVC	×	×[b]		
Matsushita	×		×	
Mitsubishi	×	×		
NEC	×	×		
Philips	×[c]			
Samsung	×	×		
Sanyo	×	×		
Sharp		×		
Sony	×[d]			
Tatung	×			
Toshiba	×	×		

[a] Daewoo announced plans to begin VCR production in Belfast in 1989.
[b] Under Thorn-EMI's ownership, Ferguson and JVC were partners with Thomson in a joint venture to manufacture VCRs in Newhaven. After the sale of Ferguson to Thomson in 1987, production was transferred to Berlin.
[c] Philips ceased production of CTVs in Britain at the end of December 1988.
[d] Sony also manufacture CTV tubes in the UK, as do Philips.

members, which put the organization into the odd position of seeking to persuade governments to support its efforts to protect the industry from the parent companies of its own members! In practice the Japanese firms sent their British rather than their Japanese managers to BREMA, with instructions not to oppose the interests of the long-standing firms such as Thorn-EMI and Philips. The Japanese firms maintained amongst themselves a parallel structure of representation through the European office of the Electronic Industries Association of Japan (EIAJ), which had been established in Düsseldorf as early as 1962. This organization maintained its own direct relationship with the Department of Trade and Industry (DTI). While BREMA membership served to defuse potential opposition to the growing presence of Japanese firms in the industry, EIAJ links served as an effective means of furthering government policies of encouraging inward investment by the Japanese.

In the 1970s BREMA became a forum for the expression of the fears of the British producers that they would be overwhelmed by Japanese competition, and a channel for 'voluntary' negotiation of trade restraints between Britain and a growing number of Far East producers. It noted the growth of Japanese imports in the early 1970s with some concern, and attributed the success of the Japanese export offensive in the US market to the close support given by the Japanese government to the industry. The *Annual Report* for 1972 posed the threat and possible responses in stark terms:

... [T]here are two methods of dealing with this particular type of highly co-ordinated industrial and commercial enterprise: either by imitating the corporate state so that government, industry and unions strive as one dynamic united organization, or alternatively for government to preserve existing systems and to limit exports by quota action, as in France or Italy, or by increased import duties, as in the United States of America. There is a third alternative, altruistic and more demanding, which is for the Japanese to recognize that they are over-producing so far as industrialised overseas countries are concerned.

The accession of Britain to the EEC in 1973, however, put paid to the second of these options, since such bilateral import quotas were illegal under the terms of the Treaty of Rome. The French and Italian quotas pre-dated the Treaty, and were allowed to continue in place. A fourth option, which was significantly omitted by BREMA, was that the British firms could undertake to improve their products and modernize their manufacturing processes so as to be able to compete effectively against Japanese imports. The reason for its omission, according to industry sources interviewed for this study, was that British managers believed that the Japanese edge arose from unfair government subsidies which allowed predatory pricing policies, and from low wages. British firms lacked first-hand knowledge of the Japanese industry; it was not until 1977 that Thorn-EMI organized a fact-finding tour of Japan for its managers and trade union officials.[4]

BREMA opted for the strategy of seeking 'industry-to-industry' talks between the Radio Industry Council (RIC—which brought the set-makers together with the components firms) and the EIAJ. The first talks took place in London in March 1973, and there were two subsequent meetings in 1973, also in London. Following the second meeting BREMA was informed by the EIAJ that it had been instructed by the Ministry of International Trade and Industry (MITI) to restrict its exports to the UK. A 'hot-line' was set up between the RIC and EIAJ to tackle urgent situations, and it was in use before the year end. The attitude of the DTI to bilateral trade restraints was to turn a blind eye.

BREMA and the leading British firms are represented through the European Association of Consumer Electronics Manufacturers (EACEM) which was established in 1978. EACEM has a rotating secretariat, and its activities are dominated by the major European producers, in particular Philips and Thomson, but Thorn-EMI also had an important voice. EACEM has tended to reflect the interests of the Europeans *against* the Japanese, in pressing for measures in respect of sensitive products such as VCRs where the European Commission has played a crucial policy-making role. In 1988 an anti-dumping complaint against two Japanese and three Korean VCR producers was made officially by EACEM, although the evidence presented in support of the complaint was compiled by Philips. In this case we have the example of a single large firm acting as the respresentative of the interests of other firms.

Trade Unions

Union representation in the electronics industry is, as elsewhere in British industry, fragmented between a large number of different unions. The most important is the Electrical, Electronic, Telecommunications and Plumbing Union (EETPU), not so much by virtue of its size, but because it has taken a leading role in recruitment in high technology sectors, and has, through Frank Chapple (who turned gamekeeper and became President of BREMA in 1986) and later Eric Hammond, adopted an overtly market-orientated rather than class-orientated stance. Incoming Japanese firms have benefited from its willingness to negotiate single union agreements, which were the envy of managers of British firms in the industry who had to negotiate with up to six unions in existing plants, including the AUEW, TGWU, ASTMS, and APEX. The EETPU has not confined its innovative industrial relations practices to new entrants, however, since it successfully bypassed existing multi-union representation at the Hitachi (earlier GEC then GEC-Hitachi) plant at Hirwaun in South Wales to secure a single-union agreement under the noses of the other unions. When Thorn-EMI opened a new TV cabinet factory in High Wycombe they signed such an agreement with the EETPU, and would have liked to do the same for their TV plants at Enfield and Gosport.[5]

Britain lacks an institutionalized role for trade unions at plant level, such as the works councils of the FRG. Their access to civil servants is restricted compared to that of employers, and the advent of the Thatcher government in 1979 diminished their national role as well as their access to ministers. But despite this, individual unions such as the EETPU and ASTMS have played an important part at the sectoral level, both through the NEDO industry committee and at plant level where restructuring has taken place. In the wake of Philips's decision to close its Pye factory at Lowestoft in 1981, and an attempt to lobby the Philips headquarters in the Netherlands, ASTMS convened a conference in 1984 of European unions representing Philips workers. Such efforts, however, need to be interpreted in the context of a political and industrial relations system which denies a *formal* role to unions in policy formation. Unions suffer the same disadvantages of fragmentation and duplication that are characteristic of British trade associations. This in part accounts for the importance we have attached to firms as political actors in Chapter 2. But it is important to stress that formal institutions are not necessarily a reliable guide to actual influence, and the role played by trade unions tends to vary between different industries. In the British consumer electronics industry trade unions played an important part in the modernization strategy, and in defining the essentially defensive stance of the British industry towards the threat of international competition discussed more fully below.

The Department of Trade and Industry

Many industry actors expressed concern at the lack of priority attached by government in Britain to manufacturing industry, which is reflected in the role of the DTI within government, at both the political and administrative levels. Since 1979 there have been no fewer than six Secretaries of State for Industry, and most commentators saw Leon Brittan's move from the Home Office to the DTI in 1984 as a demotion. Such a view of the importance of industry is also reflected in the career choices of new recruits, where potential high flyers opt in preference for the Treasury, the Foreign Office, or the Home Office. Despite its position as a low-status ministry, in 1974 the DTI was split by Harold Wilson into separate Ministries of Trade and Industry, but these were brought together once more under Cecil Parkinson in 1983.

In 1979 the leading intellectual exponent of monetarism within the Conservative Party, Sir Keith Joseph, was appointed to the D.o.I. explicitly to find ways of winding it up. In the event he was 'educated' by the then permanent secretary, Sir Peter Carey, as to the importance of industry, and after a brief hiatus the work of support for industry continued, although hardly with enthusiasm. Within the sphere of electronics there was a notable effort in information technology under a junior minister, Kenneth Baker, but the priority attached to the consumer electronics manufacturing industry has continued to be low, amounting at best to a policy of benign neglect. One of the traditional functions of the DTI was industrial sponsorship (see Chapter 3), but with the re-emergence of the DTI as the 'Department for Enterprise' under Lord Young in 1987, sponsorship was abolished and the structure reorganized as 'market' divisions to emphasize that government did not see itself responsible for the economic welfare of firms.

During most of the period of our study consumer electronics (CTV and video products) was 'sponsored' by one principal, one higher executive officer, and half a secretary, so that the abolition of this function cannot be regarded as a major change! It was in part for such reasons that the leading role in modernizing the British television manufacturing industry was taken in the mid-1970s by the Consumer Electronics Sector Working Party (SWP) of the National Economic Development Office (NEDO). The trade association did, however, lose its 'outpost' in Whitehall, which contributed further to the already well-established pattern of major firms representing their own interests in direct bilateral relations.

The National Economic Development Office

Since its formation in 1962, NEDO had participated in tripartite negotiation at a macro-economic level under successive governments. In the 1970s it developed an important meso-economic focus which almost led to the development of a corporatist strategy for the British consumer electronics industry.

The incoming Labour government of 1974 identified as part of the problem of government–industry relations in Britain the neglect of the promotion of industry because of the preoccupation of successive governments with 'regulation to prevent the activities of industry, or the abuse of its powers, damaging the interests of other sectors of the community'.[6] It called for a new, more positive relationship between government and industry which would reflect a partnership in pursuit of industrial success. While the major policy instrument, planning agreements, failed to materialize, and the National Enterprise Board emerged neutered from the process of accommodating different interests,[7] more modest initiatives at the sectoral level had some success.

An Industrial Strategy Steering Group was formed within the D.o.I. which worked in close consultation with NEDO. It identified some thirty industrial sectors which were reasonably homogeneous so that a specific *sectoral* strategy might be devised.[8] The newly created NEDO Sector Working Parties were charged with identifying the problems and prospects of each industry, with the intention of creating in many instances a 'network' of important actors drawn from government, management, and trade unions. The existing Electronics Economic Development Committee of NEDO was divided into SWPs covering capital and consumer goods and components. The Electronic Consumer Goods SWP was, until it was wound up by the Thatcher government in 1988, chaired by Jimmy Griffiths, then Managing Director of Pye, which was in deep trouble and was subsequently taken over by Philips. It comprised representatives from the big firms, trade unions, BREMA, and the DTI, and although one Japanese manager from Matsushita was co-opted for part of its work, its purpose was explicitly to promote a solution favouring the interests of long-established firms, which might include some forms of partnership with Japanese firms. The major activities of the SWP were concerned with the politics of inward investment, and the process of adjustment to Japanese competition, which are examined in the following sections.

The Politics of Inward Investment

Despite the collapse of the domestic market in 1974–5, Japanese exporters managed to improve their relative position in the British market. Part of this was due to the increased popularity of the small-screen sets which the Japanese were restricted to exporting by the terms of the PAL licence. MITI had decided against renewing the restraint agreement beyond 1975, and a Department of Trade investigation into allegations that the Japanese had been dumping CTV tubes failed to substantiate the charges. The strongly protectionist line taken by the British industry was sufficient to convince the leading Japanese firms that they would benefit from establishing factories in Britain. In 1973 Sony announced its plans to build a factory on a greenfield site in South Wales, and it was soon followed to Wales by Matsushita. These decisions prompted mixed reactions among the British firms. Some felt that the situation would be eased when the Japanese firms entered the British industry, since they would be competing on the same terms as the indigenous firms. Others, however, saw inward investment as a 'Trojan Horse', and used BREMA to lobby the government to prevent their entry, citing the subsidies available to these firms under the government's regional and selective assistance policies, which in Sony's case amounted to 28 per cent of costs.[9] This argument is reflected in the BREMA 1976 *Annual Report*'s reference to a new challenge arising from 'Japanese-owned assembly plants autocratically permitted by the government to be established inside the United Kingdom'.

By the time that the Labour government took office in February 1974 the initial strategy followed by the British firms of exclusion either through state action or through voluntary negotiation had failed. Indeed governments had undermined exclusionary attempts by actively seeking Japanese investment in the industry, which provoked a fierce battle over Hitachi's proposed factory in Washington, Tyne and Wear. This issue dominated the agenda of the SWP during its first year. An invitation to Hitachi to invest in Britain had been made by the Industry Minister, Eric Varley, and his junior minister, Alan Williams. Part of the attraction for the government of Japanese investment was its location in the depressed regions, and part was in the effect it might have on stimulating improvements in the export performance of the industry. In the course of negotiations with the D.o.I., Hitachi promised that up to 70 per cent of its components, including tubes, would be sourced locally,[10] and that 50 per cent of its anticipated production of 80,000 sets per year would be exported, with a further 20,000 expected to replace existing imports.[11]

The SWP became a focus for opposition to the plan, which involved both firms and unions acting through BREMA and the SWP, as well as direct approaches to government and to Hitachi. The SWP's analysis of the economic conditions of the industry revealed a capacity of 2.5 million sets p.a. against a domestic market of only 1.6 million, and the unions argued that up to 5,000 jobs would be in jeopardy.[12] Hitachi had recently concluded a joint venture agreement to make tubes in Finland, and the projected North-East location led to fears that its new plant would simply be a 'screwdriver' operation. The Philips subsidiary Mullard was one of the leading and vocal opponents of the planned investment, despite Hitachi's promise to source tubes from its nearby plants.

Despite the continued support of the D.o.I., Hitachi 'retired hurt' from the fray in December 1977 and cancelled its proposed investment. The SWP diagnosed the two key problems of the sector as excess capacity and import penetration—which had reached 41 per cent by 1976—and urged the government to permit inward investment only in the form of the purchase of existing capacity either through joint ventures or take-overs. The guidelines drawn up by the SWP were accepted by the D.o.I., and they acted as a block on greenfield investments in the industry until 1985. The guidelines also stated that specific agreements over local content and exports should be made with inward investors.[13]

Japanese inward investment in consumer electronics in the UK can be conveniently divided into three phases. The first, from 1973 to 1977, consisted of direct investments on greenfield sites in South Wales by Sony and Matsushita. The second phase, from 1978 to 1983, was initiated by the conflict over Hitachi's plans for a greenfield site in the North-East, and took the form of an informal veto on greenfield investment, with the Department of Industry encouraging joint ventures between Japanese firms and existing UK producers (GEC–Hitachi and Rank–Toshiba). During this period Mitsubishi took over the Scottish factory of Tandberg, and Sanyo purchased the Lowestoft factory vacated by Philips. The joint venture between Thorn, JVC, and Telefunken (J2T) was located in the ex-Thorn hi-fi plant at Newhaven.

The third, and current, phase of Japanese investment started in 1985 with Sharp locating its video recorder factory on a greenfield site in Wrexham, with some £6.5 million of government grants. By this time the informal restrictions on the Japanese had been lifted, and indeed there was considerable competition between European governments to attract Sharp. The location of subsequent investments by Orion and NEC has been determined by these companies in the light of what investment incentives have been available: Orion opted for the old Dragon home computer factory in South Wales rented from the Welsh Development Agency, whereas NEC chose a purpose-built factory at Telford. This period has also seen significant investments by Korean producers as they have followed the Japanese in seeking to overcome trade frictions by direct investments in the EEC. Samsung established a plant on Teesside in 1987 to produce CTVs, VCRs, and microwave ovens, and Daewoo announced in late 1988 an £18 million VCR plant in Northern Ireland accompanied by an undisclosed amount of government subsidy.

Each of these three phases has been marked by distinctive combinations of market conditions and government policies. In the early 1970s Japanese firms wishing to expand their CTV markets in Europe were faced by technical barriers in the PAL and SECAM systems. The PAL licence, which applied to all European markets except France, was only granted to Japanese firms for small-screen size sets. The European firms reserved to themselves the manufacture of large sets (20" and above), unless the Japanese firms located factories in Europe, in which case they would be allowed to manufacture larger sets. But a further condition of the PAL licence was that no more than 50 per cent of output could be exported, which effectively narrowed the choice of location in Europe to the two countries with the largest domestic markets: Britain and West Germany. Britain tended to be chosen by the first wave of investors for CTV because of language barriers and high wage costs in the FRG.

The preference of the Japanese for a UK location was reinforced by government policy, which sought in general to attract inward investors especially to regions with high areas of unemployment. In addition, and specific to the consumer electronics industry, Japanese investment was encouraged because Japanese firms were seen as more efficient producers whose presence alongside British firms would induce the latter to become more competitive. The agreements made between the Department of Industry and Sony and Matsushita included commitments to build up local procurement of components and exports from the UK. Market conditions during this early phase were relatively buoyant, and the Japanese firms were not seen by the domestic producers to constitute a significant threat.

The second phase was marked by a severe escalation of conflict between long-established firms and Japanese entrants. Government policy towards inward investment hardened significantly, and important conditions were attached which led to the creation of the Rank–Toshiba and GEC–Hitachi joint ventures. The collapse in demand for colour televisions which began in 1974 had hit British firms hard, and by 1977 import penetration had reached 48 per cent.[14] Fearful that they would lose out to a steady stream of more efficient Japanese firms locating in Britain with the aid of government grants, the established firms dug in their heels and fought a rearguard action to prevent inward investment adding to excess capacity in the industry. Ultimately the action failed, and the response was a steady exit of firms from the industry (see Figure 10.1 above). By 1984 the two joint ventures had collapsed, and it was evident that a policy which was intended to prod British firms into becoming more competitive had in fact cruelly exposed their weaknesses.

The Sharp decision signalled a new phase of government policy towards inward investment which reflected the reality of competition between European governments for a share of what was a rapidly expanding pool of investment, especially in video recorders. In 1984 there were 23 Japanese plants making CTV, VCR, and audio products in the EEC, of which 12 were located in Britain. In 1987 there were 32 such plants of which 18 were in Britain.[15] Thus Britain has maintained its share of such investments, arguably because it has abandoned a restrictive approach and adopted what amounts to a virtual open door policy towards Japanese and other foreign investment.

This change was an implicit admission that the policy of reconstructing the UK industry by exposing it to competition had failed. Once there is no indigenous industry to protect, it makes more sense to have foreign plants located in Britain, potentially exporting to the rest of the EC, than located elsewhere and exporting to Britain. Following the sale of the Ferguson subsidiary of Thorn-EMI to Thomson in July 1987, and the closure of the Fidelity plant in May 1988, all CTVs and VCRs manufactured in Britain (with the partial exception of those made by the Funai–Amstrad joint venture) were produced by foreign-owned firms.

In retrospect the policy of using inward investment as a lever to increase the competitive strength of the British industry was not enough by itself to ensure the survival of British firms. It became evident by 1979, at least to members of the NEDO Sector Working Party, that some positive steps needed to be taken on the supply side to induce rationalization and scale economies in the industry.

The next section examines the politics of this adjustment process, and in particular the attempt to engineer a meso-corporatist strategy.[16]

Firm Strategies and the Politics of Adjustment

Once the Hitachi affair had been resolved, the SWP turned to the urgent task of analysing the strategic position of the UK firms and their major competitors. Its chairman took the view that the position articulated by BREMA in the early 1970s was mistaken: the Japanese threat did not come from unfair competition but from the superior efficiency of its firms. The SWP wanted to avoid a knee-jerk protectionist response, and so took the bold step of commissioning the Boston Consulting Group to undertake a comparative study of the UK industry and its major competitors, the FRG, Korea, and Japan. The £30,000 cost of the study was shared between NEDO, the D.o.I. and the firms.[17]

The BCG report was received in the autumn of 1978 in conditions of great secrecy for fear that its contents, if communicated to the retail trade, would further damage the position of the UK industry. It found that, although British products were broadly competitive with those of the West German industry, there was a large gap between European and Far Eastern costs. In the case of Japan the cost advantage was achieved, not by lower wage rates, but by much more efficient production technologies, superior set designs, and the insistence of manufacturers on reliable supplies of very high quality components which reduced costs associated with repairing defective sets on the production line. Very large volumes per plant had allowed the Japanese firms to take full advantage of these benefits. The Koreans, by contrast, achieved their cost advantages largely through lower wage rates and government subsidies.[18]

The SWP urged a strategy of increasing the competitiveness of British firms, which would lead to higher exports and thus safeguard employment in the industry. Four objectives were stressed:

1. the rationalization of production units into a small number of plants, each with an annual volume of 500,000 sets compared to the then UK average of 100,000:
2. the increased involvement of the Japanese in the sector, as

a means of transferring technology and upgrading the technical
level of the British plants;
3. the incorporation of innovations in set design and manufacture
as a way of cutting costs; and
4. a concerted effort to improve the quality and supply of UK
manufactured components.

The SWP estimated that structural adjustments costing some £300
million would be necessary if its target of eliminating the sector's
balance of payments deficit by 1984 was to be reached. It argued
that government had a crucial role to play in providing financial
support for rationalization, in ensuring that inward investors
adhered to the SWP guidelines, and in making sure that it supported
the negotiation of voluntary export restraints with Far Eastern producers. But clearly the major effort would have to come from the
British firms' adopting Japanese methods and attempting to achieve
their volumes, and from the trade unions' recognizing the necessity
to accept redundancies. There is no doubt that the tripartite structure of the SWP played a crucial role in forging the consensus around
this strategy, and that the efforts of the SWP succeeded in giving
firms in the industry a more realistic analysis of the nature of the
threat to their interests. The option of a state-supported collaborative strategy of modernization to defend the industry against Japanese usurpation—akin to the 'crisis cartels' developed in the FRG
to deal with excess capacity in the steel industry[19]—had been chosen.
Ironically, however, the strategy depended on getting the Japanese
firms to co-operate in sharing their expertise.

In March 1979 the govenment accepted the SWP's plans for the
industry, and promised substantial financial assistance. The SWP
hoped that the D.o.I. would launch a special industry scheme for
the sector, amounting to additional financial assistance of £80 million. It was advised, however, that the inevitable delay in launching
such a scheme, including reference to the European Commission,
might take it beyond the election and the possibility of a Conservative government with a declared opposition toward government
intervention in industry. The SWP decided not to press for a special
programme, but to encourage applications for selective financial
assistance under Section 8 of the Industry Act 1972. D.o.I. officials
played an active role at this stage in visiting firms to persuade them
to apply for grants, but despite this the major beneficiaries of govern-

ment grants in the consumer electronics industry were the Japanese firms.[20]

In 1978 there were broadly three options available to firms in the industry:

1. *Exit.* This was the option taken by Tandberg, which had set up a factory in Scotland in 1974. It sold out to Mitsubishi in 1979. Pye, which had sold a 60 per cent stake to Philips in 1967, became a wholly owned Philips subsidiary in 1976, with the closure of two factories. In turn Philips sold the one remaining Pye CTV factory to Sanyo in 1982. Decca was sold by Racal to the Taiwanese firm Tatung in 1980. The ITT subsidiary STC withdrew from television production in 1984, as did Rediffusion. ITT had decided to concentrate its European CTV production in its German factory, which later became part of the Finnish Nokia group (see Chapter 13).

2. *Collaboration.* Recognizing the superiority of Japanese CTV manufacturing technology, two British firms decided to enter joint ventures with Japanese firms. Rank was estimated to have lost £20 million on the production of some 175,000 CTVs per year in 1974–6.[21] The firm was persuaded to enter into a deal with Toshiba whereby it contributed its two factories in exchange for 70 per cent of the new company. Toshiba made a cash investment of £3 million for the remaining 30 per cent. Rank was persuaded to enter the joint venture as a result of considerable pressure from the Department of Industry, which contributed a grant of £2 million. The D.o.I. saw the agreement as removing some of the embarrassment it had suffered in having to bow to industry pressure over the Hitachi episode. Unfortunately political compromise does not guarantee commercial success, and the venture proved short-lived, according to one observer because of the basic differences in company philosophy between the financially managed conglomerate Rank, and the product and engineering-orientated Toshiba.[22] Less than two years after the start Toshiba acquired the plants for £3 million and restarted production with 300 employees, compared to the 2,700 who had been employed when the venture started. Toshiba also had the benefit of a pioneering single-union agreement negotiated between the EETPU and the Japanese management which permitted the latter to introduce its own manufacturing and industrial relations practices.

A second joint venture was equally unsuccessful. Following Hitachi's withdrawal GEC's chairman Sir Arnold Weinstock dispatched a top manager to Japan to open talks with Hitachi, and the outcome was a 50:50 partnership based at GEC's factory at Hirwaun in South Wales. The deal was nearly two years in the making, and involved sustained efforts by the Labour government to persuade Hitachi to shrug off its earlier rebuff. As in the case of the Rank–Toshiba venture, the British firm contributed plant, machinery, and 2,000 employees and the Japanese firm £2.75m cash and technology.[23] In the first two years GEC–Hitachi managed to double its output to 300,000 sets per year, but Hitachi-branded sets outsold GEC ones by two to one, despite their being £50 more expensive.[24] It seemed clear that by 1981 the British public was convinced that the Japanese were masters of the art of television manufacturing. Once more this was a case of a joint venture riven by different manufacturing philosophies, and the divorce went through in 1983. Following that Hitachi reduced the workforce by 50 per cent, and reached an agreement with the EETPU behind the backs of five other unions to introduce a Toshiba-style agreement.

3. *Emulation*. The third strategy open to British firms was to try to go it alone and match Japanese best practice. The only firm seriously to attempt to do this was Thorn–EMI, which embarked on an ambitious scheme combining innovation with the closure of several plants, and the concentration of CTV production in two plants at Enfield and Gosport.

Plant closures were accompanied by a determined effort to upgrade the product technology for CTV and reduce assembly costs through automated insertion of components. In 1979 Thorn launched 'Project 1982', which produced a new range of chassis designs—the TX series—which drastically reduced the number of components required and the time taken to manufacure a set. A total of £13 million was invested in this project, of which £2.8 million was paid in government grants for R. & D. and specific capital projects. The new range of TX portable sets was introduced in 1983 with 25 per cent fewer components of which 84 per cent were inserted automatically. The time taken to produce, test, and pack the sets had been reduced from 3.5 to 1.4 hours. These changes made Thorn's production broadly comparable with the Japanese companies examined in the Boston report, but Japanese components were some 20 per cent cheaper than UK-sourced ones.[25]

Despite this major achievement Thorn's CTV manufacturing remained unprofitable, and in 1985 it undertook a further major reorganization costing £28 million.[26] More jobs were shed in 1986 as the Enfield plant was turned over to the manufacture of circuit boards for the entire range of CTVs, with all final assembly switched to Gosport. That it achieved its goal of matching Japanese standards of production efficiency is evident from an agreement signed in 1986 to manufacture CTVs for the Japanese company JVC. A year later, however, the Thorn management decided to focus its corporate strategy around its rental and retail businesses, and it sold the Ferguson subsidiary to the French Thomson company for £90 million. The closure of the small CTV plant operated by Fidelity the following year marked the final departure of British firms from the consumer electronics industry.

The prospect of a government-backed and subsidized modernization programme which NEDO had envisaged in 1978 had given way to a non-interventionist policy in which the Thatcher government left adjustment almost entirely to the firms. The provisions for regional and selective assistance to firms under the 1972 Industry Act remained in place, but as British firms left the industry the only firms left to benefit were foreign-owned. The major exception to this policy, which a manager of one of the hard-pressed British firms described as 'malign neglect', was the teletext initiative, which was seen by the firms as a way of escaping from the cut-throat competition in basic CTV sets, and by the government as the promotion of an indigenous British technology. Despite its success in diffusing the technology, it failed as a closure strategy, and once more the ultimate beneficiaries were the Japanese.

Teletext arose out of research conducted by the BBC into ways of providing captions to broadcast television programmes for the deaf and hard of hearing which would not be seen by the ordinary viewer.[27] As the research developed its potential for the transmission of other types of information was quickly realized, and the BBC and ITA both began to work on the introduction of a new service which would be available to those owning or renting a suitably modified television set at no extra cost beyond the additional expense of the teletext decoder. Each manufacturer saw teletext as an opportunity to gain a competitive advantage over the Japanese, but none alone was willing to bear the risk of trying to create a new market.

The slow expansion of the service was a matter of considerable concern to the hardware industry, and particularly to the Philips subsidiary Mullard—the major components supplier to the television industry—which had invested heavily in redesigning decoder chips. The price of these chips would inevitably fall with long production runs, but these depended on the development of a mass market which was in turn inhibited by the high price of the chips. Some way was needed to break out of this vicious circle.

In the course of 1980 the NEDO SWP began to press upon the Department of Industry the need for action to promote teletext. Despite their hostility to government intervention in industry, the Conservatives had been forced to recognize the strategic significance of information technology, in part by a report from the Advisory Council for Applied Research and Development (ACARD) which argued that IT would be among the most important applications for micro-electronics, and that future trading performance would depend on a competitive presence in IT products.[28] IT was in the process of becoming accepted as an exception to Thatcherite orthodoxy, symbolized by the appointment of a junior minister within the D.o.I. as Minister of Information Technology. Teletext was pounced on as a technology where the UK could be argued to have a lead over its competitors, and where there was already considerable evidence from industry that some form of intervention would be welcome.

In November 1980 the D.o.I. constituted the Teletext and Viewdata Steering Group comprising civil servants and industry representatives. The Group's objectives were to examine the issues facing teletext and viewdata, and to develop a concerted marketing strategy for the promotion of these technologies which would be acceptable to the industry and form the basis of specific commitments. It is worth stressing that the policies were to be framed as part of a consensus-forming process involving industry representatives, and they were to be implemented by industry actors and not by government itself. The latter's role was essentially one of bringing together the interested parties, and providing some finance to assist their activities.

The first act of the Steering Group was to hold a conference at which those directly involved in teletext provision and marketing were invited openly to state their commitment to the success of the initiative. This resulted in a series of specific undertakings by each party. Set-makers agreed to target sales increases of teletext sets from 80,000 in 1980 to 1.1 million in 1983. Broadcasters undertook to improve the quality of the teletext service and the rental and retail trade agreed to step up the level of staff training. Semiconductor manufacturers had already demonstrated their commitment to teletext by undertaking substantial investments, and they agreed to maintain development work in this field. More specifically they promised to give assistance to set-makers in undertaking the assembly of decoders from supplied components, and to exploit export opportunities to the maximum. Finally, the government committed itself to the role of co-ordinating the overall marketing effort, which involved a relatively small amount of financial assistance for the preparation of publicity material as the campaign got under way. It was clear that government viewed the teletext initiative as a collective enterprise by the industry which it would facilitate as far as possible, but not direct.

The Steering Group maintained an active role in monitoring the implementation of the agreements, and the D.o.I. distributed 3 million leaflets through the trade. The D.o.I. also collaborated with the retail trade association, RETRA, in running a series of training seminars for salespersons. But perhaps even more important was a tangible measure by the government to stimulate new teletext business when the Treasury approved the halving of rental down-payments and HP deposits for those acquiring teletext sets. Later a much more significant concession was made by the Treasury when, against stiff opposition from the Inland Revenue, it agreed to retain capital allowances for the TV rental industry. The Treasury had feared that the effect of this would be to increase the cash flow of the rental companies which they would use to finance the expansion of video recorder rental rather than teletext. In the end the Treasury relented after an approach from the Information Technology Advisory Panel of the Cabinet Office had stressed the significance of teletext in gaining consumer acceptance for IT.

Government involvement in the promotion of teletext was scaled down as it became apparent that the initiative was having a considerable degree of success. Consumer offtake of teletext sets in the first year of the campaign was 50 per cent higher than the combined total for the previous four years. The success of teletext has not, however, simply been the expansion of the market in Britain. The British teletext system has become the world standard for teletext and is now being used in seventeen countries. Moreover 98 per cent of teletext chips in use world-wide were designed and made in Britain. Teletext is an all-too-rare example of a British invention being successfully brought to a mass market through the combined efforts of the industry and government. Despite this, however, British firms were unable to match the Japanese manufacturers' success in the television industry and teletext offered them only a relatively short breathing space. In another crucial area, that of video cassette recorder technology, the British industry had no chance of resisting usurpation through innovation, and the enormous expansion of the VCR market was almost entirely to the advantage of the Japanese.

Usurpation Through Innovation: The VCR Case

In CTVs the major European firms—although not, as we have seen, the British—were able to offer some defence against Japanese competition. In the late 1980s, however, the ability of the Japanese to achieve a mass market for an entirely new product against European competition was demonstrated by the outcome of the video format war. Unable to win the market battle, the Europeans turned to political measures, and a voluntary export restraint agreement was signed with MITI. When this failed to secure the European technology, Philips-Grundig adopted Japanese technology, and succeeded in raising tariffs on VCR imports. By this time the Koreans were beginning to emerge as VCR producers, and the European firms began to try to resist competitive pressure through antidumping complaints. Continual Japanese innovation in VCRs, first with camcorders and then with improved definition formats and the application of digital technology, forced the Europeans to follow suit as the low-cost Asian producers were snapping at their heels.

The enormous growth in the world-wide market for video recorders in the 1980s took industry experts as well as policy-makers by surprise, and created much more intense pressures for political intervention than were evident in response to competition in television sets. In 1979 the Japanese industry was predicting that the value of its production of VCRs would not reach 700 billion yen until 1990;[29] in fact that figure was surpassed in 1981! Between

1980 and 1981 VCR production in Japan doubled and video recorders became the single most important product by value to the consumer electronics industry[30] and by 1982 Japan accounted for 94 per cent of world-wide production. By 1985 Japan was producing over 30 million VCRs per year with a home market of less than 5 million, which underlined its considerable success in export markets throughout the world. In 1983 exports of VCRs were 19 per cent of total electronics industry exports (i.e. consumer electronics, industrial electronics, and electronics components), with over 4.5 million recorders exported to the EC.[31]

Unlike the United States, which absorbed the bulk of Japanese VCR exports, Europe did have its own indigenous VCR technology. Philips had introduced its first domestic VCR in 1974, and in the late 1970s significant markets for VCRs began to develop in West Germany, Britain, and the Netherlands. Despite the introduction of a new long-play model in 1977, Philips was in a relatively weak position when the Japanese VHS and Beta systems began to be sold in Europe in 1978 and 1979.

The VHS system, which has now become the dominant world-wide video format, was developed by the Japan Victor Company (JVC), a subsidiary of the giant Matsushita corporation.[32] JVC was a relatively small company by Japanese standards, and unlike Sony, producer of the rival Beta format, chose to attack European markets by collaboration with the main competitor to Philips in each of the major European markets. In 1977 JVC concluded deals with Thorn-EMI in Britain, Telefunken in West Germany, and Thomson in France which enabled those companies to market their own-brand VCRs supplied by JVC from Japan. The Thorn deal in Britain was pivotal, because of Thorn's ownership of a major part of the TV rental industry and its software interests through EMI. The deals also contained provision for the eventual manufacture of VCRs in Europe, which began in 1982 when the J2T joint venture between JVC, Thorn, and Telefunken began production of JVC-designed VCRs at Newhaven and Berlin.

Philips responded to the Japanese challenge with a newly designed VCR, the V2000, which was introduced in 1981, its third system in seven years. At the same time Philips was in the process of marketing for domestic use its LaserVision videodisc system which was eventually introduced in 1982. Its commercial strategy in video was to market the V2000 primarily as a time-shift machine to enable

TABLE 10.2 *Sales and production of video recorders in the UK 1977–1986*

Year	Cumulative Sales[a] ('000)	% Penetration	Production ('000)
1977	20	—	—
1978	85	—	—
1979	200	1	—
1980	550	3	—
1981	1,520	7	—
1982	3,600	17	20
1983	5,780	27	180
1984	7,285	34	300
1985	8,885	40	400
1986	10,690	46	950

[a] Total sales less an estimate of machines scrapped

Source: BREMA; BIS-Mackintosh.

users to record programmes off-air to watch at another time. They expected the software rental market to develop through videodiscs, thus thinking rather optimistically that many consumers would be prepared to buy both kinds of machine! JVC also had its own videodisc system, the VHD, but its launch, which was due in the UK in 1982, was abandoned shortly afterwards when Thorn and JVC perceived rather earlier than did Philips that the rapid penetration of VCRs, and the enormous growth in independent software rental outlets, were providing insurmountable constraints to the development of a mass market for videodiscs. Table 10.2 shows the rapid build-up of VCR sales in the UK from 1980 onwards, with 17 per cent penetration of homes by the end of 1982. In 1983 it was estimated that Philips had captured only 8 per cent of the British market with their V2000 system, compared to 70 per cent for the JVC system and 22 per cent for the Sony Beta system.[33]

The situation in other European markets, where Philips and Grundig had their production bases, was somewhat better, with V2000 capturing 34 per cent of the West German market and 60 per cent of the Austrian. But it was becoming clear that in an unrestricted market the European producers would be unable to compete against the Japanese, and late in 1982, just after the French had begun to restrict Japanese VCR exports to France by funnelling them through an obscure customs post at Poitiers, Philips and Grundig initiated an anti-dumping suit clearly intended to provoke the

EC into taking action to reduce its £7.5 billion trade deficit with Japan.[34]

Negotiations between EC Commissioners Viscount Davignon and Wilhelm Haferkampf and MITI concluded with an agreement in February 1983 to restrict Japanese VCR exports to Europe for a period of three years. The agreement, the first ever negotiated by the EEC rather than by individual countries, provided for a maximum shipment of 4.55 million sets (compared to 4.9 million in 1982) at a floor price set in effect by Philips-Grundig's production costs for their V2000 model (estimated to be some 30 per cent higher than equivalent Japanese costs). The figure also included 600,000 kits supplied by JVC for assembly at its British and German factories, and it was expected that it would enable Philips and Grundig to sell 1.2 million machines annually. This agreement effectively meant that Philips and Grundig would set the price, it would be the consumer who would lose out, and it would be the Japanese producers who would gain by enhanced profits. Nothing in the agreement had altered the fundamental lack of competitiveness of the European producers *vis-à-vis* the Japanese.[35] Shortly afterwards Philips and Grundig withdrew their anti-dumping suit, and at the end of April France abandoned its Poitiers ploy. Both measures had succeeded in their prime aim of provoking the EEC into protectionist action against the Japanese.

The British government and the trade association BREMA were relatively uninvolved in these events, since with the exception of J2T the British industry unlike the German was not involved in VCR production, and unlike the French Thomson company, which had been shut out of the JVC consortium by the French government, Thorn-EMI had no plans to undertake its own independent production of VCRs. The British Trade Secretary, Lord Cockfield, had even before the EEC–MITI agreement been pressing the Japanese for more investment in VCR production in Britain, so that the British government had a general interest in protectionist measures which would accelerate such inward investment. The inclusion of a limit on kits in the MITI quota was initially seen as disappointing for Britain, because of fears that it would remove the incentive for Japanese firms to locate in Europe as a way of avoiding quota restrictions. Sanyo and Mitsubishi had already announced their intention of producing VCRs in Britain, and their decision to go ahead with these investments, and subsequent decisions to invest in VCR production in Britain by Toshiba and Sharp, indicate that these fears were unfounded, and perhaps also that the Japanese expected the protectionist mood in Europe to harden still further. In any case the quota on kits was raised for 1984 to take account of growing Japanese production in the EEC.

The EEC–MITI agreement is of considerable interest, not only because its effects were precisely the reverse of what was intended, but also because it signalled a shift in trade policy determination from national capitals to Brussels. The accord failed in securing its principal objective—the preservation of indigenous European technology in VCRs—when Philips decided to secure a licence from Matsushita to manufacture VHS recorders in 1983, and then the following year decided to abandon the V2000 format altogether in order to try to stem the growing losses in its video division which amounted to 1,800 million fl. (£228m.) between 1983 and 1985.[36] Philips management agree in retrospect that the V2000 system was already doomed by the time the EEC–MITI accord came into effect, and the downturn in the European VCR market in 1984 meant that the quota had no effect on restraining the level of imports from Japan. By the time the three-year agreement reached its end there was no enthusiasm for its extension, and with effect from January 1986 it was replaced by an increase in the tariff from 8 per cent to 14 per cent.

The effect of the accord on the determination of trade policy in VCRs is likely to be more long-lasting. The DTI has in effect reserved this area to the European Commission, and efforts by Philips to secure local content rules are directed towards Brussels. It did however put considerable energy in 1983–4 into a campaign to persuade the Japanese to extend VCR manufacture in Britain, with visits to Japan by both ministers and senior civil servants, as well as from the Welsh Development Agency. The most intensive efforts were aimed at the Sharp Corporation which was deciding between a British or West German location for its European VCR plant. Its decision to opt for a factory in North Wales occasioned quite exceptional amounts of regional assistance from the DTI, over £6 million in 1985–6, making it the biggest single recipient of regional aid of any of the Japanese companies in Britain.

The success of the government's campaign to attract inward investment in VCRs is evident from the spate of investments in 1986–8 which brought the total number of VCR producers in Britain to twelve, more than in any other European country. What is less clear is the extent to which these constitute manufacturing operations rather than assembly plants for components imported from abroad. Unlike CTVs there are no legal requirements for a specified level of local sourcing, although all the firms interviewed claim to be working to reach 45 per cent, and such undertakings have been sought by the DTI as part of the negotiations over discretionary regional assistance. Philips and Grundig are pressing for the EEC to adopt a 60 per cent rule, but many express doubts as to whether that level is feasible given the difficulty of procuring key components in Europe (such as the mechanical deck, including the head assembly which is the biggest single component by value in a VCR). One solution, which amounts in practice to a further Japanization of the European industry, would be for Japanese component manufacturers to locate in Europe, and indeed this process began when Alps Electric established a plant in Milton Keynes in 1985 to produce VCR components.

Conclusion

The combination of increasing foreign ownership of the industry, the abstentionist industrial policy pursued by the Conservative government since 1979, and the active role in trade policy issues played by the EEC has served to weaken government–industry ties within the consumer electronics sector in Britain. The role of the trade association has diminished as its protectionist ambitions have been compromised by the overwhelming weight of Japanese production in the UK. Apart from the acquisition of Ferguson by Thomson, Britain has been left out of the process of restructuring through mergers and take-overs at the European level which is discussed in Chapter 13. Governments have restricted their role to providing as favourable conditions as possible for foreign investment in the industry, leaving its future in the hands of boards of directors meeting in Tokyo, Paris, and Eindhoven. While the Japanese firms are likely to remain as manufacturers in Britain in order to gain access to the EEC, the introduction of new television technologies in the 1990s will make the future of the non-Japanese manufacturers in Britain increasingly uncertain.

Notes

1. Electronic Consumer Goods SWP, *Progress Report 1978* (London: NEDO, 1978).
2. *Business Monitor* (1975).
3. E. Arnold, *Competition and Change in the British Television Industry* (London: Macmillan, 1985).
4. Interview.
5. Interview.
6. Department of Industry, *The Regeneration of British Industry*, Cmnd. 5710 (London: HMSO, 1974).
7. T. Forester, 'Neutralising the Industrial Strategy', in K. Coates (ed.), *What Went Wrong?* (Nottingham: Spokesman Books, 1979).
8. K. Middlemas, *Industry, Unions and Government* (London: Macmillan, 1983), p. 94.
9. M. Sharp, 'Japanese Investment in Consumer Electronics', in M. Brech and M. Sharp, *Inward Investment: Policy Options for the United Kingdom* (London: Routledge & Kegan Paul, 1984), p. 69.
10. *Engineer*, 28 July 1977.
11. *Financial Times*, 8 Dec. 1977; *Electronics Weekly*, 1 June 1977.
12. Electronic Consumer Goods SWP, *Progress Report 1978*.
13. According to our interviews, such agreements had earlier been drawn up with Sony and Matsushita in 1973 and 1975. In the case of Sony, company lawyers had advised that such agreements were not legally enforceable. Ironically the company has since won the Queen's Award for Exports.
14. BREMA, *Annual Report 1978*.
15. BIS-Mackintosh, 'Towards a Community Strategy for a New Audio-Visual Technology: The Consumer Electronics Industry', unpublished report for DG XIII of the European Commission (1987).
16. For a discussion of the concept of meso-corporatism, and some case-studies drawn from other sectors, see Alan Cawson (ed.), *Organized Interests and the State: Studies in Meso-Corporatism* (London: Sage Publications, 1985).
17. Initially it proved difficult for the SWP to persuade the firms that such a study was needed, and that they should help to pay for it (interview).
18. Electronic Consumer Goods SWP, *Progress Report 1979* (London: NEDO, 1979).
19. See Martin Rhodes, 'Organized Interests and Industrial Crisis Management: Restructuring the Steel Industry in West Germany, Italy and France', in Cawson (ed.), *Organized Interests and the State*.
20. An analysis of regional assistance to consumer electronics firms, compiled from announcements in *British Business*, shows that from 1984

100% of aid has gone to foreign firms, mostly Japanese but since 1987 also Korean.

21. *Financial Times*, 24 Aug. 1978.
22. M. Trevor, *Toshiba's New British Company: Competitiveness through Innovation in Industry* (London: Policy Studies Institute, 1988), pp. 14–15.
23. A. Kransdorff, 'Learning to Live in Harmony', *Financial Times*, 1 June 1981.
24. *Sunday Times*, 11 Apr. 1982.
25. Interviews.
26. *Financial Times*, 10 Jan. 1986.
27. See Alan Cawson, 'The Teletext Initiative in Britain: Anatomy of Successful Neo-corporatist Policy-Making', Economic and Social Research Council, *Corporatism and Accountability Newsletter* (1986).
28. Advisory Council for Applied Research and Development, *The Applications of Semiconductor Technology* (London: HMSO, 1978).
29. G. Gregory, *Japanese Electronics Technology: Enterprise and Innovation*, 2nd edn. (Chichester: John Wiley, 1986), p. 94.
30. Electronic Industries Association of Japan, *Electronic Industries in Japan* (Tokyo: EIAJ, 1984).
31. Ibid.
32. For a history of the development of the VHS VCR by JVC, see P. R. Nayak and J. M. Ketteringham, *Breakthroughs!* (New York: Rawson Associates, 1986), ch. 2.
33. Economist Intelligence Unit, *Home Electronics* (London: EIU, 1983).
34. *Financial Times*, 15 Dec. 1982.
35. *Financial Times*, 15 Feb. 1983.
36. *Financial Times*, 25 Mar. 1987.

11

France: The Illusion of State Control

Introduction

The French consumer electronics industry is a highly concentrated industry, largely dominated by two firms, Thomson and Philips-France (through its subsidiary La Radiotechnique). Unlike the British industry examined in the previous chapter, existing firms have not been usurped by Japanese competitors, and have benefited from a mode of closure underpinned by the policies of successive French governments. Several key aspects of this closure regime are examined in this chapter: the maintenance of incompatible technical standards for CTVs which segregated the French market more rigidly than other national markets, the privileging of Thomson as a national champion, the strict controls applied to inward investment, and the use of informal quotas to cartellize the French market. The chapter shows how this regime has been undermined by a number of pressures towards internationalization, arising from changes in firm strategy as well as from the shift in the determination of trade policies from national capitals to Brussels.

Three features of the pattern of closure arising from a direct relationship between the state and large firms are of particular interest in the context of government–industry relations. Firstly, over the last twenty years as the French government developed the notion of certain companies as 'national champions', Thomson took on this role, with government support. This did not mean, however, that the government controlled either Thomson or Philips. Secondly, the nature of Thomson itself, which was, in ways which will be considered further below, an ill-co-ordinated and at times conflict-ridden conglomerate, combined with the government's problems in defining, especially after the 1981 nationalization, an appropriate relationship with the company. In the event the French Industry Ministry was widely regarded as a mouthpiece for Thomson's own interests. A third, more recent, feature of the development of the industry has been active, but indirect, state support for Thomson as it has sought to expand within the world-wide electronics industry. Despite its status as a nationalized industry, Thomson has increasingly become a genuinely multinational company, in effect an 'international champion'.

This chapter first examines the French consumer electronics sector in terms of its markets and the actors within it. The relationships between these actors are considered in the second part of the chapter, and finally the effects and operation of these relationships are demonstrated through an account of the French companies' strategy and actions concerned with VCR production. This case-study provides in effect a 'French' view of the events surrounding the Grundig–Thomson negotiations that are described from a German angle in Chapter 12. Since French consumer electronics production is heavily concentrated on colour televisions (CTVs) most of the analysis will be concentrated on CTVs although our case-study turns to VCRs as a separate issue.

Products and Markets[1]

In 1985 CTVs accounted for 55 per cent of total French production of consumer electronics products. The other significant item was car radios where French production has consistently exceeded demand. VCR production has also recently begun, but on a modest scale, notably in J2T, which is now a JVC–Thomson joint venture.

In the core business of colour televisions (CTVs) Philips and Thomson each have a market share of about 30 per cent. Estimates vary, but in 1985–7 Philips and Thomson probably each produced about 600,000 CTVs in France. Océanic, now owned by the Finnish Nokia group (formerly owned by ITT and later by Electrolux), took 8–9 per cent of the CTV market. In 1987 Nokia also bought the SEL Consumer Electronics division, another former ITT subsidiary, from the French CGE group who had acquired it as part of the telecommunications deal described in Chapter 6. Grundig's French production seems to have been comparable to that of Océanic.

Japanese investment in this sector in France has been a recent phenomenon. Figures on total output by Japanese producers are not readily available, but given their absence from the main CTV field and the importance of Philips in car radios, it seems likely that Japanese production of consumer electronics in France is of the order of 25 per cent of the sectoral total.

In 1985, CTV imports took 30 per cent of apparent consumption with just over half the imports being from the EEC (50 per cent), mostly Germany (38 per cent). A striking feature of the French industry has been Thomson's willingness to establish supply bases in Asia (sometimes owned, sometimes not). Hence a high percentage of imports are actually by 'French' firms (60 per cent in 1984–5). The pattern of trade has in fact begun to alter in the late 1980s with the somewhat belated European-wide rationalization of Thomson and Philips. Japanese CTV imports, severely restricted by quotas, have been slightly less than imports from Singapore (a Thomson base). Japanese imports have been more successful in other CE products and have taken about 18 per cent of the French market (36 per cent of total imports) in 1985. Sony is estimated to have had 5 per cent of the French CTV market in 1985.

The Industrial Actors

The rise of Thomson-Brandt

The relatively stable structure of the consumer electronics industry has been profoundly affected over the years by government hostility to foreign investment which lasted until about 1982. While foreign investment was discouraged, successive governments sought to promote the Thomson group as the national champion in electronics. The firm Thomson SA is, at the time of writing, state-owned. It is the product of successive mergers. The original Houston-Thomson company was set up around the turn of the century by French investors who bought the rights to exploit the patents of the American engineers Houston and Thomson. An analogous company was set up in the UK. Houston-Thomson sold its telecommunications interests to ITT in the 1920s. In the 1960s the environment was very favourable to mergers such as that of Houston-Thomson with Hotchkiss-Brandt. Thomson-Brandt, as it became, was the rising star of French electronics under the entrepreneurial leadership of its Président Directeur-Général (PDG) Paul Richard, who did not, however, own a controlling interest in the equity. The group was spread across a vast variety of electrical, electronics, consumer durable, and engineering activities, including small arms. One senior manager observed that the culture of Thomson-Brandt was that of provincial business with managers recruited from outside the traditional *pantouflage* élite. Its business was concentrated in consumer markets away from the heavy hand of the state.

In 1967 it took a step which brought it into the embrace of the state. Thomson-Brandt took a majority stake in the CSF electronics group. CSF was commercially and politically locked into the government apparatus. Heavily dependent on miltary contracts, its management had formed intimate links with the Defence Ministry, where it enjoyed a position analogous to that of Siemens as the Bundespost's 'court supplier'. The acquisition of CSF brought Thomson more closely into the world of state subsidies for *'grands projets'*. It also posed the question of rivalry with the CGE group, at that time perceived more as a financial holding company than an industrial concern. In 1969, with the blessing of the public authorities, CGE and Thomson made a 'Yalta' agreement which divided the electronics market into spheres of influence, with Thomson taking consumer electronics and CGE telecommunications, although Paul Richard resented their loss.

The merger of Thomson-Brandt and CSF was never fully consummated: Thomson-CSF remains a partially owned subsidiary. According to interview sources in government and in the firm, the pre-1981 Thomson group was not run as a coherent whole. Thomson-Brandt had acquired a vast number of disparate plants, while the CSF management formed a separate empire, highly privileged by the Defence Ministry and later by the Industry Ministry. Thomson-Brandt's management did not control Thomson-CSF, which entered telecommunications in 1976 (see Chapter 6). But the parent group was responsible for underwriting the financial position of CSF, which became very difficult. Thomson-CSF was also one of the major recipients of the huge subsidies for exports of capital equipment.

It seems that the interest of the public authorities in more glamorous (and seemingly lucrative) areas of electronics induced Thomson-Brandt to treat consumer electronics as a milch cow. The protected market sustained sales, but Thomson began to move production outside France in the late 1970s. Its internationalization had two elements, European and Asian.

Thomson's Vidéocolor TV tube subsidiary had initially been part-owned by RCA. RCA had developed tubes for SECAM but was prevented from exporting to France by manipulation of safety regulations,[2] and therefore entered into a collaboration agreement with Thomson for the establishment of Vidéocolor. By the 1970s Vidéocolor was substantially autonomous, was headed by Abel Farnoux (later of the Mission de la Filière Électronique), and was expanding in Europe. In the late 1970s Thomson-Brandt began to acquire smaller consumer electronics firms in Germany, evidently with a view to exploiting their brand images and building on their market shares. Vidéocolor took over, and shut down, Telefunken's tube factory in Ulm.

At the same time Thomson was beginning to build up production facilities in audio in Singapore: this move was somewhat unusual. Thomson-Brandt and Rhône-Poulenc were the only two big French firms to go in for major 'outward processing' activities of this sort.[3] The state had very little real alternative to underwriting the strategy of the national champion it had fostered, though even in the 1970s it had potential veto power. In common with most of the big conglomerate 'national champions' Thomson was getting into financial (and political) trouble in the late 1970s. Despite the much criticized export and R. & D. subsidies,[4] the group was beginning to lose money above all due to telecommunications, and getting into debt. Within consumer electronics, in addition to the weakening of traditional protectionist barriers, the firm was coming under public attack for its import strategy, and its abandonment of new products, notably videodiscs. Thomson-Brandt did little R. & D. in new products, especially in France, and in fact as German firms with R. & D. facilities were acquired, Thomson's consumer electronics R. & D. concentrated in Villingen in Germany. Thomson's strategy was essentially to avoid entering new markets until other producers had established which products would succeed, and then to produce under licence. Meanwhile Farnoux's Vidéocolor tube production was unprofitable and he was opposed by the head of Thomson's consumer electronics, Jacques Fayard, who saw the firm's future lying substantially in cheap imports from Asia. Farnoux argued, within the firm and elsewhere, for co-operation with Philips on new products, but was dismissed in early 1981.

Philips in France

In the light of French governmental hostility to foreign investment Philips has trodden a delicate path; its subsidiaries have retained

French names, French top management, less than 100 per cent ownership by Philips, and a consistent commitment to idiosyncratic French standards such as SECAM. Philips has never attempted to usurp the privileged position of Thomson, nor challenge publicly policies of selective state intervention. Offers by Philips-France for co-operation with Thomson in 1977[5] reflected the company's long-standing desire to be a good corporate citizen in France. The Philips group in France consists of a wholly owned parent Philips-France, and a range of subsidiaries mostly less than 100 per cent owned by Philips. Philips-France acts as a holding company and as a sales organization for the group. In consumer electronics the key elements have been La Radiotechnique which produces final products, above all CTVs, and RTC which makes components. The group has recently restructured with La Radiotechnique becoming a holding company like Thomson SA with product group divisions under it. The firm claims to be moving in line with Philips's goal of a product-based corporate structure, even faster than the rest of Philips.[6] Philips-France remains a separate legal entity, co-owner with Philips NV of the majority of La Radiotechnique's shares.

The pressures on the Philips-France group to be properly 'French' have been subtle and varied. Philips took 100 per cent control of La Radiotechnique after the wartime management were accused of collaboration, but it was advised to reduce its stake quickly to around 50 per cent. La Radiotechnique has a *conseil d'administration* drawn from the French politico-business élite, not from Philips in Holland. The company reports of both La Radiotechnique and its operating subsidiary reveal that non-executive directors in 1985–6 included Ambrose Roux (ex-head of CGE), one person also on the boards of another Philips-France subsidiary and of Thomson CSF, but no one *visibly* from Philips. The brand images, Schneider, Radiola, as well as Philips, have traditionally been seen as French, and Philips-France has taken an active part in the development of the SECAM system. La Radiotechnique's recent annual reports refer somewhat elliptically to the need to strengthen links with Philips. But La Radiotechnique, according to its managers, was always treated as Philips's French Consumer Electronics division for the purposes of the Philips 'federal' structure at Eindhoven. Its senior managers are responsible to Philips and join group corporate planning meetings. The aim of the 'Francization' has been to secure perception by the consuming public of La Radiotechnique's products as truly French, and to convince the authorities of its loyalty for the purpose of obtaining public procurement contracts and research subsidies. In many ways Philips-France has been at least as 'French' as Thomson; RTC participated in the '*Plans Composants*' of the 1970s and La Radiotechnique has received important state-regulated orders, including 'minitels' for the French videotext system.

Japanese companies in France

Having long restricted foreign investment, France was not in the 1970s a welcome environment for Japanese investment. A combination of events in 1982 changed this, and led the French government to reconsider its exclusionary practices. At a macro-economic level the government began to prize the inflow of foreign exchange and ultimately of jobs, and industrially it became harder to find French *repreneurs* to rescue firms in trouble. Accordingly the government sent missions to Tokyo seeking to attract Japanese firms. The threat of increased protectionism also increased the willingness of Japanese firms to invest in Europe; many observers see this as an aim of the decision to force all imported VCRs to undergo customs clearance at Poitiers, though this probably imputes excessive coherence to a panic move. Thus, for reasons of push and pull, a major flow of Japanese establishments began in 1982. Between 1968 and 1982 only five Japanese plants were set up in France, including, in 1980, Sony. These plants employed an estimated total of 1,000 workers. In 1982–4 19 Japanese companies entered France, employing altogether 6,000 people. 3,500 jobs were accounted for by Sumitomo's acquisition of Dunlop-France, and consumer electronics investments accounted for half the rest, with Clarion, Pioneer, Sony (again), Trio, and Akai (two stages in Honfleur).[7] Apart from the J2T plant, and Akai's VCR plant, Japanese production in France has been mainly in audio products and tapes, presumably because of the unattractiveness of CTV plants dedicated to SECAM. Alsace-Lorraine has been an attractive location to Japanese firms aiming to export to Germany. Sony-France has stated its intention to export 90 per cent of its production. Perhaps in the light of French sensitivities, Japanese investments in France have typically been slightly smaller than elsewhere in Europe (an average of 251 employees per plant compared with 334 in the UK).[8]

Public Policy and Governmental Actors

Public policy on television in France has probably been less concerned over the last twenty years with the 'hardware' than with
the 'software' of programme content (notably regarding political
and linguistic content) and the regulation and liberalization of
broadcasting.[9] Hardware and software, however, interact: recently,
for example, a market for TV signal decoders has arisen as a result
of the Socialist government's creation of the pay-tv Canal-Plus.

Nevertheless, relations with the French state form an ambiguous
and paradoxical background to consumer electronics production.
Managers interviewed insisted that the determinant of success or
failure is the consumer market-place, where the state is seen as
having no part to play; but on the other hand even in this sector
the attitude and actions of the state are a presence which can never
be ignored.

The consumer electronics sector has in recent years seen active
government intervention, but until the late 1970s it was not considered 'noble' enough to benefit from major state aid, beyond protection, after the effort of the early 1960s to develop SECAM. Many
factors that have impinged on the consumer electronics industry
have been spin-offs from policies with more general aims. The manufacturers of consumer electronics products are multi-product firms
whose strategies in this sector and relations with the state cannot
be viewed in isolation from their wider activities and their broader
links with the government, via civil and military public procurement, and support for R. & D. Thomson, above all, and Philips
to a very major degree, have been beneficiaries of heavy state spending in areas of electronics that seem more glamorous than consumer
electronics, such as the various 'Plans Calcul' and the programmes
for semiconductors, as well as being major contractors in defence
and telecommunications. Thus to the extent that firms produce
across sectors, the effects of a tight regime of closure in one sector
can have much wider implications for government–industry relations in other sectors.

At the apex on the administrative structure is the President of
the Republic. His intervention is rare and determinant chiefly
through his role in the nomination of key individuals and their
subsequent relationship with him. For example, in 1982 Mitterrand
appointed his left-wing Research Minister Jean-Pierre Chevènement

as Minister for Industry. His attempts to interfere in management decisions led to his isolation in the government, and his resignation in early 1983 followed protests directly to the President of the Republic by Thomson's PDG, Alain Gomez, and other PDGs of state firms. Gomez is a former top civil servant, once a political associate of Chevènement and an ex-paratrooper. He had been Finance Director of St-Gobain. His appointment in 1982 was a last minute choice by Mitterrand, not part of a strategy by Chevènement.

The Industry Ministry

Any closure strategy based on the nurturing of a national champion relies for its effectiveness on the capacity of the government to turn its public policy goals into corporate decisions of the firm. In turn this depends on the power and expertise of the sponsoring department.

During the 1970s and 1980s Thomson's official interlocutor inside the government was the DIELI, the electronics directorate of the Industry Ministry whose bargaining power was extremely weak in the consumer electronics sector. Its objectives tended to be diffuse and macro-economic and while it could demand that firms take a long-term perspective, it did not have the power or the expertise to force its own analysis on the firm, or indeed to oppose short-run profit maximizing strategies when these were required by the Finance Ministry. For example during the late 1970s the Industry Ministry was openly hostile to Fayard's strategy of relying on cheap imports from Asia.

Thomson's bargaining power with the Industry Ministry was, even in the period after nationalization, substantial. If pressure was exerted by ministry officials, or by state-appointed members of Thomson's conseil d'administration, the PDG would retort that he would settle the matter with the President of the Republic. Once profitability by 1985 had become the government's aim the Industry Ministry lost most of its leverage. The firm was much more able to dictate the stance of the ministry on such matters as trade policy than vice versa. Confidential Industry Ministry papers on consumer electronics policy reflected the stance of the firm. One Industry Ministry official conceded that it was natural that this should be so; everyone knew, he said, that the Industry Ministry was a mouthpiece for business, private or public, and discounted it accordingly. Ministry officials did not make any claim to being able to regulate the firm once the 1983 restructuring plan had been allowed to go through. They could monitor performance and seek to persuade, but, according to Industry Ministry officials, Thomson was subject to regulation by the market not the state. The Industry Ministry itself had few incentives to offer the firm. It did represent the French industry in negotiations in Brussels and was able to support Thomson in conflicts with the Finance Ministry. According to one official, Thomson and the Industry Ministry would always establish and defend a joint position before any negotiations with the Finance Ministry. Officials in other ministries saw the matter in the same light, regarding the Industry Ministry as weak and dominated by industrialists. Indeed the decision of the Chirac government's Industry Minister Alain Madelin in 1986 to abolish sectoral directorates including the DIELI reflected the widespread perception that they were ineffectual. After the restructuring initiated by Thomson and CGE and backed by the Élysée (see Chapter 6) Industry Ministry officials saw that they would have to accept the basic strategic decisions of the firm. They depended heavily on the firm itself for information, though under the Socialists the practice grew up of commissioning consultants' reports.

The Finance Ministry

While, during the 1970s, Thomson-Brandt's consumer electronics strategy was its own, the internationalization which it then initiated could not have occurred without the authorization of the Finance Ministry. Despite opposition elsewhere in the administration Thomson's consumer electronics boss Jacques Fayard was able to persuade the Finance Ministry that moving into Spain and Singapore was useful expansion by France.

Officials in both the Industry Ministry and the Finance Ministry suggested that the latter ministry was mainly concerned with immediate balance of payments and budgetary matters, including a desire to minimize subsidies given to state firms and to maximize revenues from them. Finance Ministry officials can read a balance sheet as well as anyone and are thus better placed to monitor what concerns them than is the Industry Ministry.

Other ministries

As we have seen, the wide scope of the companies in the consumer electronics industry inevitably means that other ministries are involved with them, though from the point of view of specifically consumer electronics strategies such involvement has on the whole been marginal. The PTT Ministry has affected the consumer electronics sector through its demands for minitel terminals. Shortly after the arrival of the Socialist government La Radiotechnique tendered to produce an experimental minitel terminal. La Radiotechnique's design was approved by the DGT who were however ordered to give this business to Thomson; Thomson's model was less satisfactory because its telecom branch (CSF) had designed it, whereas Radiotechnique had used its threatened black and white TV team, who were well placed to make the item. Radiotechnique made known that if its tender for the main order was not accepted it would have to close a black and white TV factory which was in the constituency of the PTT Minister Louis Mexandeau. Unexpectedly the minister announced in a speech to his constituency that Radiotechnique would get the order.

Although on paper the PTT Ministry was linked to the Industry Ministry for most of the 1980s there was a functional separation and the DIELI had neither the technical capability of the CNET (see Chapter 6) nor the DGT's public procurement role. DIELI and CNET did not act in concert: the traditions of the two institutions, as embodied in the *corps* from which their senior staff are chiefly drawn—the *corps des mines* in the DIELI and the telecommunications engineers in the CNET—are totally different.

The Planning Commission, unlike the Finance Ministry, was opposed to Fayard's internationalization strategy,[10] criticizing the implications for import penetration and explicitly calling for repatriation of consumer electronics production activities into France. After nationalization it was kept out of the process of formulating planning contracts between the state and the companies, and was even instructed not to supply macro-economic projections to state firms, who were enjoined to formulate their own independent hypotheses.

Under Chevènement the Research Ministry asked Abel Farnoux to establish a study group, the Mission de la Filière Électronique. Inspired by a school of thought which stressed the need to promote vertical linkages along *filières*, or chains of production from components to finished goods, the Mission, which analysed the whole electronics sector, sought to prevent France from becoming nothing more than an assembler or importer of consumer goods. Components production had to be promoted too. Farnoux called for a 'European alliance' between Thomson and Philips. But other ministers were never united behind this initiative of Chevènement. The publication of the Mission's report[11] coincided with the investiture of new heads for the state firms, but at this point it was made very clear that the government did not accept Farnoux's plan for a co-ordinated electronics policy under a 'Secrétariat de la Filière Électronique' which would have required a fundamental alteration in the balance of power between the big firms and the state. Only the name 'Programme de la Filière Électronique' was retained for the Industry Ministry's budgetary allocation for electronics; this has misled some people into supposing that Farnoux's plan was actually accepted.

Government and Industry: Issues and Strategies

The nature of the relationships between the various actors described above can further be illustrated and analysed by considering the main issues relating to the development of the French consumer electronics sectors which have arisen over the past two or three decades. Among the policy influences of a more narrowly industrial character which have influenced the development of the consumer electronics sector, one might single out two major factors. The first is protection which has long been enforced by technical barriers and by quotas and also by tight regulation of foreign investment; and secondly the consumer electronics industry has been strikingly affected by more general policies, linked to the fostering of 'national champions', for industrial concentration and subsequently nationalization and restructuring. These two factors, absent in Britain, help to account for the greater degree of closure in the French consumer electronics industry, and for its more stable industrial structure.

Protectionism: standards quotas and trade policy

France is renowned for the use of technical barriers to restrict the import of consumer electronics goods. For many years black and white TV transmissions used a unique 809-line system, and since the 1960s France has had the idiosyncratic SECAM colour system. This was originally intended to spread French technology worldwide, not to isolate France.

France has a fairly rigid quota system on TV imports, which is officially recognized by the EEC who have permitted France to use measures under Article 115 of the Rome Treaty to bar Japanese goods coming in via other member states.[12] Without such authorization, individual countries cannot effectively impose quotas on their own national markets apart from global EEC restrictions. The import regime is the product of high-level bargaining between the big firms and top political figures and of low-level collaboration between the Industry Ministry and trade associations.

The consumer electronics trade association SYMAVELEC (chaired by J.-C. Bonnet of Philips-France), a member of the federation of electrical and electronics industries associations (FIEE), is officially consulted on technical matters and offers a view on inward investment. But neither it nor the employers' confederation (CNPF) plays a major part in grand strategy on imports, which clearly results from negotiation between Thomson and Philips and the offices of the Prime Minister or the President, with the occasional involvement of the Finance Ministry.

Thomson, along with Philips, is one of France's leading importers. The Industry Ministry consults with members of the producers' trade association SYMAVELEC and SECIMAVI, the importers' association. The ministry then allocates the total quotas among individual firms or their local agents. The Japanese producers are forced to curtail their sales, and object strongly to the fact that Philips's and Thomson's quotas come out of a fixed total. But the established Japanese importers in return are guaranteed some quotas and the benefits of high prices in the segmented French market. The maintenance of the system requires the tacit collaboration of all the firms involved and the state in what amounts to a state-run market-sharing cartel. Smaller firms such as Océanic get 'mathematically' fair allocations of quotas according to the chosen formula. But the EEC's internal market initiative if fully implemented will eliminate the scope for France to segment its market in this way. The fact that 'voluntary' export restraints work in other markets without state licensing suggests that a natural consequence of the abolition of measures such as France's TV quotas will be either their continuation without any legal basis, as has happened for VCRs (see below), or else *de facto* market sharing agreements by the firms themselves.

This system of protectionism is nevertheless subject to increasing pressures. Japanese firms based in the UK can easily produce—or assemble—SECAM and PAL sets, and the EEC's internal market programme threatens to undermine France's ability to exclude them even though a large retail chain such as the FNAC group buys from manufacturers or their agents, on whom they depend for matters such as after-sales service, and would not consider disrupting established commercial circuits by buying from cut-price wholesalers in other EEC markets with looser restrictions on Japanese imports.

Even the Socialist government before its defeat in 1986 was increasingly coming to the view that protection at a national level was ineffective. But one senior Thomson executive stated that in his view national measures to control imports should remain in place even while the EEC's internal market unification programme is put in place. If in fact the EEC abolishes the use of Article 115 of the Rome Treaty, individual member states will no longer be able to exclude Japanese products legally imported into (or assembled in) another member state. Another senior executive of the firm suggested that Europe's trade policy towards Japan should be settled 'by the industry itself', a single pan-European trade association should negotiate export restraint with the Japanese, even if this meant cartellization of the world market. However, Thomson's views on protectionism have evolved as they increase their overseas production, and the firm appears to recognize even more than Philips-France, that it has a substantial interest in maintaining its own access to low-cost imports.

Like national import quotas, technical barriers are due to be phased out within the EEC. In fact SECAM has given France very little protection in recent years and has served more as an export barrier, with UK-based Japanese firms having recently become able to produce SECAM and PAL sets on the same production line.[13] In 1980, the French introduced a requirement that all CTV sets had to have a *péritélévision* socket which allowed the connection of non-SECAM equipment. This was an idiosyncratic requirement, but involved a European norm developed by Philips.

Philips in fact have been active participants in the isolation of the French market. They developed SECAM tubes, and have been active in the technical work of the trade association. One of the consequences of this has been that Philips came to be regarded by the Socialist government as a true 'European champion' in whom hopes could be vested once the era of national champions was over. French officials said that they had often had to speak up for Philips in EEC discussions when the Dutch government was being insufficiently forceful. A Finance Ministry official who observed the Thomson–Grundig affair closely remarked: 'The French government tried to transfer its mercantilist ambitions on to a European plane'.

Inward investment

The issue of inward investment, especially by the Japanese, is clearly closely linked to the problems of the import regime. As we have seen, the number of Japanese firms established in France has increased markedly since 1982 and the inflow continues. The official view has come to be that since the Japanese invest in Europe anyway, it is preferable to have them in France. The FIEE has not sought to oppose this except where it claims there is already excess capacity on French soil: according to FIEE staff they opposed, in vain, a 51 per cent Japanese Clarion car radio plant. The French attitude still retains an element of caution. When rumours appeared in autumn 1986[14] that Thomson might want to sell its consumer electronics division probably to a Japanese buyer, an Industry Ministry spokesman said that this would be unwelcome, though reports continued that the firm was pursuing the idea of selling its consumer interests to the Japanese, until Thomson eventually decided to go for expansion into the UK and US rather than divestiture in consumer electronics.

Nationalisation and Restructuring

Largely due to cost overruns in telecommunications, the Thomson group was in severe financial trouble in 1981. Had the Right won the elections, the firm would have had to request government-guaranteed loans from the banks, and a new government-approved PDG would have been appointed, probably Gerard Théry.[15] Just before the elections, the group appointed J. Bouyssonnie, the head of Thomson-CSF, as PDG of the parent firm, in the hope that the close relations between CSF and the administration might allow the top management to survive nationalization unscathed should the Socialists win.

But in 1982 President Mitterrand appointed Alain Gomez as PDG.[16] The appointment was well received within the firm, and Gomez has since built up a formidable reputation, and has remained in post through successive changes of government. In 1982 Gomez was an outsider and felt obliged to demonstrate his authority both within the firm and *vis-à-vis* the administration. Gomez had to make profound changes within the firm while being seen to resist the pressures of the Industry Ministry. In 1982 the newly nationalized firms were required to negotiate a 'planning contract' with the state, defining corporate strategy in relation to national policy (see Chapter 6). Both the state and Thomson, however, gave an absolute minimum of commitments. The primary concern of Gomez, the Finance Ministry, and after March 1983 the Industry Ministry was not planning for growth, but restoration of Thomson's profitability. Thomson lost 2.2 billion fr. in 1982 and 1.2 billion in 1983, and had a chaotic management structure.

Thomson-Brandt had been unusual among French conglomerates in acting both as a holding company and as a manufacturing unit. Gomez created a new holding company, Thomson SA, above the subsidiaries, not all of which, notably CSF, were 100 per cent owned. Thomson Grand Public, the consumer products division, was 75 per cent consumer electronics and 25 per cent 'white goods'. Vidéocolor became a subsidiary reporting to Thomson Grand Public. Surprisingly perhaps, Thomson Grand Public was itself reorganized rather less than some of the other divisions. Fayard remained its head, along with other former associates of Paul Richard, including Fayard's eventual successor, P. Garcin, even though the new government disapproved of Thomson Grand Public's international strategy. But Fayard's commercial astuteness impressed Gomez who now sought to divest chronic money losers elsewhere. Forbidden to sell his medical electronics subsidiary CGR, he opened negotiations with Georges Pebereau of CGE to achieve the restructuring discussed in Chapter 6. Gomez did however share one idea with Abel Farnoux in seeking to exploit synergy between semiconductor and consumer products, although this has since given way to integration with the Italian firms SGS.

During the '*contrat de plan*' negotiations the firm was ordered to produce a long-term strategy of its own. It was widely acknowledged that, although the government could demand that the new management rectify the chaotic internal state of Thomson, divided between Thomson-Brandt and CSF and lacking any overall corporate strategy, nevertheless it did not have the competence to determine the contents of the strategy.

Considerable ambiguities in the relationship remained until spring 1983, however. In 1982 government policy encouraged firms to expand employment and Fayard judged it politically prudent to agree to expand hi-fi production in France. In 1986 the firm decided to shut the hi-fi plant at Moulins, after taking time to secure the necessary permission to close it; no French firm, public or private, could at that time lay off workers without Ministry of Labour authorization. One Thomson executive attributed the losses incurred in consumer electronics in the early 1980s to its French hi-fi factory. When financial policy became tighter it was easier to get permission to sack workers, but this was always a politically sensitive issue, and the firm refrained from making some demands that it knew the government could not accede to. The firm moreover was aware that its public image in Germany was also at stake. The pressures on Thomson to keep factories open were not much greater than those applied to private firms, but while the Industry Ministry saw itself as leaving Thomson largely free to determine its own strategy, Thomson executives interviewed saw themselves subject to constant pin-pricks of interference. They conceded that after 1984 they had been able to adopt their own corporate strategy, but under Chirac eagerly anticipated the liberation of an eventual privatization, a hope subsequently thwarted by the return of a Socialist government.

Philips-France and the French state

Philips-France also in the 1980s found itself curiously dependent on the state. When the authorities were inclined, as they increasingly have been, to treat it as a French firm, it was included in state-sponsored programmes of research, and has been awarded '*Marché d'études*' contracts by the DGT. Philips subsidiaries have been involved in state-promoted development of electronic payments systems and RTC has been involved in the *Plans Composants*. Even more strikingly the diversification plans of La Radiotechnique in the early 1980s were totally dominated by orders secured in semi-public markets. Worried about becoming dependent on a highly vulnerable CTV market, La Radiotechnique set about entering new markets. It did well, but only for a short period in video games, and its foray into VCRs (see below) was a commercial failure. Despite some political opposition, La Radiotechnique won orders for decoders for Canal-Plus and, as we have seen, from the DGT for minitel terminals.

But despite their important contribution along with pay-tv decoders to home sales minitels have had limited export success, and La Radiotechnique needs to develop a new approach to consumer markets. A senior executive remarked that the only marketing required for the diversification into minitels and Canal-Plus decoders was a few phone calls by the chairman and the chief executive.

Mergers and Videos

The relatively stable pattern of state-enforced closure in the French consumer electronics sector was, as we have seen, undermined by difficulties in the relationship between the state and its national champion, by the relaxation of the policy of excluding Japanese inward investment, and by the shift in the determination of trade policy from Paris to Brussels. Further pressures arose from the arrival of the VCR, since this was a product in which Thomson had no technological capability, and was faced with the choice of acquiring its technology from either the Japanese or Philips-Grundig. Both these alternatives involved reducing the isolationism of the French industry; the choice between them proved to be unusually difficult and protracted.

The 'Grundig affair'[17]

In 1981 Thomson-Brandt initialled a proposed video deal with JVC, Thorn-EMI, and Telefunken, the so-called 'J3T' deal, but was ordered to freeze it by the Industry Ministry under both Giscard and Mitterrand. In the past Fayard had successfully persuaded officials to let him take over foreign firms, but this time Thomson was to be in a minority in the enterprise, despite protests that he planned to take over Telefunken and gain a 50 per cent stake. Regardless of the legal basis of the ban on J3T, Fayard judged it imprudent to challenge the ruling. In its desire to promote European collaboration, the new government made it clear that it wanted to see Thomson and Philips collaborate. So did Abel Farnoux, of the Mission de la Filière Électronique.

In spring 1982 Farnoux proposed to both Grundig and Thomson a deal whereby Grundig would be a joint subsidiary of Philips and Thomson, and a test-bed for new products. Fayard opposed the plan. Gomez was interested at first, but wanted total control of Grundig or nothing. Thomson offered in autumn 1982 to buy Max Grundig's 75.5 per cent share in his firm. Philips held 24.5 per cent and an option on the rest. In fact, in the late 1970s Philips and Thomson had agreed a plan to stop the German consumer electronics falling into Japanese hands as the UK industry had done. Philips was to take over Grundig if necessary, while the smaller firms were left to Thomson: Nordmende, Dual, Saba, Telefunken. Philips actually held an option on at least one of the firms Thomson took over. For Thomson to go for Grundig was breaking the agreement. Moreover in 1982–3 Thomson's financial position was disastrous: Philips feared that if it took over a loss-making Grundig the two might be dragged down together, a fear shared by Fayard.

Philips also wanted to maintain Grundig's use of the V2000 system, which had 25 per cent of the German VCR market, and its tube sales to Grundig. It had the power to stop Thomson, but it was under pressure from the French government to agree to the sale, and did not wish to seem obstructive. Thomson was under even stronger pressure to proceed with the deal, though this does not seem to have been the initiating factor. Philips demanded assurances of a commitment by Thomson-Grundig to the V2000 system and on tubes. Gomez, despite or perhaps because of pressure from the French government, was very unwilling to commit himself to V2000 before securing control of Grundig. Fayard convinced Gomez that V2000 was doomed and argued strongly against the Grundig deal.

Gomez was losing interest and while he was negotiating with Grundig, Fayard kept the lines open with JVC and Telefunken, which Fayard had always wanted to take over, but which Grundig now proposed to take over itself. The German Cartel Office indicated that Thomson-Grundig-Telefunken with a 24.5 per cent Philips stake would be unacceptable. But contrary to some accounts its final ruling declared that Thomson could buy Grundig alone if Philips withdrew. This amounted to a veto. An appeal by Thomson would have been futile since Philips could still have blocked the sale. In February 1983, therefore, Thomson announced the acquisition of Telefunken which had by then signed a 'J2T' deal with JVC; Thomson was able to enter this arrangement by the back door.

Gomez knew that the President's office and Industry Minister Chevènement were keen on the Grundig take-over and may have considered it politically prudent to allow it to be quashed by circumstances beyond his control. It seems no one in the government forced Gomez to follow the Grundig path. Mitterrand met Dekker, the President of Philips; Chevènement publicly declared that adoption of the V2000 system was an acceptable price to pay. But once Chevènement had intervened, it became crucial for the internal politics of Thomson that Gomez should not be seen to give way to him. Meanwhile the serious French financial position in 1982–3 set Jacques Delors and the Finance Ministry against the Grundig deal, which they would have had to finance in Deutschmarks. The French Embassy in Bonn was thus receiving conflicting signals from the Finance Ministry and the President's office. If the deal had been agreed by the Cartel Office and Philips before March 1983, the President might well have overruled the Finance Ministry's objections, but had negotiations dragged on after the financial crisis of March 1983, it is possible that Thomson would not have got the money.

Gomez was apparently pursuing a double strategy all along, wanting to explore both the Grundig and the JVC link-up before finally committing himself. By making a play for Grundig he ensured he got Telefunken. The difficulty of interpreting this episode is compounded by the apparent secrecy with which all negotiations were conducted. Thomson's *conseil d'administration* was only told the day before the Telefunken deal was publicly announced. Seen from the French side the affair does not appear to be part of any grand strategy, although its coincidence with the bizarre Poitiers affair has led many commentators to assume a connection.

VCR issues: protection and production

The disagreement over VCR formats was one element in the frustration of the Thomson–Grundig deal. From the government's point of view VCRs were crucial; arguing essentially from a macro-economic viewpoint the Industry Ministry insisted that France could improve her trade deficit with Japan if she could produce VCRs at home.

In November 1982 France forced all VCRs to be cleared through the customs post at Poitiers, and inspected to ensure that all instruction books were in French. Many reasons were given at the time. The only one that cannot be taken seriously is that given by a Trade Ministry official in an interview: that the primary issue was the cultural one of linguistic usage. The desire to block imports, and in particular to delay them until payment of a supplementary tax on VCRs came in in January 1983, is entirely consistent with a hope that domestic production would replace imports. The Poitiers measures were imposed by the Finance Ministry, though the subsequent EEC-wide Japanese voluntary export restraint (VER) was policed, in France, by the Industry Ministry which acquired trade policy responsibility in March 1983.

In retrospect French officials have claimed that the Poitiers measures were a lever in securing the signature of the VER. The Poitiers measures were embarrassing to the EEC Commission who had to defend Paris against complaints from Japan, while protesting on behalf of other member states because the Poitiers controls also obstructed intra-EEC trade. The VER seemed to offer a useful political solution. However the Germans were insistent that any VER signed with Japan had to respect the integrity of the EEC internal market. Quotas should apply to the whole EEC, and not be divided nationally. France agreed to this on paper, but ignored it in practice. Japanese firms were not allowed to allocate their sales as they wished in Europe, but were given quotas for the French market, which were respected because administrative pressures could be brought to bear even in the absence of Article 115 measures.

French attitudes to Japanese inward investment in consumer electronics were, as we have seen, evolving rapidly in 1982–3. The earlier hostile attitude reversed itself almost totally. The Poitiers measures are held to have stimulated Japanese investment in Europe. Indeed officials complain that the VER agreement, for which they claim the credit, brought more Japanese investments in other EEC states. In fact the U-turn on inward investment took until about 1984 to crystallize, and the Poitiers measures appear to have been a panic move rather than part of a concerted strategy with the Grundig plan.

Thomson's VCR factory: Tonnerre v. Longwy

The Grundig affair led to one acute conflict between the government and Thomson over the siting of the factory allegedly intended to produce one million VCRs in France by 1985. Thomson wanted to use an obsolescent black and white TV factory in Tonnerre. The government wanted to have a factory sited in Longwy in Lorraine, scene of severe disturbances over steel closures. After protracted negotiations Thomson agreed to split the plant between the two sites, though company statements make it clear that the intention was to start at Tonnerre with Longwy as a follow-up. Thomson's long-run commitment to VCR production in France is unclear. The Longwy plant was eventually transferred to J2T. The declared aim of producing a million VCRs in France in 1985 was unreal, and the trade association reports that in 1985 'imports essentially covered the French market'.[18] But in order to maintain credibility as a seller, Thomson must actually produce some of the products it markets. However, as with its 1986 decision to raise CTV production in Singapore by 60 per cent, the location decisions of Thomson are increasingly becoming those of a conventional multinational rather than those of the national champion of France.

The limited production by Thomson was the only fruit of the Poitiers measures apart from the plant set up by Akai in Honfleur, which in 1984 announced it had reached 40 per cent French valued added. Océanic re-examined its decision to import VCRs rather than manufacture, but kept to its original strategy. Philips did however temporarily produce V2000 VCRs in France.

Philips and VCRs in France

In 1981 Philips announced it would begin production of V2000 VCRs in France in 1982. Philips's motives were mixed. In 1981 it probably still retained hopes that the V2000 format could survive and even prosper. There was thus a chance that this investment might pay off commercially. Any such hope seems to have vanished quite soon. The plan was maintained even as the prospects for

V2000 became dimmer, as a way of signalling to Thomson and to the French government the serious commitment to V2000. It seems that, even in 1982, Philips genuinely felt V2000 could keep up a major market share in Europe if Thomson agreed to adopt it instead of VHS. Fayard was of course bitterly opposed to this, and within Philips-France it is now readily conceded that for Thomson in 1982 it would have been an error to adopt V2000. The investment by La Radiotechnique in V2000 in France was characterized as both 'commercial' and 'political' by Philips sources. The latter motive seemed dominant, but it does not appear to have been the case of a firm responding to political pressures; if anything it was trying to give political signals to the government and Thomson. Philips-France's VCR production was abandoned when V2000 was dropped.

Thomson: international champion?

The French consumer electronics industry has been subject to a curious mixture of political and commercial pressures, in which ultimately the latter have predominated. Under the 1981–6 Socialist government, the political element reached a peak and then receded. Thomson began to develop a world-wide production and marketing strategy. Its management sought to turn it into a thoroughgoing multinational, like Philips, instead of a national champion.

In 1986 Fayard, who believed that Thomson could never be anything more than a follower in consumer electronics, was shifted to the role of 'special adviser' to Gomez. He was replaced by Pierre Garcin, one of the Thomson-Brandt 'old guard'. In autumn 1986 press reports backed by Japanese industry sources suggested that Thomson planned to dispose of its consumer electronics activities. An Industry Ministry spokesman stated that any sale to a Japanese firm would be viewed unfavourably. Gomez could contemplate this as a result of his successes elsewhere, notably in selling the RITA system to the Pentagon. It seems likely that this was an example of a process such as was seen in the Grundig affair—the exploration of two options, double or quit. In fact only Dual in Germany was sold. Instead Thomson bought up the Ferguson subsidiary of Thorn-EMI including part of its stake in J2T, which became a 50:50 joint venture between Thomson and JVC. In the same year it acquired the US General Electric's RCA consumer electronics division, approximately doubling Thomson's consumer electronics output. Gomez was able to dispose of his medical electronics activities in this deal as he had long wished, but it also required $600 million in cash, and was pushed through against Fayard's advice.[19]

Thomson has overtaken Philips as Europe's largest CTV producer. It now has a foot in Europe, North America, and South-East Asia, with around 17,000 employees in consumer electronics in each. The firm is gambling that it will be able to pull off the rationalizations it had not managed to accomplish during earlier periods of expansion. Thomson has increased its R. & D. effort, and is a major partner with Philips in the Eureka High Definition Television Consortium. It claims to be at the leading edge in digital optical recording technology, but has so far been slow into the market with compact disc products. The dream of a link with Philips to form a pan-European force in consumer electronics is as far away as ever.

Thomson continues its policy of shifting alliances and trying to gain market share by acquisition. Its success in the military field and the restoration of profitability in consumer products in 1986 have been sources of strength. But the firm has paid vast sums at the height of the stock market boom for what could prove lame duck assets. In 1987 1.8 billion fr. of the 2.2 billion fr. profit made by the Thomson group as a whole was from financial placements of advance payments for military hardware. This strategy is not without risk: Thomson found itself caught up in the rescue plans for the failing Al Saudi Bank in Paris.[20]

The 1988 Socialist government did not reverse its stance as the hands-off shareholder. But an Industry Ministry adviser to the new government noted sourly that there are firms who invest, like Sony, firms who can follow someone else's idea within six months, like Toshiba, and firms which wait a year or two before seeking licences, like Thomson.[21] If Thomson's gambles pay off, we shall have seen an interesting example of successful state capitalism, where the public shareholder provided cash when almost certainly the market would not have done so. But success, if it comes, will be based on managerial rather than state initiative. If things do go wrong, experience suggests that all the government would be able to do would be to replace Gomez, decide the level of state funds to be invested, and hope for the best.

Conclusion

As we have seen in this chapter, in consumer electronics as in the telecommunications case examined in Chapter 6, France had adopted a sectoral industrial policy of state-backed market closure sustained by a number of measures, the most important of which were the promotion of Thomson as a national champion, the adoption of incompatible television transmission standards, a policy of hostility towards inward investment, and the use of import quotas. The degree of protection they gave to the French industry stands in marked contrast to the British case, explored in the previous chapter, and the German case, which is the subject of the following chapter. There have been new entrants to the French industry and some changes in ownership, but no departures, and no case of a French company selling out to a foreign competitor. Indeed, the reverse has been true: the policy has enabled Thomson to make extensive acquisitions and become a genuine multinational big enough to compete at a global level with Philips and the major Japanese firms. This process has occurred, however, at the same time that the specific mechanisms through which closure was achieved have largely ceased to operate: technical change, a transformation in the state–firm relationship, internationalization, and the extension of EEC prerogatives have all worked to undermine the isolationism of the French industry, and reduce the scope of state interventionism. It has become clear that France can no longer go it alone in consumer electronics, and that political strategies to reinforce the market power of firms such as Thomson and Philips in their struggle against the Japanese will need to be fashioned on a European basis.

Notes

1. Data in this section have been compiled from a variety of French industry publications.
2. R. B. Cohen, R. W. Ferguson, and M. F. Oppenheimer, *Non-Tariff Barriers to High Technology Trade* (Boulder, Colo.: Westview Press, 1985), p. 15.
3. H. Bertrand, C. Mansuy, and M. Norotte, *Vingt Groupes industriels français et le redéploiement* (Paris: Direction de la Prévision / Ministry of Finance, 1981).

4. P. Galambert, *Les Sept Paradoxes de notre politique industrielle* (Paris: CERF, 1982).

5. J.-M. Quatrepoint, 'Un échec exemplaire: L'Affaire Grundig', *Revue d'économie industrielle*, 27 (1984), 31–40.

6. *Nouvel Économiste*, 7 Aug. 1987.

7. W. Andreff, 'L'Après-Poitiers des multinationales', *La Tribune de l'économie*, 9 Apr. 1985.

8. *Nouvel Économiste*, 20 Nov. 1987.

9. See, for example, S. Nora and A. Minc. *L'Informatisation de la société* (Paris: Documentation Française, 1978), and J.-H. Lorenzi and E. Le Boucher, *Mémoires Volés* (Paris: Ramsay, 1979).

10. See the Industry Commission Reports of the VIIth and VIIth Plans, Commissariat Général au Plan (Paris: Documentation Française, 1976 and 1979).

11. A. Farnoux, *Rapport de la Mission de la Filière Électronique* (Paris: Ministry of Industry, 1982).

12. See P. Holmes, 'Rules of Origin in Intra-EEC Trade, Article 115 and Some Sectoral Issues for the UK and France', University of Sussex, International Economics Research Centre, Discussion Paper 87/46 (1987).

13. J. Pelkmans and R. Beuter, 'Standardisation and Competitiveness: Public and Private Strategies in the EC Colour TV Industry', Paper presented at the INSEAD symposium on the economics of standards (1986); and R. Levacic, 'Government Policies towards the Consumer Electronics Industry and their Effects: A Comparison of Britain and France', in G. Hall (ed.), *European Industrial Policy* (London: Croom Helm, 1986).

14. *Usine nouvelle*, 6 Nov. 1986.

15. Interview with government official.

16. Autonomy for the PDGs of nationalized firms was implicit in the nationalization legislation, for example by the removal of the right to dismiss PDGs from the firms' *conseil d'administration*. This term is often misleadingly translated as the 'board of directors' but it consists largely of external non-executive directors and in some ways resembles the German supervisory board. The Président-Directeur-Général of a French firm legally embodies the functions of a chairman and chief executive (though the latter function can be devolved to a separate Directeur-Général); indeed the chief executive often exercises many of the managerial functions collectively exercised by a board in the UK.

17. This account is based on a combination of published sources, notably J.-M. Quatrepoint, 'Un échec exemplaire' and E. Cohen and M. Bauer,

Les Grandes Manœuvres industrielles (Paris: Belfond, 1985), and interviews in France and Germany.

18. Groupement des Industries Électroniques, *Annual Report 1986* (Paris, 1986), p. 34.

19. Fayard, still an adviser to Gomez, apparently argued that it would take over 100 years for the RCA purchase to pay for itself. See *Nouvel Economiste*, 11 Nov. 1988.

20. Ibid.

21. Ibid.

12

Germany: Holding the Ring?

Introduction

In the post-war 'boom' which ended around 1974, the German consumer electronics industry flourished. The German industry was the biggest and strongest in Western Europe. Its leading firms— Grundig and Telefunken—became household names and Max Grundig was seen as the prototype of the successful German entrepreneur of the 'economic miracle'. The Telefunken laboratories especially were pioneers of technological innovation in the industry. It was here that the PAL colour TV format was born. The possession of the PAL patents provided the German industry with strong protection against foreign competition in the largest segment of the market. Despite constantly rising productivity, employment in the industry almost quintupled between 1950 and the early 1970s. The issue of protection or an interventionist strategy for the industry simply did not arise during this period: state-backed closure strategies such as those examined in France in the previous chapter were unnecessary as long as the firms maintained their power in the market-place.

In the late 1970s and early 1980s, however, the industry's situation and prospects changed radically. The expiry of the PAL patents began to expose its colour TV segment to increasingly intense competition. More seriously, the industry failed to establish a foothold in expanding product markets, especially that for VCRs. The export offensive of the Japanese plunged the German industry into a profound crisis. Numerous smaller firms became insolvent or were taken over by bigger German or foreign competitors, and the former flagships of the industry turned to the state or to each other to try to secure their longer-term survival. In 1980, the industry began to call for assistance from the government—'help so that it could help itself', as its trade association said.[1] Under pressure from the industry and drawn into its affairs by the dictates of competition law, the federal government retreated some way from the non-interventionist stance which it had adopted towards the industry in the period of the post-war 'boom'. This policy change manifested itself in the federal government's acquiescence in trade agreements between the EEC and Japan in which the Japanese 'voluntarily' limited their exports of VCRs to the EEC states and the 'industry-friendly' interpretation of competition policy which it urged on the Federal Cartel Office BKA (see below). The role of political champion of the industry was taken up more strongly by the government of the states (*Länder*) in which the threatened firms were predominantly located, such as Bavaria. The German government did not, however, contemplate direct measures to assist its firms to develop counter-usurpation strategies. Its support for the rescue of AEG-Telefunken was indirect (see below) and there was no attempt to develop a national champions policy to protect the stronger firms.

During the post-war boom, in which the relationship between the state and the industry was primarily of the arm's length kind corresponding to the philosophy of the 'social market economy', the state had played an important 'tin-opening' role by introducing new mass communications media, such as television, and participating in the determination of technical standards. But otherwise it confined itself to 'holding the ring' for the firms competing in the market. The processes referred to above thus constituted a new development in government–industry relations. The Grundig affair and the voluntary export restraint agreement between the EEC and Japan were milestones on this path. Before analysing these developments in detail, however, the main actors in government–consumer electronic industry relations in the FRG are portrayed.

The Actors

The industry

All the noteworthy firms in the German consumer electronics industry, and most of the smaller ones, are organized in the consumer electronics sub-association of the ZVEI. All firms with consumer electronics manufacturing facilities in the FRG are entitled to join the sub-association; those firms which only market products in the FRG are accepted solely with the unanimous support of existing members. (Thus two Japanese firms are extraordinary members of the sub-association without voting rights.) The Japanese firms which 'manufacture' in the FRG are sub-association members, but their membership and role in the sub-association is controversial. Whereas the 'doves' among the German firms (the big, export-orientated German firms, supported by the sub-association secretariat) prefer to have the Japanese 'around the table to discuss problems with them' the 'hawks' (mostly the smaller firms) want neither to speak to nor to have anything else to do with them. This conflict has hitherto prevented any Japanese firm being elected on to the sub-association's advisory council (*Beirat*).

The strongest incentive to belong to the sub-association is the chance to participate in the work of its technical commission, which is the industry's spokesman in talks with the Bundespost on standards issues and through which the firms can keep informed about technological trends and seek to win allies in market conflicts over standards. The sub-association also has a significant role in the conduct of industry-to-industry talks with the Japanese, the formulation of common policies on attendance at trade fairs, and the representation of the German industry's interests in the EEC. Three main groupings or 'camps' of firms are identifiable in the sub-association, one comprising Philips and Grundig, another the German Thomson subsidiaries (Telefunken, Nordmende, Saba), and a third, a 'loose confederation', comprising Bosch and Siemens (joint owners of Blaupunkt) and (before the sale of its consumer electronics division to Nokia in 1988) SEL.

Reflecting the 'power of the market share', the big firms are more influential in the sub-association than the small. Philips, now the biggest firm in the German industry, has an effective veto power in the organization: 'When Philips says no, then there is no point in trying to do something'. The Philips–Grundig axis has held the chair of the sub-association in recent years. However, the trade association is no longer the critical channel for the representation of industrial interests to the federal government. The reason why the sub-association declined (in one view) from a once 'very significant' organization to a 'club of statisticians' was attributed by a former company chairman to the impact of competition law and the BKA, which declared commercial agreements reached between firms in the sub-association to be illegal. In relation neither to trade policy nor to the implementation of competition policy in the industry is the sub-association perceived to be a significant actor. In this respect trends in the FRG have paralleled those in France and

Britain, leaving bilateral contacts between government and large firms as the most significant form of government–industry relations.

The roles of the electrical engineering trade association as a whole and of the umbrella industrial and business organizations, the BDI and the DIHT, are even more marginal. The Federal Economics Ministry is reputed to try to use the umbrella interest organizations as buffers to shield it from the particularistic demands of individual trade associations or firms. However, our case-studies of consumer electronics politics do not support this thesis.

The principal industry actors in government–industry relations are the firms. Firm–government relations are not institutionalized as they were in Britain in the NEDO sector working party. They are *ad hoc* and 'not rigidly organized'. Interviews suggested that contacts between company executive board chairmen or other members and ministers or high-ranking ministry officials are abundant. At the informal level, 'continuous talks' are said to take place. Trade exhibitions and similar events provide plenty of opportunities for meetings between industrialists and politicians or civil servants. The firms typically try to talk to the 'highest possible levels' in the Economics Ministry, but their access to decision-making circles varies according to firm size and the local content of their products: thus it listens more closely to the manufacturers than to those firms which simply market foreign products. At least in respect of VCRs, this amounts to saying that the ministry is more sympathetic to the demands of Philips than to those of other firms in the German industry.

Philips sees itself as being dependent on 'first class contacts' with business associations, political parties, and the governments in the FRG and the other EEC states and on being able, when necessary, to speak to them directly. Since the early 1980s, the status of the company's Bonn office, which had formerly been no more than a 'listening post' and 'relay station', has been upgraded. This is attributed by Philips to a change in company philosophy following on a change in the firm's Eindhoven management. It may not be a coincidence, however, that the Bonn office's upgrading occurred almost simultaneously with Philips's effective take-over of Grundig, which enhanced its potential political weight in the FRG, and with Philips's abandonment of its traditional support for free trade in favour of protection of the European consumer electronics industry from Japanese competition. Philips's conversion to protectionism was followed, in turn, by the Bonn Economics Ministry's adoption of a more benevolent attitude to protectionism (see below). Philips's lobbying activities in Bonn are paralleled by those in Brussels, where the EEC bureaucracy has shown itself more responsive to Philips's demands than the German government: 'When Philips goes to Brussels, all the doors fly open'.

In contrast to the giants of the industry, a small, traditionally family-owned firm like Loewe-Opta maintains few direct contacts to the Economics Ministry—it channels its problems and protests (as best it can) through the trade association. The Japanese firms profess not to have access to federal ministries. Their political interests are represented in the EEC by the Japanese industry's trade association (see Chapter 13) and the Japanese government. The picture at the level of the state and local governments, however, is different. They vie with each other and with other EEC governments to attract Japanese investment. All the German state governments, and many local governments, have agencies whose task it is to attract new investors, using, among other instruments, public subsidies.

The banks

The relatively high interpenetration of industrial and banking capital in the FRG (see Chapter 3) raises the question of whether the big German banks constitute important actors in German consumer electronics politics. In the German business community, oblique references are sometimes made to a 'mafia' consisting of Siemens, Bosch, Daimler Benz, and the Deutsche Bank. However, we found no evidence that, as claimed in one source, the Deutsche Bank played a decisive role in combating Thomson's attempted take-over of Grundig in 1982–83.[2] Other German and Swiss banks had more to do with Grundig than the Deutsche Bank. In the reorganization of the German consumer electronics industry, the banks' role was less to prevent Thomson (or any other firm) taking over their industrial clients than to persuade the firms' owners to sell, or where the banks already owned the firms, themselves to find buyers for them. This is not to deny, however, that, by threatening to allow a firm to go bankrupt and/or close it down, the banks can exercise considerable power over political decision-makers—as they did, for example, during the rescue of the insolvent AEG-Telefunken in

1982, forcing the federal government to guarantee the credits they granted to keep the second biggest firm in the German electrical engineering industry afloat. The industrial 'fire-fighting' role occasionally performed by the big universal banks eases the pressure on the government to intervene to rescue failing firms.

Organised labour

Tripartite co-operation between government, business, and labour is generally held to be an identifying characteristic of the 'German model' of industrial and economic crisis management alluded to in much of the literature on the political economy of the FRG. However, the degree of integration of organized labour in company and industrial restructuring may vary considerably by sector, influenced by differences in union and worker co-determination rights (which are most extensive in the iron and steel and coal industries) and the level of unionization and militancy of workers in the industry or region. The union which organizes workers in the German consumer electronics industry, IG Metall, is not closely integrated into the making of governmental decisions on consumer electronics issues, such as trade relations with Japan. It has been reticent about formulating policies for individual industrial sectors. The union prefers to avoid 'sectoral egoism' (the maintenance of jobs in a particular sector at all costs). This policy is related to the structure of the union, which organizes the entire West German metalworking industry. The high export dependence of many of these sectors makes the IG Metall 'very cautious' of supporting protectionism. Similarly, since it organizes workers in competing firms, it hesitates to demand subsidies for individual firms. Thus, during the AEG crisis in 1982, the union as a whole 'held back to a certain extent', allowing the lobbying for state intervention to rescue the firm to be conducted primarily by the AEG works council and the union's representatives on the company supervisory board. The task of representing the interests of labour in particular firms tends to be performed by the company works councils more than by the unions.

Federal, state, and local governments

The primary policy-making responsibility for the consumer electronics industry in the federal government lies with the federal Economics Ministry, the traditional guardian of the 'social market economy' in the federal bureaucracy. Within the ministry, several sections and/or divisions are typically involved in formulating policy on consumer electronics issues. In the industry division (one of five in the ministry), the electrical engineering industry section is responsible for issues relating to consumer electronics. It is always involved in formulating ministerial policy on such issues. It is not necessarily or always the industry's advocate in the ministry, but it is renowned as being more sympathetic to industry demands than other divisions—which see their task as being to resist particularistic demands from the industry or from 'its' section in the ministry 'in the interests of other sectors'. In contrast to the electrical engineering industry section, whose contacts are primarily with the trade association or individual firms, other sections and divisions maintain closer relations to the umbrella business organizations, such as the BDI and DIHT, from which they expect to obtain opinions representative of industry or commerce and industry as a whole. On issues of trade policy relating to consumer electronics, sections in the ministry's trade and European policy divisions are involved in policymaking. They are highly conscious of the policy implications of the export orientation and dependence of German industry: 'import and export considerations must always be weighed up against each other'. On merger and take-over issues, the competition policy section is involved in policy-making, together with the BKA (see below). In cases of conflict, the various sections try to resolve their differences amongst themselves—where this fails, the issue is passed up to the minister for decision. In the industry, the political leadership of the ministry is occasionally seen to be more sympathetic to industry demands than are the permanent officials.

Other ministries which may be involved in formulating policy affecting the consumer electronics industry include those of Finance, Research and Technology, and Post and Telecommunications. The Finance Ministry is involved when the question at stake is whether subsidies are to be paid to firms and these cannot be provided under programmes for which the 'spending' ministries have already negotiated funding from the federal budget. Thus, the Finance Ministry collaborated closely with the Economics Ministry in the government-organized financial rescue of AEG-Telefunken in 1982. The Post Ministry, as the controller of the Bundespost, which has a monopoly of the telecommunications network, is involved in making decisions concerning television standards—such as those concerning European satellite television (D2-MAC). The Research and Technology Ministry may subsidize research or the development of new technologies relating to consumer electronics. Thus, within its 1984 programme for the information and communications technologies, the ministry provided grants for firms to co-operate with a view to developing a common European standard for high definition television. Finally at the federal level, the Chancellor's Office may be the object of industrial lobbying and, when the issue is politically explosive, as it was, for example, in respect of the AEG-Telefunken, may itself intervene in the policy-making process.

As the federal agency responsible for implementing competition policy, the BKA has been a major actor in conflicts over mergers and take-overs in the consumer electronics industry. The BKA is (according to the statute which created it) an 'independent federal administration' subject to the general supervision—and directives—of the federal Economics Ministry. German competition law prescribes that the BKA must be informed of any planned mergers or take-overs if the two firms each have a turnover exceeding 1 billion DM or one of them has a turnover of more than 2 billion DM. The acquisition of a shareholding of 25 per cent or more is held to give a firm a controlling interest in another. By law, the BKA must reject any proposed merger which, in its view, would lead to the emergence of a position of 'market domination'. If, through a merger or take-over, the firm(s) involved would acquire a market share of 33 per cent or more, the BKA is required to investigate *whether* this would establish a dominant market position. This implies that the BKA enjoys some discretion and flexibility in interpreting and implementing competition law. While, on the one hand, the relevant 'market' for the BKA is the German one, it can, on the other, take account of potential or actual foreign competition in deciding whether a market share of one third or more constitutes a dominant market position.

Decisions of the BKA may be contested in the courts (although the time taken to resolve such cases may dissuade firms from exercising this option) and, after an adverse ruling by the BKA, firms may appeal for permission to proceed with mergers or take-overs from the federal Economics Minister. The latter is empowered to grant such permission when it is justified by an 'overriding public interest' or 'macro-economic benefits', which competition law says may relate to competitiveness on export markets, employment, and defence or energy policy.

The BKA is generally reputed to be fairly independent of the federal government. None the less, although the Economics Ministry is said not to 'apply pressure' on or 'issue directives' to the BKA, it may let it be known that it would prefer a certain decision and not another. The BKA chairman's participation in the weekly meeting of the ministry's division heads also institutionalizes an opportunity for political pressure to be brought to bear on the office. As well as by the firms themselves, including those which oppose proposed mergers or take-overs, the BKA is lobbied by state and local governments, politicians, trade unions and works councils, and commercial interests (which are affected by concentration tendencies in the industry). Interventions by organized labour and local governments—which generally have to do with the employment implications of mergers or take-overs—are said to have no influence on the BKA's decisions.

In so far as 'industrial policy' for the consumer electronics industry has been pursued in the FRG, state governments have been as much its perpetrators as the federal government. Their interventions, or attempted interventions, in the industry have typically been motivated by employment preservation objectives. Thus, the state governments—through their respective economic promotion agencies—have been avid seekers of Japanese consumer electronic investments, supplementing grants paid under federal regional policy with their own subsidies. After the UK, the FRG is the most favoured location for Japanese investment in the EEC. On merger and take-over issues, state governments are often lobbyists of the federal Economics Ministry and/or the BKA, to which they have the right to make formal submissions. Or they may adopt an active crisis managing role themselves, advocating their own company crisis 'solutions', as in the case of the Bavarian state government and Grundig. They are more likely than the federal government to intervene to try to alter company plans to cut back employment or close factories.

The Grundig Affair

The background

Faced with the growing challenge of Japanese competition, the major European consumer electronics firms, including the German, pursued a dual closure strategy. On the one hand, they lobbied the EEC governments and the Commission for measures of at least temporary protection against Japanese imports to give them a 'breathing space' to build up or modernize their production capacities and become more competitive and/or to force the Japanese to produce in Europe under the same conditions as they did. On the other hand, they sought, via take-overs, mergers, or co-operation agreements, to reorganize and regroup forces with the aim of achieving similar economies of scale as those enjoyed by the most formidable Japanese firms.

The foundations of the Grundig 'affair', the conflict which arose around the attempt by Thomson to take over Grundig, were laid in the late 1970s, when Thomson had swallowed up several smaller German firms—Nordmende, Dual, and Saba—unable to survive alone in the face of intensifying Japanese competition. Confronted with the joint challenge of the Japanese and Thomson to its position in the German market, Philips reacted in 1979 by taking a 24.5 per cent stake in Grundig—at this time, the BKA ruled out Philips's assuming a controlling shareholding since this would in its view have given Philips a dominant position on the colour TV market. Since the Second World War, a close commercial relationship had existed between Grundig and Philips, which supplied Grundig with TV tubes. Philips had long been interested in increasing its influence over Grundig. Max Grundig himself saw Philips's participation in his firm as a first step towards its assumption of control of the firm after his retirement. Philips was granted a veto power over the sale of Grundig's own remaining shareholding in the firm—a decision which was to have a crucial impact on the outcome of the Thomson take-over four years later.

By 1982, Grundig's financial position was deteriorating rapidly, primarily as a result of its mounting losses in VCR manufacture. Max Grundig acknowledged that, in the medium term, Grundig, given its lack of technological resources and expertise, could not survive as an independent firm in the consumer electronics market. In 1982, he floated the idea of creating a European consumer electronics 'super firm' centred on Grundig, but also involving Bosch, Siemens, SEL and Telefunken. Quite apart from the insuperable competition law obstacles which the realization of such a plan (which resembled that also proposed by Farnoux in France—see Chapter 11) would have encountered, most of the prospective participants were unenthusiastic about becoming involved in such a venture.

The Thomson take-over bid

The outcome of Grundig's search for a stronger partner to keep the firm afloat was Thomson's bid for a 75.5 per cent shareholding in November 1982. Thomson's motives in trying to take over Grundig, and the divisions within the firm on this issue, were explored in the previous chapter. There were several reasons for Philips's interest in thwarting such a take-over and extending its own influence over Grundig. First, Philips wanted to protect its components trade with Grundig—worth some several hundred million marks a year. Second, Thomson's take-over of Grundig would have made it the biggest consumer electronics firm on the German market and thus turned the existing balance of forces on the market on its head. After the USA, the German market was Philips's biggest, so that to be trumped by Thomson would have been a considerable blow for the company as a whole. A further consideration which might have played a role in Philips's thinking relates to the issue of whether Thomson would serve as a 'Trojan Horse' for Philips's Japanese competitors and whether its take-over of Grundig would not be followed by its forming a technological alliance with the Japanese. Given the Thomson consumer electronics division's known preference for co-operating with the Japanese rather than with Philips in respect of VCR technology, the danger of such a development taking place must have seemed very real.

A final factor which contributed to Philips's decision not to allow Grundig to be taken over by Thomson was the certainty that Thomson and its subsidiaries would not have been prepared to adopt Philips's V2000 VCR technology—the format in which Grundig manufactured VCRs. Philips was forced to abandon this technology later in any case, but at this stage it still hoped to be able to maintain it against the VHS format. Grundig's departure from the V2000 camp would have meant the technology's certain demise.

At the outset, however, Philips maintained a low profile in respect of Thomson's Grundig bid. One can hypothesize that Philips would have preferred the BKA to stop the bid to avoid being seen to be (co-)responsible for preventing the creation of a common European consumer electronics front to resist the Japanese challenge.

The question arises, of course, as to why Philips did not immediately bid for a controlling shareholding in Grundig, but instead held back and allowed Thomson to make the running. There are two factors which together might account for the tactics it adopted. The first has to do with its possession of a veto power over Max Grundig's sale of his own shares. Thomson's purchase of Grundig could not go through unless Philips agreed not to make use of its prior right to buy out Max Grundig. The longer Grundig's financial situation deteriorated and Philips could postpone making a bid itself, the better (that is, the cheaper) was the take-over deal which they could expect to be able to force Max Grundig to accept.

The second had to do with competition law and the BKA. Up until November 1982, both Philips and Grundig had thought—possibly correctly—that the BKA would prevent Philips assuming control of Grundig, just as it had done in 1979. When Grundig and Philips began talking about the possibility of Philips assuming a controlling shareholding in Grundig in 1981, Grundig's initial soundings at the BKA and Federal Economics Ministry suggested that neither was as yet prepared to accept a Philips take-over of Grundig.[3] Philips was thus in a position where it could prevent any other firm taking over Grundig, but could not take it over itself. In these circumstances, since, irrespective of whether the BKA approved Thomson's bid, Philips could block it, the BKA's response to Thomson's take-over attempt could provide Philips with a strong clue as to how it might fare if it later sought to take a controlling shareholding in Grundig.

Thomson's bid for Grundig immediately became a major issue in domestic German politics and in Franco-German relations. Among the German political parties and organized economic interests, there seemed to be hardly a single one which was not opposed to the proposed take-over. The Grundig works council and the trade unions resisted the deal because Thomson's personnel policies at its other German subsidiaries and in particular its recent closure of the Vidéocolor television tube factory in Ulm had earned it the reputation of being a 'job killer'. They were backed by the SPD, whose Bavarian organization even advocated Grundig's nationalization to prevent it falling into Thomson's hands. The consumer electronics retail trade also appeared to be united in opposing Thomson's take-over bid, presumably because greater concentration in the industry would weaken retailers' bargaining power *vis-à-vis* their suppliers. The Deutsche Bank was reputedly also opposed to the planned Thomson–Grundig deal. It has close ties to the two biggest German electrical engineering firms, Siemens and Bosch (see above), both of which are represented in the bank's supervisory board and had a strong interest in preventing Thomson's taking over Grundig (see below). In industrial and conservative media circles, the deal was also opposed on the grounds that Thomson (since 1982) was a *state-owned* firm—it was even argued that, in offering his firm for sale to Thomson, Max Grundig was 'defecting to a different economic system'.

Such arguments found a strong echo within the Christian Democratic parties, especially in the states of Lower Saxony and Bavaria, the ones most affected by Thomson's plans. The CDU Economics Minister in Lower Saxony described Thomson as a 'highly subsidized, loss-making enterprise which, in the interests of the [French] state, buys up brand names in other countries', exporting knowhow to France and unemployment abroad. As most of Grundig's production facilities (and two-thirds of the firm's workforce) were located in Bavaria, the Bavarian state government was especially perturbed by the prospect of Thomson's taking over Grundig. Following the reduction in jobs which Thomson had implemented at its German subsidiaries, the Bavarian government feared that it would transfer production capacity and jobs at Grundig to France—a development which would have been 'catastrophic' for the economic situation in Nuremberg, the second biggest Bavarian city, where Grundig's biggest factories were located, and possibly also for some smaller Bavarian towns where Grundig had production sites. The state government also anticipated negative knock-on employment effects through a reduction of orders to Grundig's Bavarian sub-contractors and suppliers, especially in its micro-electronic component orders from Siemens (a third of whose electronic components sales, according to the Bavarian Economics Minister, were to the consumer electronics industry). Political and business opinion in Germany was thus overwhelmingly hostile to Thomson's plan to take over Grundig. But the BKA and the federal Economics Ministry, which would have to decide a request for special ministerial permission for the take-over if the plan was rejected by the BKA, were also exposed to contrary pressures. If Thomson was prevented from taking over Grundig and no other buyer could be found for the firm, the danger existed that it would go bankrupt.[4] At the BKA, the financial position of Grundig was regarded as 'critical'. If the only alternative to Grundig's being taken over by Thomson had been for it to go bankrupt, it would have been difficult for the BKA and / or the Economics Ministry ultimately to veto the take-over plan.

A second factor which would have made it difficult for the federal government to be seen to block the deal was the French government's (at least initial) support for the Thomson initiative, which President Mitterrand underlined in a summit meeting with Chancellor Kohl. If the government were seen to be responsible for thwarting Thomson's take-over of Grundig, this could have had a negative impact on Franco-German relations. The federal Economics Minister, the Liberal Count Lambsdorff, thus had particularly good reasons for taking no public stance on the issue—which the ministry justified by reference to the possibility of its later being called on by the firms to override a negative decision by the BKA and approve the take-over plan.

Informally, however, Lambsdorff is said to have intimated his preparedness to approve the take-over plan. According to Max Grundig's financial adviser Ludwig Poullain, who staged talks with Lambsdorff on the issue, Lambsdorff had undertaken to direct the BKA that it should use EEC rather than German market shares for assessing whether Thomson's take-over of Grundig would secure it a 'dominant' position on the consumer electronics market. On this basis, the BKA would have had no choice but to approve Thomson's taking over Grundig—in which case the federal Economics Ministry would conveniently have been relieved of itself having to make the decision. Poullain's claim is substantiated by the fact that, contrary to most expectations at the time the take-over bid was launched, the BKA ultimately sanctioned the Thomson–Grundig deal, if only on the condition that Philips forfeited its Grundig shareholding (see below). It is also supported by the perception held at the Bavarian Economics Ministry that the federal Economics Ministry was neither for nor against Thomson's taking over Grundig, but rather in favour of a 'market economy solution'—that is, in this case, of allowing the firms to decide Grundig's fate among themselves.

The 'German solution'

Motivated by employment policy considerations, the Bavarian state government was not prepared to adopt a similarly *laissez-faire* policy on the issue. The Bavarian Economics Minister launched an attempt to find a 'German solution' to the Grundig crisis. In essence, this involved preventing Thomson achieving control of Grundig by persuading several German electrical engineering firms, but principally Siemens and Bosch, to buy shareholdings in the firm. Neither of these firms welcomed the initiative. As the controversy over the proposed deal continued, Siemens indicated that it might be prepared to take a minor shareholding in Grundig, but that it had no interest in buying a controlling stake in the firm. Siemens's reluctance to participate in Grundig, despite its 'certain' opposition to a Thomson take-over, which could have cost it much of its components trade with Grundig, did not relate only to the price issue. With its enormous cash reserves, Siemens could easily have bought a controlling shareholding in Grundig if it had wanted to. A more important consideration was the fact that Siemens, as a predominantly investment goods manufacturer, lacking the appropriate marketing expertise and organization for consumer products, did not want to extend what would be a risky involvement in the consumer electronics industry beyond its modest shareholding in Blaupunkt.

As long as Philips blocked the Thomson bid, Siemens could count on being able to attain its objective of keeping Thomson out of Grundig without itself having to make a risky financial investment. It is 'certainly conceivable' that, behind the scenes, Philips, which supplied Grundig with TV tubes, and Siemens, which supplied it with other components, had reached an agreement that, in the event of Philips assuming control of Grundig, the firm would continue to buy Siemens's components. Siemens in fact intimated publicly that Philips constituted the natural alternative to Thomson as a majority shareholder in Grundig.[5]

Bosch was no more keen than Siemens to get involved in a 'German rescue' of Grundig. This had partly to do with the personal animosity which prevailed between Max Grundig and the Bosch chairman, Hans Merkle. But, apart from this, Bosch was interested more in scaling down than expanding its involvement in the consumer electronics industry—Merkle is said to have wanted Grundig to take over Blaupunkt rather than vice versa! With respect to VCRs, Bosch, via Blaupunkt, had just launched a joint venture with Matsushita. It could hardly therefore have been interested in helping Grundig (and Philips) out of their difficulties with the V2000.

Furthermore, Bosch viewed itself as an 'international firm' which, by implication, did not want to serve as the executor of the Bavarian state government's industrial policy—all the less, one may assume, since it is based primarily in Baden-Württemberg.

In March 1983, the BKA announced that it would approve Thomson's take-over of Grundig, but only if Philips forfeited its existing shareholding in the company and Max Grundig sold his own shareholding in Philips. Its decision confounded the expectations that most participants in the Grundig saga had held at its outset. It is unclear whether the decision was attributable to Grundig's intervention at the federal Economics Ministry and the latter's subsequently directing the BKA to decide the case on the basis of whether the Thomson–Grundig deal would give the firms a dominant position on the EEC rather than just the German consumer electronics market (see above). The BKA says that its stance was not influenced by the federal ministry. It justified its decision (although the combined colour TV market shares of Grundig and Thomson's existing German subsidiaries amounted in 1983 to some 38 per cent) presumably with the argument that it later used to justify its approval of Grundig's take-over by Philips: intensified foreign competition had changed the consumer electronics market so radically since 1979 that even market shares of 40 to 50 per cent could not be interpreted as giving the firms in question a 'dominant market position'.

By insisting on Philips's withdrawal from Grundig as a precondition of approving its take-over by Thomson (and on Max Grundig's sale of his shareholding in Philips), the BKA ruled out a three-way link-up of Grundig, Thomson, and Philips, which together at this time would probably have held more than a half of the colour TV market in the FRG. However, the failure of such a deal to materialize can not be attributed primarily to the negative attitude of the BKA which the firms, if they had wanted to join forces in Grundig, could have tried to persuade the Economics Minister to reverse. Both Philips and Thomson wanted a controlling influence over Grundig and neither was prepared to settle for less.[6] After the BKA had announced its judgement, Philips was forced to abandon its cover and declare that it would not part with its stake in Grundig. Only the French government could conceivably have forced Philips to withdraw from Grundig, but it is doubtful whether any sanction which the French government could have imposed on Philips on the French market would have been as unpalatable to Philips as its losing its stake in Grundig to Thomson. In any event, political divisions within the French government ensured that it would be difficult for it to take action (such as the withholding of government contracts) to try to move Philips to withdraw from Grundig (see Chapter 11).

Implications of the Grundig affair

The failure of Thomson's bid to take over Grundig and the BKA's decision in respect of the take-over attempt cleared the way for Philips's assumption of a controlling stake in Grundig in 1984. Since the combined German market shares of Philips and Grundig were not significantly greater than those of Grundig and Thomson's German subsidiaries would have been, the BKA could not say no to Philips's take-over of Grundig. If Grundig's strategy from the outset had been to use the Thomson bid to clear the political obstacles to an eventual take-over of the firm by Philips (see above), then it had succeeded.[7] In retrospect, Thomson's bid for Grundig appears to have been a cause in which only the Thomson management and the French Industry Ministry could be counted as its convinced supporters. Philips's take-over of Grundig was the work of Philips alone.

Thomson's reaction was immediately to acquire the AEG subsidiary, Telefunken. The combined market shares of Telefunken and Thomson's existing German subsidiaries were not so high as to pose competition law obstacles to this second take-over bid. The banking consortium which owned AEG had been seeking a buyer for the conglomerate's loss-making consumer electronics subsidiary. Initially, Grundig had been the prime candidate to acquire Telefunken. However, negotiations between Grundig and the AEG's banking consortium over the terms of the transaction had got bogged down and Grundig had withdrawn the offer early in 1983, since it was evident that the BKA would not have approved Thomson's bid for Grundig if the latter were simultaneously to acquire Telefunken. The AEG banks entertained no objections to selling Telefunken to Thomson—they were pleased to be rid of it. According to one source, Thomson's strategy all along had been to make an 'artificial' bid for Grundig—which it knew would not succeed—and thereby soften the opposition to a subsequent take-over of Telefunken. Certainly, Thomson's consumer electronics division and its head (although not the overall company chairman) wanted the firm to take over Telefunken rather than Grundig since this would give them access (through the J2T joint venture) to Japanese video technology of which they had been deprived by a decision of the newly elected French Socialist government in 1981 (see Chapter 11).

Thus, within roughly a year in 1983–4, the two former flagships of the German consumer electronics industry, Telefunken and Grundig, the one effectively bankrupt and the other near enough to it, had fallen under the control of other European multinational electronics firms. Only three firms worthy of mention, Blaupunkt (Bosch–Siemens), Schneider, and Loewe-Opta, accounting at the most for one-sixth of the jobs in the German industry, remained in predominantly German hands.[8] For the most part, these were firms which had pursued successful niche strategies (such as Loewe-Opta in 'de luxe' CTV sets) or diversification strategies (such as Schneider into the home computer market). The level of concentration in the industry had increased sharply, bearing out the BKA's own judgement that its capacity to influence developments on the consumer electronics market was 'very limited'.

The outcome of the Grundig affair illustrates clearly the inability or unwillingness of the various actors to close ranks in defence of any conception of a 'German' consumer electronics industry. The Bavarian state government's rescue plan collapsed because it could persuade neither other firms nor the federal government to take part. The firms involved were reluctant to buy into Grundig for the different reasons explored above; such reluctance might have been overcome had the federal government endorsed the plan with enthusiasm and attempted to use its leverage with, for example, Siemens over the other parts of its business such as telecommunications. But, crucially, the federal government chose to stand apart from the situation, and it was never put to the ultimate test of facing a choice between an interventionist solution or the bankruptcy of Grundig. The evidence suggests strongly that the federal Economics Ministry wanted at all costs to avoid being seen itself to be determining the outcome of Thomson's bid for Grundig—and thus departing from its role as custodian of the 'social market economy'. It was, however, prepared to ensure that the BKA's interpretation of what would constitute a 'dominant market position' would not pose an obstacle to the take-over of Grundig. In this sense German government policy was a recognition of the imperative for consumer electronics firms to increase their market power to counter the Japanese, and a recognition that this involved abandoning any conception of 'national' firms and a 'national' market. The ultimate significance of the Grundig affair was that it confirmed the role of the major firms as the crucial actors in government–industry relations. The tendency of German government policy to bend in the direction of the interests of the major firms was further shown in its acquiescence to the voluntary export restraint agreement for VCRs, to which we now turn.

The German Politics of VCR Protection

The background

By the time a potential market for VCRs had developed in the EEC states in the late 1970s, the Japanese industry had already built up massive production capacities to serve not just the Japanese but also the American market, which it had cornered without any competition from the European firms. With the advantage of much greater economies of scale, the Japanese firms swamped the rapidly growing German VCR market between 1978 and 1982. In this period, German imports of VCRs increased almost tenfold. Whereas, in 1982, the value of the FRG's colour TV exports exceeded that of its imports by more than twofold, the picture on the VCR market was exactly the reverse.

Of the German firms, only the largest, Grundig, in collaboration with Philips, attempted to develop its own VCR production capacity. The two firms brought the V2000 VCR on to the market in 1980. Telefunken could not contemplate building up an independent production capacity for VCRs—it had no option but to seek a licence to produce either V2000 or Japanese VCRs. After negotiations with Philips and Grundig had failed, Telefunken signed a joint venture deal with JVC, aligning itself to the Japanese rather than to the European camp.

In 1982, there were massive cuts in the prices of Japanese VCRs on the EEC market. Consequently, the V2000's market share began to decline sharply, exacerbating Grundig's already precarious financial position. Grundig and Philips spoke of the possibility of mass redundancies, factory closure, and firm bankruptcies on the scale of those of AEG.[9] Against this background, the two firms lodged a dumping complaint against the Japanese exporters with the EEC Commission. According to the complaint, the price of Japanese VCRs on the EEC market had been cut within a year by 60 per cent and they were now being sold at prices below production costs. The market share of the European manufacturers had fallen in the previous few months by more than half. If nothing were done, some 20,000 jobs would be destroyed in the European consumer electronics and component manufacturing industries.[10]

The VCR export restraint agreement

Philips and Grundig waged their campaign for protection from Japanese VCR imports through the European and national trade associations, the EEC member governments, and the EEC Commission. Among the EEC governments, the French, which was about to impose the Poitiers 'blockade', was the most receptive to their case. Traditionally a strong supporter of free trade in the EEC, the Dutch government was divided on the issue of protecting the European VCR industry, but came down ultimately on the side of Philips. Hitherto, the German government had proven the most resistant in the EEC to industry demands for protection. Securing its support for or acquiescence in protection for the VCR industry was a key to the success of the Philips–Grundig campaign.

Majority opinion in the ZVEI consumer electronics sub-association was in favour of protectionist measures against the Japanese. Until the early 1980s, Thomson had been the strongest advocate of protection among the major European consumer electronics firms. Philips, on the other hand, had traditionally championed free trade. Its shift into the protectionist camp was decisive for the change in the balance of opinion in the German industry. Thomson's attitude on the VCR protection issue was probably more ambivalent, certainly more so than that of Philips and Grundig, which orchestrated the protectionist campaign. At this time, since it marketed imported Japanese VCRs, it would have been negatively affected by the imposition of import quotas or higher tariffs. On the other hand, it was aiming in the longer term to develop an independent VCR production capacity—there were reports at the time that Thomson was planning to build a VCR factory in France—and the imposition of measures and political pressure which could help to force the Japanese firms to set up production facilities, especially in joint ventures with indigenous firms, in Europe could serve to further this objective. At the same time, the intensifying VCR price war was already making it more and more difficult for firms such as Thomson which merely sold Japanese VCRs under their own labels.

The other V2000 marketers in the sub-association (Siemens, Metz, Loewe-Opta) sided with their suppliers, Philips and Grundig. With the exception of Thomson (i.e. its German subsidiaries), the importers of Japanese VCRs were opposed to protectionist measures. The strongest opponent was Telefunken. It had just signed a very favourable deal with JVC which the imposition of import quotas or higher tariffs could spoil. Blaupunkt, too, belonged to the opponents of protection. Only two months before Grundig and Philips launched their dumping suit, its majority owner, Bosch, had negotiated the establishment of a joint VCR venture with Matsushita.[11] However, even Blaupunkt had some sympathy with Philips's and Grundig's cause and recognized that if the Japanese 'invasion' of the EEC market was not halted, the European VCR industry would be destroyed.

The Philips–Grundig axis also succeeded in obtaining the acquiescence of the ZVEI as a whole in its demand for protection. This was by no means self-evident: the electrical engineering industry is highly export-orientated and therefore 'basically in favour of free trade'. The protection lobby was assisted, however, by the fact that other branches in the industry besides the VCR manufacturers were also irate over perceived unfair Japanese trading practices and by the fact that, since some 80 per cent of the industry's total exports were to other Western European states (and hardly any to Japan), the imposition of protectionist measures against the Japanese VCR industry would not expose it to the danger of damaging retaliatory measures by the Japanese. Moreover, the Philips–Grundig axis also enjoyed the support of the biggest German electronic components manufacturer (and electrical engineering conglomerate), Siemens, for which the consumer electronics industry as a whole constituted a crucial market. The ZVEI's electronic components' sub-division, in which Siemens has probably a dominant voice, was strongly in favour of protection for the European VCR manufacturers.

The ZVEI's acquiescence in the protectionist demands of its consumer electronics sub-association presumably enhanced the legitimacy of the Philips–Grundig cause within the federal government. However, it is doubtful whether the sub-association exercised a decisive influence on government policy on this issue. According to one source in industry, the trade association was 'badly informed' on this issue, had not been asked for its opinion, and had not been advised as to what was going on. All the big firms with a vested interest in the issue intervened directly in both Bonn and Brussels. The trade unions, on the other hand, were not involved at all in government policy-making on VCR trade, but supported the protectionist line.[12]

The Philips–Grundig 'case' for protection consisted of four main components. The first stressed the alleged unfairness of Japanese trading and industrial policy practices, often alleged to be orchestrated by the Japanese MITI, of industrial targeting or 'laser-beaming'—that is, the building up of enormous production capacities in particular sectors and the flooding of the corresponding world markets. The second, which carried most weight with governments, stressed the imminent consequences of the Japanese export offensive for employment in the European consumer electronics industry. The firms pointed, thirdly, to the potential loss of research and development capacity and knowhow in the European consumer electronics industry and growing danger of European dependence on imported technologies. Finally, particular emphasis was laid on the implications of the decline of the European consumer electronics industry for the maintenance of an independent European microelectronics components industry.[13]

The Japanese industry wanted at all costs to avoid an anti-dumping case. In negotiations with the EEC Commission, the Japanese government promised that the industry would restrain its exports to the EEC in exchange for Philips's and Grundig's dumping claim being withdrawn and the Poitiers VCR blockade (see Chapter 11) being lifted. Philips and Grundig, which had initially demanded an increase in tariffs on Japanese VCRs, consulted each other and decided to acquiesce in the deal, parts of which, however, were strongly criticized in the European industry. The criticism was directed in particular against the floor price for VCRs included in the agreement, which, according to various firms, allowed the Japanese exporters to rake in massive profits on VCR sales, and the European Commission's too optimistic assessment of the growth of the European VCR market, which was to put the Japanese industry in a position to achieve a greater market share with the concrete VCR quotas which it was granted by the EEC in the self-restraint agreement. Of crucial importance to Philips and Grundig were the 'local content' provisions of the agreement—which meant that the quotas applied not just to VCRs manufactured and assembled in Japan, but also to the VCR 'kits' assembled in what the European manufacturers described as 'screwdriver factories' in the EEC.

Within the Bonn Economics Ministry, attitudes to the (proposed) self-restraint agreement, which required the EEC Council of Ministers' approval, varied, according to the various sections' or divisions' closeness to the industry. Hitherto, the ministry had always opposed protectionist proposals in the council. The ministry's electrical engineering industry section proved relatively sympathetic to the protection advocates' case. This section was interested in maximizing the local content of VCRs sold on the European market and preserving jobs in the industry. Other sections in the ministry's industry division and the other divisions involved in trade and European policy-making appear to have adopted a much more sceptical attitude to the proposed agreement or even to have opposed it 'to the last'. Here there was a stronger adherence to the ministry's free trade ideology—which was conceivably strengthened by the opposition of commercial interests to VCR protection.

The motives for these divisions' ultimate acquiescence in the agreement (despite their agreeing that it would not work) had less to do with their concern for the plight of Philips and Grundig or for employment in the industry than with their concern (after Philips had brought the Dutch government into the protectionist boat) not to become isolated within the EEC on the issue and their belief that, if the European VCR industry was to be protected, then a self-restraint agreement represented the least undesirable policy option available. To impose import quotas, such as Philips and Grundig are said to have demanded, was 'always rather spectacular' and to impose them unilaterally was illegal under GATT rules. A self-restraint agreement, on the other hand, did not expose its instigator so clearly to the accusation of practising protectionism. The Economics Minister himself (Lambsdorff) probably had no principled objections to the self-restraint agreement—his opposition to Japanese 'laser beaming' was well known and he had already played a key role in persuading the Japanese car industry 'voluntarily' to restrain its exports to the FRG.[14]

The aftermath

Retrospective judgements on the impact of the self restraint agreement vary according to the original division of opinion within the industry. Philips sees it as having been one factor which helped to improve the EEC trade balance in VCRs and as having made a 'useful contribution' to improving the European industry's competitiveness *vis-à-vis* the Japanese. One thing, however, is certain: the agreement did not save the Philips–Grundig V2000 format. Within a year of its adoption, both Philips and Grundig announced that they were beginning to manufacture VHS VCRs and by the time the agreement expired at the end of 1985, the two firms had stopped manufacturing V2000 VCRs altogether. The VHS had established itself as the dominant VCR standard in Western Europe.

The European industry's dissatisfaction with the concrete quotas allocated to the Japanese in the agreement led to bilateral industry-to-industry talks and the Japanese firms agreeing not to exhaust their quotas in 1984 and 1985. They had seen that otherwise the 'Europeans would shout more loudly for protection'. Even after the formal expiry of the agreement, the Japanese industry continued in practice to exercise export self-restraint. This, and other practices, such as the sub-contracting of TV manufacture to local producers, corresponded to the firms' objective of creating 'a good atmosphere' in the EEC and thus avoiding being subjected to tougher protectionist measures.

At the same time, the self-restraint agreement and the danger of the EEC market's increasingly being closed to Japanese exports—along with other developments, such as the appreciation of the yen—motivated the Japanese firms to invest increasingly in VCR production facilities in the EEC. The first to do so was Sony, which had taken over the German firm Wega in 1975 and since then been engaged in CTV production. Sony and Sanyo, which in the same year took control of Fisher Hifi, remained the only notable Japanese investors in the German consumer electronics industry until the early 1980s, when, in quick succession, JVC (J2T in Berlin) and its parent company, Matsushita (Matsushita–Bosch), Sanyo (Fisher), Hitachi, and Toshiba all established VCR production facilities in the FRG. The wave of Japanese investment in the FRG thus occurred later than in Britain (see Chapter 10) and the investors were generally already established in the British industry. 'Closeness to the market' was the most frequently cited motive for the firms' additional investments in the FRG. The availability of adequate skilled workers and component suppliers—more so than government subsidies—also attracted investment. Whether such investments, mainly in small production facilities and in addition to those already made in Britain, made commercial sense may be questioned. Conceivably, they were aimed rather, or just as much, at securing the political goodwill of the German federal and state governments in trade conflicts.

An ironic consequence of the growth of Japanese VCR investment in the EEC between 1982 and 1985 was that when the self-restraint agreement was superseded by an increased tariff on VCR imports, the Japanese firms manufacturing in the EEC belonged to its supporters and beneficiaries. In particular, the higher tariff helped to protect them from the competition of the more cheaply producing South Korean and smaller Japanese firms, whose share of the EEC VCR market was rising sharply in the market for lower-priced VCRs and CTV sets. The joint pressure of the European and Japanese manufacturers for protection from the 'Korean challenge' began to precipitate a similar response from the Korean firms to that of the Japanese in the early 1980s. Thus, in 1986 the fear of protectionist measures led the Korean firm Goldstar to decide to set up a factory to manufacture CTVs and VCRs in the FRG.[15]

The pressure for the increase in the tariff on imported VCRs— after the Japanese government had insisted on the formal termination of the self-restraint agreement—came from the same firms whose pressure had initially led to the Japanese acquiescence in self-imposed export moderation. The German government abstained in the vote on the increase in the tariff in the EEC Council of Ministers, but the federal Economics Ministry was not so torn about accepting this measure as it had been about accepting the self-restraint agreement. Its acquiescence in the increase was eased by a simultaneous cut in the tariff on semiconductors, which made the overall package compatible with GATT rules.[16]

Japanese export self-restraint and the increase in the tariff on imported VCRs failed, however, to bring about a lasting improvement in the competitiveness of the VCR manufacturing industry in the FRG. In 1988, Grundig demanded the imposition of 25 to 30 per cent tariffs on Far Eastern VCRs, otherwise the firm would be forced to transfer production abroad and cut back its workforce.[17] Philips threatened that if the EEC Commission did not launch an investigation into CD player dumping by Japanese firms, it would close down its entire European production.[18] The wheel seemed to have turned full circle and landed back where it had stood in 1982.

Conclusion

In the period from the late 1970s to the middle of the 1980s, the German consumer electronics industry underwent a massive reorganization and contraction. Employment in the industry declined from 108,000 in 1977 to little more than 60,000 in 1983. The number of factories manufacturing consumer electronics products fell between 1980 and 1986 from 290 to 230. Production processes were extensively rationalized and automated: in less than a decade, the average time required to manufacture a colour TV set was cut from eight to one and a half hours. At the same time, foreign penetration of the German market advanced rapidly: imported products accounted for roughly 80 per cent of sales in value in 1986, compared with about 50 per cent in 1980. The colour TV market was the only one in which German-based producers retained a dominant position against foreign competitors. The firms which remained in the industry sought to survive through the formation of product-specific alliances, against or, as in Thomson's case in respect of VCRs, with the Japanese.[19]

At the same time as they tried to regroup and reorganize, the big consumer electronics firms also stepped up their pressure on the German federal government and the EEC for protective state intervention or, in respect of competition policy, benevolent state non-intervention. But where the state did intervene at the industry's behest, the development of the VCR market in the FRG illustrated that the market could not be steered—and the European manufacturers could not be effectively protected—with such trade policy instruments as 'voluntary' self-restraint and (moderately) higher tariffs. Where, as in the VCR market, both private standards prevail and the government does not constitute a significant customer, the capacity of government actors to influence the development of the industry and the market may be particularly tightly circumscribed.

To speak in the German case of the capacity or incapacity of government actors to intervene in and steer structural change or market trends in the consumer electronics industry is to tell no more than half the story. Despite the massive upheaval and contraction of the consumer electronics industry, the federal government at no stage aspired to formulate or implement an industrial strategy or policy for consumer electronics. The federal Economics Ministry acquiesced in or supported *ad hoc* interventionist measures and also displayed increasing understanding for the majority of the industry's pleas for protection from Japanese and other Far Eastern competition. But it did not become a full-blooded advocate of the industry and its protection from East Asian competition either in the federal government or in the EEC.

In addition state governments had a limited capacity to influence company strategies in a highly internationalized market increasingly dominated by multinational conglomerate firms. The responsibility of the EEC for the trade policy of its member states has made the process of policy-making on consumer electronics issues a transnational one, inhabited not only by the national and state governments and 'national' firms, but also by multinational and foreign firms, supra-national institutions, and foreign governments, either within or beyond the EEC. This internationalization or at least Europeanization of consumer electronics and its implications are discussed in the following chapter.

Notes

Note: Unless specifically cited, quotations in this chapter are drawn from interviews.

1. See ZVEI, *Fachverband Unterhaltungselektronik, Kommunikations und Unterhaltungselektronik in Deutschland: Perspektiven und Probleme* (Frankfurt: ZVEI, 1980).

2. See 'Das Riesen-Monopol der Deutschen Bank', *Der Spiegel*, 11 Feb. 1985, pp. 63–66.

3. It is interesting, however, that the then Economics Minister Count Lambsdorff is reported to have said in 1979 that he had 'nothing against Philips and Grundig getting together' (*Die Zeit*, 17 Aug. 1979: 'Das Ende eines Solos'). This suggests that the responsible minister personally was in favour of Philips taking over Grundig from the outset, although the remark need not be interpreted as meaning that Lambsdorff supported a take-over of Grundig by Philips rather than, for example, closer co-operation between the two firms.

4. In fact, according to our interviews, the overall head of Philips's consumer electronics division at the time is said to have been advised from within Philips to let Grundig go bankrupt.

5. 'Neue Gespräche über Grundigs Zukunft', *Süddeutsche Zeitung*, 9 Dec. 1982.

6. 'Kartellamt will Beteiligung von Thomson bei Grundig genehmigen', *Stuttgarter Zeitung*, 25 Feb. 1983.

7. Following Philips's decision to take over Grundig, Grundig's financial adviser Poullain said: 'It is perhaps slightly exaggerated and arrogant to say now that the negotiations with the French [i.e. Thomson] were only conducted to prod Philips into action, but this is the effect they had' (quoted in *Die Zeit*, 18 Mar. 1983). In an interview with one of the authors, he confirmed that this had been Grundig's strategy.

8. Until 1984/5, Loewe-Opta had actually been controlled through 'dummy' firms by Philips. After Philips's influence over the firm had become known, the BKA forced it to withdraw from Loewe-Opta as a price for its being permitted to take over Grundig. A group of managers of the firm subsequently took a majority shareholding in the firm and the automobile manufacturer BMW a minority shareholding.

9. 'Der Druck verstärkt', *Der Spiegel*, 8 Nov. 1982.

10. 'Antidumping Klage gegen japanische Videorecorder', *Handelsblatt*, 15 Dec. 1982. According to one industry source, the material submitted by the firms to the Commission would have justified the imposition of a 29% duty.

11. The attitude of the Japanese firms which belonged to the ZVEI's consumer electronics sub-association will not have been relevant to the formation of the sub-association's policy on the trade issue, as none of them was represented on its executive council or committee (see introduction).

12. 'IG Metall fordert Importrestriktionen', *Süddeutsche Zeitung*, 16 Nov. 1982.

13. According to an interview in *Welt am Sonntag*, 21 Nov. 1982, Grundig argued that the consumer electronics industry consumed 50% of the components industry's output, but this is disputed by other sources. There seems to be agreement, however, that this issue was not decisive in determining the atttitude of the German Economics Ministry, but it may have played a greater role in EEC states such as France with a stronger mercantilist tradition.

14. As reported from an interview with Lambsdorff in *Handelsblatt*, 6 May 1986.

15. 'Koreaner bauen VideoWerk in Worms'. *Süddeutsche Zeitung*, 11 June 1986.

16. One industrialist described the increase in VCR tariff from 8 to 14% as 'chicken feed'. Hermanus Koning, as quoted in an interview in *Der Spiegel*, 23 Sept. 1985, p. 68.
17. As reported in the *General-Anzeiger*, 16 Apr. 1988.
18. European Commission official quoted in *Die Zeit*, 7 Oct. 1988.
19. The most significant such 'alliance' in the period after the reorganization of the industry in 1982–3 was an agreement between Grundig and Blaupunkt according to which the former would manufacture CTVs for the latter and the latter car radios for the former.

13

European Consumer Electronics: The Rise of the Transnationals

Internationalization amidst Technological Uncertainty

In the last three chapters we have presented an overview of the development of government–industry relations in each country. It became evident from the spate of transnational merger and alliance activity in the 1980s, and from the increasing role played by the European Commission, that national industries are no longer the key unit for analysis. This process of internationalization is a complex one, fuelled by political developments, market trends, and technological innovations. We need to be careful to distinguish the forces which propel major companies such as Philips and Thomson to emulate their main Japanese competitors like Sony and Matsushita in developing global strategies, from the simultaneous process of the emergence of a European focus for political activity over trade and industrial policy issues. The pull towards internationalization in terms of world markets may have the effect of undermining the prospects for European collaboration.

The probable arrival of new technologies to achieve high definition television (HDTV) in the 1990s is a major stimulus for European companies to develop global strategies. Their principal competitors are the Japanese firms, who are already well established in the United States, as well as secure in their domination of their own domestic market in Japan and, through direct investment and component supply, well placed in the fast-growing consumer markets of the ASEAN countries.[1] In 1986 it seemed as if the only route to HDTV lay in entirely new systems at each stage of origination, transmission, and reception. The issue was whether there would be a single (Japanese) world standard, or whether Europe would succeed in developing its own standard. Thus the Eureka HDTV project, led by Philips, was intended to establish a new system based on the MAC-packet family of standards. It seemed that the adoption of this standard by the EC in 1986 would offer the kind of 'passive protection' in the future that Europe enjoyed by virtue of having adopted its own PAL and SECAM colour television standard in the 1960s.

The pace of innovation in television technology is so rapid, however, that these assumptions seem questionable. The arrival of 1 megabit chips, and the prospect of cheap 4 megabit chips within two or three years, offered an alternative route to high definition based on the processing of existing signals within the television set. This route was equally available to the Americans with their existing transmission equipment and standards, as it was to the Japanese and the Europeans. The possibility arose that consumer electronics manufacturers would be able to follow this route independently of the tortuous political process of standard-setting which involves national broadcasting organizations and national governments.

The imminent involvement of the private sector in Direct Broadcast by Satellite (DBS) in Europe was accompanied by further uncertainties in technological choice. In 1989 two DBS satellites began to offer British viewers a wide range of additional (to the existing terrestrial) channels. The uncertainty arose from the intention of the Sky channel, at least initially, to broadcast in PAL rather than MAC, which removed the need for a special decoder (at extra expense) to allow new programmes to be received on existing sets. If MAC channels have to compete for a mass market against PAL–DBS channels, then the possibility of enhanced definition by signal processing rather than through the development of high definition MAC becomes more likely. The closure strategy employed by the consumer electronics majors, led by Philips, and the state-owned national broadcasting organizations would be at risk on its home territory with no chance of adoption in other markets.

At the time of writing it is difficult to judge the outcome of the intense competition to be the first to make money from satellite television, but the process does illustrate that even a coalition of large oligopolistic firms and public sector monopolies (not unlike those we have earlier analysed in telecommunications) is vulnerable to erosion from outsiders. The creation of new markets for as yet unproven technologies is risky enough, without the intervention of maverick entrepreneurs such as Rupert Murdoch of Sky and Alan Sugar of Amstrad. What was clear was that this was to be a race between international coalitions—the MAC family and the mavericks—and was not confined to national industry or sector frontiers. Indeed, the most threatening characteristic of satellite broadcasting for national governments with regulatory ambitions was precisely that it takes place across frontiers.

Broadcasting inherently brings consumer electronics firms within the constraints set by other organizations, including governments, but there are indications that many other technological developments also have this effect. The move within compact disc from stand alone music players to a new publishing medium brings with it new challenges for the firms. We saw in earlier chapters that the failure of the European V2000 VCR format was in part due to Philips underestimating the importance of available video software in the early stages of market development. Unlike the case of teletext examined in Chapter 10, VCR market development was left entirely to firms. Governments stood on one side, with the French government taking a negative role in terms of trying to restrict market growth as long as there was no indigenous French producer. With CD-based products aimed at the consumer the links between software and hardware are vital, and these have spawned a complex set of joint ventures examined later in this chapter.

The 'home bus', which some argue will allow a domestic network to link home appliances and offer security functions, again brings 'brown goods' manufacturers into contact with a number of different partners, among them the quite unfamilar 'white goods' community.[2] The Eureka framework has proved a useful way in which to encourage such links to develop across sectoral and national boundaries. If the project proves successful and results in marketable home systems and products, it is likely that Philips's own involvement in manufacturing will be augmented by a number of joint ventures.

Finally, there is the prospect of further erosion of the previous distinctions between professional and consumer electronics as many products become 'personal' and sold on to mass markets. This has happened most obviously with personal computers, but not far behind are personal mobile communications (cellular radio), personal photocopiers, fax machines and the like which have encouraged the Japanese to talk about 'personal office automation'. The Japanese vision of the home of the future is that a good deal of work will take place there as well as play.

From Industry Sectors to Clusters of Firms

The major problem that has faced European firms in the last fifteen years has been how to cope with the competitive threat mounted by Japanese companies. As we have seen from earlier chapters, one of the most common responses of the British firms was to leave the industry, retreating to 'safer' segments such as defence electronics and telecommunications. In Germany the major part of the industry passed from German to foreign control, but few producers actually folded. The structure of the industry remained the same, but the pattern of ownership was transformed, particularly as Philips and Thomson divided the diminishing spoils between them, with Nokia as a late arrival at the ball. As in Britain this process was facilitated, if not actually encouraged, by the indifference of the government to the national origin of investment capital. This was in sharp contrast to France, where until very recently government policy was overtly neo-mercantilist, geared towards protecting what were seen as French interests by the promotion of the French national champion, Thomson.

The formation of the single market in the EEC, which is under way, but which will take rather longer than 1992 to achieve, has encouraged firms to look towards European strategies. In the case of Philips and Thomson there is the problem of integrating European strategy within the framework of a global approach. In this section we will look at the industry structure which has emerged from the process of internationalization in consumer electronics. This process can be traced back to 1973, when the first Japanese manufacturing investment was made by Sony at Bridgend in Wales.[3] By 1988 there were sixty-three consumer electronics plants in the EEC wholly or partly owned by the Japanese, and significant Taiwanese and Korean investments as well.[4] All four firm clusters—Philips-Grundig, Thomson, Nokia, and the Japanese—are attempting to develop a coherent international strategy which treats Europe at least potentially as a single market, and which treats plants in different countries as part of the strategic whole.

Philips[5]

Philips is the biggest and oldest European consumer electronics firm,[6] with operations in sixty countries, and is perhaps the one which was facing the most difficult set of challenges. In 1981 it began a radical restucturing of its activities, trying to change from being a loose confederation of nationally oriented subsidiaries to become a genuine transnational corporation with a co-ordinated global strategy. Its oft-repeated goal was to split its manufacturing and sales roughly one-third each between Europe, North America, and the Far East. This strategy involved a painful process of rationalization and plant closure, as well as an attempt at the more difficult problem of changing organizational structure and corporate culture. Philips has always been fiercely proud of its role as an innovator, and among other new products has introduced the tape cassette and compact disc. It has, however, had expensive failures, the most important of which was the abortive V2000 VCR system which has already been discussed at length.

The losses incurred on the V2000 led the main board in Eindhoven to consider in 1983 the possibility of withdrawing from consumer electronics altogether. In the end the board decided that the rest of the company was crucially dependent on consumer activities, despite their slipping from 47 to 23 per cent of total turnover from 1975 to 1985. There were few signs that Philips intended to relinquish its role as a pioneer, and it has been investing heavily in CD applications, and, perhaps more important in the long term, flat-screen and projection alternatives to the cathode ray tube. It has been, however, a frequent criticism of Philips, especially within the technology policy sections of the EEC, that it failed sufficiently to exploit its own inventions, leaving the Japanese firms to develop the full potential of the product and with it the lion's share of the profit.

In five years from 1981 Philips closed one-third of its European plants, but as late as 1986 still had some 170, including nine CTV plants.[7] Plant closure has been a difficult political problem for Philips, especially in those smaller countries where withdrawal would mean the end of manufacturing activity in consumer electronics. In deciding such matters, the central board has often been swayed by the adverse impact that this might have on its lobbying efforts in Brussels. With a relatively small country, the Netherlands, as its home, Philips has found it useful to try to gain the support of the German, French, and British governments in particular. This reasoning long affected decisions about the future of the one remaining CTV plant in Britain, which was finally closed in December

1988, and can plausibly be argued to have lain behind the short-lived assembly of V2000 VCRs in France. With new products Philips has been able to achieve economies of scale by locating in a single country: it chose to centralize all its compact disc player manufacture in a single plant in Belgium.

At the same time that it was trying to compete against the more efficient Far Eastern producers by cutting costs,[8] Philips pressed the EEC to increase the effective protection offered by tariffs, arguing in 1984 for a standard rate of 19 per cent for existing products such as hi-fi and VCR, and suggesting that eight new product groups be covered by specific higher tariffs.[9] While this claim was not conceded, Philips did manage to achieve a 19 per cent rate for compact disc players, reducing to the now standard rate of 14 per cent after three years. More recently Philips has led the campaign by European producers to persuade the EEC to clamp down on so-called 'screwdriver' plants by extending anti-dumping measures from finished products to component imports and to adopt new rules for EEC value added for VCRs. The Philips credo has been continually expressed in terms of 'reciprocity' and the metaphor of the 'level playing field': until the removal of non-tariff barriers in Japan—the most important of which is argued to be the tied distribution system through which retail stores deal only with the goods of a single manufacturer—Philips management believes it has a right to protective measures in Europe.[10] Publicly and privately, many EEC officials concede that Philips was among the most persuasive lobbyists at the European Commission, maintaining an impressive organization in Brussels devoted to that task.

Thomson

By contrast, Thomson has only very recently emerged as a serious challenge to Philips as a European-based international consumer electronics company, and has tended to try to influence Brussels through the agency of the French government. As we have shown earlier, Thomson was groomed for many years as the 'national champion' of successive French governments, but this meant neither control of Thomson by the state, nor any necessary harmony between Thomson's objectives and state policy. The latter problem arises from the conflicts between departments: at the same time that Thomson had persuaded the Industry Ministry to back its

'Asian' strategy of getting into VCR production through the JVC link, the Finance Ministry stunted the growth of the French VCR market by introducing a special tax on VCR ownership.

Nationalization of the firm in 1981 paradoxically inaugurated an era of exceptional commercial freedom. Thomson's ambitious attempt to become a global producer through acquisitions received the backing of the Finance Ministry when it purchased the RCA division of the US General Electric Company[11] and the Ferguson division of Thorn-EMI within the space of a few weeks in 1987. These acquisitions put Thomson into third place in the world CTV league, after Philips-Grundig and Matsushita. Thomson's PDG, Alain Gomez, survived the rolling of heads of the nationalized industries undertaken when the Chirac government was elected in 1986, surely because he had succeeded in turning around a 2 billion fr. loss in 1982 to a small profit in 1986. Gomez chose to concentrate Thomson's activities into consumer electronics, semiconductors, and defence electronics by relinquishing computers, telecommunications, and medical equipment.[12] In 1987 consumer electronics amounted to 52 per cent of Thomson's wholly owned activities, with defence systems 45 per cent.[13]

Thomson's early move into Germany, through the acquisition of Saba, Nordmende, and Dual, led to the 'Grundig affair' and the take-over of Telefunken. Had Thomson's bid for Grundig succeeded, and had Thomson joined forces with Philips in VCR technology and components manufacture, then European consumer electronics might look very different now. The strengthening of the link with JVC, first through the Telefunken and then through the Thorn-EMI-Ferguson purchase, has had important benefits for Thomson which the Philips link would have denied it. Like Philips, Thomson's board considered exit from consumer electronics in 1985, and, again like Philips, it decided the links between consumer electronics and components were, at least potentially, crucial. Thomson managed to negotiate the most far-reaching technology transfer agreement with JVC, permitting it to manufacture video cassette recorder mechanisms. In 1988 Thomson maintained ninety people in Japan engaged in technology acquisition, and it has married this to the exploitation of French government-backed chip design.[14] This kind of activity was seen by Gomez as an essential part of its global strategy, the transition from French national champion to international champion neatly symbolized by his changing the French title Thomson Grand Public to the Thomson Consumer Electronics Division.

Nokia

The Finnish-owned conglomerate Nokia was the most recent arrival on the European consumer electronics scene. As recently as 1984 its core businesses were such areas as paper and electric cables, but in 1987 two-thirds of its sales came from electronics, telecommunications, and information systems. In February 1984 Nokia bought Luxor of Sweden and Salora of Finland to become the leading TV producer in Scandinavia, manufacturing each year the same volume of sets as Ferguson in the UK. Then, within four months in 1987, Nokia bought France's third biggest CTV maker, Océanic, from Electrolux of Sweden, and SEL, the former ITT German consumer electronics subsidiary, which had passed from ITT to the French CGE group as part of the restructuring process in the telecommunications industry we analysed in Chapter 8. Nokia thus became the third force in the European CTV industry, after Philips and Thomson, with a combined production of 2.5 million sets per year. The former SEL plant was Europe's biggest, producing 1.25 million sets a year,[15] and SEL has pioneered digital CTV circuitry. In addition Nokia bought in 1987 an 80 per cent share of Ericsson's data systems division, and was the leading European producer of mobile telecommunications equipment and computer monitors.

In the rapid upheavals of the European electronics industry of the last five years, Nokia fashioned a structure and a broad information technology strategy which closely resembled those of the leading Japanese firms, in that it depended on manufacturing and market experience in consumer electronics to feed back into professional areas and information systems. Unlike the IT strategies of the leading British firms, Nokia's did not rest on the two legs of computing and telecommunications; like the Japanese companies, Nokia had consumer electronics as its third leg. In this respect Philips, Thomson, and Nokia shared a broader conception of IT than any of the British firms.

The Japanese in Europe

In 1988 there were twelve Japanese CTV plants in the EEC. They started on a relatively small scale, and even the largest plant, the ex-GEC factory in Wales now run by Hitachi, had only a modest output of 320,000 sets per year, only a quarter of the normal volume of Far Eastern plants. Japanese companies accounted for about 14 per cent of EEC CTV output in 1986. Their position was stronger with respect to VCR production, where Japanese companies (including their share of joint venture operations) accounted for 45 per cent of EEC production in 1986 (but 37 per cent of European production). As with CTV, the production volumes of Japanese VCR plants in Europe were tiny compared to that of Far Eastern plants: an average between 150,000 and 200,000 compared to those million-plus norm in Japan, or even the 400,000 output of the Philips and Grundig plants in Austria and Germany.

The pace and direction of Japanese inward investment in consumer electronics has been dictated by trade frictions. These forced Hitachi and Toshiba into 'shotgun weddings' in Britain with GEC and Rank respectively, despite the willingness of the British government to encourage greenfield investment to continue. French hostility to inward investment dominated policy until 1981, and since then investment has been channelled into products, such as audio, where indigenous French production is weakest. Of the nine Japanese consumer electronics plants in France in 1987, none was in CTV, only one was in VCR, and the remainder produced hi-fi, car audio, and compact disc products. By contrast Britain had only one Japanese audio plant. In Germany the pattern of inward investment has been different again, with Sony taking the unusual step of entry by acquisition, by buying Wega, and Matsushita developing a 'voluntary' joint venture with Bosch. But most of the activity in the German industry arose from the expansion of Thomson, Philips, and latterly Nokia.

European Strategies

At first the Japanese plants tended to be very tightly controlled by their parent companies, with very little if any communication between the subsidiaries of the same company in different EEC countries. In some cases, such as that of Toshiba, even the sales and production divisions of the same company reported separately to the appropriate parent division in Japan. What links existed, in terms of defining and defending a 'Japanese' interest within Europe, were fostered by the Electronic Industries Association of Japan, which has maintained a European office in Düsseldorf since 1962, and whose European Director had been in the same job for twenty-five years, longer than any of the Japanese or European managers and civil servants with whom he dealt.

This pattern began to change as Japanese companies as well as European ones geared up to the prospect of a single European market. The Japanese companies were facing fierce competition from the Koreans in particular, which forced them to retreat from the lower end of the CTV and VCR markets and produce ever more innovative products with higher value added and higher profit margins. Some managers of Japanese companies even expressed a common interest with European firms in protectionist measures against Korea. Future closure strategies for both European and Japanese firms would seem to depend on innovation in order to create higher value added products.

One response, not surprisingly pioneered by the first inward investor into Europe, Sony, was to regroup its European CTV operations under a single management structure based in Stuttgart.[16] Sony's aim was to supply all of its European sales from European plants by 1989, and then to concentrate specific functions in different locations within the group. Germany offered superior engineering skills and expertise for CTV and VCR product development, but research and software skills in the UK may be sufficient for Sony to locate its future European R. & D. headquarters in Britain. Likewise, Matsushita, the second inward investor, has become deeply committed to joint ventures with Bosch and Grundig for manufacture and component sourcing. Other major Japanese firms are likely to reorganize along European lines, with variation in the precise location of consumer activities within their overall IT strategies.

Perhaps the most significant recent trend has been the entry into Europe of Japanese components producers, which has recently accelerated with the effect on their home activities of the rising yen, the move offshore by their major customers, and the local content rules and anti-dumping moves by the EC (see below). Alps Electric opened a factory in Milton Keynes in 1986 to produce VCR components, and was soon followed to Britain by two other Japanese component firms. While the big firms like Matsushita are anxious to become integrated into European supply chains, the smaller VCR producers may begin to reproduce within Europe the pattern of component procurement they operate in Japan. 'European content' may become 'Japanese–European' content, with the 'European' industry becoming more 'Japanized'.[17]

The future development of the consumer electronics industry is likely to involve families of new systems and products emerging in uncertain ways as innovations in digital technology (HDTV, CD, and DAT), optoelectronics (CD), domestic networking (IHS), and so on feed through into product development strategies. Although the Japanese have become technological leaders in consumer electronics, they will have to consider afresh the links between R. & D., manufacturing, and marketing in the European context. It may be difficult to develop next generation products entirely in Japan, especially as they become parts of systems and not simply stand-alone products. To the extent that software (video and music as well as computer) is becoming more important for the success of hardware products, and that more of the value of the whole system is located in the software, Japanese companies will have to move activities from Japan to Europe and the United States. Sony's acquisition for $2 billion in 1987 of the world's largest record company, CBS Records, is a significant pointer to this future.[18]

Philips-Grundig was perhaps the only European grouping which could match the spread and ambition of the Japanese majors, and was in many respects better placed than any one of them to exploit future opportunities in consumer electronics. Philips also owned a major record company, PolyGram, but unlike Sony had major strengths in telecommunications via the link with AT&T and in semiconductors through its participation with Siemens in VLSI projects. The most obvious Japanese parallel was with Matsushita, with whom it had a joint venture, first in lighting and later in semiconductors, going back to the 1950s. The reversal in Grundig's fortunes which followed its absorption into the Philips group suggests that Grundig was beginning to play the same role vis-à-vis Philips that JVC did vis-à-vis Matsushita.[19]

EEC Policy towards the Consumer Electronics Industry

European consumer electronics policy since the mid-1970s has been dominated by the politics of international trade. The television industries of the member states have only slowly emerged from the mosaic of national industries whose identity was protected by incompatible national standards and a very low level of intra-EEC trade. But as VCR became as important to consumer electronics trade as CTV, and the threat posed by the Japanese firms became more intense, the situation changed markedly. The engineering and technical skills required to produce VCR machines were such that very few European firms could even think of joining the game. Philips had pioneered VCR technology, but had lost its early lead to Sony and JVC. Its development of the V2000 in collaboration with Grundig gave Europe a stake in the VCR industry, and thus a reason to contest Japanese dominance, which was lacking in the United States.

As the driving force in European VCR, Philips was handicapped in being domiciled in the Netherlands. Only the German government had a material stake in defending the VCR industry, but its policy was in general supportive of free trade and suspicious of protectionist measures. Philips and Grundig realized that their interests in European markets would need to be protected by the EEC, rather than by the actions of individual governments. Their political campaign to swing public policy behind European VCR technology found an ally in the French government, which was alarmed by the rising level of VCR imports, and keen to get Thomson involved in VCR manufacture. At the same time the EEC was in negotiation with Japan in the context of the GATT, trying to get the Japanese to take more positive steps to open their home market to European exports.

It was in this context that the VER agreement was negotiated between Viscount Davignon and MITI in 1983. Philips and Grundig had filed an anti-dumping allegation against one Japanese manufacturer who had offered an OEM contract for Beta machines at very low prices.[20] The European Commission was severely embarrassed by the unilateral French action at Poitiers (see Chapter 11), and the Davignon initiative appeared to offer a satisfactory way out. In the event as we saw in Chapter 12 the VER worked almost entirely to the advantage of the Japanese, because the quota allocated to the V2000 firms was unrealistically large given the slump in VCR sales which hit the industry in 1984. Almost as soon as the agreement was signed, Philips sought access to VHS technology to produce machines for export, and before it had finished Philips was using its quota to get rid of unsold stocks of V2000 machines and build up its sales of VHS machines in Europe. These sales were launched in a market where Japanese machines were sold at a floor price related to European rather than Japanese costs of production. European consumers were thus protecting the inefficient production of Japanese technology in Europe!

But more serious for trade politics than the interests of consumers was the hostility that developed amongst the European firms. The Davignon agreement had also covered kits of parts for assembly in European plants, which meant that Thorn-EMI and Thomson-Telefunken were subject to quotas in respect of their J2T collaboration with JVC. Just as Thomson, as a major importer of own-label Japanese VCRs, had been hit by the Poitiers restrictions, so was it damaged by the VER agreement with MITI. By the end of the three-year agreement, all parties, including Philips and Grundig, were agreed that it had failed to meet its main objective of safeguarding European VCR technology. But the chances of collaboration between Thomson and Philips had also been damaged. Philips's executives complained bitterly in the following years that Thomson had turned its back on compact disc technology, leaving Philips as the only European producer competing against several Japanese firms, and the French firm had declined to collaborate in a joint venture to produce VCR components. Thomson preferred to strengthen its already close relationship with JVC, and it remains to be seen how the formal collaboration between Philips and Thomson in various Eureka projects works out in practice. The strengthening of Thomson's global ambitions following the Ferguson and RCA take-overs is unlikely to have made this collaboration any easier.

The *de facto* VHS standard for VCR was achieved in the competitive market-place after a bitter struggle over rival formats. Philips and Sony both lost very large sums of money in trying to establish their proprietary technologies, and both were ultimately forced to manufacture VHS machines under licence in order to stay in the industry. This stands in stark contrast to television transmission standards, which are negotiated in international bodies in which national governments rather than leading firms are the key actors. The battle continued, however, over camcorder standards between the Sony-led 8mm. camp and the JVC-led VHS camp. JVC's introduction of the Super-VHS (S-VHS) format in 1987 offered enhanced performance as well as a greater measure of world-wide compatibility.[21] But the major challenge still lies in the future, with the potential for a fully digital standard for television and video.

The European firms and governments, after several years of negotiation and compromise, adopted a new standard for Direct Broadcast Satellites, which was expected to make a major impact on European broadcasting from 1989 onwards. The MAC-packet standard offered a better quality picture, with a clear path towards HDTV in the 1990s. It also offered the beguiling prospect for Philips, Thomson, and others of a measure of protection against the Japanese, because the latter would only have access to MAC on negotiation of a licence and payment of the appropriate royalty. In 1990 the CCIR was due to consider a world standard for HDTV, with one of the contenders a MAC derivative developed in a Eureka project under the leadership of Philips. The rival Japanese standard was developed by the Japanese state broadcasting authority NHK in collaboration with Japanese firms. Sony led the development of a studio standard and professional equipment for HDTV, but this could be used independently of the Japanese transmission standard MUSE.

It is possible, if not probable, that Europe and Japan will adopt separate, and at first incompatible, standards for HDTV. The American position is unclear, but seems to have changed since 1986 when the US backed the Japanese proposals at the CCIR meeting in Dubrovnik. By 1988 several research teams in the US (including two in the subsidiaries of Philips and Thomson) were working on different proposals for achieving HDTV, and the American Electronics Association set up a task force with the encouragement, but not at least initially with the financial backing, of the Commerce Department and the US Congress Office of Technology Assessment.[22] The task force included telecommunications and computer firms such as AT&T, Apple, and IBM, and was an indication that the US industry had at last realized the significance of HDTV for a wide variety of broadband communications activities—something the Japanese industry had made no secret of for some years.

In the 1960s, when Europe adopted two incompatible standards for CTV in PAL and SECAM, the semiconductor industry was entirely based around discrete components. In the 1980s advances in chip technology meant that conversion between standards could be achieved with very little increase in the cost of receivers. This cast doubt on the assertion that conversion between MUSE and MAC represented a difficult technical barrier, as the proponents of each system claimed. Nor indeed was it clear that a new transmission technology was actually necessary to deliver HDTV pictures to consumers. Moreover, the decision of Sky to offer DBS broadcasts using PAL rather than MAC called into question the path favoured by the coalition of European broadcasting authorities and major firms which formed around MAC. The issue seemed to be whether the outcome would be left to consumers to decide through their purchases, as happened with VCR standards, or whether European governments and the Commission would attempt to legislate MAC into existence.

The European Commission was facing an acute dilemma, with a sharp conflict between industrial policy and competition considerations. On the one hand the Commission tried to force the pace of industrial collaboration between European firms, through programmes such as ESPRIT and RACE (although these programmes reflected an understanding of information technology which neglected the potential of consumer electronics). Although not directly responsible for Eureka, the EEC supported the concept and tried to co-ordinate its own efforts with Eureka projects. On the other hand the competition directorate tried to prevent national governments from discriminating in favour of their national firms through subsidy and preferential public purchasing, and frowned on the unseemly scramble to attract Japanese investment. In addition the external relations directorate was responsible for negotiations with Japan over trade frictions, and carried the responsibility for investigating allegations of dumping.

Trade Policy and Politics

Trade politics exposed the contradictory strategies of the leading European firms, Thomson and Philips, within the EEC. Publicly, spokesmen for these firms continued to plead unfair trading practices by the Japanese and Koreans, while at the same time they sought to establish barriers within Europe to protect them against competition. We have noted that the preferred policy instruments of the Commission shifted from voluntary restraint, through increased tariffs, to action on local content and a stricter interpretation and enforcement of anti-dumping laws. In each case the outcome of the policies was perverse: they sharpened the competitive thrust of the Japanese firms and damaged the interests of the firms which sought them.

Tariff penalties have the effect of forcing the penalized to find new ways of cutting costs and improving efficiency. It is of course possible in theory to impose tariffs at a level which would render efficiency increases quite impossible to achieve, but given the international framework of the GATT such levels are out of the question. In CTV industry estimates suggested that the current 14 per cent tariff was roughly equal to the cost advantage held by the Japanese. In VCR the Japanese appeared to have a 30 per cent advantage, which meant that by adopting a pricing policy geared to European rather than Japanese production costs, the Japanese firms could make healthy profits and thus subsidize sub-scale investments in the EEC undertaken for purely political reasons.

As we have already suggested, local content regulations can have the unintended effect of accelerating the inward investment of Japanese component suppliers, and through this put extra pressure on European component firms. Curiously many, if not most, firms appeared to behave as if local content regulations were already in force for VCRs, whereas in fact the legal position was that the 45 per cent rule only applied to CTVs where pre-Treaty of Rome import quotas did not already exist. For VCRs, as long as the component importers paid the appropriate tariff, finished VCRs, even those put together with a screwdriver, were legally in free circulation within the EEC, so that it was illegal to prevent their importation from one EEC country to another. Yet in public statements firms continually appeared to accept 45 per cent as a condition for an EEC 'label of origin'. Even if such a law had existed, its implementation would have been problematic. As the chairman of Sony, Akio Morita, pointed out, most inward investors need several years to develop the kind of relations with component suppliers that ensures quality products.[23] But then the intention of the European firms was to try to force the Japanese to manufacture under the same conditions as they did.

'Dumping' poses even more difficult problems of interpretation. The relevant European legislation deriving from GATT rules stated that dumping takes place when exporters sell at a price lower than the cost of production in their own domestic market. Moreover for a suit to be successful, the complainant has to show that dumping has caused injury to European firms. One problem of enforcement arises in determining prices and costs for each product, since what counts as a strictly comparable product is not at all clear. The definition of a 256K DRAM chip may be unambiguous, as may be sheet steel or bulk polyethylene, but when it comes to VCRs, what counts as the same product in home and export markets can be arbitrary. The exporters of dot matrix and daisy wheel printers complained that the EEC has compared their low-cost personal products with professional printers not usually attached to personal computers. A second point is that cost comparisons reflect prevailing exchange rates, so that if a country like Korea maintains the value of its currency at what is regarded as an artificially low level, its products are likewise 'artificially' low-priced. Yet it is the firms rather than the governments which carry the penalty.

Under what economic logic would a firm engage in dumping? The usual explanation is that once market share is gained through dumping, the successful monopoly producers raise their prices and extract monopoly profits from consumers. This may be a problem if only one firm were involved, but given the likelihood of many competing firms, anti-cartel rather than anti-dumping legislation would appear to be more appropriate to deal with this problem. Some argue that if policy-makers were really concerned to protect the consumer (rather than the producer) they would impose penalties on firms which charged higher prices in the EEC than in their domestic markets.[24] The possibility that the injury to European producers is self-inflicted is ruled out *ab initio*, and exporting firms are penalized by temporary levies unless and until they are found innocent. Anti-dumping is argued by Philips managers among others to be part of the process of levelling the playing field, yet in 1988 Philips was selling CD players in the US at lower prices than obtain in Europe because fiercer competition in the US had driven prices lower than in Europe.

Standards and trade policy issues have in common that they are predominantly determined by power struggles. In the case of VCR standards it was a relatively unfettered competitive struggle between firms which decided the outcome, and despite the attempt by Philips-Grundig to mobilize political power in support of market position, the outcome was determined by consumer preference. In the case of PAL–SECAM television standards market competition and technical progress following the expiry of patent protection eventually eroded the political settlement. Tariffs reflect the ability of producers to influence public policy, but can be undermined by a process of market usurpation from outside, or through inward investment. Anti-dumping measures again reflect the exercise of political power by domestic producers, but there was little evidence that they could offset the market power of successful producers, and their main consequence was the acceleration of internationalization.

Competition and Collaboration between Firms

The recourse to political strategies of support for protection has not been the only response of European firms to the export offensive of the Far East producers. Many have adjusted by trying to match Japanese best practice, and by attempting to develop new products and processes. In consumer electronics such strategies have often led to new forms of collaboration in addition to the processes of merger and acquisition we have discussed above. In the final section of this chapter we look at the negotiation of strategic alliances and joint ventures as a response to the extension of consumer electronics markets to the global level. To what extent can these phenomena be explained by technological factors, and what conclusions can we draw from their increasing frequency for the study of government–industry relations? Should governments tear up their competition policies and encourage firms to collaborate?

The European Commission has played an active part in fostering collaboration between European firms in high technology sectors. It has inaugurated three major programmes in the IT, telecommunications, and manufacturing technology areas—ESPRIT, RACE, and BRITE—but even in the IT programme there was no project specifically concerned with consumer electronics, although the IT task force set up by the Commission to administer ESPRIT sponsored several studies of the industry.[25] This gap was filled in June 1986, when the Eureka ministerial conference in London approved a proposal to develop a high definition television system sponsored by Philips, Thomson, Bosch, and Thorn-EMI. The participants came together on the understanding that, since Eureka was not a Commission initiative, the EEC was unlikely to commit funds to the venture, but that the various national governments involved could be expected to pay 50 per cent of the costs. This expectation initially proved unrealistic in Britain, where the government at first refused to allocate extra money to Eureka and in doing so drew strong criticism from the leading IT firms.[26] Thorn was given responsibility for development work on HDTV receivers, but the take-over of Ferguson by Thomson in 1987 led to Thorn's eventual withdrawal from the project. In due course the Eureka EU95 HDTV project became an important part of the Commission's technology policy, and the consortium received substantial EEC subsidies.

A second consumer electronics Eureka project started a year later, involving Philips, Thorn-EMI, Thomson, Siemens, Mullard, GEC, and Electrolux in a £12 million investment to develop compatible standards for a central interactive system to control electrical appliances and services within the home, and linked to the outside via the telephone network. This project linked directly to the work of the IHS task force of the NEDO consumer electronics EDC, and the specific aim was to develop a European standard which could offer some degree of protection against Japanese competition. In neither this programme nor the HDTV one were European subsidiaries of Japanese firms involved, although in the HDTV case Philips's Japanese subsidiary Marantz was an associate member.

In addition to multi-firm projects facilitated by European governments, such as those discussed above, there has been considerable activity in negotiating specific agreements, alliances, and joint ventures involving European firms. As can be seen from Table 13.1, these have more often involved collaboration with Japanese firms than with other European firms.

The reasons for this are complex, but apparently not always to do with the superior technology of the Japanese. Cultural and language barriers within Europe make technical co-operation difficult, and in many cases it appears that European–Japanese alliances are easier to forge. The two British joint ventures should be excluded from this conclusion, however, since neither was desired by the Japanese partners, and there developed irreconcilable differences over product strategy and quality control. Apart from these two failures, and the demise of the involvement of RCA in the two Euro-American tube ventures, all the other alliances in consumer electronics continued to flourish. We did not, however, find any example of an alliance between the European subsidiaries of different Japanese firms.

The two Eureka projects were more ambitious ventures, however, and the value of such a framework for co-operation remains unproven. The HDTV project had a clear goal and precise timetable: the partners had to achieve a working system for reaching HDTV on an evolutionary path (i.e. without rendering all existing CTV equipment obsolete) by the next CCIR sessions in 1990. Both

TABLE 13.1 *Joint ventures and alliances in European consumer electronics*

Firm	Firm	Nature of venture
Within Europe		
Philips	Grundig	Collaboration on VCR technology
Thorn-EMI	Telefunken	Collaboration (with JVC in J2T) on VCR production
Eureka HDTV Project	Philips, Thomson, Bosch *et al.*	Development of new transmission studio, and reception equipment for High Definition Television
Eureka IHS Project	Philips, Thomson, Bosch, *et al.*	Development of new standards for home automation equipment
Grundig	Bosch	Collaboration on CTV and car audio
Europe–USA		
Thomson	RCA	Joint venture for colour tube manufacture
Thorn	RCA	Joint venture for colour tube manufacture
Europe—Japan		
Philips	Matsushita	Joint venture in lighting and components since 1952
Philips	Marantz	50% stake since 1980
Philips	Sony	Collaboration on CD, CD-I, and CD-V standards
Philips	Kyocera	Joint venture in CD and CD-I technology
Philips	Toppan	Joint venture in optical publishing for CD-ROM and CD-I
Philips	Yamaha	Joint venture in interactive media
Philips	Pony-Canyon	Joint venture in interactive media
Rank Radio International	Toshiba	Joint venture for CTV production
GEC	Hitachi	Joint venture for CTV production
Thorn-EMI	JVC	Joint venture for VCR production (J2T)
Telefunken	JVC	Joint venture for VCR production (J2T)
Thomson	JVC	Licence agreement to manufacture VCR mechanisms; continued JT joint venture for VCR manufacture
Bosch	Matsushita	Joint venture for VCR production
Grundig	Matsushita	Collaboration on VCR components manufacture
Amstrad	Funai	Joint venture for VCR manufacture

Eureka projects were formed overtly to mount a challenge to rival Japanese efforts, but they also involved co-ordinating a range of technologies into a system. The Eureka HDTV project linked studio equipment, transmission, and reception, and involved the participation of several firms and broadcasting organizations which had been undertaking R. & D. in different aspects of the problem. IHS linked the 'brown' and 'white' goods and the telecommunications industries. In both cases the projects involved the complementary development of application specific integrated circuits (ASICs), so that the collaboration of chip designers was also necessary.

The trend towards families of products and systems which cut across industrial sectoral boundaries poses particular problems for European firms, which are commonly less diversified than their Japanese competitors. A project such as IHS can be developed *within* a firm such as NEC whose activities span consumer electronics, telecommunications, computers, and semiconductors. Industrial collaboration between firms raises knotty financial, organizational, and intellectual property issues. Collaboration between several different divisions of a single firm may also require innovative organizational solutions, but it is in principle easier to achieve than international inter-firm collaboration. In consumer electronics Philips, Thomson, and perhaps in the future Nokia are the only firms of sufficient scale and diversification to match the Japanese. Philips could have gone its own way in developing HDTV and IHS, but a partnership framework was more likely to pre-empt the possibility of other European firms developing rival systems with rival standards. Philips was bruised severely by the VCR format battles of the early 1980s, and its collaboration with Sony in the final stages of compact disc development was an indication of its reluctance to repeat the experience. For Philips Eureka was a useful means of legitimizing its dominant position, but it did not necessarily mean that the Eureka firms would be immune from usurpation by the Japanese. Thomson in particular has not found that co-operation as a junior partner to Philips fits in with its global ambitions, and it may well decide that joining the Japanese is a surer route to commercial success than trying to beat them.

Joint Ventures for Compact Disc Development

The European firm with the largest number of collaborative ventures with the Japanese is Philips itself. Philips failed to persuade Thomson to join it in the early stages of CD, and chose to develop CD—Interactive through a complex web of alliances involving firms in Europe, Japan, and the United States. CD-I is a development of the audio compact disc in which high quality graphics are coupled with text and sound which can be retrieved in a sequence determined by the interaction of the consumer and the CD-I system. For example a single 4.75″ disc, with the equivalent storage capacity of 1000 floppy discs, might contain recordings of the entire works of Beethoven, together with all the scores, and a substantial amount of textual and graphic material on the composer's life and works. By coupling a disc player to a microprocessor and screen with suitable operating software, the consumer can, for example, follow the scores while listening to the music, interrupting the programme at any time to retrieve textual information. Other potential applications include DIY manuals and recipes, and a variety of ideas which combine education and entertainment, for which Philips has coined the ugly word 'edutainment'. It should be distinguished from the associated technology of CD-ROM (compact disc—Read Only Memory), which uses the CD format as a means of storing primarily textual material for retrieval by computer. This technology is in the process of being widely adopted in professional applications, such as library catalogues and spare parts inventories where the requirement is for large quantities of data readily updatable within a short period, but not instantly as is the case with on-line databases for applications such as stock market information. CD-I is seen as primarily a consumer product with a potential mass market in the home.

Measured by its speed of penetration of homes world-wide, CD—audio has been the most successful single product in the history of consumer electronics, outpacing VCR and CTV. There was, however, no doubt in the consumers' minds about what kind of a product it was, and its successful marketing required the relatively simple task of co-ordinating hardware (players) and software (discs), which brought together the consumer electronics and record firms. Philips-PolyGram and Sony-CBS brought both aspects within the structure of the leading firms.

For CD-I the picture was completely different. Not only was the technology more complex, but the nature of the product, and thus the extent of the potential market, was uncertain. The rapid rise and fall of the home computer industry illustrates the difficulty of finding a use for the new technology: apart from the games market and word processing applications, there is not much evidence that consumers want interactivity in their electronics products.[27] VCR and CD—audio involved the consumer in a passive role; CD-I required active consumers who may have to be persuaded that they ought to be active. But on the other hand the increasing familiarity of young consumers with home computers, and the willingness of older ones to embrace interactivity with a machine when there is a specific purpose to it, such as getting cash from a hole in the wall when the banks are closed, were sufficient to persuade a large number of industry actors to believe that CD-I might tap a very large consumer market.

One thing was clear from the outset: CD-I players would not sell unless they were launched on to the market together with a wide range of easily available software. The CD-I system involved a new hardware specification, jointly developed with Sony and in the final stages with the participation of a large number of potential producers of CD-I equipment. In addition it required various kinds of software, including an operating system for retrieval and display of the information, as well as the CD-I discs themselves. Philips and other leading players such as Sony recognized the importance of involving other firms as partners, where they command necessary expertise which the major firms could acquire only slowly and expensively. The perils of going it alone into new areas were illustrated by the short-lived involvement of the Digital Equipment Corporation (DEC) in publishing its own CD-ROM software.[28]

The network of alliances shown in Figure 13.1 illustrates this point, and also shows the recognition by Philips that global markets for software of this kind could not be sourced from a single location, even if there were no such thing as trade friction. For this reason Philips created through its PolyGram subsidiary three new companies to develop CD-I software: European Interactive Media, American Interactive Media, and Japan Interactive Media. In Japan additional participation from a large record company, Pony-Canyon, was required given the relatively small role of PolyGram in Japan. In both the United States and Japan Philips formed a new company together with a large firm which was already involved in electronic publishing: in Japan it joined forces with Toppan to form Denshi Media Services, and in the US, Philips and R. R. Donnelly formed Optimage Interactive Services. Three further joint ventures with American firms covered various aspects of hardware and software. Philips–Dupont Optical was to manufacture CD-I discs at plants in the United States, Britain, Germany, and France. Optical Storage International, a joint venture with Control Data Corporation, was concerned with developing the computer interface, and Philips joined Sun Microsystems in a joint venture (Sun–Philips New

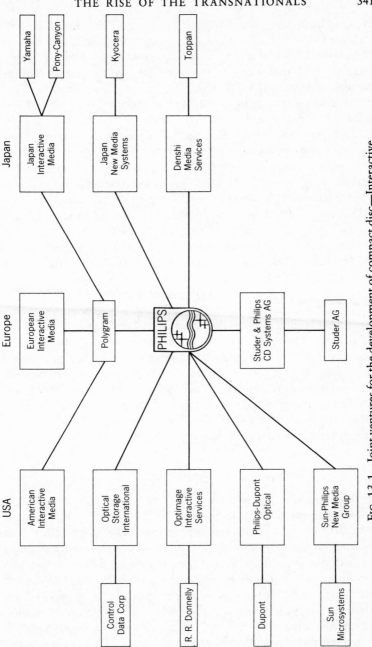

FIG. 13.1. Joint ventures for the development of compact disc—Interactive

Media Group) to provide workstations for CD-I authors. A joint venture between Philips and Kyocera, based in Japan, was formed to develop CD-I players, to be manufactured in Japan and probably Belgium (Philips's world centre for CD players). Finally Philips formed a new company based in Switzerland with Studer AG, a leading manufacturer of professional electronics, to produce CD-I studio systems.

All of this CD-I activity for potential consumer markets was firmled with very little tangible government support. An exception to this was the subsidies given by the Italian government through the state holding company IRI towards a joint project with Philips called 'Benventane' which aimed to produce mixed media classical music CD-I discs.[29] The Italian government was already funding optical publishing projects concerned with recording Italian culture through pictures and text on LaserVision discs, in the same way as the BBC–Acorn–Philips Domesday project. The Italian state broadcasting organization RAI funded demonstration HDTV projects using the Japanese standard, but was also an associate member of the Eureka HDTV project, as were the BBC and IBA. It is possible that governments might play a more important role in developing markets for CD-I in the future, following the pattern whereby the British government co-ordinated the teletext initiative discussed in Chapter 10. CD-I faced rival optoelectronic technologies, however, and the density of the network of alliances was an indication of the complexity of the technology and the uncertainty of the diffusion path. Collaboration may not be a guarantee of success, but many firms took the view that non-collaboration multiplied the risks of failure.

Towards a European Industrial Policy?

Philips also saw a role for the EEC in offering tariff protection against imports as well as reduced VAT during the initial stages of marketing CD-I and related products. But the impact of such new technologies is a long way off, and for the next few years at least the industry will continue to be dominated by just two products, CTV and VCR. A report to the EEC in 1986 on the future of the European consumer electronics industry pointed out that the Japanese exempted new technology products from sales taxes, and advocated such policies as preferable to higher tariffs.[30] The report suggested that Europe was faced with a choice between attempting to achieve competitiveness on a world scale, and retreating into a 'Fortress Europe' stance. Discounting the European firms' constant complaints about 'unfair trade', the report suggested lower tariff rates together with measures to stimulate European demand. The approach taken by the consultants, Booz-Allen & Hamilton, contrasts strongly with a subsequent report to the Commission from BIS-Mackintosh, which advocated a co-ordinated industrial policy on the supply side to encourage more collaboration between manufacturers in core technologies, including as appropriate collaboration with the Japanese firms, especially in the development of an appropriate components infrastructure.[31]

Booz-Allen suggested that, if demand for consumer electronics products in Europe were to reach American or Japanese levels, then the industry would benefit through higher sales and lower costs through greater economies of scale, and governments would benefit from a higher tax take (despite lower tax rates) and lower expenditures on unemployment benefits. In order to take advantage of a bigger market, however, the CTV and VCR industries would have to be rationalized into a smaller number of larger plants. Public policy in the past few years has had the effect of subsidizing the establishment of sub-scale Far Eastern plants: Booz-Allen estimated that from 1980 to 1985 the Japanese had invested 450–650 million ECUs, and had received subsidies of 90–130 million ECUs from national governments. The projection of the scale required for the Europeans to compete against the Japanese suggested between 11 and 14 CTV plants (against the 1985 figure of 45) and 4–7 VCR plants (against 18).

While the adjustment process we have described is leading towards fewer plants and bigger volumes of production, it is hard to see how the kind of plants closures envisaged by Booz-Allen could be achieved without massive state intervention by an EEC rather more powerful vis-à-vis national governments than it is today. While, as this chapter has shown, we are in the era of international champions with global strategies, these are easier to achieve with new products than they are with mature products. Philips was able to make its decision to locate all CD player manufacture in a single plant on commercial criteria alone. The decision, made in 1988, to close several existing CTV plants and relocate production in another country was highly contentious, however, and risked making the achievement of other goals more difficult. Philips had, after all, been trying to rationalize CTV production since 1981.

In the case of VCR, where most of the sub-scale plants were Japanese-owned, it is hard to see how rationalization could be effected unless much stricter controls on imports of finished goods and components were adopted. Such controls would have the effect, at least in the short term, of driving up costs and choking the expansion of the market. If rationalization were to be planned in sequence with import controls, it would require both a Community industrial policy (which is as far off as ever) and a co-ordination of this with external trade policy and negotiations in the GATT. Such policy prescriptions tend to presume an institutional nexus of government–industry relations which is vastly different from the hands-off approach that we have argued in this book to have been the main feature of the consumer electronics industry. The movement towards the completion of the internal market in 1992 is likely to reinforce the concentrative dynamic which benefits the major players, but there is no certainty that the beneficiaries will be European-owned firms. In this case, as in the telecom case, we are observing a *process* of change, rather than a stable pattern of government–industry relations.

Notes

1. The American industry faced the Japanese offensive in television exports in the 1960s, and there remained only one US-owned TV producer, Zenith, in mid-1988. There are signs, however, that the American industry hopes to fight back through HDTV. Spurred on by the chip-makers, who envy the captive markets held by their Japanese competitors' consumer divisions, the American Electronics Association has formed a special task force to devise a strategy for the 1990s. (*Financial Times*, 11 June 1988.) For the link between HDTV and global strategy, see A. Watson Brown, 'The Campaign for High Definition Television: A Case Study in Triad Power', *Euro-Asia Business Review*, 6/2 (1987), 3–11.

2. Philips is one of the few European firms which manufactures both colours of electrical goods. Thorn recently sold both its white goods (to Electrolux) and its brown goods activities (to Thomson) but it retains an interest in the Eureka project and has a demonstration 'smart house' in its Central Research Laboratories at Hayes. So far the Japanese firms (like Hitachi and Mitsubishi) have not sought to acquire or invest in white goods manufacture in Britain.

3. This remains true for the recent period despite the international nature of Philips which very early on found that growth necessarily took it beyond the boundaries of the tiny Netherlands home market. Philips was 'multinational' in the sense that many national companies existed, but not 'international' in the sense of having global market and production strategies.

4. This figure includes components manufacturers and associated consumer products such as tapes, batteries, and microwave ovens. If we restrict the sector to video and audio equipment, there were 48 Japanese plants in the EEC in early 1988. *Journal of the Electronics Industry* (Feb. 1988).

5. This section is based on a large range of documents and more than fifteen interviews in Eindhoven, Brussels, Paris, Hamburg, and London. Unless specifically cited the material comes from interviews.

6. Philips ranks 12 in the *Fortune International 500*, just behind Matsushita which is ranked 10, but well ahead of Thomson (rank 54) and Nokia (209) (*Fortune*, 1 Aug.1988). This ranking excludes US companies. In the *Times 1000 1987–88* (London: Times Books, 1987), Philips ranks 33 among the world's top industrial groupings, and Matsushita ranks 27. Philips, however, is the world's largest manufacturer of colour televisions.

7. G. de Jonquieres, 'Breaking out of the Past', *Financial Times*, 25 Apr. 1986.

8. In 1987 Philips announced its intention to reduce its white collar staff in Europe by 20,000.

9. This claim was pressed once Philips accepted that the voluntary export restraint agreement with MITI was not working to its advantage.

10. See the interview with Jan Timmer, main board member responsible for consumer electronics, in the *Financial Times*, 25 July 1988.

11. In an asset swap in which GE acquired Thomson's medical equipment division and an undisclosed amount of cash (estimated at $600–700 million in *Le Point économie*, 13 June 1988).

12. Thomson merged its semiconductor activities into a joint venture with SGS of Italy in 1987 to become the second biggest European chipmaker, after Philips but ahead of Siemens. *The Economist*, 28 Mar. 1987.

13. *Le Point économie*, 13 June 1988. Industry sources estimated that in 1988 some 80% of Thomson's profits arose from advance payments on defence contracts.

14. Thomson developed its VCR chips by acquiring technology from the CNET laboratories in Grenoble, which produced a design with 50 fewer components which could be made more cheaply than the equivalent JVC design.

15. Output figures should be treated with caution, as they are generally closely guarded secrets. This and subsequent figures in this section were estimated by BIS-Mackintosh for 1986.

16. *Financial Times*, 24 June 1988.

17. See Alan Cawson, *The Japanization of Europe?* (London: Sage Publications, forthcoming).

18. 'Sony sees more than Michael Jackson in CBS', *The Economist*, 28 Nov. 1987.

19. Matsushita has a majority holding in JVC, but has always allowed JVC an important degree of autonomy. In the 1970s JVC developed its VHS system in direct competition to Matsushita, which had a rival but ultimately inferior VCR technology. JVC has taken the lead in VHS, which permits Matsushita to adopt a 'wait-and-see' attitude, having preferential access to JVC patents as required. But it can also maintain a foot in both camps, as it has done with 8mm., manufacturing 8mm. camcorders on an OEM basis for other companies. Recently Grundig has pioneered up-market innovations in CTV and VCR, for example a VCR incorporating a teletext chip which allows the consumer to programme the VCR by moving a cursor on the television screen to identify the desired programme. It seems unlikely that Philips will submerge Grundig and simply use it as a Philips brand.

20. It should be remembered that in 1983 the Beta group, led by Sony, was locked in a fierce struggle with the VHS group, led by JVC and Matsushita. The Beta firms were mainly trying to expand their market share against the VHS firms rather than Philips-Grundig. There are good reasons to doubt whether the Philips-Grundig case could have been substantiated had it reached the European Court.

21. The standard S-VHS specification includes full PAL–SECAM compatibility, so that the same machine will operate anywhere in Europe.

22. *Financial Times*, 11 June 1988.

23. *Financial Times*, 20 June 1988.

24. Martin Wolf, 'The Dumping Inquisition', *Financial Times*, 28 July 1988.

25. The task force also played an important part in alerting the European industry to the threat posed by the attempt by the Japanese to pressure the CCIT to adopt their HDTV standard. The task force (now DG XIII) has made intelligence about the Japanese industry a particular priority.

26. *Financial Times*, 11 Oct. 1988. For the background to the establishment of Eureka, see Margaret Sharp and Claire Shearman, *European Technological Collaboration* (London: Routledge & Kegan Paul, 1987). Thorn-EMI were invited to apply for a discretionary industrial assistance grant under Section 8 of the Industry Act, but were advised

by the DTI that the extra administrative and travel costs involved in European collaboration could not be subsidized; for the purposes of the grant it had to be assumed that European collaboration took place entirely in the UK!

27. See Ian Miles, *Home Informatics* (London: Frances Pinter, 1988) for a cautiously optimistic view of the market potential of interactive consumer electronics products.

28. *CD-I News*, 1/1 (Nov. 1986), p. 4.

29. *CD-I News*, 1/8 (June 1987), p. 8.

30. Booz-Allen & Hamilton Inc., 'EEC Consumer Electronics Industrial Policy: Final Report' (Brussels, 1985) (unpublished).

31. BIS-Mackintosh, 'Towards a Community Strategy for a New Audio-Visual Technology' Report to the Commission of the EC (1987) (unpublished).

14

Conclusions

The Shifting Contours of Government–Industry Relations

This book has reported the results of research on the relationships between government and industry at a *sectoral* level. The research was based on the hypothesis that there would be considerable variations in these relationships between sectors: the pattern of reciprocal influence in a single country between industry and government in telecommunications was likely to be different from that in consumer electronics. A detailed examination of these contrasting patterns would help to distinguish sectoral effects from *national* policy characteristics.

The examination of the relative importance of sectoral and national influences can only go so far, however, in a study restricted to a single country. Thus our research design extended the sectoral comparison to a three-way national comparison between Britain, France, and West Germany. In this way we could be sure that we had identified powerful sectoral effects if we found a sector which exhibited common characteristics in three countries with very different national settings. If, on the other hand, we found very different ways of organizing government–industry relationships in a single sector across the three countries, we would be able to conclude that national institutional factors outweighed sectoral effects. The examination of inter-sectoral similarities and differences in the context of international comparisons would enable a much richer analysis of industrial policies and politics than is obtained from the use of national stereotypes.

This kind of static comparison of cases certainly yields ample evidence of the complexity of sectoral and national effects. If we had taken a 'snapshot' of government–industry relations in 1975, we would have been able to observe the following pattern:

1. Telecommunications was a natural monopoly and was everywhere organized in a similar way which gave rise to the same kinds

of government–industry relations whatever the characteristics of the national state. Every government established a single national telecommunications administration (PTT) which procured its equipment from a small number of 'court suppliers'. Quite independently of the institutional characteristics of the state, or the ideological character of the ruling parties, telecommunications was a public function managed by a public bureaucracy which negotiated with private firms for the equipment it needed and the price it had to pay. These closed procurement relationships were justified by the monopoly characteristics of the service, and the relationship was very similar to that found in the defence sector. There was no substantial difference between Britain, France, and Germany in their institutional set-up, save that Germany reserved telecommunications to the state under its Basic Law or constitution. There were, however, considerable variations in the *quality* of service, which in France amounted to a national scandal.

2. In consumer electronics, the pattern of government–industry relations varied according to preferred national policy objectives. Unlike the situation in countries which produced their own telecommunications switchgear, consumer electronics products were traded internationally and sold to final consumers rather than public bureaucracies. Firms and industry associations in Britain and West Germany were left to adjust to competition from Japan, first in radio and tape recorders, but by this time also in colour televisions. Japanese firms wishing to set up production facilities or take over existing firms were encouraged to do so. In France, however, relationships in the sector were quite different from the other two cases. The domestic television industry was protected by an idiosyncratic transmission standard, and the French market was too small compared to other European markets for exporters to consider it worthwhile making extra investments to cope with differences in technology and taste. Beyond this the French industry is more concentrated, and one firm, Thomson, had been identified as a 'national champion' in the sector, receiving public investment and support in exchange for actions in support of the French national effort in electronics.

The conclusions drawn from such a comparison would be that the pattern of government–industry relationships can be moulded by both sectoral and national effects, with national influences more important than sectoral ones in France as compared to Britain and Germany. Telecommunications, along with defence and agriculture, was part of a group of sectors relatively insulated from the competitive market by state intervention. In France this mode of intervention extended also to consumer industries where particular sectors and firms were granted privileges in exchange for conformity to national political objectives. The sectors have a real economic and political identity which made it easy to identify German telecommunications, British consumer electronics, and so on.

In the late 1980s, however, the picture given in this snapshot has become transformed. National firms serving predominantly national markets have been rapidly changing into international firms addressing increasingly global markets. Firms which have failed to adapt to the internationalization of markets have been forced out or taken over by those that have. National governments, led by the British, have turned from selective industrial policies towards market-driven policies involving privatization and deregulation. These policies have had less effect on consumer electronics than on telecommunications, where the Thatcher government has acted as a usurper of the privileges previously bestowed on the equipment makers. Patterns of government–industry relations in which trade unions and trade associations were important intermediaries have shifted into bilateral links between large firms and governments. The EEC has emerged as an important transnational quasi-state system which has carved out powers for itself at the expense of the power of national governments.

In short, government–industry relations have changed markedly. Just as we were beginning to realize that it was necessary to disaggregate national political economies into their sectoral components, those very sectors are losing their distinctiveness. It is not just that national boundaries are less salient than once they were, but also technological changes are beginning, slowly but unmistakably, to erode sectoral boundaries. The transmission and reception of information in digital form is the common thread which is beginning to bind together the information technology industries, which include consumer electronics and telecommunications, together with other electronic hardware and the software (computer and entertainment) industries. These changes have yet fully to work their effects on the organization of the firm, but the rash of joint ventures and mergers which we have examined in this book is unmistakable evidence that this process is in train. If we were beginning this study in 1989 rather than in 1985, we would have organized our research on the electronics industry in terms of a comparison of the relationship between governmental and intergovernmental strategies and internationally orientated business firms rather than by choosing to look at discrete sectors.

The empirical studies analysed in earlier chapters show how these changes have affected government–industry relations. It is the task of this concluding chapter to bring this material together in order to trace the dynamic of change which has 'Europeanized' both sides of the relationship. It will be done by focusing attention on five crucial dimensions of change:

1. *Internationalization*: the increasing scope of markets from the national, to the European, and ultimately to the global level. The pace of change on this dimension has been forced by US and Japanese multinationals, together with the emergence of major firms from the newly industrialized economies of the Far East.

2. *Political strategies*: government policies intended to encourage adjustment to internationalization have diverged sharply. Some governments have adopted state-led strategies intended to insulate their economies from the destructive effects of international competition; others have sought to use competitive pressures as a means of levering change.

3. *Technological change*: the introduction of digital technologies, first in telecommunications and most recently in consumer electronics, have had a profound effect on the economics of these industries. New products and services have emerged to challenge the existing structures of regulation and competition.

4. *Boundary erosion*: the effect of technological change has been to reward innovating firms and punish those which fail to adapt. At the heart of this innovation lies the creation of the information industries, which involve establishing synergies between different branches of electronics and information processing which cut across traditional industry boundaries.

5. *Changes in the structure and organization of firms*: the impact of the above four dimensions of change has been felt most crucially at the level of the firm. In order to survive firms have had to address bigger markets, and to develop new products and processes requiring new skills. Firms have emerged as the most important carriers

of these changes, and the capacity of national governments to control them has been reduced. Older forms of indicative planning have given way to government measures to strengthen the competitive position of firms, which in the wake of internationalization has become intervention at the European level rather than at the level of national governments.

These interrelated dimensions of change have not developed evenly between different countries, industries, and firms. National differences remain as major influences on this uneven development—in legal systems, capital markets, training, industrial relations, and importantly in the capacity of national state systems to provide incentives for firms to develop appropriate competitive strategies. The process has had the effect of reducing the influence of three kinds of collective actors—trade unions, trade associations, and national governments—and of increasing the influence of a fourth: the firms.

Changes in the Relative Influence of Different Actors

The stress that we have given in this book to bilateral relations between major firms and governments reflects in part the very high levels of concentration in telecommunications and consumer electronics compared to many other branches of industry. There are many reasons, some of them specific to our chosen sectors, why other actors have become less significant players. In this section we review our findings on the four most important kinds of organizational actors: trade unions, trade associations, governments, and firms. In the case of the last two we emphasize the necessity of understanding these 'actors' as complex organizations with multiple goals and often conflicting strategies.

Trade unions

Trade unions have at various periods been regarded as potentially significant actors within the industrial policy arena. Our research findings confirmed wide variations, both nationally, and between the sectors we studied, in the scope and nature of their influence within the pattern of government–industry relations, but against these variations there was a common tendency for trade union influence to decline.

Institutional factors help to explain differences between countries in the extent of trade union influence. The West German co-determination system provides for the presence on supervisory boards of representatives from the trade unions. In the Bundespost five of the members of the administrative council are representatives of the staff and the unions, and the staff councils (*Personalräte*) are dominated by the unions. This gives the one union that organizes over 70 per cent of the Bundespost's employees important access to information about policy and a means of early intervention in the policy-making process. This influence, however, is used primarily to protect the conditions and careers of Bundespost employees. The union is, for example, strongly opposed to moves which might jeopardize the public status of its members or risk a decrease in employment. The institutional status of the unions is particularly strong in the public sector in West Germany. We did not find the same degree of union influence, even of a 'blocking' nature, on the firms with which we were concerned.

In Britain, as in West Germany, the extent of the unionization of employees especially in the public sector helps to explain the nature and influence of the unions. In the absence of a well-defined legal institutional framework for union participation in policy-making by firms or public corporations, numerical strength is one of the unions' main resources. Until the late 1970s, as we have seen, the British Post Office management was anxious to maintain good relations with the two main unions, and they had an important voice in the opposition to the removal of the Post Office's telecommunications monopoly. In the early 1980s, however, in a climate in which trade unions were weakened by unemployment and a legislative offensive by the Thatcher government, their numerical strength proved inadequate to resist privatization. The best that they could do was to work with the management to prevent the break-up of British Telecom; in this they succeeded but were not the decisive influence.

Numerical strength is undoubtedly an important factor in determining variations in the extent of union influence. The degree of fragmentation in union representation is another such factor. In the British Post Office there were eight separate unions, although two dominated. In the British consumer electronics industry the extent of fragmentation was greater. Nevertheless despite the absence of formal institutional frameworks and the handicap of a degree of duplication and fragmentation, the British unions played a much larger part in the modernization strategy of the consumer electronics sector than did their counterparts in France and West Germany. Despite having limited access to government, especially after 1979, British unions were able to exercise some influence at the level of the firm. The EETPU, for instance, has recruited actively in this sector, and has deployed its commitment to a market-orientated strategy and to a new style of industrial relations in order to establish single-union agreements both with new entrants and, as in the case of the Hitachi factory at Hirwaun, in existing plants. Unions have thus been important when firms have wished to modernize or innovate at plant level. During the 'industrial strategy' period of the Labour government, they were able to act within the tripartite NEDO Sector Working Party, but this policy-making role has disappeared in the latter years of the Thatcher government.

In France the unions have neither a strong institutional position, nor numerical strength, and their fragmentation is along strongly ideological lines, which makes inter-union co-operation virtually impossible. The unions are consequently largely excluded from the tight networks of personal contacts which characterize relationships within the political, administrative, and industrial élites. Our research findings confirm those of other studies of France which suggest that the unions have been effectively marginalized within the policy-making structures that deal with industrial sectors (though not within policy-making related to welfare conditions—sickness and unemployment benefit for example). The reforms of the Socialist government after 1981 improved the institutional framework for the unions in some respects, giving them rights to nominate representatives to the boards of nationalized industries. Our research suggests that, while this certainly meant that the management of the firms were forced to pay greater attention to presenting, explaining, and justifying their policies, the effect of the reforms was on the firms' exposition of their strategies rather than upon their formulation.

Although unionization has traditionally been much higher in the French public sector than in the private sector, the unions have not played a part in the French PTT that is comparable to that of the unions in the Bundespost and British Telecom, although they did induce the government to be cautious in moving to change the DGT's status. It should not be forgotten that the *corps*, such as that of telecommunications engineers, who do play an important role in affecting the development of strategies for telecommunications, are not unions. They are groups of professionals, all recruited and trained through the same institutions, and part of an official hierarchy and career structure. In some respects they act like a union, for they certainly have a sense of a collective interest in their career patterns and opportunities, but in other respects they are more like a particular division or branch of an enterprise or administration.

We can conclude that the different combinations of factors such as institutional arrangements, fragmentation, degree of unionization, and vision of the appropriate stance and role for a union help to account for variations in the role and influence of the unions both nationally and between sectors. These variations do not fully conform to some stereotypes. In the country (Britain) with the weakest institutional arrangements for union participation in policy-making, we none the less observe the strongest degree of union influence in the consumer electronics sector.

Internationalization is likely to weaken union influence further, given the greater difficulties faced by unions as compared to management in collaborating across frontiers. In addition the development of new telecommunications services outside the public sector will restrict the scope of union participation in the information industries. Differences in union influence between countries are likely to remain, but these will become less significant to the extent that union power is felt less at the national and sectoral levels and more at the level of individual plants—an important corollary of the growing importance of the firm.

Trade Associations

The sectoral and industrial interests of firms may find their expression through trade associations. In so far as these give voice to the general concerns of those involved within sectors they might be expected to play a fairly major role within any policy-making process affecting the sector. Our research, however, has not confirmed this expectation. Firms in all three countries are organized into trade associations, and in the case of France, for example, these associations are grouped within the Conseil National du

Patronat Français. This has important functions in relation to social policy matters, for example in the tripartite administration of unemployment and industrial injury benefits. The trade associations themselves undertake executive functions on behalf of the government, chiefly the collection of statistics, and the administration of some export promotion measures. But we found no evidence to suggest that the trade association played any part in policy-making or the determination of industrial strategies. Responses to changing market conditions and technologies were not considered by the trade association, nor were policies that deeply affected the firms in the sector, such as the measures that for so long inhibited foreign inward investment, the result of trade association pressure. If this seems surprising, given the institutionalization of tripartite *concertation* through the national planning system and through the 1958 constitution in the shape of the Economic and Social Council, the explanation may lie in the fact that these bodies are concerned with economic policy in its very broadest sense and with the endorsement of governmental and political priorities rather than with detailed strategies.

If the firms in the consumer electronics sector in France could until the 1980s take as axiomatic governmental hostility to inward investment, on the basis of deeply entrenched 'Gaullist' views about the development of French industry, this was not true of Britain, where the trade association has been active in lobbying the government for the stable and orderly development of the market, and in practice for a degree of protection against first Japanese and now Korean firms. But the British representation of sectoral interests is weakened by fragmentation; separate associations organize the equipment and the components producers and electrical equipment manufacturers. We found that many within the sector regarded this fragmentation as inhibiting the development of closer government-industry relations, and it seems symptomatic that the British subsidiaries of Japanese firms who are members of BREMA did not regard it chiefly as a means through which to influence government, but as a forum for defusing potential opposition to their presence and development.

In telecommunications the nature of the market and of the associated industrial structures determines the way in which sectoral interests are expressed. The existence of *clubs* or of *court suppliers* has meant that the interests of the industry have been expressed directly in the close relationships between the suppliers and their public sector customers. The impact of deregulation, of British privatization, and of greater competition has coincided with the Europeanization and internationalization of the structure of the industry. The large firms continue to see their interests as best protected through direct contact with the governments who are their main customers; they are large enough not to need the umbrella of a body to represent the aggregate of sectoral interests. Where bodies do exist of which the firms are members, the difficulty of containing competitive pressures may result in a low profile approach. This is the case in the FRG, where the peak organization, the BDI, has been faced with the problems of containing the conflicts between two of its member trade associations both containing telecommunications manufacturers, and also of representing simultaneously the interests of both producers and users of telecommunications.

The role of trade associations in representing sectoral interests in telecommunications is thus very limited indeed. But associations may also seek to represent the interests of the users of telecommunications services. In France before the mid-1970s dissatisfaction with the supply of services was sufficiently general to render it a political issue. In the FRG the users, perhaps because of a more satisfactory overall level of service, have generally been seen as docile; apart from the VPB, whose adversarial stance and poor relations with the Post Minister have excluded it from influence. In Britain, however, the organizations of users have been effective and influential. The POUNC, despite its problems in representing both business and residential users, contributed to the generally critical climate which led to the division of the Post Office and the ending of the monopoly. In this climate the business users, through the TMA and the TUA, were able to be particularly forceful in urging improved services and a more commercial and competitive approach. Our research findings support the view that in relation to specifically sectoral interests the firms seldom find advantages in collective representation rather than personal, individual, and often informal contacts. This may be both cause and consequence of the marginalization and fragmentation which increases the lack of effectiveness of the trade associations. Only when groups whose members are not necessarily direct competitors have a clear and limited objective, as in the case of the British telecommunications users, have they had an important impact on government–industry relations.

Government

All our research findings have emphasized the difficulty of aggregating the interests subsumed under the general appellation 'industry' or even 'sector'. Our findings point clearly to the key role of individual firms, rather than any bodies which might represent industry-wide, or even sectoral, interests. A similar finding in relation to the 'government' term of the government–industry equation is another major element to emerge from our inquiries.

The term 'government' needs to be closely examined in every context in which it is used. A fundamental distinction which we wish to emphasize is that between the political executive—government as the team of ministers in power—and 'government' as the administrative agencies of the state. The relationships that we have studied have tended on the whole to be between these latter agencies and the firms, and often involve ongoing, rather routine contacts where the views and actions of the members of the political executive have little direct impact. As one of our interviewees pointed out, firms are taxpayers, employers, producers, owners, and occupiers of land and property, and in all these areas there is constant and regular contact with officials at a variety of levels.

The political executive may, however, under certain conditions, have a decisive role in setting the framework within which firms operate, and this in turn affects the firms' strategies. We found very little evidence that the policies which determine such broad frameworks are influenced specifically by any particular consideration of the strategic needs of a particular industry. Given the party political nature of political executives, they seem far more to relate to a broad orientation towards the future shape of society and the nation's place in the world. Thus the French 'national champions' policy was conceived largely as a response to France's need for modernization which was held to be a condition of her retaining her status within the international community of nation-states. Similarly, President Giscard's support for a huge programme of investment in telecommunications was part of the outcome of a programme for modernizing French society which formed an important element of his appeal to French voters in 1974. The ideological nature of Mrs Thatcher's commitment to deregulation and privatization which made possible the developments for British Telecom outlined in Chapter 5 needs no emphasis here. In France it is arguable that it was not so much the 1981 nationalizations which led to changes in the firms, but the Socialists' rediscovery of the virtues of the 'enterprise' and ministers' insistence, from 1984, that nationalized companies get out of the red. Likewise, privatization after 1986 changed less than might have been expected because the nationalized firms were already responding to market pressures.

All these key 'governmental' factors arose from the presence in power of leaders with a broad and rather simple political strategy which set the parameters within which firms operate, and provided them with arguments that they could use in the course of their negotiations with 'government'. Where firms were operating within less ideologically determined environments, the role of 'political' decisions becomes less crucial. This is the case in the FRG, given the effect of coalition government and of federalism, combined with a political culture which ensures that politics are conducted 'within the centre'.

At the other end of the spectrum, individual firms may be affected by decisions taken for reasons which may be primarily electoral and local. The efforts of the *Land* government of Bavaria to influence the future of Grundig, and the pressure on Thomson to locate in both Longwy and Tonnerre, are cases in point. Such intervention is inevitably sporadic and unpredictable.

For much of industry much of the time, however, the political executive is not the part of the 'government' with which they are concerned. Their relationships occur with the multifarious administrative agencies which make up the state. To stress that 'government', in the sense of the complex of individual ministers and officials within a whole range of state organizations, is far from monolithic is neither particularly original nor new. But our research provides strong support for this interpretation. It is clear that functional differences are amongst the strongest determinants of the different approaches of various parts of government. Distinctions may, for example, be drawn between 'government as customer', 'government as financier', 'government as producer', 'government as researcher', 'government as regulator'. Many of these distinctions, however, can be summed up in what seemed to us to be one of the key variables; the distinction between 'government as enterprise' and 'government as administration'. To talk of 'government–industry relations' in respect of telecoms, for example, is misleading as long as it blurs the differences between those government agencies whose functions and mode of operations effectively cause them to be 'enterprises within the state'—the DGT (now France Télécom) is an example of such an agency—and those parts of the state structures concerned with administration—of financial affairs, for example, or employment concerns. 'Enterprises within the state' tend to have objectives which are similar to those of other enterprises, their relationship with firms and with other parts of the state structure tends to resemble commercial relationships, and provided that the financial backing they require can be obtained they tend to resist attempts to impose broader objectives upon them, as do nationalized companies or even private firms.

Such a distinction, while it serves to illuminate many of the conflicts of interest that we have observed within 'government', is too simple to encompass all the complexities; for example, the governmental enterprise may, as in the case of the Bundespost, or British Telecom before privatization, also be the regulator; the Bundespost's monopoly of the supply of telephone handsets, like British Telecom's powers to license equipment to be attached to the network, are potentially capable of being used in ways which support essentially commercial objectives. One trend, now an explicit EEC policy, is a movement towards a greater clarification and separation of these various functions.

Our finding that certain parts of state structures may be 'captured' by outside interests as a part of the 'closure' strategies of those interests, and that conflict between such interests occurs within, as well as outside, administrative bodies is nowadays taken to be a commonplace. Our research has demonstrated the complexities of such phenomena. We have discussed the influence which the firms' monopoly of expertise may give them within certain parts of the administration; we have observed that in France the existence of *corps* supports networks within and outside state bodies and, for example, provided a particular impetus to strategies supporting the autonomy of the DGT. In Britain the extent of governmental powers, through the political legitimacy of a single party political executive and its domination over the legislative process, lessens the likelihood of capture strategies making much headway against determined political opposition. It is not the least of the paradoxes which we observed that in the UK the scope for imposition of a centrally determined interventionist strategy is greatest, but there has been little attempt to utilize this potential in the industrial field.

Firms

One of the most important findings of our study is that even where governments were acting strategically in the promotion of industries and products, outcomes were ultimately decided by the strategies of firms. For example, our main conclusion about the French tele-communications sector is that the success of the strategy of the DGT was due to a unique conjuncture of events in the late 1970s that allowed it to take on the characteristics of a management-controlled industrial enterprise: from 'government as adminis-tration' it became 'government as enterprise'. In securing and defend-ing its autonomy the DGT laid claim to the kind of resources which are the principal source of the independent power of the business firm, i.e. technical and commercial expertise which is not available to administrative agencies. The other side of this coin is that firms—including here 'governments as enterprises'—can demand and get incentives and subsidies if they are asked by elected governments to pursue non-commercial strategies towards political objectives.

Government agencies are unable to exercise detailed controls over firms because they lack their personnel resources, marketing know-ledge, technical ability, collective memory, and strategic orien-tation. Although many large firms (such as Thomson or GEC) have a conglomerate structure, they nevertheless tend to be less frag-mented than governments. Relations between firms and govern-ments thus often take the form of a relatively centralized organization confronting and negotiating with a number of different departments with various and often conflicting objectives. In such circumstances firms have considerable structural advantages in addition to those conferred by their superior technical and commer-cial expertise. The information available to governments concerning costs, technology, and future prospects tends to come from the industry itself. In an uncertain world it is difficult to test wisdom by first principles, and the critical element of strategic judgement is based on information which cannot easily be queried by civil servants.

The power of the firm, paradoxically, depends on the interventio-nist ambitions of the state. Where governments are committed to specific political objectives, such as job creation and preservation, or regional development, it is commonplace to observe that firms may more easily extract subsidies or preferential policies. What is less obvious, but which has emerged strongly from our research, is that where governments can credibly claim *not* to be responsible for the level of output or employment, firms may have less freedom of manœuvre. Governments may impose fewer constraints on firms, but equally are less likely to free firms from constraints arising from the market. What this implies is that state intervention in production confers privileges on firms, which involves a degree of market closure reinforced politically. Far from firms losing power as a consequence of state direction, they *gain* power, at least in the short term, and at least in so far as technology and market conditions remain relatively constant. Non-intervention confers autonomy, but the power of each individual firm then becomes subject to its performance in the market. In the case, for example, of the British consumer electronics firms, the refusal of the Thatcher government to embark on a state-supported modernization programme exposed the British firms' weaknesses in the face of foreign competition, and led to their disappearance from the industry.

Here, however, we must distinguish between different kinds of state intervention and their effect on the power of firms. If governments set *performance* objectives, such as, for example, the creation of a strong domestic electronics industry, they are in effect trying to determine both the means and the ends, which increases the bargaining power of the firms whose specific actions are necessary to achieve the ends. If, however, governments set *structural* objectives, such as are embodied in privatization or competition policies, and are indifferent to the fate of specific firms, then the outcomes are less likely to be determined by the power of individual firms. With respect to the relationship between government and an individual enterprise, intervention can be most effective where governments regulate with respect to a single parameter, such as the French government's insistence that the nationalized firms return to profit (irrespective of the industrial policy implications of how they achieve it), or the British government's insistence that following privatization BT's price increases remain 3 per cent below the rate of inflation.

Neither firms' nor governments' power is a constant. Changing market conditions, and especially technological change, continually rewrite the parameters of the relationship. Relatively closed power relationships, dependent on the conferment by government of privileged status, are susceptible to erosion through technical change, as in the case of the 'telecom clubs'. Existing firms which have failed to innovate are threatened by those who have, as in the case of consumer electronics. Radically new technologies open up new market opportunities, and introduce new actors. The political problems associated with intervention which takes the form of discrimination between existing firms are absent. Governments may decide themselves to act as 'collective venture capitalists' in the early stages of the development of new technologies, but our experience suggests that sooner or later such enterprises fail or develop the autonomy of firms.

One form of reaction to the uncertainties created by technical change is collective action between firms. Firms whose market position is threatened by the expansion of the geographical scope of the market (in the shape of '1992' as well as the globalization of markets) may seek to take over, merge, or form joint ventures with others. The increasing complexity of the products and services in consumer electronics and telecommunications, especially as digitalization erodes market boundaries and introduces new kinds of competitors, leads to the obsolesence of traditional closure strategies and the relentless search for new ones. Our research emphasized relations between firms, and between firms and governments, rather than stressing the internal relationships within firms. But it became obvious that different kinds of firms face a variety of adjustment problems, and that the issues of power, autonomy, and the capacity to defend interests through different kinds of closure strategies are crucially dependent on factors such as internal organization, the distribution of expertise within the firm, horizontal as well as vertical channels of communication, and management calibre.

Technological Change and the Erosion of Sectoral Boundaries

Technological change is the main reason why the sectoral specificity of telecommunications is breaking down. Hitherto distinct sectors, like computing and consumer electronics, are beginning to merge with the telecommunications sector. The origins of this sea change lie in the convergence of data processing and communications, a process whose theoretical beginnings can be traced back to research done as long as fifty years ago. However, such convergence did not become a commercial reality until powerful and inexpensive micro-electronic devices were widely available. The most modern digital communications systems being installed today are designed to handle all types of information—voice, data, text, graphics, and full video transmission—in exactly the same form. Hence digital exchanges (or switches) are generically identical to computers, while the once separate functions of the telephone, the data terminal, and the television are starting to merge. At the present time television technology contains 'digital islands in an analogue sea', but few doubt the trend towards the islands' combining into a continental land-mass. In both telecommunications and consumer electronics software and design skills, especially in the production of application specific integrated circuits (ASICs), will become an increasingly important part of firms' competitive strategies.

Sectoral convergence, or boundary erosion, is still in its infancy and is only beginning to be reflected in firms' structures and strategies. Firms in each of the convergent sectors are finding that it is far from easy to lever their strength from one sector into the other. Two important examples of this are the difficulty which AT&T has had in trying to break into the computer market, and the problems which IBM have experienced in diversifying into telecommunications. The basic reason for this is that the skills appropriate in one market are not identical to those required in another.

Technological convergence means that firms are faced with a dilemma: should they try to develop new competence in-house or should they collaborate with a firm from an adjacent sector? In other words should telecom firms seek to acquire data processing capabilities or should they form an alliance with data processing firms? Should consumer electronics firms build up expertise in publishing and computing, or seek to acquire such skills through joint ventures? Should software expertise be generated internally or bought in? To date both options have been followed, with a bias towards inter-firm collaboration.

In addition to the erosion of sectoral boundaries we are also witnessing the gradual erosion of national boundaries in telecommunications, which is beginning to travel the road that the consumer electronics industry has been on since the 1960s. There are two major reasons for this: (1) the escalating costs of developing new generations of digital public exchanges mean that more than one national market is needed to amortize the original R. & D. outlay and (2) deregulation makes it more difficult for firms to think of reserving the whole of their domestic market to themselves. Hence we see a new phenomenon in telecommunications, namely, the internationalization of markets. However, this process should not be exaggerated because nationally based telecom firms still account for the lion's share of the orders from 'their' PTT, and this is especially the case in the FRG. And, even though the European Commission is trying to introduce a more competitive regime in the Community telecommunications market, we have seen that its directive on public procurement seeks to privilege EEC producers— a perfect example of a policy which combines elements of both competition and closure!

Nevertheless, internationalization is under way and this is making it more difficult for a firm, like Alcatel for example, to equate its interests directly with the interests of the French state. In consumer electronics the internationalization of Thomson has had the same effect: its manufacturing interests in Britain and Germany have severed the tie between its own strategy and French neo-mercantilism. The wide spread of Alcatel's interests in the wake of the merger with ITT suggests that Alcatel, like Thomson, will henceforth have to spread its lobbying activities across the Community. Moreover the internationalization of the French domestic consumer electronics industry, consequent on the acceleration of Japanese investment in France, is likely to make it more difficult for French industrial policy to privilege firms on the basis of French ownership.

Internationalization makes it even more difficult to treat the firm as a unitary actor. For example, the big effort which Siemens has made in recent years to become a major player in the US means that it cannot uncritically support protectionist policies in the Community without assessing the consequences for its US subsidiary. The CGCT case illustrated the conundrum here. By going head-to-head with AT&T in the fight for CGCT, Siemens was threatened with a backlash against its US subsidiary. There is ample scope here for 'turf fights' within multinational firms between different national factions. Philips's disingenuous position in opposing the 'dumping' of Japanese and Korean VCRs on the European market while at the same time selling its CD players in the US at below the 'normal' European price illustrates neatly the way in which diversities in national markets are reflected in the form of contradictory policy impulses within the firm.

Another boundary that seems to be losing its integrity is that between manufacturing and services in the telecommunications sector. The main reason for this is that some traditional equipment markets, like public switching, are growing slowly, while growth is exploding for such services as cellular radio and VANS. The equipment suppliers in the UK, France, and the FRG are thus trying to diversify into this service segment. The most spectacular example of this to date is Racal, once a military communications equipment supplier, and now one of the UK's cellular operators. In just over three years of operating, its Vodaphone subsidiary has been valued at £1.7 billion, which is comparable to the value of some of Europe's major electronics companies.

National Differences in Decline

Despite the beginnings of the erosion of sectoral boundaries, increasing internationalization, and the effects of both 'homegrown' and imported deregulation, there remain substantial differences between the patterns of government–industry relations in the three countries. Why should this be so, given that each country has faced broadly similar pressures?

Telecommunications

We cannot hope to explain the new institutional structures in telecommunications simply by referring to 'technological change'. The very fact that France and Germany are 'late' in liberalizing their telecom regimes, and show no signs of privatizing their national carriers, provides a powerful antidote to this kind of technological determinism. Clearly, technological change can be negotiated and accommodated in different forms, be it at a corporate or a national level. How then are we to explain the divergent paths? As regards the uneven development of regulatory regimes we can point to a number of variables which help to explain why the UK distinguished itself from France and the FRG with respect to liberalization and privatization. In these cases as we have seen the pattern of closure was sustained by a stronger coalition of political forces, and the pressures towards usurping the dominant position of the privileged firms were weaker.

Legal and Constitutional Constraints. There can be little doubt that legal and constitutional constraints were greater in France and the FRG, hence the scope for radical political reform was that much more limited than in the UK. These constraints have been most powerful in the FRG where the Basic Law stipulates that the Bundespost must be an 'administration owned by the Federation', and a two-thirds majority in the Bundestag is required to remove this particular constraint. Unlike BT, which was already a public corporation before it was privatized, the Bundespost and the DGT are both governmental organizations imbued with a strong public service tradition. This form of closure through the state rules out the kind of usurpation strategy practised in Britain, where a neo-liberal programme legitimated by user interests provided sufficient leverage to breach the telecom monopoly. In France and the FRG closure in telecoms was sustained through political and constitutional arrangements whose unlocking would require a more complex alliance of political interests than was evident in Britain.

The Veto Power of Organized Labour. The PTT unions in France and the FRG have been fervently committed to the public monopoly in telecommunications, partly because this bolsters their bargaining power. In the case of France the Chirac government was loath to tamper with the public status of the DGT for fear of antagonizing the PTT unions before the presidential elections. In the FRG the trade union role has been even more prominent, with the DPG represented on the administrative council in such a way that it was able to exercise greater influence over telecommunications policy than its counterparts in France and the UK. Overall what is significant here is that rightist governments in France and the FRG have been reluctant to confront the entrenched power of organized labour, in sharp contrast to the UK where the Thatcher government launched an offensive against public sector unions, so much so that liberalization and privatization were partly seen as a means of circumventing the POEU. In Britain telecom deregulation was but one part of a broader strategy of usurping trade union privileges; the erosion of trade union power in telecoms was made easier by the success of this broader strategy.

Status of the Telecom Club. The French and German clubs never attracted the same degree of criticism as did the British club. This can partly be explained by the fact that the continental clubs were perceived to have performed relatively well, helped no doubt by the fact that the investment programmes of the DGT and the DBP exceeded BT's by a substantial margin in the decade to 1985. In

France the rapid and successful modernization of the network earned the DGT considerable prestige within both government and industry. In the FRG the Bundespost may have lagged behind both France and the UK in digitalizing the network but the excellent performance of its installed analogue base muted criticism from the telecom user community. As regards the supply side of the club the French and German equipment suppliers could lay claim to a better export record than their UK counterparts. Hence the status of the continental telecom clubs was that much greater than in the UK although, as we shall see, the UK club faced a much more demanding business user community. Thus in the UK closure could be presented as damaging to UK economic performance, and the link between efficiency and competition could be more readily drawn.

Character of the Ruling Party. Although the distinction between left and right parties should not be taken too far, the fact that France was governed by a Socialist administration between 1981 and 1986 helps to explain why liberalization and privatization were low on the French political agenda at the time when the UK was going through a sea change in telecommunications policy. What is more significant is that major ideological differences remained even when rightist parties were in goverment in all three countries. The fact is that the conservative administrations of Chirac and Kohl proved to be far more cautious than the Thatcher administration. Even though the ruling parties in France and the FRG laboured under greater political constraints, this is both cause and consequence of their ideological pragmatism. In both France and the FRG we see a greater degree of 'industrial patriotism' so far as state policy towards the telecom sector is concerned, born of an anxiety about potential threats to the indigenous industry. (The main contrast here is between the FRG and the UK: while the German industry enjoyed immense political prestige and was closely integrated in the process of rethinking regulatory policy, the UK industry commanded very little political support, with the result that it was barely consulted in the process of telecom policy reform.) Whereas telecom *producer* interests were paramount on the continent the Thatcher government ascribed far more importance to (business) *user* interests, particularly those of the financial community. In the eyes of the Thatcher government the interests of the indigenous industry counted for little as compared with the wider goals of attracting foreign capital to Britain, boosting the international competitiveness of the City, reducing the PSBR, and laying the foundations of a 'share-owning democracy'.

Structure and Role of the Business User Population. The demands placed on the PTTs varied a good deal so far as the business user population was concerned. Of the three countries the UK has the most concentrated industrial structure, biased as it is towards multinationals. These large multi-site companies have considerable technical expertise and sophisticated needs, especially for data communications. The sophisticated nature of the UK business user population is evidenced by the fact that the UK alone accounts for over 25 per cent of all the private data networks in Western Europe. The poor performance of the UK club in meeting these needs helps to account for the readiness of large users to endorse the usurpatory ambitions of the Thatcher government.

The transition to digital technology destabilized the traditionally cosy PTT–Supplier relationship in Britain, France, and Germany. In the case of Britain this took the form of shaving the number of traditional suppliers from three to two and, later, of introducing foreign technology from Ericsson. In the French case a byzantine process of industrial restructuring occurred, which resulted in Alcatel having to tie up with ITT. Finally, in Germany the transition to digital technology showed Siemens to be lagging, so much so that it spelt the end of the single technology policy of the Bundespost. But technical change was not by itself sufficient to translate instability into structural change in the telecom regimes. Closure was a multifaceted process underpinned by a specific coalition of producer, user, and political interests. The changes which occurred in the UK case were not mirrored in France and the FRG, where few voices could be heard demanding radical changes. But despite being relatively protected from usurpatory demands at home, the French and German national clubs now face a challenge from what is perhaps the most important new entrant to the 'telecom game'— the European Commission.

Manufacturers and PTTs view the Commission as one of the most powerful agents for liberalization in the EEC telecommunications market. But, as we have sought to emphasize, the European Commission cannot and should not be conceived as a unitary or homogeneous actor. There are at least two important divisions within the Commission, namely between DG IV and DG XIII, respectively the directorates for competition policy and tele-communications. The former appears to be more pro-competitive, with the emphasis on market-based outcomes, while the latter seeks to strike a balance between liberalization of telecom markets on the one hand and promoting the interests of the indigenous telecom industry on the other. Striking a balance between users and pro-ducers in the EEC is a very delicate task indeed. The best illustration of this to date was in the directive which the Council of Ministers issued on public procurement which, as we saw, tried to open the public procurement market in such a way as to benefit local (i.e. European) producers.

With the exception of the UK there has been limited change in the European telecom sector. More change is surely on the way, as a result of pressure from the European Commission and from US interests (government, producers, and users). However, radical institutional change should not be inferred from technological change because the former is in no way an epiphenomenal form of the latter. There are many factors which will slow down the pace of liberalization in Europe, like the newly elected Socialist government in France, which is trying to orchestrate opposition to the pace of change envisaged by the European Commission.

Consumer electronics

The consumer electronics industries of Britain, France, and Ger-many in the early 1970s were more open than the telecommunica-tions industries, but there were significant differences in the degrees of closure between the three countries which account for the differ-ent outcomes as each country's industry faced the growing interna-tionalization of the industry and the intensifying competitive threat from Japan. We noted in the last section the destabilizing effects of product innovation in telecoms, but concluded that closure was sustained in France and Germany by political and institutional fac-tors. In the consumer electronics case outcomes were much more closely tied to the closure strategies of individual firms. France alone of the three countries sought to privilege its domestic producer, but its technological weakness placed severe limits on this strategy.

During the 1970s and early 1980s, when the industry's expansion was concentrated on the rapid growth of colour television, different technical standards and segmented markets offered an important

degree of protection to television manufacturers. Until the advent
of cheap integrated circuits in the late 1970s, which permitted the
production of multistandard CTV sets at little extra cost, the French
industry in particular was able to benefit from the unique SECAM
standard. In addition bilateral import quotas put in place before
the Treaty of Rome permitted the French government to resist Japanese import penetration in a way openly envied by CTV makers
in Britain and Germany. The British firms had to rely on voluntary
restraint agreements with the Japanese, but these were overtaken
by the Japanization of the British industry that we examined in
Chapter 10. In CTVs the response to Japanese competition led to
the formation of multinational groupings, centred on the French
company Thomson, and the Finnish company Nokia, which,
together with Philips, allowed the European industry to retain a
major share of the European CTV industry. These differences
account for the survival of the European television industry compared to that in the United States, where all but one of the US-owned
CTV makers were driven out of business by the unrestrained ferocity
of Japanese producers who shared the common NTSC standard.

The relatively strong position in CTVs must be contrasted with
the effect that product innovation in consumer electronics has had
on the European consumer electronics firms. In the late 1970s the
development of the domestic VCR unleashed a ferocious competition between Japanese and European firms around three incompatible VCR formats. The VCR, unlike the solid state CTV set,
contains electro-mechanical parts which demand precision manufacturing processes and sophisticated assembly operations which
put it outside the reach of the smaller European CTV manufacturers. None of the British, French, or German firms had the expertise or resources to enter VCR production by itself, so that for
these firms the choice was whether to collaborate with Philips or
with the Japanese. Of the Japanese contenders, Sony was unwilling
to manufacture its Beta VCRs with the brand names of other firms,
whereas JVC sought out European firms and offered them an inexpensive route into the VCR market. The formation of the J2T joint
venture embraced Telefunken and Thorn, and excluded Thomson
only because the French government vetoed its participation in
search of a French, or at least a European, solution. Grundig alone
chose to ally with Philips in the search for a European VCR technology.

As we saw in earlier chapters, the market struggle in VCRs proved almost ruinous for the Philips–Grundig alliance. Grundig was unable to survive as an independent firm, and the enormous losses made by Philips before it decided to abandon its V2000 system almost resulted in Philips's withdrawal from its core activities in consumer electronics. The closure through technical standards, which had allowed some protection into the 1980s for television manufacture, was not an option for VCR producers. Philips's failure in this technology, when compared to previously successful innovations such as the compact cassette tape recorder which is now an undisputed *de facto* world standard (at least in the present pre-digital era), arose from its inability to marry a successful marketing strategy to its innovation strategy. Philips chose to promote videodisc and videotape technologies at the same time, and misread consumer preferences. Had other European firms, and in particular Thorn and Thomson, backed the V2000 standard European technology would not have been so precariously dependent on the commercial strategy of a single firm. The agreement between Philips and Sony on compact disc standards, which was the key to the very rapid diffusion of CD into the market from 1982, is testimony to the extent to which Philips absorbed the lessons from its failure in VCR.

Faced with a set of extreme difficulties for the success of their attempt to close through product innovation and market domination, Philips and Grundig tried to use their political influence to restrain the Japanese. The voluntary export restraint agreement, which was negotiated between EEC Commissioner Davignon and MITI without consulting national trade associations or firms, demonstrated the extraordinary political power which Philips was able to exert both in Brussels and in the national capitals of EEC member states. An opportunistic anti-dumping complaint against the Japanese, in the aftermath of the infamous Poitiers measures applied by the French government, and the relentless lobbying of Philips's management at the Commission, created a climate in which even the usually liberal inclinations of the German government were stifled. It was a victory for Philips, but ultimately a Pyrrhic one. Far from guaranteeing the future of the V2000 it allowed Japanese firms to repatriate super-profits in the regulated European VCR market of 1983-6. Moreover it had the effect of accelerating the location of VCR plants by Japanese manufacturers in Europe. As far as the interests of individual European *firms* are concerned, European manufacture by Japanese firms constrains the extent to which they can react to failure in the market-place with trade policy measures. Now that VERs are recognized not to be an effective means of market closure, and tariff rates are constrained by GATT rules, the European firms have turned to anti-dumping complaints as a means of defending themselves against Far Eastern competitors. Significantly the anti-dumping charges filed by the European trade association EACEM at the behest of Philips in August 1988 refer to three Korean firms and two minor Japanese firms; the major and long-established firms have achieved the status of club members.

In recent years new competitive threats have emerged in consumer electronics from the newly industrialized economies of the Far East. The technology of CTV, VCR, and CD production has been transferred to Korea, Taiwan, Hong Kong, and Singapore, and firms in these countries have made major inroads into the European market. Although firms such as Philips and Thomson have themselves established Far Eastern plants, especially for audio products, Japanese firms have played a major role in establishing consumer electronics production in the NICs. The Japanese firms are less vulnerable to competition from the NICs for a number of reasons. As integrated electronics firms, most of them continue to benefit from supplying components to the NICs, and indeed have transferred much of their own production of basic CTV, VCR, and audio products to those countries. The Japanese firms are pursuing a strategy of relentless product innovation, hoping that returns from higher value added products such as camcorders, digital VCRs, DAT machines, and increasingly HDTV will compensate for the loss of markets in mature products to the NICs.

The major Korean firms, Samsung, Goldstar, and Daewoo, have recently followed the Japanese in seeking to avoid protectionist pressures by locating plants within the EEC. While the European firms press the EEC Commission for tighter rules on local content to outlaw 'screwdriver' plants, the competitive struggle between the Japanese firms and the Europeans is becoming enmeshed in a race to determine standards for the next generation of television systems. Autonomous commercial strategies, such as those which we have examined in our analysis of CTV and VCR, have given way to inter-firm alliances backed by governments. The most important of these, the Eureka EU95 project to develop a European HDTV system, is in effect a research cartel embracing the public sector broadcasters and the European firms. Its closure strategy is dependent on the achievement of a technical standard for HDTV through which they will be able to control the conditions under which different categories of firms have access to European technology.

For the European firms, who are fighting to survive in Europe, have almost no foothold in Far Eastern markets, and are outgunned in the enormous US market, the stakes are huge. Their interests are inextricably bound up with the extent to which European governments and the EEC are prepared and able to defend European national interests against outsiders. The position is made much more complicated by the burgeoning strength of the Japanese firms within Europe. Led by firms such as Sony, Matsushita, and Hitachi, the Japanese majors are busily reorganizing their European operations so that hitherto independent subsidiaries in different European countries are becoming 'Euro-Japanese' firms. Moreover joint ventures such as JVC–Thomson and Matsushita–Bosch are indicators of the conscious policy of digging their roots deep into the fabric of the European industry.

It thus remains to be seen to what extent inter-firm collaboration in the development of new consumer electronics technologies can be organized in such a way as to exclude the Japanese. British governments in the 1970s and 1980s were engaged in assisting the Japanese efforts to usurp the position of the British firms, and this policy was so successful that by 1987 the last major firm in the industry, Thorn, had sold its CTV operations to Thomson, and in 1988 Philips had decided to close its last CTV factory in Britain. With a domestic industry now almost completely dominated by the Japanese, and a broadcasting policy explictly aimed at deregulation, it is difficult to see how Britain can champion the interests of the Eureka HDTV cartel if that means damaging the interests of the British-based Japanese firms. The French position is less complicated by such factors, since French CTV production is almost entirely in the hands of Philips, Thomson, and Nokia. The German industry is almost equally divided between European-owned and Japanese-owned firms, but with only one major German-owned firm left, German public policy is likely to remain scrupulously neutral between the Japanese and the Europeans.

The aggregate of the balance of national interests within Europe is unlikely to produce a consensus for a strongly interventionist

European strategy to defend the European-owned consumer electronics firms. Outcomes are much more likely to arise from the competitive struggle between firms, and in this struggle the ability of firms to create markets for new products is likely to prove decisive. If technological prowess, as shown both by efficient manufacturing technologies and successful new products, is going to determine which firms will be market leaders in the 1990s, then the experience of the last fifteen years of the industry, which we have analysed in this study, suggests that as far as consumer electronics hardware is concerned, the Far Eastern multinationals are likely to prosper, given their strong position at the global level. But innovation in consumer electronics is tending towards the creation of new *systems* of products cutting across the traditional boundaries which divide consumer electronics from other branches of the electronics industry such as telecommunications and computers. In these evolving families of products much of the added value will lie in sophisticated components and software, in which *design* skills will be crucial. The real differences in national markets, which become more important as a consequence of sectoral boundary erosion, will have to lead to changes in the strategies of all firms, including the Koreans and the Japanese. We can thus expect that the pace of change, which we have seen accelerating during the years covered by our research, will continue, and the structure of the industry will be subject to continuous pressures in the future.

Conclusion: GIR and the Politics of the Firm

The research reported in this book challenges many of the assumptions made in the study of government–industry relations. We have shown that the stereotype of state versus market which is characteristic of much of the literature is based on a false dichotomy between politically determined decision-making and supposedly 'automatic' mechanisms of the market-place. In the heavily protected and relatively closed world of telecommunications such findings hardly come as a surprise, but in consumer electronics it is important to stress that outcomes depend only partially on the competitive strength of firms.

Our research has led us to the unmistakable conclusion that at the present time the key to unlocking the complexities of industrial politics lies in the corporate strategies of the major firms. Other

actors—trade unions, trade associations, even governments—are
far less significant as the drivers of change than are the firms. In
the period of our study, roughly from the time of the first oil crisis
of 1973 to the present, the importance of firms within the pattern
of government–industry relations has been growing steadily.
Government intervention can provide opportunities for firms, and
can constrain their behaviour, but it cannot substitute for their role.

We have suggested that a purely economic analysis of the firm
fails to capture the variety of influences upon its activities. By making
use of a perspective drawn from neo-Weberian political economy,
we have identified the central impulse of firm behaviour as the
attempt to evade constraints, whether arising from the operation
of markets or the actions of political authorities. Such *closure* strategies can take many forms, but the different kinds of strategy have
in common the search for a means to protect the interests—of
managers, workers, shareholders—that are embodied in the firm.
In favourable market conditions the preferable closure strategy is
one of successful competition within the market, in which the firm
seeks to insulate itself from competitive pressure by successful autonomous enterprise. Such a strategy is always subject to the possibility
of usurpation by other competitors, unless a regime is created in
which regulation sets up barriers to entry.

As we have seen in the telecommunications case, however, usurpation is not always the prerogative of competitor firms. Government policy can be specifically directed towards the removal of firms'
privileges where these are judged to be detrimental to some other
set of interests, such as those of other firms, consumers, or voters.
Conversely, in some cases where the competitive position of national
firms is being usurped by others—as in the case of the European
consumer electronics firms against the Japanese—governments may
attempt to regulate the effects of the competition and privilege national interests. The patterns of closure, in their mix of economic
and political dimensions, vary considerably between different countries as we have shown in our examination of the different trajectories of change in Britain, France, and West Germany.

Within this complexity, as we have shown, several trends are
apparent which are shifting the ground. The process of internationalization changes the boundaries within which the process of closure
takes place. At the least protectionism at the national level within
Europe is giving way to the definition of *European* interests, and

this has markedly affected both the commercial practices and the lobbying behaviour of the firms, as well as inhibiting national governments from attempting to privilege firms' interests on the basis of national ownership. Technical change is tending to undermine sectoral boundaries, leading to new combinations of products and markets which can undermine the effectiveness of existing closure strategies. Firms are increasingly looking towards co-operative solutions in the form of mergers, joint ventures, and alliances which leave little scope for the influence of national governments. Trade unions and trade associations are searching for new institutional forms at the European level, although perhaps inevitably this process is occurring much more slowly than adjustment at the level of the firm.

We have emphasized time and again in this book that technological development is a crucial independent variable in accounting for outcomes, but its effects are tempered by the scope for autonomous decision-making on the part of firms and governments. The impact of technical change cannot be considered in isolation from politics and markets, and in accounting for the extent to which technological change has knock-on social, economic, and political effects, we must be alive to the extent to which different constellations of power within the market determine the pace of diffusion of technological change. In discussing both telecommunications and consumer electronics we have emphasized the extent to which the industrial structure and political context constrain the impact of new technologies. Certainly new technology upsets the balance of forces which underpins specific patterns of closure, but it does not predetermine the responses of different actors to such upsets. It is still possible, at least in the short run, for actors to acquiesce in the mobilization of state power around protectionist measures. Adjustment through innovation strategies can be extremely painful for established firms whose interests have been forged around historic patterns of economic advantage, and whose capacity to exercise political power derives from those patterns.

Our cases show a considerable range of such responses, but unmistakably this range is narrowing as state-led strategies become less common, even in France where there remains relatively recent experience of successful state intervention in telecommunications, rail transport, and nuclear power. It is possible that the current period is one of transition where national policies are giving way to European-level initiatives, and that it is not state intervention itself that is waning but the salience of the nation-state level within Europe. Competitive pressures, leading to the collapse of the enlarged European firms which our study has described in their formative phase, may give rise to a new interventionist dynamic in the 1990s. The form that intervention may take in the future is, of course, in the realm of speculation. We can, however, be sure that studies of industrial politics must in future be conceived in a framework which gives due attention to the European and wider world market dimensions, and that the politics of the firm must be at the centre of the picture.

Bibliography

Advisory Council for Applied Research and Development, *The Applications of Semiconductor Technology* (London: HMSO, 1978).

ARNOLD, E., *Competition and Change in the British Television Industry* (London: Macmillan, 1985).

Arthur D. Little, Inc., *World Telecommunications Information Program: France* (Cambridge, Mass.: Arthur D. Little, 1985).

BAUER, M., and BERTIN-MOUROT, B., 'Enterprises publiques et mouvement patronal: Le Cas français', unpublished paper for colloquium 'The Politics of Private Business and Public Enterprises', European University Institute, Florence, 1986.

BAYLISS, B., and BUTT-PHILLIP, A., *Capital Markets and Industrial Investment in Germany and France* (London: Saxon House, 1980).

BEAUCHAMPS, X., *Un état dans l'état?: Le Ministère de l'économie et des finances* (Paris: Bordas, 1976).

BEESLEY, M., *Liberalisation of the Use of the British Telecommunications Network* (London: HMSO, 1981).

BENN, T., *Out of the Wilderness: Diaries 1963–67* (London: Arrow Books, 1988).

BERGER, S., 'Lame Ducks and National Champions: Industrial Policy in the Fifth Republic', in Andrews, W., and Hoffman, S. (eds.), *The Fifth Republic at Twenty* (Albany, NJ: State University of New York Press, 1979), pp. 292–310.

—— (ed.), *Organizing Interests in Western Europe: Pluralism, Corporatism and the Transformation of Politics* (Cambridge: Cambridge University Press, 1981).

BERTHO, C., *Télégraphes et téléphones de Valmy au microprocesseur* (Paris: Livre de Poche, 1981).

BERTRAND, H., MANSUY, C., and NOROTTE, M., *Vingt Groupes industriels français et le redéploiement* (Paris: Direction de la Prévision / Ministry of Finance, 1981).

BIS-Mackintosh, 'Towards a Community Strategy for a New Audio-Visual Technology: The Consumer Electronics Industry', unpublished report for DG XIII of the European Commission (1987).

BONNETT, K., 'Corporatism and Thatcherism: Is There Life After Death?', in Cawson, A. (ed.), *Organized Interests and the State: Studies in Meso-corporatism* (London: Sage Publications, 1985), pp. 85–105.

Booz-Allen & Hamilton Inc., 'EEC Consumer Electronics Industrial Policy: Final Report', unpublished report (Brussels, 1985).

BRENAC, E., JOBERT, B., MALLEIN, P., PAYEN, G. and TOUSSAINT, Y.,

La DGT et le Plan Câble (CEPS/CERAT, University of Grenoble II, 1986).

British Radio and Electronic Equipment Manufacturers Association, *Annual Report 1978* (London: BREMA, 1978).

British Telecom Unions Committee, *The Battle for British Telecom* (London, 1984).

BRUCE, R., CUNARD, J. and DIRECTOR, M., *From Telecommunications to Electronic Services* (London: Butterworths, 1986).

CAWSON, A., *Corporatism and Political Theory* (Oxford: Basil Blackwell, 1986).

—— 'The Teletext Initiative in Britain: Anatomy of Successful Neo-corporatist Policy-Making', Economic and Social Research Council, *Corporatism and Accountability Newsletter* (1986).

—— 'In Defence of the New Testament: A Reply to Cox', *Political Studies*, 36 (June 1988), pp. 309–15.

—— 'Reply', *Canadian Journal of Political Science*, 21 (1988), pp. 819–22.

—— 'Is there a Corporatist Theory of the State', in Duncan, G. (ed.), *Democracy and the Capitalist State* (Cambridge: Cambridge University Press, 1989), pp. 233–52.

—— (ed.), *Organized Interests and the State: Studies in Meso-corporatism* (London: Sage Publications, 1985).

—— HOLMES, P., and STEVENS, A., 'The Interaction Between Firms and the State in France: The case of Telecommunications and Consumer Electronics', in Wilks, S., and Wright, M. (eds.), *Comparative Government–Industry Relations: Western Europe, the United States and Japan* (Oxford: Clarendon Press, 1987), pp. 10–34.

CECCHINI, P., *The European Challenge: 1992* (Aldershot: Wildwood House, 1988).

COHEN, E., and BAUER, M., *Les Grandes Manœuvres industrielles* (Paris: Belfond, 1985).

COHEN, R. B., FERGUSON, R. W., and OPPENHEIMER, M. F., *Non-tariff Barriers to High Technology Trade* (Boulder, Colo.: Westview Press, 1985).

Commission of the European Communities, *Communication from the Commission to the Council on Telecommunications*, Com (84) 277 (Brussels: CEC, 1984).

——*Report of the Commission to the Council on R&D Requirements in Telecommunications Technologies as Contribution to the Preparation of the R&D programme RACE*, Com (85) 145 (Brussels: CEC, 1985).

——*On the Coordinated Introduction of ISDN in the European Community*, Com (86) 205 (Brussels: CEC, 1986).

—— *Completing The Internal Market* (Brussels: CEC, 1986).

—— *Telecommunications in the US: Report of the EC Fact-Finding Mission, 16–27 June 1986* (Brussels: CEC, 1987).

—— *Green Paper on the Development of the Common Market for Telecommunications Services and Equipment*, Com (87) 290 Final (Brussels, 1987).

—— *Towards a Dynamic European Economy*, Green Paper on the Development of the Common Market for Telecommunications Services and Equipment, DG XIII/195 (87) Draft Version (Brussels: CEC, 1987).

—— *Towards a Competitive Community-Wide Telecom Market in 1992*, Com (88) 48 (Brussels: CEC, 1988).

Committee to Review the Functioning of Financial Institutions, *Report and Appendices*, House of Commons Session 1979–80, Cmnd. 7937, 2 vols. (London: HMSO, 1980).

COOMBES, D., and WALKLAND, S. A. (eds.), *Parliaments and Economic Affairs in Britain, France, Italy and the Netherlands* (London: Heinemann, 1981).

CORRÉ, J., 'Formation professionelle en commutation électronique', *Revue française des télécommunications*, 21 (1976).

COX, A., 'The Old and New Testaments of Corporatism', *Political Studies*, 36 (June 1988), pp. 294–308.

CYERT, R. M., and MARCH, J. G., *A Behavioral Theory of the Firm* (Englewood Cliffs, NJ: Prentice-Hall, 1963).

DANG NGUYEN, G., 'Telecommunications: A Challenge to the Old Order', in Sharp, M. (ed.), *Europe and the New Technologies* (London: Frances Pinter, 1985), pp. 87–133.

Department of Industry, *The Regeneration of British Industry*, Cmnd. 5710 (London: HMSO, 1974).

—— *Report of the Post Office Review Committee*, Cmnd. 6850 (London: HMSO, 1977).

—— *Evidence to the Review Committee*, Appendix to Cmnd. 6850.

—— *The Future of Telecommunications in Britain*, Cmnd. 8610 (London: HMSO, 1982).

Department of Trade and Industry, *The Future of Telecommunications: Government Policy Explained* (London: HMSO, 1983).

—— *Revised Government Proposals for the Future Licensing of Value Added and Data Services* (London: HMSO, 1986).

DE ZOETE and BEVAN, *British Telecom* (London, 1984).

DONDOUX, J., 'L'Impact de la déréglementation internationale: Le Point de vue français', *Financial Times* World Telecommunications Conference, London, 4 Dec. 1985.

—— 'Towards a European Telecommunications Market', address to the

Financial Times World Telecommunications Conference, London 11–12 Dec. 1984.

DORE, R. P., *British Factory—Japanese Factory* (Berkeley, Los Angeles, and London: University of California Press, 1973).

DREYFUS, F., and D'ARCY, F., *Les Institutions politiques et administratives de la France* (Paris: Economica, 1985).

DYSON, K., 'The Politics of Economic Management', in Paterson, W., and Smith, G. (eds.), *The West German Model: Perspectives on a Stable State* (London: Frank Cass, 1981), pp. 35–55.

—— 'West Germany: The Search for a Rationalist Consensus', in Richardson, J. (ed.), *Policy Styles in Western Europe* (London: Allen & Unwin, 1982), pp. 17–46.

Economist Intelligence Unit, *Home Electronics* (London: EIU, 1983).

Electronic Consumer Goods Sector Working Party, *Progress Report 1978* (London: NEDO, 1978).

—— *Progress Report 1979* (London: NEDO, 1979).

Electronic Industries Association of Japan, *Electronic Industries in Japan* (Tokyo: EIAJ, 1984).

ERGAS, H., *Regulation, Monopoly and Competition in the Telecommunications Infrastructure* (Paris: OECD, 1986).

Eurodata Foundation, *Data Communications in Western Europe in the 1980s* (London, 1980).

European Parliament, *Report of the European Parliament on Telecommunications in the Community*, Doc. 1–477/3 (1984).

FARNOUX, A., *Rapport de la Mission de la Filière Électronique* (Paris: Ministry of Research and Technology, 1982).

Federal Communications Commission, *Regulatory Policies and International Telecommunications*, Docket No. 86–494 (Washington, DC: FCC, 1987).

FINER, S., *Adversary Politics and Electoral Reform* (London: Anthony Wigram, 1975).

FORESTER, T., 'Neutralising the Industrial Strategy', in Coates, K. (ed.), *What Went Wrong?* (Nottingham: Spokesman Books, 1979), pp. 74–94.

FRIEDBERG, E., 'Administration et entreprises', in Crozier, M. (ed.), *Où va l'administration française?* (Paris: Éditions Ouvrières, 1974).

GABRIEL, P., *L'État patron c'est moi* (Paris: Flammanion, 1985).

GALAMBERT, P., *Les Sept Paradoxes de notre politique industrielle* (Paris: CERF, 1982).

GALBRAITH, J. K., 'How Keynes came to America', in *Economics, Peace and Laughter* (Boston: Houghton Mifflin, 1971), pp. 42–59.

—— 'Power and the Useful Economist', *American Economic Review*, 63 (1973), pp. 1–11.

GALLIE, D., 'The *Lois Auroux*: The Reform of French Industrial Relations', in Machin, H., and Wright, V. (eds.), *Economic Policy and Policy-Making under the Mitterrand Presidency 1981–1984* (London: Frances Pinter, 1985), pp. 205–21.

GEC, *Annual Report and Accounts* (1985).

—— *Offer for Plessey* (1985).

GIDDENS, A., *Central Problems in Sociological Theory* (London: Macmillan, 1979).

GILHOOLY, D., 'WATTC 88—Keeping the Luddites at Bay', *Telecommunications* (International Edition) (Jan. 1988).

—— 'Unlocking The Network', *Communications Week International* (July 1988).

GIST, P., and MEADOWCROFT, S., 'Regulating for Competition: The Newly Liberalised Market for Private Branch Exchanges', *Fiscal Studies*, 7/3 (1986), pp. 41–86.

GRANT, W., *The Political Economy of Industrial Policy* (London: Butterworths, 1982).

—— (ed.), *The Political Economy of Corporatism* (London: Macmillan, 1985).

——, PATERSON, W., and WHITSTON, C., 'Government–Industry Relations in the Chemical Industry: An Anglo-German Comparison', in Wilks, S., and Wright, M. (eds.), *Comparative Government–Industry Relations* (Oxford: Clarendon Press, 1987), pp. 35–60.

GREEN, D., 'Strategic Management and the State: France', in Dyson, K., and Wilks, S. (eds.), *Industrial Crisis: A Comparative Study of the State and Industry* (Oxford: Martin Robertson, 1983), pp. 161–92.

GREGORY, G., *Japanese Electronics Technology: Enterprise and Innovation*, 2nd edn. (Chichester: John Wiley, 1986).

Groupement des Industries Électroniques, *Annual Report 1986* (Paris, 1986).

HALL, P., *Governing the Economy: The Politics of State Intervention in Britain and France* (Cambridge: Policy Press, 1986).

HAYWARD, J. E. S., *The State and the Market Economy: Industrial Patriotism and Economic Intervention in France* (Brighton: Wheatsheaf Books, 1986).

HENNESSY, P., *Cabinet* (Oxford: Basil Blackwell, 1986).

HILLS, J., *Deregulating Telecoms: Competition and Control in the US, Japan and Britain* (London: Frances Pinter, 1986).

—— *Information Technology and Industrial Policy* (London: Croom Helm, 1984).

HOFFMAN, K., 'Digitale Fernsprechvermittlungstechnik bei der deutschen Bundespost: Das Präsentationasverfahren', *Jahrbuche der Deutschen Bundespost* (Bad Windsheim, 1984).

HOLMES, P., 'Rules of Origin in Intra-EEC Trade, Article 115 and Some Sectoral Issues for the UK and France', University of Sussex, International Economics Research Centre, Discussion Paper 87/46 (1987).

HOSKYNS, J., 'Whitehall and Westminster: An Outsider's View', *Parliamentary Affairs*, 36 (1983), pp. 137–47.

House of Commons, Public Accounts Committee, *Sale of Government Shareholding in British Telecommunications*, HC 35 (London: HMSO, 1985).

——Select Committee on Defence, *Fourth Report of the Defence Committee: Westland PLC: Government Decision-Making*, Session 1985–6, HCP 281 (London: HMSO, July 1986).

——Select Committee on Expenditure, *Eleventh Report*, Session 1976–7, HCP 535–I–II–III.

——Select Committee on Nationalized Industries, *The Post Office* (London: HMSO, 1967).

HUBER, P., *The Geodesic Network: 1987 Report on Competition in the Telephone Industry* (Washington, DC: US Department of Justice, Anti-Trust Division, 1987).

JORDAN, A. G., 'Iron Triangles, Woolly Corporatism and Elastic Nets: Images of the Policy Process', *Journal of Public Policy*, 1 (1981).

—— and RICHARDSON, J. J., *British Politics and the Policy Process* (London: Allen & Unwin, 1987).

LABETOULLE, D., 'Le Juge administratif et l'interventionnisme économique de l'état', in Institut de l'Entreprise, *Relations entre état et entreprises privées dans la CEE* (Paris: Masson, 1979).

LACORNE, D., 'La Politique Giscardienne des exportations ou le Colbertisme dans les moyens en vue du libéralisme comme fin', in Smouts, M.-C. (ed.), *La Politique extérieure de Valéry Giscard d'Estaing* (Paris: Presses Universitaires de France, 1985).

LE DIBERDER, A., *La Production de réseau de télécommunications* (Paris: Economica, 1983).

LEHMBRUCH, G., and SCHMITTER, P. C. (eds.), *Patterns of Corporatist Policy-Making* (London: Sage Publications, 1982).

Le Monde, *Dossiers et documents: Bilan économique 1984* (Paris: Le Monde, 1985).

LEVACIC, R., 'Government Policies towards the Consumer Electronics Industry and their Effects: A Comparison of Britain and France', in G. Hall (ed.), *European Industrial Policy* (London: Croom Helm, 1986), pp. 227–44.

LIBOIS, L.-J., *Le Genèse et croissance des télécommunications* (Paris: Masson/CNET, 1983).

LOCKSLEY, G., '1992, the European Commission and Strategies for Telecommunications', Paper presented at MIT Conference on World Tele-communications (June 1988).

LORENZI, J.-H., and LE BOUCHER, E., *Mémoires Volés* (Paris: Ramsay, 1979).

LUTHJE, B., 'Regulierungskrise in Telekommunikationssektor in der BRD', unpublished manuscript (Frankfurt-on-Main, 1986).

MACDONALD, M., 'The Future of Privatisation in France: A Crisis of Confidence', *Modern and Contemporary France*, 31 (Oct. 1987), pp. 1–9.

McKinsey & Co Inc., *Performance and Competitive Success: Strengthening Competitiveness in UK Electronics*, report prepared for the National Economic Development Council's Electronics Industry Sector Group (London: NEDC, 1988).

MARCH, J. G., and SIMON, H., *Organizations* (New York: John Wiley and Sons, 1958).

Microelectronics Design Associates, *Independent Telecommunications Networks: Report to the DoI* (London, 1980).

MIDDLEMAS, K., *Industry, Unions and Government* (London: Macmillan, 1983).

MILES, I., *Home Informatics* (London: Frances Pinter, 1988).

Monopolies and Mergers Commission, *The General Electric Company plc and the Plessey Company plc* (London: HMSO, 1986).

—— *British Telecommunications plc and Mitel Corporation* (London: HMSO, 1986).

MORGAN, K., 'Breaching the Monopoly: Telecommunications and the State in Britain', Working Paper Series on Government–Industry Relations, No. 7 (University of Sussex, 1987).

—— and PITT, D., 'America Against Itself: Re-regulating Telecommunications in the US', Berkeley Roundtable on the International Economy Monograph, University of California (Berkeley, 1989).

—— and SAYER, A., *Microcircuits of Capital: 'Sunrise' Industry and Uneven Development* (Cambridge: Polity Press, 1988).

—— and WEBBER, D., 'Divergent Paths: Political Strategies for Telecommunications in Britain, France and the Federal Republic of Germany', *West European Politics*, 9/4 (1986), pp. 56–79.

MURPHY, R., *Social Closure: The Theory of Monopolization and Exclusion* (Oxford: Clarendon Press, 1988).

National Enterprise Board, 'Report on Telecommunications', unpublished (London: NEB, 1978).

NAYAK, P. R. and KETTERINGHAM, J. M., *Breakthroughs!* (New York: Rawson Associates, 1986).

NORA, S., and MINC, A., *L'Informatisation de la société* (Paris: Documentation Française, 1978).

OFFE, C., 'The Attribution of Public Status to Interest Groups: Observations on the West German Case', in Berger, S. (ed.), *Organizing Interests in Western Europe; Pluralism, Corporatism and the Transformation of Politics* (Cambridge: Cambridge University Press, 1981), pp. 123–58.

OFTEL, *BT's Procurement of Digital Exchanges* (London, 1985).

—— *Annual Report for 1985* (London, 1986).

Organization for Economic Co-operation and Development, *Telecommunications: Pressures and Policies for Change* (Paris: OECD, 1983).

—— *Review of Innovation Policies* (Paris: OECD, 1986).

PANITCH, LEO, 'Review of Corporatism and Political Theory', *Canadian Journal of Political Science*, 21 (1988), pp. 813–18.

PARKIN, F., *Marxism and Class Theory: A Bourgeois Critique* (London: Tavistock, 1979).

—— *Max Weber* (Chichester: Ellis Horwood, and London: Tavistock, 1982).

PARRIS, H., PESTIEAU, P., and SAYNOR, P. J., *Public Enterprise in Western Europe* (London: Croom Helm, 1987).

PELKMANS, J., and BEUTER, R., 'Standardisation and Competitiveness: Public and Private Strategies in the EC Colour TV Industry', Paper presented at the INSEAD symposium on the economics of standards (1986).

PFISTER, T., *La Vie quotidienne à Matignon au temps de l'union de la Gauche* (Paris: Hachette, 1985).

PIGÉAT, H., and VIROL, L., *Du téléphone au télématique* (Paris: Documentation Française/Commissariat au Plan, 1980).

PITT, D., *The Telecommunications Function in the British Post Office* (Farnborough: Saxon House, 1980).

Plessey, *Reject the GEC Bid* (London: Plessey, 1986).

Post Office, *Evidence to the Post Office Review Committee*, Appendix to Cmnd. 6850, 1976.

Post Office Engineering Union, *The Telephone Ring: It's Time to Investigate* (London: POEU, 1962).

—— *Evidence to the Post Office Review Committee*, Appendix to Cmnd. 6850, 1976.

—— *The Modernisation of Telecommunications* (London: POEU, 1979).

—— *Making the Future Work: The Broad Strategy* (London: POEU, 1984).

Post Office Users' National Council, *Annual Report for 1979–80* (London: POUNC, 1980).

—— *Annual Report for 1980–81* (London: POUNC, 1981).

QUATREPOINT, J.-M., 'Un échéc exemplaire: L'Affaire Grundig', *Revue d'économie industrielle*, 27 (1984), pp. 31–40.

—— *Histoire secrète des dossiers noirs de la Gauche* (Paris: Alain Moreau, 1987).

R. Caves and Associates, *Britain's Economic Prospects* (London: Allen & Unwin, 1968).

REID, A., *The ISDN: A Presentation of Related Policy Issues* (Paris: OECD, 1986).

REINHARD, M., SCHOLZ, L., and THANNER, B., *Gesamtwirtschaftliche und sektorale Perspektiven der Telekommunikation in der Bundesrepublik Deutschland* (Munich, 1983).

RHODES, M., 'Organized Interests and Industrial Crisis Management; Restructuring the Steel Industry in West Germany, Italy and France', in Cawson, A. (ed.), *Organized Interests and the State* (London: Sage Publications, 1985), pp. 192–220.

ROSS, G., 'The Perils of Politics: French Unions and the Crisis of the 1970s', in Lange, P., Ross, G., and Vannicelli, M., *Unions, Change and Crisis: French and Italian Union Strategy and the Political Economy* (London: Allen & Unwin, 1982), pp. 13–93.

Roundtable of European Industrialists, *Clearing the Lines: A User's View on Business Communications in Europe* (Brussels, 1986).

RUGES, J.-F., *Le Téléphone pour tous* (Paris: Seuil, 1970).

RYLAND, W., *Life and Letters: The Sixth STC Communication Lecture* (London, 1976).

SAINT GEOURS, J., *Pouvoir et finance* (Paris: Fayard, 1979).

SAUVANT, K., *International Transactions in Services: The Politics of Transborder Data Flows* (Boulder, Colo., and London: Westview Press, 1986).

SCHMITTER, P. C., and LEHMBRUCH, G. (eds.), *Trends Toward Corporatist Intermediation* (London: Sage Publications, 1979).

SCHUMPETER, J. A., *Capitalism, Socialism and Democracy* (London: Allen & Unwin, 1943; 4th edn. 1954).

SCOTT, J., and GRIFF, C., *Directors of Industry: The British Corporate Network* (Oxford: Martin Robertson, 1983).

SEDGEMORE, B., *The Secret Constitution* (London: Hodder & Stoughton, 1980).

SHARP, M., 'Japanese Investment in Consumer Electronics', in Brech, M., and Sharp, M., *Inward Investment: Policy Options for the United Kingdom* (London: Routledge & Kegan Paul, 1984), pp. 63–86.

—— and SHEARMAN, C., *European Technological Collaboration*, Chatham House Papers 36 (London: Royal Institute of International Affairs/ Routledge & Kegan Paul, 1987).

SMITH, A., *The Wealth of Nations* (London: Methuen, 1950).

SOLOMON, J., 'Telecommunications Evolution in the UK', *Telecommunications Policy* (Sept. 1986).

STEEL, D. R., 'Review Article: Government and Industry in Britain', *British Journal of Political Science*, 12 (1983), pp. 449–503.

STEVENS, A., 'The Higher Civil Service and Economic Policy-Making in France', in Cerny, P. G., and Schain, M. A. (eds.), *French Politics and Public Policy* (London: Frances Pinter, 1980), pp. 79–100.

STEWART, M., *The Jekyll and Hyde Years: Politics and Economic Policy in Britain* (London: Dent, 1977).

STOFFAES, C., 'The Nationalisations 1981–4: An Initial Assessment', in Machin, H., and Wright, V. (eds.), *Economic Policy and Policy-Making under the Mitterrand Presidency 1981–1984* (London: Frances Pinter, 1985), pp. 144–69.

STONE, R., 'Political Economy, Economics and Beyond', *Economic Journal*, 90 (Dec. 1980), pp. 719–36.

STREECK, W., and SCHMITTER, P. C. (eds.), *Private Interest Government: Beyond Market and State* (London: Sage Publications, 1985).

SULEIMAN, E., *Politics, Power and Bureaucracy in France* (Princeton, NJ: Princeton University Press, 1974).

—— *Élites in French Society* (Princeton, NJ: Princeton University Press, 1978).

TEECE, D., 'Joint Ventures and Collaborative Arrangements in the Telecommunications Equipment Industry', in Mowery, D. (ed.), *International Collaborative Ventures in US Manufacturing* (Cambridge, Mass.: Ballinger, 1988).

TEXIER, M., *La Stratégie des commandes publiques dans le secteur des télécommunications 1966–1980* (Paris: DGT, 1981).

TREVOR, M., *Toshiba's New British Company: Competitiveness through Innovation in Industry* (London: Policy Studies Institute, 1988).

UNGERER, H., 'The European Community's Telecommunications Policy: A Global Approach', in Garnham, N. (ed.), *Telecommunications: National Policies in an International Context* (Windsor: Communications Policy Research Conference, 1986).

VAN TULDER, R., and JUNNE, G., *European Multinationals in Core Technologies* (Chichester: Wiley, 1988).

VISSER, J., 'Dimensions of Union Growth in Postwar Western Europe', European University Institute, Working Paper No. 89 (Florence: EUI, Feb. 1984).

—— 'The Positions of Central Confederations in the National Union Movement: A Ten-Country Comparison', European University Institute, Working Paper No. 102 (Florence: EUI, May 1984).

WATSON BROWN, A., 'The Campaign for High Definition Television: A Case Study in Triad Power', *Euro-Asia Business Review*, 6/2 (1987), pp. 3–11.

WEBBER, D., 'The Framework of Government–Industry Relations and Industrial Policy-Making in the Federal Republic of Germany', Working Paper Series on Government–Industry Relations, No. 1 (University of Sussex, 1986).

—— 'The Politics of Telecommunications Deregulation in the Federal Republic of Germany', Working Paper Series on Government–Industry Relations, No. 3 (University of Sussex, 1986).

—— 'Die ausbleibende Wende bei der Deutschen Bundespost: Zur Regulierung des Telekommunikationswesens in der Bundesrepublik Deutschland', *Politische Vierteljahresschrift*, 27/4 (1986), pp. 397–414.

WEBER, M., *Economy and Society*, ed. Roth, G., and Wittich, C., 2 vols. (Berkeley and Los Angeles: University of California Press, 1978).

WHITE, H. C., 'Where do Markets come from?', *American Journal of Sociology*, 87/3 (1981), pp. 517–47.

WILKS, S., 'Liberal State and Party Competition: Britain', in Dyson, K., and Wilks, S. (eds.), *Industrial Crisis: A Comparative Study of the State and Industry* (Oxford: Martin Robertson, 1983), pp. 128–60.

—— *Industrial Policy and the Motor Industry* (Manchester: Manchester University Press, 1984).

—— 'Government–Industry Relations: A Review Article', *Policy and Politics*, 14 (1986), pp. 491–506.

—— and WRIGHT, M. (eds.), *Comparative Government–Industry Relations: Western Europe, the United States and Japan* (Oxford: Clarendon Press, 1987).

WILLIAMSON, O., *Markets and Hierarchies* (New York: Free Press, 1975).

—— 'The Economics of Organization: The Transaction Cost Approach', *American Journal of Sociology*, 87/3 (1981), pp. 548–77.

WILLIAMSON, P. J., *Corporatism in Perspective* (London: Sage Publications, 1989).

WITTE, E., *Neuordnung der Telekommunikation: Bericht der Regierungskommission Fernmeldewesen* (Heidelberg, 1987).

YOUNG, S. C., *An Annotated Bibliography on Relations Between Government and Industry in Britain 1960–82*, 2 vols. (London: Economic and Social Research Council, 1984).

Zentralverband der Elektrotechnischen Industrie, *Fachverband Unterhaltungselektronik, Kommunikations und Unterhaltungselektronik in Deutschland: Perspektiven und Probleme* (Frankfurt: ZVEI, 1980).

ZYSMAN, J., *Governments, Markets and Growth* (Berkeley and Los Angeles: University of California Press, 1983).

Index

Action Programme for
  Telecommunications (1984) 185–
  194
  industrial collaboration 189–90
  market, opening of 190–4
  network, future development 187–8
  standards 188–9
Advisory Council of Applied Research
  and Development (ACARD) 252
Advisory Group on System Definition
  (British Telecom) 107
AEG 294
  and 'Round Table' 183
  VCR industry 307
AEG–Telefunken 58–9, 62, 157, 293,
  295
agency capture 8
Aiwa 228
Akai 228, 268
Alcatel
  and digital switching project 137–9,
    140–3
  in Germany 157
  and 'intelligent' equipment 201
  and merger with Thompson 197–8
alliances, see collaboration
Alps Electric 327
Amalgamated Union of Engineering
  Workers (AUEW) 239
American Interactive Media 340
American Telephone and Telegraph
  (AT&T) 80, 185
  alliance with Philips 199
  and CGE 134–5, 140
  enhanced business services 201
  and HDTV 331
  intercompany agreements 210, 212–
    14
  as manufacturer 205
Amstrad 29, 31
  and CTV 221, 236, 246
  joint ventures 337
ANT Nachrichtentechnik 157
Apple 331
application specific integrated circuits
  (ASICs) 364
Association des Ingénieurs de
  Télécommunications (AIT) 122,
  127

Association Francaise des Utilisateurs
  du Téléphone et des
  Télécommunications (AFUTT)
  122
Association of Post Office Users (VPB,
  Germany) 156, 357
Association of Professional and
  Executive Staffs (APEX) 239
Association of Scientific, Technical and
  Managerial Staffs (ASTMS) 239–
  40
associative action and closure 22–3

Baker, K. 241
banks / banking
  and consumer electronics industry
    293–4
  in Germany 61–2
  nationalized in France 62–3
Barclays Bank and private telecom
  consortium 93
bargaining and corporatism 6, 8
Basic Law (Germany) 40, 43, 49
  and Land 39–40
  and Minister of Posts and
    Telecommunications 151–2
Basic Research in Industrial
  Technologies in Europe (BRITE)
  335
Bavaria: government of and Grundig
  Affair 300–3
Benventane 342
Beta VCR format 226, 255–6
Blaupunkt 291, 303, 309
Bonnet, J.-C. 274
Bosch
  in CTV market 221
  and Grundig Affair 298, 301, 303–4
  and HDTV 335
  joint ventures 230, 327, 337
  and ZVEI 291
Boston Consultancy Group report
  (1978) 247–8
Boublil, A. 133
Bouyssonnie, J. 276
Britain
  Cabinet, role of 41–2
  and civil service 54–5

Britain (*cont.*):
  constitutional and legal frameworks
    39–44
  and consumer electronics industry
    233–61; adjustments in 247–54;
    firms in 235–6; Japanese
    investment in 230, 236–7, 242–7,
    258; and national differences 371;
    production 220; trade in 228–9;
    unions in 239–40
  economic attitudes 46
  financial institutions 61, 63
  government, role of 358–9
  innovation and VCRs 254–9
  and labour unions 55–6
  and mergers 198
  parliament, role of 42
  and pattern of government-industry
    relations (1975) 348–9
  plant closure in 250
  Prime Minister, role of 42
  privatization 48
  and size of firms 59
  and sponsorship 51–2
  telecommunications 81–4; Bulk
    Supply Agreement 97–8;
    liberalization of 366–9; monopoly
    88–9, 91–3, 95–7
  trade associations 356–7; in
    consumer electronics industry 236–
    9
  trade unions 239–40, 353
  Treasury, role of 50
British Gas 48
British National Oil Corporation 48
British Petroleum 48
  and private telecom consortium 93
British Radio and Electronic Equipment
    Manufacturers Association
    (BREMA) 60, 223, 247, 356
  and Japanese firms 236–7, 243
  strategies and imports 238–9
  and VCRs 257
British Telecom 24, 30, 48, 81, 184,
    190, 200
  charges (tariffs) 102–3
  enhanced business services 201
  and government 360
  and ISDN 187
  intercompany agreements 212
  liberalization 93–5
  and Mitel affair 101–2
  new alliances 202–3

  privatization 93, 95–6, 97
  public switching 106–14; engineering
    110–13; and project management
    109–10; rivalry 107–9
  reorganization 102
  and specialized services 94–5
  and Thorn–Ericsson controversy 99–
    100
Brittan, L. 240
Bull 130
  intercompany agreements 207–9, 211
  and 'Round Table' 183
Bundespost 184
  and digital switching equipment 168–
    71
  and EWS-A technology 163–5
  and German telecommunications
    industry 151–60; and parliament
    154–5; and Post Ministry 151–4;
    suppliers 156–61; users 155–6
  and government 360
  and ISDN 187
  and restrictions on trade 204
  and single technology policy 166–7;
    abandonment of 173–4
  staff councils 155
  switching technology 161–2
  and trade unions 353
  and ZVEI 291

Cable & Wireless 93
cable TV 94, 96
CAD and System X engineering 110
Caisse Nationale des
    Télécommunications 123
car audio 230
Carey, Sir P. 241
cartels in French telecommunications
    industry 129
cartel-oriented closure strategy 22–3,
    31–2
CDC 340
cellular mobile telephone network 94,
    96
Central Telecommunications
    Equipment Approval Office (ZZF,
    Germany) 151
Central Telecommunications Office
    (FTZ, Germany) 151–2, 157–8,
    160
  and digital switching equipment 170
  and EWS-A technology 162–5
  and single-technology policy 166–8

Centre Nationale d'Études des
   Télécommunications (CNET)
   122–3, 125, 128–9, 272
   and DGT 129
   and digital switching project 137, 140
CGCT 130, 134–5, 199
   net profits 132
CGE 122, 144
   and Alcatel NV 142
   CTV in France 263
   and digital switching project 137,
      140, 141
   failure in US markets 141
   intercompany agreements 207–9, 211
   mergers: in Europe 202; with ITT
      135–6; with Thomson 133, 140
   nationalization 131
   net profits 132
   privatized 135
   in public sector markets 132–3
   and 'Round Table' 183
Chaban-Delmas, J. 138
Chapple, F. 239
Chevènement, J. P. 131, 133, 269–70,
   272, 281
Chirac, J. 41, 48, 127, 135, 141, 144–
   5, 278, 368
CIT-Alcatel 122, 131
   intercompany agreements 207–11
civil services, structures 53–5
Clarion 268, 276
closure, 9
   by government interests 360
   and CTV standards 319
   and competition 16–18, 122
   in consumer electronics industry in
      France 262, 270, 279
   criteria for 28
   dual 28
   and European Commission Green
      Paper 195
   exclusion and usurpation 28–31
   and HDTV 373–4
   and innovation 327
   and public switching system 108–9
   strategies of 22–4, 32–3; and the firm
      376; in Germany 298
   telecommunications: French 143–4;
      German 156, 160
   and teletext technology 251
   in export restraint agreements 372–3
   see also exclusion
Cockfield, Lord 257

collaboration
   among telecommunications firms
      197–203
   of British firms in consumer
      electronics industry 249–50
   and competition between firms 325–8
   for Eureka HDTV project 335–7
   of European companies 183, 187
   industrial, in EEC 189–90
   in new technologies 374
   see also joint ventures
CTV (colour television)
   French public policy 269–73
   Japan: imports 235; investment in
      Europe 230
   joint ventures in 337
   markets: segmentation of 224–5; in
      France 263–4
   national differences 370–1
   production in Europe 222
   Thomson as largest producer 285
   transmission standards 223–5, 331–2
Comité Consultatif International du
   Radio (CCIR) 225, 331, 336
Comité Consultatif International pour
   Téléphone et Télécommunications
   (CCITT) 166
Commission Nationale des
   Communications et Libertés 128
communications infrastructure in
   Germany 47
compact disc 227–8
   and home computing industry 339–40
   innovations 328
   Japanese investment in Europe 230
   joint ventures 340–2
   standards 372
   systems 338–9
competition 9, 15, 18–19
   avoidance of 22–3
   and closure 16–18, 22
   and collaboration between firms 325–
      8
   defined 16
   in EEC 64
   from Korean firms 327
   and monopoly 24
   and satellite TV 319–20
   within European Community 196
   see also Japan
competitiveness
   of British consumer electronics firms
      247–8

competitiveness (*cont.*):
  in VCR industry in Europe 313
computers and CD-I 339–40
Confederation of British Industry (CBI)
  59
Conference on European Post and
  Telecommunications
  Administrations (CEPT) 184, 188–
  9, 202
Confédération Française Démocratique
  (France) 56
Confédération Générale du Travail
  (France) 56
Conseil National du Patronat Français
  (CNPF) 59, 60, 355–6
Conseil Supérieur de l'Audiovisuel 128
consumer electronics industry
  and banks 293–4
  in Britain 233–61; unions 39–40
  competition and collaboration
    between firms 325–8
  and European Economic Community
    policy 328–32
  European industrial policy 342–4
  European market 220
  in France 262–88; and ministries
    270–3; pressures 284–5; and state
    269–70
  future innovations 328
  in Germany 289–317; Grundig Affair
    305–6; role of governments 294–7
  internationalization of 318–20
  Japanese investment 229–31
  joint ventures 327, 337; for compact
    disc development 338–42
  and major firms 219–23
  national differences, decline of 370–5
  and newly industrialized countries
    373
  and pattern of government–industry
    relations (1975) 349
  production 220, 223–8
  rationalization 343–4
  sectors, and clusters of firms 321–6
  strategies in Europe 326–8
  trade: international 228–9; policy
    and politics 332–5
Corning Glass 210, 212, 213, 214
corporatism 5–9
CSF group 265

Daewoo 221, 245
DAT 328

Davignon, Viscount E. 183, 257, 329,
  372
DEC 201, 202
Decca 249
Dekker, W. 281
Delors, J. 131, 281
Denshi Media Services 340
Department of Industry (D.o.I.)
  and Japanese firms in Britain 243–4,
    247–8
  and Post Office 88, 90–1; and reform
    of (1981) 92–3
  and System X 109–12
  and teletext 252–3
Department of Trade and Industry
  (DTI) 237, 242, 259
  and consumer electronics industry
    240–1
  and GEC–Plessey take-over 105
deregulation 30–1
  of British Telecom 30
  in Germany 176–7
  in telecommunications 80
Detewe 157, 161–2, 165, 167, 169–
  71
Deutsche Bank 293
  and Grundig Affair 301
Development Aid Ministry (Germany)
  159, 172, 174
DGT, *see* Direction Générale
digital audio tape 220, 228
digital exchanges 99–100
digital switching
  in Britain 106–14, 138–9
  in France 136–43
  in Germany 168–72
digital technology 328
digital telecommunication equipment
  78–9, 364
  'contest' for orders 168–72
  specification (Germany) 166–7
Direct Broadcast by Satellite (DBS) 225,
  319, 331–2
Direction des Industries Electroniques et
  l'Informatique (DIELI) 52, 55, 270–1
Direction Générale de l'Industrie 52
Direction Générale des
  Télécommunications (DGT) 360–1
  autonomy, reduced 125–6
  and digital switching project 136–7,
    141
  modernization 123–4, 129–30, 134,
    138

monopoly of 126–7
role of 121–2
see also France Telecom
Dirigisme (planning) in France 121–50
Donnelly, R. R. 340
Donodoux, J. 125, 131
Dual 280, 284, 298, 324
dumping 231, 327, 333–4
in Germany 307–8, 310

Economics Ministry (Germany) 153,
158, 159, 292, 295–7
and Grundig Affair 300–2, 304, 306
and VCR market 311, 313
Electrical, Electronic,
Telecommunications and Plumbing
Union (EETPU) 239–40, 354
Electrolux 336
Electronic Data Systems 202
Electronic Industries Association of
Japan (EIAJ) 223, 237–8, 326
Elf Aquitaine 47
EMD switching technology in Germany
162, 168
employees in telecommunications 82
emulation of Japanese firms 250
Ericsson 130, 135
and collaboration 187
and digital switching project 137–8,
142
in France 122, 128
in Germany 160, 167
intercompany agreements 208, 209
mergers in Europe 202
and Thorn 99–100
Eureka HDTV project 318, 332, 338,
342
closure strategy 373–4
collaboration for 320, 332, 335–7
Europe
industrial policy 342–4
intercompany cooperation 207–14
strategies: in consumer electronics
326–8; in telecommunications
182–217
and trade with US 203–6
European Association of Consumer
Electronics Manufacturers
(EACEM) 32, 221, 239, 373
European Commission 182, 184
and collaboration 335
Green Paper (1987) 186, 194–7
industrial policy instruments 332

and ISDN 187
and Japanese investment in consumer
electronics 231
markets, opening of 191
public procurement directive 206
and trade with US 204–5
telecommunications: 'Action
Programme for (1984) 185–6;
standards 188–9; strategies for
185–94
and VCR market 310
European Economic Community (EEC)
6, 32, 64
agreement with MITI 257–8
consumer electronics market 220
and French import quotas 275
and industrial collaboration 189–90
as market for telecommunications
equipment 182–3
opening of markets 190–4
and Philips 323
policy towards consumer electronics
328–32
powers 65–6
single market and competition 321
and tariffs for consumer electronics
industry 342–3
European frameworks 63–6
European Interactive Media 340
European Strategic Programme for
Research on Information
Technology (ESPRIT) 189, 198,
332, 335
European Telecom Standards Institute
(ETSI) 189
EWS switching technology in Germany
162–5, 166, 172–4
exclusion
and closure 28–31
and corporatism 5–6, 7
policy over Japanese firms in Britain
243–4
export restraint agreement 282
and closure 372–3
and European Commission 329–30
in Germany 308–14; aftermath 312–
14
exports
of telecommunication equipment
from Germany 159
of VCRs by Japan 255

Fabius, L. 131, 133, 134

Farnoux, A. 266, 272–3, 277, 280, 298
Fayard, J. 266, 270, 271, 277–9, 280,
 284–5
Federal Cartel Office (BKA, Germany)
 153, 160, 162, 171, 173–4, 281,
 291, 295
 and Grundig Affair 298–302, 304–5
 and mergers in Germany 296–7
Federal Constitutional Court
 (Germany) 43–4
Federation of German Employers
 Association (BDA) 59
Federation of German Industry (BDI)
 155, 292, 295, 357
Finance Ministries
 France 271
 Germany 153, 177, 295
finances of Post Office 90
financial institutions 61–3
firms
 changes in organization 351–2
 and closure strategy 27
 clusters of in Europe 321–6
 collective action by 363
 in consumer electronics industry 219–
 23; in Britain 235–6; competition
 and collaboration in 325–8;
 options, 248–9
 and government–industry relations
 361–2, 375–8; in Germany
 292
 internationalization of 365
 small 58–9
 strategies 26–7, 361–3
 as systems of power 24–5
Fisher Hifi 312
Force Ouvrière (France) 56, 122
frameworks
 constitutional and legal 39–44
 European 63–6
France
 banking 62–3
 civil service structure 53–4
 and collaboration 187
 and constitution 44
 constitutional and legal frameworks
 39–44
 consumer electronics industry:
 Japanese investment in 230;
 mergers in 279–85; and national
 differences 371; nationalization
 276–9; production 220; products
 and markets in 263–4; public

policy in 269–73; restructuring of
 276–9; trade in 228–9
 economic attitudes 45–6
 and European Commission Green
 Paper 194–5
 government: and industry 273–6;
 role of 358
 industry and ministries 49–50
 Japanese companies in 268
 and nationalization 47–8
 parliament, role of 42
 and pattern of government–industry
 relations (1975) 348–9
 and Philips 266–8
 political regime in 40–1
 state control, illusion of 262–88
 stock market 61
 telecommunications 81–4; closure in
 143–4; liberalization of 366–9;
 and mergers 134–5, 198;
 modernization of business 143–4;
 nationalization of 130–1, 144;
 quality of service in 121–3, 143,
 349; restrictions on 128–36
 and Thomson-Brandt 264–6
 trade associations 60, 355–6
 tutelle 52
 and unions 56–7, 354
 and VCRs: inspection at Poitiers
 281–2, 308, 329–30, 372;
 production 281–3
France Télécom (formerly DGT) 121,
 184, 187, 360
Funai
 and CTV 221, 236, 246
 joint ventures 337
Fédérations des Industries Électriques et
 Électroniques (FIEE) 274, 276

Galbraith, J. K. 24–6
Garcin, P. 277, 284
GEC 239, 244, 246
 and HDTV 336
 and industrial collaboration 189
 intercompany agreements 208, 211
 and Japanese investment 326
 joint ventures 337
 merger with Plessey 104–6, 197–8,
 199
 public switching system 107, 111,
 112–13
 and 'Round Table' 183
 strategies 104

supplier to British Telecom 103
and Thorn–Ericsson controversy
99–100
GEC–Plessey Telecom (GPT) 200–1
Geisco 202
General Agreement on Tariffs and
Trade (GATT) 6, 64, 329, 333,
373
and telecommunications services 184,
204–5
VCR import quotas 311, 313
General Electric Company (USA) 324
German Chamber of Industry and
Commerce (DIHT) 155, 292, 295
German Trade Union Federation (DGB)
57
Germany
administrative agencies 359–60
banking 61–2
and BDA 59
and civil service 54
and collaboration 187
concertative style of government
39–40
and constitution 43
constitutional and legal frameworks
39–44
and consumer electronics industry
290–3; banks and 293–4;
governments and 294–7; Japanese
investment in 230; labour and 294;
national differences in 371–2;
production 220; trade in 228–9
and digital switching technology
168–72
and European Commission Green
Paper 195
government, role of 359
industrial policy 50–1, 52–3
and nationalization 47
parliament: politics and organized
labour 154–5; role of 42–3
and pattern of government–industry
relations (1975) 348–9
political attitudes 44–5
small firms in 58
stock market 61
telecommunications industry 81–4;
equipment suppliers 156–61;
liberalization of 366–9; mergers
296–7; regime 151–60; switching
technology 161–2; users 155–6
trade associations 357

unions 57–8, 353
VCR, protection of industry 307–14
Germany Mechanical Engineering
Association (VDMA) 155, 160
Germany Post Office Workers Union
(DPG) 176
Giscard d'Estaing, V. 122–3, 125, 138,
143, 279, 358
Goldstar 221, 313
Gomez, A. 133, 270, 277, 280–1,
284–5, 324
governments
and 1969 Act 90
changes in role of 358–60; and
control over firms 361–2
France: industry in 273–6;
nationalized industries in 131;
public policy 269–73; socialist
125, 127, 130–1, 144
Germany: consumer electronics
industry in 294–7;
telecommunication reform in
175–6
and Grundig Affair 300–1
institutions 49–53
and inward investment in consumer
electronics 258–9
liberalization of British Telecom 93–5
and Mitel–BT merger 102
policies: and GEC–Plessey take over
105–6; and Japanese investment in
Britain 245–7
and Post Office monopoly 88
and privatization of British Telecom
95–6
government–industry relations
approach to 4–14
changes in 350–1
and corporatism 5–9
and firms 361–2; politics of 375–8
introduction to 1–4
patterns of 348–52
perspectives of 9–13
GPT
and 'intelligent' equipment 201
mergers in Europe 202
Grant, W. 55
Griffiths, J. 242
Grundig
joint ventures 327, 337
mergers in France 279–81
VCR industry 226, 227, 307–12
and ZVEI 291–2

Grundig Affair 279–81, 297–307
   implications of 305–7
   solution to 302–5
   and Thomson take-over bid 299–302
Grundig, M. 280, 289–304
GTE 211, 213
   alliance with Siemens 199
   as manufacturer 205

Haferkampf, W. 257
Hammond, E. 239
Hancher, L. 51
HDTV (high definition television) 225,
      318–19, 328, 373
   and collaboration 335–8
   standards 331
hifi 230
Hinari 337
Hitachi
   in Britain 239, 243–4, 246, 326, 354
   in consumer electronics market 220
   joint ventures 337
   trade in Europe 229
   VCR production in Europe 312
Hotchkiss–Brandt 264
Houston–Thomson 264

IBM 32, 188, 201, 202, 331
   in Germany 155, 156, 160, 177
   intercompany agreements 211–14
ICI 93
IG Metall 294
IHS 328, 336, 338
industrial policy, attitudes to 44–6
Industry Ministry (France) 270–1
information technology (IT)
   in Britain 252–4
   collaboration 335
integrated broadband communications
      (IBC) 187, 190, 193
intercompany cooperation by European
      telecommunication companies
      207–14
   intra-European 207–9
   with Non-EDC firms 210–14
International Monetary Fund (IMF) 6
International Telecommunications
      Union (ITU) 204
International Telecommunications
      Users Group (INTUG) 32, 184,
      196
internationalization
   changes in 351

consumer electronics under technical
      uncertainty 318–20
   of firms 365
   in telecommunications 79
intervention
   by government 269–70, 361–2
   kinds of 362
investment
   inward: in Britain 236–7, 242–7,
      258; in Europe 229–31, 326, 333;
      in France 258–9, 276, 282; by
      Japan 326, 333
   Post Office, cut in 90
IRI 342
ISDN (Integrated Services Digital
      Network) 187–8, 190, 193
   implementation 200–1
ITT 122, 130–1, 134–5, 207
   in Britain 236, 249
   and digital switching project 138,
      140–2
   in France 263
   in Germany 157, 167–8
   merger with CGE 135–6
   and Nokia 325

J2T (JVC–Thorn–Telefunken, later
      JVC–Thomson)
   in Britain 244
   and import quotas 330
   merger 230, 281, 284, 306, 324;
      blocked by French government
      227, 279
   VCR production 221, 257, 263, 268
Japan
   in European consumer electronics
      market 199, 220–1, 224;
      components manufacture 327;
      CTV 223; and compact disc 227–
      8; joint ventures 337, 338–40;
      VCRs 225–7, 254–6, 308–10
   firms: in Britain 235–6, 237–8; in
      Europe 325–6; in France 268; in
      Germany 293
   investment: in Britain 243–5; in
      Europe 229–31; in France 263–4
   as market for telecommunications
      equipment 182–3
Japan Interactive Media 340
Japanese State Broadcasting
      Organization (NHK) 331
Joint Electronic Research Committee
      107

joint ventures
  for compact disc 338–42
  for consumer electronics 327, 337
Joseph, Sir K. 93, 241
JVC 251, 279, 280–2
  in CTV market 221
  joint ventures 230, 337
  VCRs 226, 227, 255–7; formats 330;
    industry in Germany 307, 309;
    production in Europe 312
JVC–Thomson, see J2T

Kohl, H. 302, 368
Korea 327, 373
Kyocera 337, 342

La Radiotechnique 267, 272, 279, 284
labour 55–8
  and consumer electronics industry in
    Germany 294
Lambsdorff, Count 53, 302, 311
Laservision 342
liberalization
  and business user population 369
  and labour, power of 367
  legal and constitutional constraints
    366–7
  and ruling parties, character of 368–9
  and telecom clubs, status of 367
  of telecommunications: in Britain 93–
    5, 366–9; in France 144–5; in
    Germany 178–9
  of terminal equipment market 195–6
local content regulations 231, 327–8,
    333
Longuet, J. 128

MAC (Multiplexed Analogue
    Components, CTV transmission
    standard) 225, 318–20, 331–2
Madelin, A. 52, 128, 271
Managed Data Network Services
    (MDNS) 202–3
Marantz 336, 337
Market Access Fact Finding (MAFF)
    204
market-oriented closure strategy 22,
    31–2
markets
  for consumer electronics in Europe
    220
  in Europe: fragmented 182; opening
    of 190–4, 196–7

outsiders in 29–30
  relationships 17, 20–1
  and the state 19–20, 23–6
  as systems of power 15–37
  varieties of 21
Marx, K. 11, 18
Matra 135, 208, 210
  and collaboration 187
Matsushita 303, 309, 312
  in consumer electronics market 220,
    221, 226
  in Europe 324, 326, 327
  and inward investment in Britain
    244
  joint ventures 230, 337
  trade in Europe 229
Mercury 102
  enhanced business services 201
  private consortium 93, 94–5
mergers
  and BKA 296–7
  of European companies 184
  in telecommunications industry 197–
    203; in France 134–5
  and VCRs 279–85
Merkle, H. 303
MET 135, 144
Mexandeau, L. 272
Ministry of Defence and GEC–Plessey
    take-over 104–5
Ministry of Information Technology
    252
Ministry of International Trade and
    Industry (MITI, Japan) 238, 242,
    254, 372
  agreement with European
    Community 257–8
  and export restraint agreement 329–
    30
  and VCR imports to Europe 310
Ministry of Posts and
    Telecommunications (Germany)
  and consumer electronics industry
    295–6
  and digital switching equipment 170,
    173
  and parliament 154–5
  politics 152–3
  and reform of Bundespost 176
  and single-technology policy 166
  structure 152
  and telecommunications regime
    151–4

Ministère des Postes, des Télécommunications et de Telediffusion 121–4, 127–8
and consumer electronics industry 272
and digital switching project 141
Mission de la filière Electronique 272–3, 280
Mitel 101–2, 212
Mitsubishi 244, 249, 257
Mitterrand, F. 47, 56, 131, 302
and consumer electronics industry 269–70, 277
and Grundig Affair 279, 281
mobile telecommunications services 200, 202
modernization
of DGT 123–4, 129–30, 134, 138
of telecommunication business in France 124, 143–4
Monopolies & Mergers Commission 101
monopoly 24
of DGT 126–7
in Germany: of Bundespost 172–4; and digital switching equipment 171; lapse of 177; in switching technology 161–2; telecommunication regime 151–60
Post Office as 88–9; ending of 91–3; and privatization 95–7
in telecommunications industry 77
Moran, M., 63
Motorola 202
Mullard 336
multinationals, see transnational
Multiple Sub-Nyquist Encoding (MUSE) 331
Murdoch, R. 319
Murphy, R. 10, 31

national boundaries, erosion of in telecommunications 364
National Economic Development Council (NEDC) and sector working parties 56
working parties 56
National Economic Development Office (NEDO) 240
EDC 336
modernization of consumer electronics in Britain 251
Sector Working Party in consumer electronics 242–4, 246–8

National Television Standards Committee (NTSC – CTV transmission standard) 223–4
nationalization 46–9
in France 130–1, 144; of banks 62–3; of Thomson 276–9, 324
NEB and System X 111–12
NEC 244–5
networks 187–8, 191
networking 328
Nixdorf 156, 183
Nokia 249
CTV in France 263
in consumer electronics market 220
growth of 325
Nordmende 298
and Thomson 324
and ZVEI 291
Northern Telecom 167, 211, 213
alliance with STC 199
enhanced business services 201

Offe, C. 5
Oftel
duties 94
and GEC–Plessey take-over 105–6
success 97
and Thorn–Ericcson controversy 99–100
oil crisis 45–6
Olivetti
intercompany agreements 207, 209, 213, 214
and 'Round Table' 183
Omnibus Trade and Competitiveness Act (US 1988) 203
Open Network Provision (ONP) 193–4
Open systems interconnection (OSI) 188
Optical Storage International 340
Optimage Interactive Services 340
optoelectronics 328
Orbitel 187
organization 16, 25
Orion 244
outsiders in markets 29–30

PAL 245
CTV transmission standard 223–5, 331–2, 334
produced by Japanese 275
Parkin, F. 24, 28

Parkinson, C. 240
parliament
  role of 42–3
  and telecommunication policy
    (Germany) 154–5
parochialism, end of in European
  telecommunications 182–217
participation in markets 17–18
Pebereau, G. 133, 134, 136, 140–1,
  277
Philips
  alliance with AT&T 199
  in Britain 235–6, 239, 240, 249
  and closure 32, 33
  and compact disc 33, 227
  and competition in Europe 332
  in consumer electronics market 220,
    221, 225
  in France 263, 266–8
  in Germany 157, 169
  and Grundig Affair 280–1, 298–300,
    302–5
  and HDTV project 313–19, 335–6
  imports into France 274–6
  intercompany agreements 207, 208,
    210
  joint ventures 337; in compact disc
    340–2
  and market strategies 27
  restructuring of 321–3
  and 'Round Table' 183
  and Thomson 324, 330
  and VCRs 226, 227, 255–6, 258;
    early lead 329; in France 283–4;
    industry 307–12
  and ZVEI 291–2
Philips–Dupont Optimal 340
Philips–France 278–9
Philips–Grundig 254, 256, 328
Pioneer 268
PKI 157, 169–70
Plan Câble 125–6
Plan Télématique 124–5
Plessey
  and collaboration 188
  intercompany agreements 207, 209,
    211–13
  merger with GEC 104–6, 197–8, 199
  public switching system 107, 111,
    112–13
  and 'Round Table' 183
  strategies 104
  as supplier to British Telecom 103

and Thorn–Ericsson controversy 99–
  100
political parties and telecommunication
  policy (Germany) 154–5
political regime in France 40–1
political strategies, changes in 351
politics of inward investment in Britain
  242–7, 258
Polygram 340
Pony–Canyon 340
  joint ventures in Europe 337
Post Office (Britain)
  and 1969 Act 88, 90
  duties 87–8
  finances 90
  as monopoly 88–9
  reform (1981) 92–3
  review (1975) 90–2
  structure of 91
  and suppliers 98
  and trade unions 89, 93, 353
  see also British Telecom
Post Office Engineering Union (POEU)
  89, 90, 91, 93
Post Office Users' National Council
  (POUNC) 89, 92, 357
Post, Telegraph and Telephone
  authorities (PTT) 77–80
  compared 81–2
  demands of business users 369
  and European Commission Green
    Paper 194–5
  and ISDN 201
  new alliances 202–3
  and pattern of government–industry
    relations (1975) 349
  role of 77–80
  see also British Telecom; Bundespost;
    DGT; France Telecom; Post Office
Poullian, L. 302
presidential regime (France) 40–1
prices, Post Office, controlled 90
Private Automatic Branch Exchange
  (PABX) 78, 91, 200–1
  in Germany 160
  and Mitel affair 101–2
privatization 46–9
  of British Telecom 93, 95–7
  of CGE 135
producers in markets 20–1
protectionism 22
  in consumer electronics: in Britain
    242–3; in Europe 229, 307–11

protectionism (*cont.*):
in France 268, 273–6, 281–3
in German telecommunications
industry 160
of single European market 205
public sector in France 47–8
public switching equipment in
telecommunications 106–14, 200
Pye 249
Pye–TMC 108

quotas
on CTV in France 274–5
on Japanese VCRs 311, 312

Racal 94, 188, 249
Radio Industries Council (RIC) 238
RAI 342
Rank 244, 246, 249
and Japanese investment 326
joint ventures 337
rationalization of consumer electronics
industry 343–4
RCA 265–6, 324, 337
Rediffusion 249
regulation 16
Renault 47
Research on Advanced
Communications for Europe
(RACE) 190, 198, 332, 335
Research and Technology Ministry
(Germany) 153, 296
Richard, P. 264–5, 277
Rocard, M. 131
'Round Table' of European companies
183–4
Roux, A. 133, 267
RTC 267, 278

Saba 298
and Thomson 324
and ZVEI 291
Samsung 221, 245
Sanyo 244, 249, 257
VCR production 312
Schumpeter, J. A. 18
SECAM 245, 267, 269, 274
produced by Japanese 268, 275
transmission standard 223–5, 331,
334
Sector Working Party (NEDO)
in consumer electronics 242, 243–4,
246, 247–8

disappearance of 354
and teletext 252
sectoral boundaries, erosion of 351,
363–6
SEL 157, 160, 161–2, 165, 167–72,
208, 209, 213
and Grundig Affair 298
and Nokia 325
and ZVEI 291
SGB 207, 209
Sharp 244, 258
Shintom 337
Siemens 58, 62, 113, 135, 140
alliance with GTE 199
and collaboration 187
and deregulation 177–8
and digital switching equipment 169–
72
dominant position of 160–1
and EWS-A technology 163–5
and German telecommunications
150, 156–61
and Grundig Affair 298, 301, 303,
306
and HDTV 336
and 'intelligent' equipment 201
intercompany agreements 207–9, 213
and 'Round Table' 183
and single technology policy in
Germany 166–8
switching technology 161–2
in US markets 200
and ZVEI 291
Sky Channel 319, 332
SLE–Citeral 137
Smith, A. 16
Socotel 129
Sony
8-mm. format 226, 330
and compact disc 227–8
in France 268
and internationalization of consumer
electronics 321
and inward investment in Britain 244
reorganization in Europe 327
trade in Europe 229, 312
and VCRs 226, 227
Sotélec 129
sponsorship 51–2
state and markets 23–6
state monopoly capitalism 8
STC 249
alliance with Northern Telecom 199

public switching system 107, 111,
112–13
STC–ICL and 'Round Table' 183
Stet 183, 209, 214
Streeck, W. 59
Stromberg–Carlson 104, 211
Studen A. G. 342
Suard, P. 141
Sugar, A. 29, 319
Sumitomo 268
Sun Microsystems 340–2
System X 99, 104, 106
    and closure among suppliers 107–8
    engineering 110–13
    export of 112
    management of project 109–10
    rationalization of 113

take-overs
    and BKA 296–7
    British Telecom-Mitel 102
    GEC and Plessey 104–6
Tandberg 244, 249
tariffs 313, 332–4
Tatung 249
technical uncertainty and
    internationalization of consumer
    electronics 318–20
technology
    changes in 351, 363–6; in
      telecommunications 78–9
    convergence of 364
    single policy in Germany 166–8
    switching: and Bundespost 161–2;
      equipment 106–14, 200; EWS
      162–5, 166; public, in Britain 107,
      108, 111, 112–13
telecommunication equipment suppliers
    89, 92
    and Bulk Supply Agreements 97–8
    foreign 184
    in France 122
    hostility among 198–9
    Germany 156–61; and digital
      switching equipment 168–72;
      relations with Bundespost 157–60
    opposition to privatization 96
    private consortium 93
    telecom club, end of 98–9; *see also*
      GEC; Mitel; Plessey; Thorn–
      Ericcson
telecommunications
    boundaries between sectors 365–6

business users 84
deregulation of 80
employees 82
equipment 78, 203–6
expertise 79–80
France: flexible regime in 121–8;
    modernization 124; reform of 123;
    restrictions on 128–36
intercompany cooperation 207–14
internationalization of 79
mergers 134–5, 197–203, 296–7
national differences, decline of 366–
    70
pattern of government–industry
    relations (1975) 348–9, 350
politics, technologies, and markets
    77–86
standards 188–9
strategies in Europe 182–217
trade balances 83
unions in Germany 155–6
Telecommunications Bill (1984) 96–7
Telecommunications Managers'
    Association (TMA) 89, 92–3, 357
Telefunken 279, 280–1, 324
    and Grundig Affair 298
    joint ventures: in Europe 337; with
      Japanese 230
    and Thomson take-over 305–6
    VCR industry 226, 227, 307, 309
    and ZVEI 291
Telephone Users' Association (TUA)
    89, 93, 357
teletext 251–4
Thatcher, M. 358
Thomson 129, 251
    in Britain 239, 246
    and competition in Europe 332
    consumer electronics industry 220,
      221, 284–5
    and digital switching project 137–9,
      140
    and French government 261–2, 269–
      71
    growth of 323–5
    and Grundig Affair 280–1, 298–302,
      303–5
    and HDTV 335–6
    imports into France 274–5
    intercompany agreements 208, 210,
      211
    internationalization of 265–6, 272
    joint ventures 337

Thomson (*cont.*):
  and mergers: with Alcatel 197–8;
    with CGE 133, 140
  nationalization of 130–1, 276–8
  net profits 132
  and Philips 324, 330
  and 'Round Table' 183
  in Singapore 266
  and take over of Telefunken 305–6
  VCR industry 283, 308
  and ZVEI 291
  see also JVC–Thomson
Thomson Grand Public 277–8
Thomson–Brandt 264–6
Thorn 235, 237
  and CTV technology 250–1
  VCRs 255–7
Thorn–EMI 238–9, 246, 279, 284
  HDTV 335–6
  joint ventures 230, 337
  and Thomson 324
  and VCRs 226, 227
  see also J2T
Thorn–Ericsson controversy 99–100
Théry, G. 123–5, 129, 143, 276
TN Telenorma 157, 162, 165, 167,
    169–71
Toppan 337, 340
Toshiba 258, 326
  in consumer electronics market 220
  and inward investment in Britain 244,
    246, 249
  joint ventures 337
  VCR production in Europe 312
trade
  international, pattern of in consumer
    electronics 228–9
  liberalization of 64
  policy and politics in consumer
    electronics 273–5, 332–5
  in telecommunications 203–6
trade associations 32, 59, 60
  in Britain 236–9
  change in role of 355–7
Trades Union Congress (Britain) 55–6
transnational corporations
  and German consumer electronics
    industry 306
  Nokia as 325
  Philips as 321–3
  Thomson as 323–5
Transport and General Workers Union
    (TGWU) 239

Treaty of Rome 191, 195–6
Trio 268
tutelle (France) 52

Union of Post Office Workers (UPW) 89
unions
  in Britain: consumer electronics
    industry 239–40; fragmentation of
    353–4; and Labour Party 55–6;
    and Post Office 89, 93; and
    privatization 96; and Thorn–
    Ericcson bid 100
  decline in role of 352–5
  in France 56–7, 122
  in Germany 57–8, 154–5, 353
  and internationalization of industry
    355
United States
  in European markets 199, 203–6
  telecommunication in 80; as market
    for equipment 182–3, 185, 205
usurpation
  and closure 28–31
  in telecommunications 376
  in VCRs 254–9

V2000 VCR format 226–7
  development 329
  decline of 288, 307, 309, 312, 320,
    322–3
  and Grundig Affair 280–1, 283–4,
    299
value added and data service (VADS) 95
value added network service (VANS)
    94–5, 202
  in Europe 184, 193–4
  in France 128
Varley, E. 243
VHS VCR format 226–7
  domination of 255–6, 258
  and export restraint agreement 312
  preferred to V2000
  and Sony 8 mm. format 226, 330
VCRs (video cassette recorders)
  in Britain 254–9; sales 256
  export restraint agreement in
    Germany 308–14
  formats: and trade policy 334–5; see
    also Beta; V2000; VHS
  French inspection at Poitiers 281–2,
    308, 329–30, 372
  hostility among producers 330
  innovation in 254–9

Japanese investment: in Europe 230; in Britain 235
manufacturing in Europe 227
markets in France 263–4
mergers 279–85
national differences 371–2
Philips, in France 283–4
political campaign in Europe 329
production in Europe 222
protectionism: and production in France 281–3; in Germany 307–14
site of Thomson's factory 283
technology of and Grundig Affair 299
video disc 226–7
Visser, J. 55
voluntary export restraint, *see* export restraint agreement

Weber, M. 6, 10, 11–12
on markets 16–18, 21, 23–4, 26, 30–1

Wega 312, 326
Wilks, S. 9–10, 42, 51, 54
Williams, A. 243
Williamson, O. 21
Wilson, H. 240
Wright, M. 9

Xerox 210, 213, 214

Yamaha 337
Young, Lord 241

ZVEI (Central Association of the Electrical Engineering and Electronics Industry—Germany) 155, 156–7, 158–60, 223
and consumer electronics industry 290–1
and protection against Japanese imports 308–9
Zysman, J. 50, 60, 63